GEOFFROY OF VILLEHARDOUIN, MARSHAL OF CHAMPAGNE

A volume in the series

Medieval Societies, Religions, and Cultures
Edited by M. Cecilia Gaposchkin and Anne E. Lester

A list of titles in this series is available at cornellpress.cornell.edu.

GEOFFROY OF VILLEHARDOUIN, MARSHAL OF CHAMPAGNE

HIS LIFE AND MEMOIRS OF THE FOURTH CRUSADE

THEODORE EVERGATES

CORNELL UNIVERSITY PRESS
Ithaca and London

Copyright © 2023 by Theodore Evergates

All rights reserved. Except for brief quotations in a review, this book, or parts thereof, must not be reproduced in any form without permission in writing from the publisher. For information, address Cornell University Press, Sage House, 512 East State Street, Ithaca, New York 14850. Visit our website at cornellpress.cornell.edu.

First published 2023 by Cornell University Press

Library of Congress Cataloging-in-Publication Data

Names: Evergates, Theodore, author.
Title: Geoffroy of Villehardouin, Marshal of Champagne : his life and memoirs of the Fourth Crusade / Theodore Evergates.
Other titles: His life and memoirs of the Fourth Crusade
Description: Ithaca : Cornell University Press, 2023. | Series: Medieval societies, religions, and cultures | Includes bibliographical references and index.
Identifiers: LCCN 2023020286 (print) | LCCN 2023020287 (ebook) | ISBN 9781501773495 (hardcover) | ISBN 9781501773501 (epub) | ISBN 9781501773518 (pdf)
Subjects: LCSH: Villehardouin, Geoffroi de, - approximately 1212. | Villehardouin, Geoffroi de, - approximately 1212—Military leadership. | Knights and knighthood—France—Troyes—Biography. | Crusades—Fourth, 1202-1204. | Champagne-Ardenne (France)—Biography. | France—History— Capetians, 987-1328. | Istanbul (Turkey)—History— Siege, 1203-1204. | Latin Empire, 1204-1261.
Classification: LCC DC89.7.V55 E94 2023 (print) | LCC DC89.7.V55 (ebook) | DDC 949.5/03—dc23/ eng/20230508
LC record available at https://lccn.loc.gov/2023020286
LC ebook record available at https://lccn.loc.gov/2023020287

CONTENTS

List of Illustrations   vii

Preface   ix

Editions and Names   xiii

List of Abbreviations and Short Titles   xv

1.	The Early Years	1
2.	Marshal of Countess Marie and Count Henry II	17
3.	Marshal of Count Thibaut III	34
4.	Sailing to Byzantium	64
5.	Constantinople	82
6.	Marshal of Emperor Baldwin	104
7.	Marshal of Emperor Henry	128
8.	The Marshal and His Scribe	152
9.	The Memoirs of a *Preudomme*	169
	Epilogue	182

Appendix 1. Geoffroy of Villehardouin's Letters Patent   187

Appendix 2. Tables   189

Appendix 3. Manuscripts, Editions, and Translations   193

Bibliography   207

Index   227

Illustrations

Maps

1. The county of Champagne in 1185	19
2. Villehardouin's Champenois companions at Écry	42
3. Villehardouin's properties in Champagne	61
4. Itineraries of the Fourth Crusade	73
5. The distribution of great fiefs, October 1204	115
6. Villehardouin's march to and retreat from Adrianople, April 1205	122
7. Cities destroyed by Kalojan, 1205–7	135

Figures

1. Plan of Troyes, ca. 1170	6
2. Geoffroy of Villehardouin's earliest extant letters patent with seal, 1189	27
3. Plan of Constantinople, 1204	87

Genealogies

1. The Villehardouin	xx
2. The Counts of Champagne, Blois, and Flanders	40

PREFACE

Two marshals born in the mid-twelfth century, one in England, the other in France, are remembered today through singular accounts of their extraordinary lives. William Marshal (1147–1219) is best known for his prowess as a tournament knight, for his close relations with and service to the Angevin kings of England, and for saving the royal dynasty after the death of King John, when some of the English barons were prepared to abandon their young king, Henry III, for Prince Louis of France. William Marshal's life is known chiefly through a verse biography written in 1224–26 by a poet known only as John, who consulted the family's archive of documents and gathered the recollections of the Marshal's family, friends, and especially his trusted companion John of Earley. The *History of William Marshal* (*Histoire de Guillaume le Mareschal*) is such a remarkable depiction of a great English baron's life that it has inspired a number of modern biographies.[1]

Geoffroy of Villehardouin, marshal of Champagne (circa 1148–1212/17), chief of staff of the Fourth Crusade and marshal of the Latin empire of Constantinople, is known primarily for his memoirs (1207–8) of the crusade and its aftermath. The memoirs, essentially war memoirs, have become the template through which historians view the cataclysmic encounter between the French, Venetians, and Byzantines.[2] They also occupy a prominent place in the canon of French literature

---

1. The first, and still eminently readable, scholarly study of the Marshal's life is by Sidney Painter, *William Marshal* (1933). The most thorough analysis of the marshal's life is by David Crouch, *William Marshal* (2016), which incorporates findings from the recent scholarly edition, with English translation, of *History of William Marshal*, edited by A. J. Holden (2002–6).

2. Neither Villehardouin nor his scribe provided a title for his work. The earliest surviving manuscripts, from circa 1300, identify his text as a *histoire* of the counts of Flanders who became emperors of Constantinople, but the Venetian writer Marino Sanudo, who owned either the original transcription of the memoirs or a copy of it in 1326, called it a "libro de conquisto Constantinopolitano" (Magnocavallo, *Marin Sanudo*, 150–54).

x   PREFACE

as the earliest prose narrative in French and have been the subject of numerous literary analyses. Yet the marshal's life and deeds have received slight attention since Jean Longnon's study of Villehardouin and his family and Edmond Faral's edition of the memoirs almost a century ago.[3]

The two marshals came from modest backgrounds: William was the fourth son of a middling royal official in England and Geoffroy was the fourth son of a knight from Troyes in Champagne. They were exact contemporaries who acquired renown through military service, although they traveled entirely different paths. Neither appeared destined for great deeds, much less to be remembered eight hundred years later. How that came to pass is a story of familial relationships, force of character, military prowess, contingent events, and the good sense of Queen Eleanor, who brought William into the royal entourage, and her daughter Marie, countess of Champagne, who appointed Geoffroy as her marshal. Both men were known as "the marshal" in their lifetimes, but while William Marshal's life and deeds are now a staple of the modern historiography of medieval England, Geoffroy's life remains largely unknown, overshadowed by the dramatic events he narrated.

This book describes Geoffroy's life insofar as it can be recovered from the relatively few non-narrative documents mentioning him before the crusade and from his memoirs. It is not a history of the Fourth Crusade, of which there are numerous modern accounts.[4] It begins in Champagne, where Geoffroy was born and spent thirty years in military service, first as a knight in the count's service in Troyes, then as marshal of Champagne. When he took the cross in November 1199 for the Fourth Crusade, he was in his early fifties, a veteran of the Third Crusade and a seasoned military officer and councilor. Eight years later, when he dictated his memoirs, he was about sixty. In retrospect, he found the conquest of Christian Constantinople an improbable outcome for an expedition that had set out to recover Jerusalem after the failure of the Third Crusade. His recollections, spoken in sober but colloquial prose

---

3. Longnon, *Recherches sur la vie de Geoffroy de Villehardouin* (1939), 45–114, covers the marshal's life. The *Recherches* remains fundamental for the present work; Longnon saw virtually every document related to Geoffroy and provided a detailed catalogue of his and his family's acts. Longnon's companion volume, *Les compagnons de Villehardouin* (1978), catalogues all those mentioned by Villehardouin in his memoirs.

4. Queller and Madden, *The Fourth Crusade* (1997), describe events leading up to the election of Baldwin of Flanders as emperor of Constantinople in May 1204. For a larger perspective on the crusade and its consequences, see Angold, *The Fourth Crusade*.

PREFACE   xi

by one of the few surviving leaders of the crusade, provide a unique oral record of one of the major turning points in the history of the eastern Mediterranean.[5]

The memoirs have long been regarded by copyists, their patrons, editors, and crusade historians as a chronicle or history, but the editor and translator Émile Buchet more accurately classified them as memoirs and went so far as to honor Villehardouin for being "the creator of a genre, Memoirs, which includes many masterpieces of French literature."[6] Edmond Faral, editor of the standard modern edition of the memoirs, and Jean Longnon, who gathered most of what is known about the marshal and his companions, concurred in understanding Villehardouin's narrative as a *mémoire* or *mémoires*.[7] Beryl Smalley classified it more precisely as belonging to the genre of "war memoirs," and Yuval Harari found it to be the earliest "full-fledged military memoir" from the Middle Ages.[8] It is also the earliest original prose narrative (as opposed to translation) composed in Old French.[9]

This book has been as much a collaborative enterprise as Geoffroy of Villehardouin's memoirs. For their thoughtful comments, which saved me from errors and suggested new lines of inquiry that deepened my understanding of the marshal and his achievements, I thank Michael Angold, M. Cecilia Gaposchkin, Anne Lester, Thomas Madden, Randall Pippinger, Jeff Rider, and an anonymous reader. I also thank Lisa Russell for finding the numerous interlibrary books and articles essential to this study and Gordon Thompson for designing the illustrations that enhance the text.

---

5. Angold, "Turning Points in History," 14–25. See also Madden, *Enrico Dandolo*, 117, on the Fourth Crusade's transformation of Venice "from a maritime republic into a maritime empire."

6. Bouchet (Villehardouin, *La conquête*), 2:309.

7. Faral (Villehardouin, *La conquête*), 1:xiii–xiv; Longnon, *Recherches*, 12, and *L'histoire de la conquête de Constantinople*, 24.

8. Smalley, *Historians in the Middle Ages*, 145. Harari, "Military Memoirs," 290–91, cites Villehardouin and Joinville as the only examples of full-fledged military memoirs from the Middle Ages, meaning prose accounts by the combatants themselves rather than by cleric-observers or at-home rewriters. Harari defines military memoirs as retrospective attempts by the combatants themselves to construct meaningful narratives of their experiences in war. He excludes Robert of Clari as a memoirist on the grounds that he included little autobiographical information.

9. Edbury, "Ernoul, Eracles, and the Collapse of the Kingdom of Jerusalem," 53–54, proposes the eyewitness account of the three years preceding the battle of Hattin by Ernoul, squire of Balian of Ibelin, as possibly the earliest Old French prose narrative.

Editions and Names

Unless otherwise indicated, citations are to the following editions: Faral's edition of Villehardouin's memoirs (*La conquête de Constantinople*), §§1–500; Longnon's edition of Valenciennes's *Histoire*, §§501–694; and Dufournet's edition of Clari's *La conquête*, §§1–120.

Most personal names have been Anglicized. However, since French translators have rendered Jofroi(s), Joffroi(s), and Josfroy in the earliest manuscript copies of the memoirs as Geoffroy, I think it entirely appropriate to retain this French name for him as the author of the memoirs, which stand at the very beginning of prose narrative recorded in French.

The index identifies modern spellings and locations of place names.

ABBREVIATIONS AND SHORT TITLES

Actes
Benton, John, and Michel Bur et al., eds. *Recueil des actes de Henri le Libéral, comte de Champagne (1152–1181)*. 2 vols. Paris: De Boccard, 2009–13.

AD
Archives départementales (Aube, Marne, Haute-Marne, Yonne)

AN
Archives nationales (Paris)

Beaumanoir
Beaumanoir, Philippe de. *Coutumes de Beauvaisis*. Edited by Am. Salmon. 2 vols. Paris: A. et J. Picard, 1970–74. Translated by Akehurst as The *"Coutumes de Beauvaisis."*

BnF
Bibliothèque nationale de France (Paris)

Bullarium Hellenicum
Duba, William O., and Christopher D. Schabel, eds. *Bullarium Hellenicum: Pope Honorius III's Letters to Frankish Greece and Constantinople (1216–1227)*. Turnhout, Belgium: Brepols, 2015.

Cartulary of Countess Blanche
Evergates, Theodore, ed. *The Cartulary of Countess Blanche of Champagne*. Medieval Academy Books 112. Toronto: University of Toronto Press, 2009.

Chronique de Morée
Longnon, Jean, ed. *Le livre de la conqueste de la princée de l'Amorée: Chronique de Morée (1204–1305)*. Paris: Librairie Renouard, 1911. Translated by Anne Van Arsdall and Helen Moody as *The Old French Chronicle of Morea*.

Clairvaux
Veyessière, Laurent, Jean Waquet, and Jean-Marc Roger, eds. *Recueil des chartes de l'abbaye de Clairvaux au XIIe siècle.*

xvi   **ABBREVIATIONS AND SHORT TITLES**

	Paris: Comité des travaux historiques et scientifiques, 2004.
Cligés	Chrétien de Troyes. *Cligés*. In *Romans*, edited and translated by Charles Méla and Olivier Collet, 285–494. La Pochothèque. Paris: Librairie Générale Française, 1994.
Feoda	The rolls of fiefs as edited in Auguste Longnon, *Documents relatifs au comté de Champagne et de Brie (1172–1361)*. Vol. 1. Paris: Imprimerie nationale, 1901.
GC	*Gallia Christiana in provincias ecclesiasticas distributa*. 16 vols. Paris, 1716–1865.
Itinerarium Peregrinorum	Stubbs, William, ed. *Itinerarium Peregrinorum et gesta regis Ricardi: Chronicles and Memorials of the Reign of Richard I*. Vol. 1. Rolls Series 38. London: Longman, 1864. Translated by Helen J. Nicholson as *Chronicle of the Third Crusade*.
l.	livres
Larrivour	Cartulary of Larrivour. Archives Départmentales de l'Aube, 4 H 1, thirteenth century.
Layettes	Teulet, Alexandre, et al., ed. *Layettes du Trésor des Chartes*. 4 vols. Paris: Imprimerie nationale, 1863–1909.
"Léproserie"	Harmand, Auguste. "Notice historique sur la Léproserie de la ville de Troyes." *MSA* 14 (1847–48): 429–69.
MGH SS	*Monumenta Germaniae Historica: Scriptores in folio*. 32 vols. Hannover and Leipzig, 1826–1934.
MSA	*Memoires de la Société académique d'agriculture, des sciences, arts et belles-lettres du Département de l'Aube*
Notre-Dame-aux-Nonnains	Lalore, Charles, ed. *Documents sur l'abbaye de Notre-Dame-aux-Nonnains de Troyes*. Paris: Thorin, 1874.
Obituaires	Boutillier du Retail, Armand, and P. Piétresson de Saint-Aubin, eds. *Obituaires*

ABBREVIATIONS AND SHORT TITLES   xvii

	de la province de Sens. Vol. 4, *Diocèses de Meaux et de Troyes.* Paris: Imprimerie nationale, 1923.
Oorkonden	Prevenier, Walter, ed. *De oorkonden der graven van Vlaanderen (1191–aanvang 1206).* Vol. 2, *Uitgave.* Edited by Water Prevenier. Brussels: Palais des Académies, 1964.
Paraclet	Lalore, Charles, ed. *Cartulaire de l'abbaye du Paraclet.* Paris: Thorin, 1878.
Perceval	*Le conte du Graal (Perceval), édités d'après la copie de Guiot (Bib. nat. fr. 794).* Edited by Félix Lecoy. Les romans de Chrétien de Troyes. 2 vols. Paris: Librairie Honoré Champion, 1984.
Perceval: Concordancier	Andrieu, G., and J. Piolle, eds. *Perceval: Ou le conte du graal de Chrétien de Troyes; Concordancier complet des formes graphiques occurrentes d'après l'édition de M. Félix Lecoy.* Aix-en-Provence: Université de Provence, 1976.
PL	*Patrologiae cursus completus: Series Latina.* Edited by J. P. Migne. 221 vols. Paris, 1844–64.
Pontigny	Garrigues, Martine, ed. *Le premier cartulaire de l'abbaye cistercienne de Pontigny (XIIe–XIIIe siècles).* Paris: Bibliothèque Nationale, 1981.
Register	Hageneder, Othmar, et al., comp. *Die Register Innocenz' III.* 14 volumes. Graz: Verlag Hermann Böhlaus, 1964–.
Saint-Loup	Lalore, Charles, ed. *Cartulaire de l'abbaye de Saint-Loup de Troyes.* Paris: Thorin, 1875.
Saint-Pierre	Lalore, Charles, ed. *Cartulaire de Saint-Pierre de Troyes.* Paris: Thorin, 1880.
Villehardouin, *La conquête*	Villehardouin, Geoffroy de. *La conquête de Constantinople.* Edited and translated by Edmond Faral. 2 vols. Paris: Les Belles Lettres, 1938–39. Reprint, 2nd ed., 1961.

GEOFFROY OF VILLEHARDOUIN, MARSHAL OF CHAMPAGNE

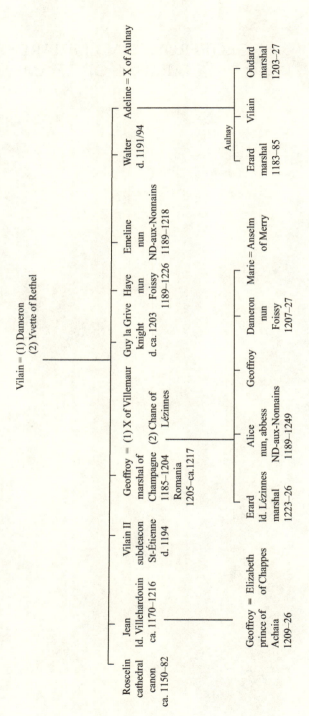

GENEALOGY 1. The Villehardouin

CHAPTER 1

The Early Years

Geoffroy of Villehardouin was born around 1148, the fourth son in a family of knights, canons, and nuns (but not monks).[1] His father, Vilain (ca. 1110–70), a younger son of Odo, lord of Arzillières, inherited the secondary property of Villehardouin, a small agricultural community originally settled by the Romans about twenty-five kilometers east of Troyes, the closest urban center (map 1).[2] At some point Vilain migrated to Troyes, where he received several grain mills in fief from the count of Champagne. Geoffroy and his siblings spent most of their lives in Troyes.[3]

---

1. Longnon, *Recherches*, 45–46.

2. I follow the detailed genealogical reconstruction of the Arzillières and Villehardouin lines in Longnon, *Recherches*, 14–18. Vilain's older brother William inherited their father's main properties at Arzillières, about 10 km south of Vitry, and at nearby Brandonvillers (see chap. 3). Baudin, *Emblématique et pouvoir en Champagne*, 374, posits two Vilains, one "of Arzillières" (genealogical table 8: Arzillières), the other "of Villehardouin" (genealogical table 21-1: Villehardouin). See also Barthélemy, "Les seigneurs et la seigneurie d'Arzillières." A cache of third-century Roman coins found at Villehardouin suggests that it had been a Roman settlement (Roserot, *Dictionnaire*, 3:1769), but the earliest reference to Villa Harduini is in Pope Eugenius III's confirmation of the properties of Saint-Loup of Troyes (*Saint-Loup*, 33–36, no. 16, 1147).

3. Vilain of Villehardouin was not alone in migrating to Troyes. Humbert of Villehardouin had a house in the suburb of Saint-Jacques of Troyes that he later gave to the canons of Saint-Loup, who held property in Villehardouin (*Actes*, 542–43, no. 435, 1176).

2   **CHAPTER 1**

Geoffroy's older brothers Roscelin and Vilain II became canons in Troyes, while Jean, a knight, inherited most of the property in Villehardouin, where he later constructed a modest moated fortification and styled himself "lord of Villehardouin."[4] As the fourth son, Geoffroy inherited only minor revenues in Villehardouin and in several outlying properties.[5] In the absence of a fortuitous collateral inheritance, the fourth son of a second son was fated to seek his fortune through marriage, a religious calling, or in service to a great lord. Geoffroy chose to enter military service with Count Henry the Liberal (r. 1152–81), who was in the process of transforming Troyes from an old episcopal city into the capital of his principality.

In the Count's Service

Shortly after Vilain died in 1170, all of his children appeared at Count Henry's court to give their consent to Roscelin's exchange of their father's grain mills in Troyes for a lifetime grain rent from the priory of Saint-Quentin in Troyes. Roscelin had been a well-known presence in Troyes ever since Abbot Bernard of Clairvaux had sponsored his reception as a cathedral canon two decades earlier.[6] Roscelin's unnamed

---

4. Jean of Villehardouin was identified as a knight (*miles*) in 1193 (*Saint-Loup*, 155–58, no. 113), but after building a modest rectangular motte and bailey fortification (97 x 147 meters) he announced himself as "lord of Villehardouin" (Longnon, *Recherches*, 187, no. 67, 1202: "Ego, Johannes, dominus de Villa Harduini"). A ten-meter-wide moat surrounded a residential complex, a chapel associated with Saint-Loup of Troyes, and an elliptical mound surmounted by a tower (demolished ca. 1890); a sketch is in Roserot, *Dictionnaire*, 3:1772. For the hilltop as it appeared in the 1990s, see Bur, *Vestiges*, 4:144–46. Today, the site is entirely overgrown, and an open field covers the former lower court. Jean of Villehardouin appears in twenty-eight charters between 1177 and 1216; a brief biography is in Longnon, *Recherches*, 20–26.

5. Vilain II was the third son and Geoffroy the fourth (genealogy 1). Since the obituaries of both Roscelin and Vilain II identify their mother as Dameron (Vilain's first wife), and since Geoffroy named one of his daughters Dameron, I conclude that Geoffroy was the fourth son of his father's first marriage. Previous genealogies have Geoffroy either as the third son of the first marriage (Baudin, *Emblématique et pouvoir en Champagne*, 564, genealogical table 21-1) or the oldest son of the second marriage (Evergates, *Aristocracy*, 263, genealogical table 16). In either case, Vilain's properties passed to his sons according to the custom of partible (but not equal) inheritance in Champagne; see Evergates, *Aristocracy*, 120–23, 134–35.

6. Longnon, *Recherches*, 18–20, estimates the dates of Roscelin's birth (before 1140) and death (ca. 1182). If Roscelin became a canon ca. 1150 at the minimum age of fourteen, he could have been born as early as 1136, which would make him about the same age as the chapter's provost, the count's brother William. In 1192 Bishop Bartholomew of Troyes recalled that Vilain of Villehardouin, a knight, had given the tithe of Villehardouin "through the hand of Bernard of Clairvaux" to the cathedral of Troyes for the lifetime support of his son Roscelin as a canon (Roserot, "Deux chartes," 282–84, no. 2).

siblings, no doubt including Geoffroy, approved of the exchange, as did the count, since the mills were held from him in fief.[7] Three witnesses at court attested to the family's web of ties: the count's marshal William Rex of Provins; Roscelin's colleague in the count's chapel, Haice of Plancy (later bishop of Troyes); and Anselm of Courcelles, a nephew who owed castle-guard in Troyes and who later managed Geoffroy's lands in Thrace after the Fourth Crusade.[8]

Geoffroy was about twenty-two years old in 1170 and likely in the count's service for the fief of Villy, a village just south of Troyes (map 3), but he is first recorded by name in 1178, in a list of Count Henry's fiefholders: "Geoffroy of Villehardouin, liege, and he owes castle-guard [*custodia*] in Troyes."[9] Forty of the count's 120 fiefholders (33 percent) were knights who owed some form of annual castle-guard; others were townsmen or canons like Geoffroy's brother Vilain, who was listed just after Geoffroy for a prebend in the count's chapel.[10] Geoffroy was among the fourteen garrison knights (12 percent) who were on permanent duty in Troyes.[11] He was about thirty in 1178, married to a sister of the garrison knight Berengar of Villemaur, and the father of two young daughters who later entered convents in Troyes.[12] As a garrison knight guarding

---

7. *Actes*, 393–94, no. 309, 1170, done in Troyes.

8. Anselm and his brother Itier of Courcelles owed castle-guard in Troyes (*Feoda*, Troyes, no. 1910). They were first mentioned in 1167, when Anselm witnessed Bishop Henry of Troyes confirm Itier's gift to Vauluisant (Cartulary of Vauluisant, fol. 43r). Geoffroy of Villehardouin later identified Anselm as his nephew who administered his lands in Thrace (Villehardouin, *La conquête*, §382).

9. *Feoda* 1, Troyes, no. 1999: "Gofridus de Ville Hardoin ligius et debet Trecis custodiam." For the date of the rolls of fiefs, see Evergates, *Henry the Liberal*, 156. The earliest reference to Villy (later known as Villy-le-Maréchal) is in Geoffroy's letters patent of 1189, in which he assigned revenues there for the support of his daughter Alice in Notre-Dame-aux-Nonnains of Troyes (*Notre-Dame-aux-Nonnains*, 8, no. 3). For the location of Villy, see map 3; for its history, see Roserot, *Dictionnaire*, 3:1846–49.

10. *Feoda* 1, Troyes, no. 2000: "Vilanus ligius." By 1186 Vilain was subdeacon of Saint-Étienne of Troyes ("Léproserie," 532–33). The canons remembered Vilain (died ca. 1194) and his mother Dameron in their necrology: "Item obiit Dameronna, mater Villani subdecani" (*Obituaires*, 4:478, 13 December). For his life, see Longnon, *Recherches*, 34–36.

11. Eight of the 128 fiefholders listed in the roll of fiefs for the castellany of Troyes owed castle-guard at Isle-Aumont. Of the remaining 120, thirty owed castle-guard in Troyes: fourteen for full-time service (*estagium, custodiam totum annum*), and sixteen for indefinite *custodiam*. The fact that Geoffroy's entry, uniquely, lists his castle-guard as being "in Troyes," and that he later succeeded two marshals who had been garrison soldiers, suggests that he, too, owed full-time service in Troyes. Of the count's 2039 fiefs in his thirty castellanies, only 7 percent owed full-time castle-guard (Evergates, *Aristocracy*, 255–56, tables C.1, C.2). The size and commercial and political importance of Troyes required a larger garrison.

12. Longnon, *Recherches*, 47 (following Petit, *Les sires de Villehardouin*, 25–26) identifies Geoffroy's unnamed wife as the daughter of Drogo Strabo of Villemaur and sister of Berengar

CHAPTER 1

Count Henry's capital city, and with social ties through his brothers to the cathedral and the count's chapel, Geoffroy was fully embedded in the urban life of Troyes in the 1170s.

Troyes in the 1170s

Geoffroy would have found Troyes a bustling urban center in full economic expansion. Unlike the count's smaller, somnolent castle-towns like Vitry and Rosnay, where his brother Jean and their relatives performed castle-guard, Troyes was the thriving capital of a principality consisting of thirty or so walled towns and fortresses, all linked by a well-policed network of roads. Merchants from Italy and northern France who attended the trade fairs helped to commercialize the economy of the city and its hinterland, enriching both the count and the religious houses and knights who shared the revenues that Count Henry collected from tolls, duty taxes, and sales taxes. The count's next largest towns of Provins and Bar-sur-Aube, both within a day's journey from Troyes, experienced a similar economic takeoff in the years following the Second Crusade (1147–50), as the fairs of Champagne became centers of international commercial exchange. The nexus of three fair towns hosting an annual cycle of six trade fairs in southern Champagne became the motor of a regional economy that rivaled, and soon supplanted, the markets of the old episcopal cities of Reims, Châlons, Langres, and Sens that encircled the county.[13]

As a garrison soldier Geoffroy would have acquired an intimate knowledge of the topography of Troyes and the walls surrounding its three quarters (fig. 1). The old city, dating from the Roman settlement, encompassed the cathedral and episcopal palace, an antiquated compound of the counts, and several monastic houses, including the Benedictine priory of Saint-Jean-en-Châtel and the Augustinian chapter of Saint-Loup, which had property and later a chapel in Villehardouin.[14]

---

of Villemaur, a garrison soldier there (*Feoda* 1, no. 342). The fact that Geoffroy placed two daughters in convents before leaving on the Third Crusade (*Notre-Dame-aux-Nonnains*, 8, no. 3), suggests that he was married with young daughters in 1178. In February 1202 Marshal Geoffroy sealed letters patent for his "dearest nephews" Geoffroy and Drogo of Villemaur (Arbois de Jubainville, "Nouvelles recherches," 371, no. 5). The marshal's son, Erard of Villehardouin, sold his mother's dowry at Villemaur to Countess Blanche (*Cartulary of Countess Blanche*, no. 119, May 1219).

13. Chapin, *Les villes de foires de Champagne*, describes the fair towns.

14. It is not known when the canons of Saint-Loup acquired the chapel in Villehardouin. Since the papal confirmation of Saint-Loup's possessions in 1147 (*Saint-Loup*, 33–36, no. 16)

THE EARLY YEARS   5

The adjacent and much larger "new town," walled in since 1125, was the commercial center of Troyes, with merchant halls, lodgings, and artisanal shops, as well as hospitals, religious houses, and a Templar house. By the late 1170s the fairs of Champagne had entered a period of high growth, as northern French merchants brought woolen cloth and Italians imported eastern spices and luxury wares to the three trade fairs held in Troyes—in mid-July (the hot fair), September (the cold fair), and January (the Fair of the Close).[15]

Abutting the old and new towns was the count's new campus. Built in the 1150s in an open field and walled in by 1170, it contained the count's residence, the attached chapel of Saint-Étienne, and twenty-five individual houses for the chapel's resident canons.[16] The count's canons constituted a new class of secular canons in Troyes who staffed his chancery and filled major positions in the comital and ecclesiastical administrations. Count Henry usually held court in the main hall of his new residence, where a flow of litigants sought his adjudications and petitioners solicited his benefactions and confirmations of their private transactions. His chancery drafted the letters patent describing his acts at court, which his chancellor sealed and presented to the beneficiaries. With the construction of the count's tomb in the early 1170s, his chapel promised to become a dynastic mausoleum as well, at a time when the monks of Saint-Denis and the cathedral canons of Reims were competing to house the mausoleum of the kings of France.[17]

Geoffroy would have witnessed the transformation of Troyes from a quiescent episcopal town into the administrative center of the count's principality and a hub of international commerce. Its location on the trunk route passing through Burgundy to the Rhône and the Mediterranean ports and through the Alps to the Italian cities also made Troyes a convenient stopover for pilgrims and ecclesiastics from northern Europe on their way to Rome and the eastern Mediterranean. Geoffroy's garrison duty, involving oversight of the trade fairs and security for merchants and travelers on the roads leading to Troyes, as well as defense of

---

does not include Villehardouin among Saint-Loup's rural chapels, it is likely that the chapel was built after Jean of Villehardouin constructed the hilltop fortress there in the 1190s and began to call himself "lord of Villehardouin."

15. For the fairs in Troyes at that time, see Evergates, *Henry the Liberal*, 85–92.

16. For the construction of the count's new campus in Troyes in the 1150s, see Evergates, *Henry the Liberal*, 35–42.

17. For Count Henry's tomb, see Evergates, *Henry the Liberal*, 140–45.

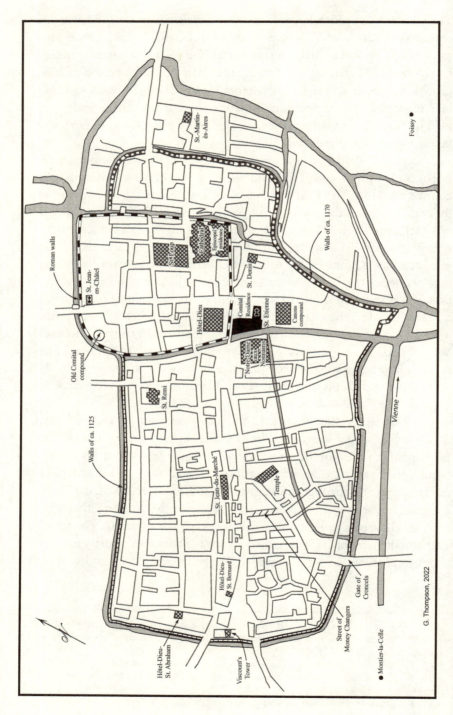

FIGURE 1. Plan of Troyes, ca. 1170

THE EARLY YEARS   7

the city's walls, defined his life for fifteen years in his twenties and early thirties (ca. 1170–85).

Given what we know about Geoffroy's family and professional activities, we can reasonably infer the following about his social life in Troyes in these years. He would have interacted with the garrison knights as well as with those who brought their wives and families with them when performing their annual tours of duty, which could range from several weeks to several months.[18] For knights who lived most of the year in the countryside on their inherited (allodial) properties and the fiefs they held from the count and other lords, castle-guard in the count's towns was an occasion for socializing with regional knights and their families, thereby contributing to the social cohesion of a class of propertied families standing between castle lords and rural tenants.

Geoffroy and Roscelin also belonged to a network of those who served Count Henry as canons and officers. Roscelin was a colleague of the count's brother William, provost of the cathedral (1152–68), then archbishop of Sens (1168–76) and Reims (1176–1202).[19] Roscelin's prebend in the count's newly built chapel also made him a colleague of Haice of Plancy, master of the chapel school and later dean of the cathedral, chancellor of the count, and bishop of Troyes.[20] Roscelin developed such a close friendship with Manasses of Pougy, first provost of the count's chapel and later bishop of Troyes (1181–90), that Manasses established anniversary Masses at the cathedral for Roscelin and himself.[21] Bishop Manasses was the brother of Count Henry's constable Odo of Pougy. The count's marshal William Rex of Provins and his chancellor William

---

18. Du Cange, *Glossarium mediae et infimae Latinitatis*, 7:573–75, gives examples of a knight's *stagium* with his family (in 1214, 1223, 1233, 1244). See also Nieus, "Pairie et 'estage,'" 41–42, for the *concordio* between Count Hugh (V of Châtillon) of Saint-Pol and his *pares*, who were required to bring their wives for their annual forty days of castle-guard in the 1230s.

19. As subdeacon in 1167, Roscelin witnessed William of Champagne resign the provostship of the cathedral chapter (*Saint-Pierre*, 29–31, no. 20, 1167 = AD Aube, G 2257) in the presence of his brother Count Henry, his uncle Bishop Henry, and the cathedral canons: archdeacon Manasses (of Villemaur, also dean of Saint-Étienne); deacon Haice of Plancy (future bishop of Troyes, 1190–93); Manasses of Pougy (future bishop of Troyes, 1181–90); and master Peter (Comestor, canon and deacon since 1143, chancellor of Paris from 1168). For William of Champagne's career, see Falkenstein, "Wilhelm von Champagne," and Williams, "William of the White Hands."

20. For Roscelin's prebend in Saint-Étienne, see Longnon, *Recherches*, 20n1. Saint-Étienne's obituary remembered Roscelin's mother (*Obituaires*, 4:273, "Obiit Dameronna mater dicti Roucelini." For Haice of Plancy, see Evergates, *Marie of France*, 131n31.

21. *Saint-Pierre*, 56–57, no. 43, 1184.

CHAPTER 1

were brothers of Bishop Mathieu of Troyes (1169–80).[22] To all appearances Roscelin was a well-connected figure in Troyes before Geoffroy entered the count's service and during his years as a garrison knight. Although Geoffroy was an unremarkable garrison knight on the face of the evidence, he would have interacted with a wide circle of those in the count's service in Troyes in the 1170s and early 1180s, including fellow knights performing castle-guard, secular canons of the cathedral and the count's chapel, the count's high officers, and the most important religious leaders residing in the capital.

Four of Geoffroy's siblings also lived in Troyes: Roscelin and Vilain as canons and his sisters as nuns, Emeline in Notre-Dame-aux-Nonnains, the aristocratic convent directly opposite the count's residence, and Haye in the Fontevrist priory of Foissy, just beyond the city walls. Despite the lack of explicit evidence of his interactions with Count Henry and Countess Marie, a garrison knight in the relatively small town of Troyes would have known their children from their earliest years—Henry II (born 1166), Marie (born 1170), Scholastique (born in the 1170s), and Thibaut III (born 1179). The fact that Countess Marie appointed Geoffroy as marshal, and that he later spoke movingly of the early deaths of Thibaut in 1201 and Marie, countess of Flanders, in 1204, suggests a close relationship with the comital family.[23] For Geoffroy and his siblings, the Villehardouin patronymic failed to capture the rich context of their lives lived within the largest and most vibrant urban center in southern Champagne in full demographic and commercial expansion.

Wars, Tournaments, Crusade

It is unlikely that Geoffroy joined Count Henry's three military expeditions beyond the county in the 1170s, since castle-guard, especially for garrison soldiers, was for defensive purposes, not for service in the field.[24] In 1172 the count sent armed forces into the lands of his brother-in-law, Archbishop Henry of Reims, who had demolished the count's fortress at Sampigny on the Vesle River, claiming that brigands used it as a refuge after attacking travelers on the road between the episcopal

---

22. For the careers of Chancellor William and Bishop Mathieu, see Evergates, *Henry the Liberal*.

23. Villehardouin, *La conquête*, §§37, 318.

24. Longnon was skeptical, in the absence of explicit evidence, that Geoffroy served in the count's expeditions; see his *Recherches*, 48–49.

THE EARLY YEARS   9

cities of Reims and Châlons. The archbishop, well known for his bellicosity, excommunicated the count for the audacity of invading archiepiscopal lands.[25] The next year Count Henry and his three brothers—Archbishop William of Sens and counts Thibaut V of Blois (the royal seneschal) and Stephen of Sancerre—joined Louis VII (and their sister Queen Adele) in supporting the sons of King Henry II of England in revolt against their father. But after two unsuccessful summer incursions into Normandy the revolt collapsed. Count Henry had returned home by October 1174.[26]

While those external matters engaged the count, a number of tournaments were being held along the northern border of his lands. Count Henry is not known to have attended any tournament after the spring of 1149, when he and the king's brother Robert of Dreux sponsored a tournament to celebrate their return from the Second Crusade.[27] It appears that after his accession, Count Henry prohibited tournaments in his lands, in large part because their sporting violence and the passage of bands of armed knights threatened the good order of the trade fairs, which were transforming the economic life of the county. The young count Baldwin V of Hainaut (r. 1171–95), who led a company of eighty knights on a circuit of events at Bussy, Rethel, and Braine, was largely responsible for popularizing tournaments in the early 1170s. According to his chancellor, Gislebert of Mons, the tournament at Braine in 1175 was attended by many knights from Champagne and the Ile-de-France.[28] It was not a coincidence that the tournament sites along the river Aisne—Braine, Roucy, Château-Porcien, and Rethel (see map 1)—were in lands held in fief from the archbishop of Reims, and that the new archbishop, William of Champagne, transferred lordship over them to his brother Count Henry in 1178.[29]

The last, most spectacular, and long-remembered tournament in this region was sponsored by fourteen-year-old King Philip II in November 1179 at Lagny, on the border between Champagne and the royal domain, to celebrate his accession. Henry the Young King of England participated with his mentor William Marshal, whose exploits were celebrated in verse four decades later by a poet who cited a still-extant tournament roll of participants identified by their region of origin: the

---

25. Evergates, *Henry the Liberal*, 108–10.
26. Evergates, *Henry the Liberal*, 133–36.
27. Evergates, *Henry the Liberal*, 27–28.
28. Gislebert of Mons, *Chronique*, 116–17 (*Chronicle*, 67–68), §77.
29. Evergates, *Aristocracy*, 23.

10   **CHAPTER 1**

Ile-de-France, Flanders, England, Normandy, Anjou, and Burgundy—but not Champagne.[30] The barons and knights of Champagne had left for Jerusalem five months earlier with Count Henry.

The allure of Jerusalem was fanned by Pope Alexander III in response to increasingly disturbing reports from the Levant that Nur-ad-Din (r. 1146–74) was posing an existential threat to the western settlements. Alexander's bull of 14 July 1165 encouraged Western leaders to organize a relief expedition to the Holy Land in hopes of repeating the success of the First Crusade.[31] Alexander promised the same spiritual benefits that Pope Eugenius had granted crusaders twenty years earlier for the Second Crusade, when Count Henry and a large number of Champenois barons and knights took the cross with Louis VII and Queen Eleanor.[32] Thereafter, a steady stream of French princes and barons journeyed to Jerusalem, some as simple pilgrims and religious tourists, others as armed pilgrims intending to aid an increasingly precarious Western occupation of Palestine-Syria, but the response in Champagne was muted.

On 29 January 1176 Alexander appealed to the king and princes of France: since Emperor Manuel Komnenos (r. 1143–80) had recovered land from the Turks, the roads were safe for travel to Jerusalem.[33] The pope sent a legate to reconcile the kings of France and England, who made peace at Nonancourt on 21 September 1177. Shortly before Christmas, Count Henry took the cross from the hand of the papal legate, Abbot Henry of Clairvaux, and promised to lead an expedition under the pope's auspices. Count Henry and Louis VII, both in their fifties, planned to travel together, reliving their experiences on the Second Crusade thirty years earlier, but Louis became too ill to travel and Henry had to go alone.[34] Just before the count's departure, Count Baldwin V of Hainaut arrived in Troyes to confirm the contract he had sealed in 1171 for the betrothal of his daughter Isabelle with Count Henry's five-year-old son Henry (II) and his son Baldwin with Henry's infant daughter

---

30. Holden, *History of William Marshal*, 1:226–55, lines 4457–4996. The poet says (page 231, line 4539) that he consulted a written source (*escrit*) for the names of the tournament participants. For tournament rolls, see Crouch, *Tournament*, 36–38.

31. *PL*, 200:384–86, no. 360, *epistolae*. For Alexander's role in promoting crusades and the protection of crusader families, see Park, *Papal Protection and the Crusader*, 82–88.

32. Evergates, *Henry the Liberal*, 16–33.

33. *PL*, 200:1063–64, no. 733. For events in the East, see Phillips, *Defenders of the Holy Land*, 225–45.

34. Evergates, *Henry the Liberal*, 150–53.

Marie. On that very day, Sunday 13 May 1179, according to Gislebert of Mons, Countess Marie delivered her second son, Thibaut.[35] Geoffroy could not have imagined at the time how Thibaut, another younger son, would inflect his own life course.

Geoffroy is not mentioned in any of the documents drawn up preparatory to the count's expedition. He might well have dreamed of visiting Jerusalem and the holy sites with the count. Growing up in the shadow of the Second Crusade, he would have heard the count and his companions reminisce about the places they had visited, notably the marvels of Constantinople and its Francophile emperor Manuel Komnenos, who had knighted young Henry during his passage through Constantinople in 1148. But Geoffroy very likely remained with the garrison in Troyes to protect Countess Marie, who would rule the county in the absence of Count Henry and his chief officers, including his marshal William Rex of Provins, chaplain Peter, almoner (and Templar brother) William, chancellor Stephen, notary William, scribe Thibaut of Fismes, and treasurers Artaud of Nogent, Milo (Breban) of Provins, and Robert of Milly.

Count Henry and his contingent of barons and knights took the southern route from Troyes, heading down the Rhône River to Marseille, then sailing to Brindisi and on to the Syrian coast, where they landed in August 1179. After an indecisive skirmish with Saladin's troops, they visited Jerusalem, Hebron, Sebaste, and Nazareth, sites that Count Henry had seen three decades earlier. But while returning home in the spring or summer of 1180, the count and his party were captured by Turks. Henry's treasurers Artaud and Milo Breban later testified that they witnessed Henry vow that, if he were liberated, he would grant a 30*l.* revenue to the cathedral of Saint-Mamas of Langres.[36] We do not know how Henry was released, but in September 1180 he appeared in Constantinople, where he witnessed the coronation of Emperor Alexios II and Countess Marie's half-sister, Agnes of France. Henry returned to Champagne in early March 1181 and died in Troyes on 16 March.[37] His

---

35. Gislebert of Mons, *Chronique*, 126 (*Chronicle*, 72), §89.

36. Artaud and Milo Breban were with Count Henry in Jerusalem (*Actes*, no. 525, 1179). They later testified in court that they were present with Henry when he made his oath after being captured by Turks (Flammarion, *Cartulaire du chapitre cathédral de Langres*, 172–73, no. 145, between 28 March and 31 October of 1182).

37. Evergates, *Henry the Liberal*, 157–66.

12   **CHAPTER 1**

marshal William Rex of Provins was among those who failed to return with him.[38]

Death of a Marshal

Among Countess Marie's first duties as regent for fifteen-year-old Henry II was the appointment of new officers to replace those lost on her husband's expedition. As her marshal she selected Lucas, a garrison knight in Troyes and son of Girard Manducator, her provost in Ervy.[39] Two years later, for unknown reasons, she replaced Lucas with Erard of Aulnay, a garrison knight in Vitry and son of Geoffroy's sister Adeline.[40] But Marshal Erard, who had a history of contentious behavior, had the misfortune to die under excommunication after tangling with the canons of Châlons.[41] In July 1185 his widow Helvide, daughter of the garrison knight Bertrand of Vitry, gathered Erard's siblings and friends (*amici*) in the cathedral of Châlons to restore his good standing with the church and to secure the salvation of his soul.

In the presence of Bishop Guy (of Joinville), Helvide made peace (*pax*) with the cathedral canons, who had excommunicated Erard

---

38. In addition to his own fief in Provins (*Feoda* 1, no. 1602), Marshal William Rex held his wife Isabelle's castellany of Chaplaines (*Feoda* 1, Sézanne, no. 1778) and a fief in Troyes (*Feoda* 1, no. 2012) that later passed with the office of marshal to Geoffroy of Villehardouin. Before leaving with Count Henry in 1179, Marshal William funded an anniversary Mass for himself and his wife at Montier-la-Celle's priory of Saint-Mesmin (a photograph of his charter can be found in Baudin, Brunel, and Dohrmann, *The Knights Templar*, 232–33, catalogue 15bis). For his family and career, see Verdier, *L'aristocratie de Provins*, 103–10, 133 (genealogy). His widow, Isabelle of Chapelaines, soon married Oger of Saint-Chéron.

39. *Feoda* 1, Troyes, no. 1920: "Luco, ligius et estagium." Lucas was the son of Girard Manducator, provost of Ervy (*Actes*, 143–44, no. 102, ca. 1150s) and may have been related to Master Peter Comestor, also known as Peter Manducator, author of the *Historia Scholastica*, a manual of biblical history; his obituary in Saint-Étienne, where he held a prebend, reads "Magister Petrus Manducator" (*Obituaires*, 4:474). In 1182 Lucas was the first witness ("Lucas, marescallus meus") to Marie's charter of franchise to "all my men in the castellany of Ervy" (Benton, "Recueil des actes," 1182g, done in Meaux). Swearing on her behalf were Erard of Aulnay, a garrison knight at Vitry and the next marshal, and Milo (Breban) of Provins, who would be appointed her treasurer (*camerarius*) in 1186.

40. *Feoda*, Vitry, no. 379: "Erardus de Alneto, ligius et estagium toto anno"; no. 382. Aulnay was likely Aulnay-l'Aître (in the département of Marne and the arrondissement of Vitry-le-François). For Adeline, see Longnon, *Recherches*, 15–16.

41. Erard's maternal aunt Gaburdis brought suit against Erard, "knight of Aulnay," for her right to dispose of her dowry property. On investigation, the court confirmed her right to alienate her inherited property, which she held as a comital fief. Erard quitclaimed his right in the presence of his sister Mathilda, her husband Philip, a knight, and their son Erard. After Count Henry agreed to the transfer, in essence an alienation of his fief, Erard's wife ("daughter of Bertrand, knight of Vitry") consented to Erard's quitclaim (*Actes*, 500–501, no. 402, 1175).

THE EARLY YEARS   13

for harming their tenants in the village of Saint-Amand near Vitry.[42] The canons were not easily mollified and peace came at a high price: surrender of all the rents and land that Helvide and Erard possessed within and beyond the village. In his letter describing the reconciliation, Bishop Guy named those in Helvide's party: Erard's brothers Oudard and Vilain, his sister Mathilda and her son Erard, several of Erard's "friends" (*amici*) identified as knights—Guy II of Dampierre and his brother Jean of Arcis-sur-Aube, Milo II of Nogent-sur-Seine, Oger of Saint-Chéron, Geoffroy of Mousson—and lastly "Geoffroy of Villehardouin, Erard's [maternal] uncle [*avunculus*]."[43] They all swore "on holy relics" (*super sanctis reliquias*) that if Helvide did not deliver the promised property, they would place themselves in captivity (*captio*), understood as honorable captivity, in Reims until she made good. Helvide's party then proceeded to Reims, where they confirmed to Archbishop William (of Champagne) the peace she had made with the chapter of Châlons and her promise to transfer the property. The archbishop sealed a confirmation of the settlement but added a clause, ostensibly to soften the blow, stating that the canons of Châlons promised to celebrate an annual Mass for Erard "as customary for a knight" (*juxta morem militum*).[44]

Soon thereafter, still in July, the archbishop's letter was presented to Countess Marie at court in Troyes in the presence of Geoffroy of Villehardouin, who was identified as her new marshal (*Gaufridus marescallus*).[45] The countess and nineteen-year-old Henry consented to Helvide's alienation of Saint-Amand to the canons "because it is our fief," said Marie, and they approved of the compensation Helvide agreed to pay both for

---

42. AD Marne G 655, 1185, original letters pendant with seal of Bishop Guy (= Robert, "La maison d'Aulnay," 186–87, no. 2). All the documents relating to Erard's death are dated July 1185. An obituary recorded at Notre-Dame-aux-Nonnains of Troyes, where Erard's sister Emeline was a nun, names him "Erard, knight, marshal of Champagne" (*Obituaires*, 4:358). See genealogy 1. The original grant of the village of Saint-Amand-sur-Fion from Count Hugh of Troyes survives: AD Marne, G 655, no. 2, April 1204, done in Troyes (= Meinert, *Papsturkunden in Frankreich*, 182–83, no. 8).

43. I follow Longnon, *Recherches*, 43, who identifies Erard of Aulnay's mother as Adeline, sister of Geoffroy of Villehardouin, who inherited property at Brandonvillers along with her brothers Geoffroy and Jean of Villehardouin. Aubri of Trois-Fontaines (*Chronica*, 852) states that Oudard's mother Adeline was the daughter of Vilain of Arzillières (understood here to be the same as Vilain of Villehardouin).

44. Longnon, *Recherches*, 152, no. 8, 1185, translated in Evergates, *Feudal Society*, 129–30, no. 98. The archbishop's letter clarified the relationships of three witnesses at Châlons: Guy II of Dampierre was the son of Helvide's unnamed sister (*consobrinus*), Guy's brother was Jean of Arcis-sur-Aube, and Geoffroy of Mousson was Erard's uncle.

45. Longnon, *Recherches*, 152–53, no. 9, 1185.

14   CHAPTER 1

the damages Erard had inflicted and "for the salvation [*remedium*] of his soul." Marshal Geoffroy also witnessed as Countess Marie confirmed a document drawn up by the Cistercian monks at Trois-Fontaines, who agreed to bury Erard in their cemetery and to remember his anniversary in return for certain pasture and fishing rights.[46]

The affair of Marshal Erard's death and how it played out illustrate several aspects of knightly society in Champagne. Erard's "friends" who supported his grieving widow were fellow knights, landed proprietors related by marriage and lineage whose ancestral lands lay between the Marne and Seine rivers in the countryside between Vitry and Troyes and who rendered castle-guard for their comital fiefs in the walled towns of Champagne. Helvide's father Bertrand, like Erard, was a garrison knight at the count's hilltop castle at Vitry, where the castellan also was on permanent duty.[47] Oger of Saint-Chéron, Countess Marie's escort Nevel of Aulnay, and Geoffroy's brother Jean of Villehardouin owed annual guard duty at the count's town of Rosnay (map 1).[48] Guy II of Dampierre, nephew of Helvide's sister, owed castle-guard in Troyes where he was viscount; he and his brother Jean II of Arcis-sur-Aube were among the count's most important resident fiefholders. [49] Of all Marshal

---

46. AD Marne, 22 H 72, no. 2 = Longnon, *Recherches*, 153–54, no. 10, original with red pendant seal, undated but clearly in July 1185, act of Countess Marie, who refers to Erard as "my former marshal." Helvide then obtained spiritual benefits for Erard by granting all that she and Erard possessed in the village of Brandonvillers (tithes, rents, and grain revenues) to the monks of Marmoutier's priory in Dampierre, with the consent of his brothers. Since she lacked a seal, she asked her lord (*dominus*) Guy II of Dampierre to affix his seal to her letter (Savetiez, "Maison de Dampierre-Saint-Dizier," 356, done at Dampierre, undated, most likely of 1185).

47. "Bertrand, knight of Vitry" (*Actes*, 500–501, no. 402, 1175), was on permanent duty (*stagerius*) at Vitry (*Feoda* 1, no. 382). He witnessed two of Count Henry's acts before 1152, both involving fiefs acquired by the Cistercians of Trois-Fontaines (*Actes*, nos. 7–8). He may have been the Bertrand listed as *sine terra* in 1153 (*Actes*, no. 30). All of which suggests that he had been a garrison knight at Vitry from the very start of Henry's rule. Erard of Aulnay's sister Matilda also was married to a knight, Philip (*Actes*, no. 402, 1175). Henry of Rethel, third son of the count of Rethel, was castellan of Vitry on permanent duty from 1171 to 1191 (*Feoda* 1, Vitry, no. 358: "mansionem per annum").

48. *Feoda* 1, Rosnay, nos. 185 (Jean of Villehardouin owed three months); 180 (Oger of Saint-Chéron, six weeks); 194 (Nevel of Aulnay, six months); see Evergates, *Marie of France*, 121n8. Oger of Saint-Chéron married the widow of Marshal William Rex of Provins in 1181 and assumed both her fief and Marshal William Rex's fief. During Oger's absence on the Fourth Crusade (in 1204), Isabelle, *domina* of Chapelaines, gave Clairvaux a grange with the consent of the five children she had with Marshal William Rex and the two she had with Oger (Verdier, *L'aristocratie de Provins*, 246n457). Oger returned to Champagne by April 1205 and died ca. 1215. For his life, see Longnon, *Les compagnons de Villehardouin*, 23–24.

49. Guy II of Dampierre (ca. 1140–ca. 1216) owed his castle-guard in Troyes for the viscounty of Troyes (*Feoda* 1, Troyes, no. 1889). His father William served as Count Henry's constable from 1152 to 1172, but it is not clear whether Guy succeeded to that office. He left

THE EARLY YEARS   15

Erard's "friends," only Milo II, lord of Nogent-sur-Seine, did not owe castle-guard at one of the count's towns.[50]

The fallout from Erard's death illustrates another aspect of knightly society in Champagne: the role played by widows, not only as regents for underage heirs, but also as appeasers and rectifiers of their husbands' sins of commission or omission, in both practical and spiritual matters. In the absence of her own children, Helvide was supported by Erard's brothers and sister, his two uncles, her own nephews, and several of Erard's companions in sorting out her husband's unfinished business. It was a wrenching experience involving the loss of substantial economic assets. Even so, the office of marshal was retained within the kinship, and Erard's friends would remain close to the comital family and to Marshal Geoffroy through the next two decades.

One witness at Marie's court in 1185 who did not appear earlier at Châlons and Reims was Milo Breban, a knight and treasury official from Provins who was, like Geoffroy, in his mid-thirties.[51] Milo had come to the attention of Countess Marie shortly after she arrived in Troyes in 1166, when she gave him a revenue for which he did homage.[52] Thereafter he often appeared at court with the count's chief treasurer Artaud as "Artaud *camerarius* and Milo Breban (or of Provins)."[53] Milo's

---

Jean of Villehardouin as guardian of his lands while he was on the Third Crusade (*Clairvaux*, 546, no. 432, undated but 1189 or 1190). For his life, see Savetiez, "Maison de Dampierre-Saint-Dizier," 16–25. His brother Jean of Arcis-sur-Aube owed castle-guard in Troyes (*Feoda* 1, Troyes, no. 1885); he died at Acre (Roserot, *Dictionnaire*, 1:17).

50. Milo inherited his castle lordship from his mother Elizabeth, an heiress who held it in fief from the abbot of Saint-Denis; see Evergates, *Aristocracy*, 239.

51. Verdier, *L'aristocratie de Provins*, 138–40, estimates Milo's date of birth and reasonably identifies Breban with the village of Bréban, formerly Brébant (département of the Marne, arrondissement of Vitry-le-François, canton of Sompuis) in the comital castellany of Rosnay.

52. Verdier, *L'aristocratie de Provins*, 251, no. 540, 1166, act of Countess Marie for Milo Brebanus with Henry's approval, done in Provins. This was a grant of the tithe and other unspecified revenues owed by five named men who may have resided in Provins, where Marie had her dower income.

53. Verdier argues persuasively (against Longnon, *Les compagnons de Villehardouin*, 48–57, and all previous historians) that two contemporaries were named Milo of Provins: one was the son of the marshal William Rex of Provins, the other was Milo Breban of Provins, often identified only as Milo of Provins (Verdier, *L'aristocratie de Provins*, 125–243). That conclusion is confirmed by an act of Count Henry II in January 1194 in Jaffa, witnessed by both "Milo of Provins" and "Milo Breban" (Delaville Le Roulx, *Cartulaire général*, 1:603, no. 954). In preparation for the Third Crusade, Milo of Provins identified himself as "son of William the marshal," his wife as Helie (of Villemaur), and his brother as Fromond (Verdier, *L'aristocratie de Provins*, 255n289, 1190, and 133, genealogical table 5). This Milo of Provins died before October 1197, when Helie on her deathbed identified herself as "widow of the deceased Milo, [son] of the marshal of Provins"; see Evergates, *Marie of France*, 154n118.

16   **CHAPTER 1**

brother Jean, also a knight in the count's service, occasionally appeared with him at court.[54] The brothers could be classified as urban knights who apparently provided security for the count's treasury, located under the church of Saint-Quiriace in Provins.[55] Artaud and Milo Breban had accompanied Count Henry on his pilgrimage to Jerusalem in 1179 and were captured and ransomed with him before returning to Troyes in March 1181. In 1186, the year after Countess Marie made Geoffroy her marshal, she promoted Milo to *camerarius*, her chief financial officer.[56] Thereafter, for more than a quarter century, Geoffroy and Milo were fast companions; they joined the Third and Fourth Crusades and spent their last years as marshal and butler of the Latin emperor of Constantinople.

The fact that Countess Marie was quick to replace Erard of Aulnay as marshal with his uncle Geoffroy suggests that she knew Geoffroy from his military service in Troyes and trusted him for his character and competence. He was typical of a new generation of comital officials, men of knightly background recruited by Marie to office and court as Count Henry's crusade companions gradually withdrew or died. Geoffroy, who had performed garrison duty in Troyes for fifteen years, was at that time best described as a professional soldier. He was in his mid-thirties and married to his second wife Chane, heiress of the knight William of Lézinnes.[57] He inherited several minor properties and revenues, acquired assets from two marriages within his knightly class, and held at least two comital fiefs, including one formerly held by the marshal William Rex.[58] His "friends" and relatives were of the same class of knights who performed castle-guard in the count's towns and canons who, like his brothers Roscelin and Vilain, acquired placements in Count Henry's chapters in Troyes, Provins, Bar-sur-Aube, and Sézanne. Geoffroy would spend the next thirteen years as marshal of Countess Marie and Henry II.

---

54. Milo Breban and Jean appeared at court in 1176 and 1178 (*Actes*, nos. 435, 469). Both held comital fiefs in 1178 (*Feoda* 1, Provins, no. 1604: Milo and Jean, both liege). Jean held a fief at Sézanne (*Feoda* 1, no. 1807) that passed to *Milo Brabannus* after his death on Count Henry's journey to Jerusalem in 1179–80. Count Henry regarded both Milo and Jean as his *servientes* (*Actes*, no. 499, 1179; no. 466, 1177).

55. Verdier's fundamental conclusion is that knights residing in towns were intimately involved with comital governance and the urban economy (Verdier, *L'aristocratie de Provins*, 211–14).

56. Verdier, *L'aristocratie de Provins*, 254, nos. 578–79, 1186: "Milone de Pruvino, camerarius noster."

57. For William of Lézinnes, see Longnon, *Recherches*, 47n2. Shortly before 1178 Count Henry granted him and his brother Renaud 100*l.* each in cash to be invested in income-generating property worth 10*l.* annually as comital fiefs (*Feoda* 1, Ervy, nos. 324, 325). For what little is known about Chane, see Longnon, *Recherches*, 48.

58. *Feoda* 1, Troyes, no. 2012, an entry added ca. 1185 to the roll of 1178.

CHAPTER 2

Marshal of Countess Marie and Count Henry II

Geoffroy of Villehardouin's horizon during the fifteen years he served as a garrison knight was limited to the city of Troyes and its immediate vicinity. From 1185 his purview as marshal extended across the entire county of Champagne with its thirty or more walled towns and fortified sites located between the royal domain in the west, the German empire in the east, Burgundy in the south, and Hainaut in the north. The county as constituted in 1185 was relatively new, having existed only since 1152 when Count Henry imposed a template of castellany districts over his diverse collection of lands and began construction of a new comital residence in Troyes, where he held court. His chancery produced his letters patent and internal administrative records, notably the fief rolls of 1178, which inventoried his fiefholders and their castle-guard obligations according to the new castellany template. Marshal Geoffroy, as he later indicated, became intimately familiar with the military disposition of the 1800 knights and barons recorded in those rolls.[1] The consolidation of the county as a political entity coincided with rise of the fairs of Champagne, which made the count's largest towns—Troyes, Provins, and Bar-sur-Aube—centers of international

---

1. *Cartulary of Countess Blanche*, 294–95, no. 333.

18   **CHAPTER 2**

commercial exchange and stimulated an economic takeoff that made Champagne part of the "new France" of the late twelfth century.[2]

During his seventeen years as marshal of Champagne (1185–1202), Geoffroy confronted a political landscape in flux after the long reign of Louis VII (r. 1137–79). The arrival of Philip II, a young and assertive king (r. 1179–1223), complicated the endemic conflicts among the princes of Flanders, Hainaut, and Namur. For Countess Marie, who ruled as regent for Henry II from March 1181 to July 1187, it was a troubling family affair. Philip was her half-brother, son of Louis VII and Count Henry's sister Adele, and so the political became intensely personal. One of fourteen-year-old Philip's first acts was to alienate his Champenois relatives—his mother the queen and her brothers, the royal seneschal Count Thibaut of Blois, and Archbishop William of Reims. He then flaunted his independence in 1180 by marrying Isabelle of Hainaut, who had been promised in marriage to Countess Marie's own son Henry. After a brief armed conflict ended with the peace of Crépy-en-Valois on 11 April 1182, Countess Marie restored good relations with Philip and Archbishop William became the king's loyal prelate, although comital-royal relations never recovered the genuine bond that Count Henry the Liberal and Louis VII had formed on the Second Crusade.[3] The political and military flash point shifted to the northern principalities, which resisted Philip's intrusion into their lands. As that regional conflict became enmeshed with the Third and Fourth Crusades, it unleashed challenges quite unlike those faced by earlier marshals of Champagne, challenges that required considerable personal and diplomatic skills beyond purely military ones. Marshal Geoffroy brought those skills to the Fourth Crusade.

Marshal Geoffroy's duties can only be inferred from much later records. They suggest that he was in charge of the count's stable (he later demonstrated a good eye for horses) and the logistics of Countess Marie's travel and lodging.[4] Several community charters state that the marshal was responsible for leading local militias in the absence of the count or his high officers (the seneschal, butler, and constable).[5] Indirect evi-

---

2. For the state of the county in 1181, see Evergates, *Henry the Liberal*, 170–76. Sivéry, *L'économie du royaume de France*, suggests that a new commercializing economy had divided the kingdom into two economic zones by 1180, with Champagne and Flanders being part of the "new France."

3. Evergates, *Marie of France*, 30–33, 41–42.

4. Longnon, *Recherches*, 51–53, lists the duties of later marshals.

5. For example, Henry the Liberal exempted his men in Avize from military service except when he appeared in person or sent his constable or marshal to lead them (*Actes*, no. 344,

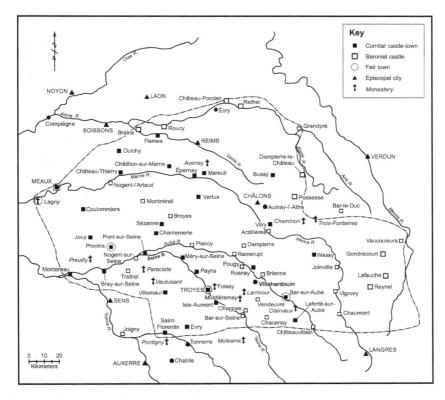

MAP 1. The county of Champagne in 1185

dence suggests that he also oversaw the security of merchants traveling with their goods to the fairs.[6] By all accounts his knowledge of military affairs was practical, acquired through his years of garrison duty in Troyes and as marshal responsible for the defense of the county. There is no evidence that he had any formal schooling or acquired proficiency in Latin beyond what was required to process administrative records like the rolls of fiefs, which allowed him to monitor the disposition of the count's fiefholders and their castle-guard. Count Henry owned a personal copy of Vegetius's *De re militaris*, a fourth-century manual

---

1172). The count's grant of a commune to Meaux required their military service whenever he needed it, under the command of either himself or his butler, constable, or marshal (*Actes*, 630–35, no. 507, item #24, 1179).

6. Marshal Erard of Aulnay witnessed Countess Marie's act in 1184 authorizing the leper house in Troyes to hold a fair on 1 May and extending her protection (*conductum*) over those coming to the fair with their goods ("Léproserie," 530–31).

20   **CHAPTER 2**

popularized by John of Salisbury's *Policraticus* (1159), but if its observations regarding military training, tactics, and strategy were discussed by the literate clerics in the count's company, it is unlikely that Villehardouin, who was still only a garrison soldier when the count died, was part of that conversation.[7]

Geoffroy, at heart a military man, gives no indication that he was interested in the literary culture of his time. Yet he must have acquired a passing familiarity with the popular "romances of antiquity" written within his own lifetime and with the Arthurian-branded stories composed by Chrétien de Troyes in the 1170s, at the very time when Geoffroy was performing castle-guard in Troyes. Chrétien's Byzantine-themed romance *Cligés*, completed by 1176, celebrated a double *translatio*: of Greek and Roman learning passing to France, as the poet claimed, and of French chivalry passing from the court of King Arthur to the imperial court in Constantinople. Geoffroy may also have heard of the *Eracle* romance written about the same time by Gautier of Arras, which deals with an imperial succession in Constantinople. Both stories attest to an interest in Constantinople and the East during the rule of Emperor Manuel Komnenos, which would have resonated with veterans of the Second Crusade who had visited the city with Count Henry in October 1147, on the way to Jerusalem, and in 1180, on returning from Jerusalem.[8] Geoffroy certainly must have heard tales of their overseas adventures, especially from Milo Breban, who had been captured with Count Henry and had seen Constantinople in 1180.[9]

If Villehardouin cannot be linked explicitly to the vernacular poets of the time, he did move within the social world of the clerics and knights who "rubbed shoulders" at court.[10] In his first two years as marshal he attended at least four sessions of Countess Marie's court. On two occasions he witnessed transactions involving the leper house outside the

---

7. John of Salisbury mentions Count Henry's copy of Vegetius in a letter to Henry; see John of Salisbury, *Letters*, 2:336–37, no. 209, ca. 1166–67, and Evergates, *Henry the Liberal*, 120. For John of Salisbury's use of Vegetius in the *Policraticus*, see Allmand, *The "De Re Militari" of Vegetius*, 83–91.

8. For interest in the East, see Ciggaar, *Western Travellers*, and for specific interest in Constantinople, see Devereaux, *Constantinople and the West*, and Dufournet, *Les écrivains de la IVe croisade*, 1:113–20. It seems unlikely that Villehardouin knew of the romance *Florimont*, which deals with the foundation of Philippopolis, a city he would come to know well after 1204. For Count Henry's time in Constantinople, see Evergates, *Henry the Liberal*, 22–27, 162–63.

9. Evergates, *Henry the Liberal*, 163.

10. Putter, "Knights and Clerics at the Court of Champagne," 258, captures that context of social interaction at court.

MARSHAL OF COUNTESS MARIE AND COUNT HENRY II

Croncels gate of Troyes in the presence of Marie's chaplain Andreas Capellanus, who was in the process of writing his *De amore*, a treatise on amorous conundrums requiring resolution by great ladies at a "court of love."[11] But it is difficult to imagine Villehardouin being amused by Andreas's moral quandaries or Chrétien's fanciful Arthurian tales. He was more in his milieu when he appeared at court with Guy II of Dampierre to witness their companion Milo II of Nogent-sur-Seine grant one-third of his castellany to the Templars.[12] Also witnessing on that occasion was Countess Marie's new chief treasury official, Milo (Breban) of Provins, who would become Geoffroy's closest companion through the next quarter century.

Geoffroy served Countess Marie for only two years before Henry II succeeded as count of Champagne on 29 July 1187. The marshal knew Henry as a young man with a disposition quite unlike that of his liberally educated father.[13] Henry at twenty-one was a generation younger than Geoffroy but already accomplished in arms, having followed the tournament circuit while still in his mid-teens with a band of well-born young men in the company of Arnold V of Ardres, who traveled with a personal trainer in martial arts.[14] Even before his accession, the young count immersed himself in the treacherous politics of northern France, where King Philip played a dangerous game of changing alliances with the princes of Flanders, Hainaut, and Namur. In what appeared as a shrewd move at the time, Henry extricated himself from his betrothal to Yolande of Hainaut, the younger sister of Queen Isabelle, who earlier had been betrothed to Henry, and contracted a more promising alliance with Ermesinde, the infant heiress of Count Henry the Blind of Namur.[15]

---

11. In 1185 Marie resolved a dispute over land next to the leper house given as an entry gift for a *conversa* there; witnesses included Andreas Capellanus, Brother William almoner (and Templar), and "Geoffroy marshal" ("Léproserie," 531). In 1186 Geoffroy, Andreas Capellanus, Artaud the treasurer, Milo (Breban) of Provins, and Marie's almoner, the Templar brother William, witnessed as Marie granted the leper house a revenue equal to a prebend in the comital chapel of Saint-Étienne, in effect circumventing the Third Lateran Council's prohibition of assignments of future prebends ("Léproserie," 532).

12. AN, S 4967, no. 2, 1186 = Benton, "Recueil des actes," 1186g. See also Evergates, *Aristocracy*, 239.

13. Arbois de Jubainville, *Histoire*, 4:11–72, provides a brief history of Henry II's rule. For Henry's years before 1190, see Evergates, *Marie of France*, 67–73.

14. Lambert of Ardres, *History of the Counts of Guines*, 125, §92.

15. Gislebert of Mons, *Chronique*, 195–96, 197–99 (*Chronicle of Hainaut*, 107–9), §§129, 132.

CHAPTER 2

We do not know whether Marshal Geoffroy was involved in the young count's maneuvers in the extremely fluid political events in northern France in the late 1180s, compounded as they were by the never-ending war between Henry II of England and Philip II of France. Count Henry clearly recognized that the entangling and rapidly shifting alliances involving the two monarchs and the counts of Hainaut and Namur jeopardized the trade fairs of Champagne, which were pillars of his county's economic life. In a revealing document he admitted that a regional war between the king and the count of Flanders would reduce the revenues from sales taxes on commercial transactions and rents from lodgings at the fairs of Saint-Ayoul in Provins, thus jeopardizing fief-rents, prebends, and pensions assigned on those revenues.[16] If that prospect did not deter Henry from his youthful bellicosity, events in the Levant soon rendered moot both the threat of war at home and his new betrothal.

News of Saladin's stunning victory at the battle of Hattin on 4 July 1187, followed by the capture of Jerusalem on 2 October, led to talk of a crusade to recover Jerusalem. Saladin sent the "true cross," discovered by the First Crusaders in 1099, to Damascus, and barred Christian pilgrims from Jerusalem. Only a narrow band of coastal cities—mainly Antioch, Tyre, and Tripoli—and several inland fortresses remained under Western control. Frederick I of Germany was the first of the three Western monarchs to respond; the kings of England and France followed by agreeing to a truce on 21 January 1188 at Gisors, where they publicly embraced in a kiss of peace and promised to liberate Jerusalem. The next day, 22 January, after the archbishops of Tyre and Reims preached crusade, the two kings took the cross in the presence of a large assembly of lords and prelates. Count Henry II of Champagne was among the many who did likewise, as did his relatives, the bishops of Beauvais (Philip of Dreux) and Chartres (Renaud of Bar-le-Duc), the duke of Burgundy (Hugh III), and the counts of Flanders (Philip I), Bar-le-Duc (Henry I), Blois (Thibaut V), and Perche (Rotrou III).[17] It was a reenactment of the great cross-taking at Vézelay four decades earlier in March 1146, when a young Henry the Liberal took the cross with Louis VII for the Second Crusade. The chroniclers mention only the great men at Gisors in

---

16. Lalore, *Cartulaire de Montier-la-Celle*, 42–43, no. 35, 1187. On the importance of commercially generated fair revenues to both religious communities and fiefholders, see Evergates, *Henry the Liberal*, 75–82.

17. Rigord, *Gesta*, 244–46 (Rigord, *Deeds*, 101–2), §62.

January 1188, but in view of subsequent events it is clear that Marshal Geoffroy and the other officials with him at Gisors also took the cross in the expectation that they would accompany Henry overseas, just as his officers had accompanied his father to Jerusalem in 1179.[18]

If Geoffroy returned to Troyes to prepare for the expedition, he must have witnessed the great conflagration in the old city and the commercial quarter on the evening of 23 July 1188, which caused substantial loss of life and building stock.[19] Shortly thereafter, Count Henry suffered a serious political reversal when King Philip decided that the inheritance of Namur and its fiefs should pass to the heir of Hainaut, effectively nullifying Henry's marriage contract with Ermesinde of Namur and his future succession to the county of Namur.[20] The loss of Namur and its heiress, following the loss of his betrothed to Philip in 1180, permanently damaged relations between the two cousins, born only a year apart, Philip on 21 August 1165 and Henry on 29 July 1166. If there was any consolation for Henry, it was the prospect of joining his other royal cousin, Richard I of England, a kindred spirit in military affairs with whom he would develop a close working relationship in the war against Saladin.

The Third Crusade

Like most territorial lords, Count Henry provided for the good order of his lands in the event he did not return from overseas. Sometime between the fire of 23 July 1188 and his departure in April 1190, his chancery drew up lists of his fiefholders by castellany, just as it had for his father a decade earlier for the benefit of Countess Marie.[21] Chancery clerics first emended and updated the rolls of 1178, noting when a fiefholder was still living or had been replaced (by an heir, widow, or another) or when a fief had been transferred or confiscated or had reverted to the count's domain.[22] Geoffroy of Villehardouin was listed for a fief in Troyes formerly held by the marshal William Rex of Provins and very likely reserved as compensation for the marshal's service, what

---

18. Ralph de Diceto, *Ymagines historiarum*, 2:51. Roger of Howden, *Chronica*, 2:334–35.

19. For Countess Marie in Troyes, see Gislebert of Mons, *Chronique*, 215–19 (*Chronicle of Hainault*, 117–19), §142. For the fire in Troyes, see Robert of Auxerre, *Chronicon*, 253; translated in Evergates, *Feudal Society*, 130, no. 99.

20. Gislebert of Mons, *Chronique*, 242–43 (*Chronicle of Hainaut*, 132–33), §156, 1 September 1189.

21. Evergates, *Aristocracy*, 24–26.

22. Evergates, *Aristocracy*, 206 (table C.3).

24   **CHAPTER 2**

later was called "the fief of the marshal."[23] A fair copy of currently valid information was made on a new set of rolls, one for each castellany, and deposited in the treasury of the count's chapel after being recopied in a codex volume. Milo Breban, the count's treasurer (*camerarius,*) later reported that he witnessed the rolls being transferred from the chancery to the count's chapel of Saint-Étienne and that Count Henry took the codex copy with him overseas as a record embodying the very structure of his principality.[24] Geoffroy, as he later indicated, was familiar with the template of the fief rolls representing a county of walled towns defended by garrison knights and enfeoffed knights living within castellany districts connected by roads to the capital city of Champagne, a template not unlike the one he would view in post-conquest Constantinople, a land of dispersed walled cities defended by small garrisons of French knights.

The second critical issue pertained to an orderly succession to the county in the event that the unmarried Henry perished overseas. Countess Marie would rule in his absence, since his closest heir was his eleven-year-old brother Thibaut. And so, probably in the late spring of 1190, the count's barons were convened at the centrally located town of Sézanne, where they swore to accept Thibaut as Henry's successor in the event that he failed to return. Count Philip of Flanders, also childless, had done the same in 1177, summoning his barons to Lille, where they swore to accept his sister Margaret and her husband as his heirs in the event he did not return from overseas.[25]

No record was made of the swearing at Sézanne, but twenty-three years later it became a major issue regarding the succession in Champagne. In October 1213 the papal legate and the bishops of Soissons and Meaux held an inquest to determine "whether Count Henry, going overseas, had his land sworn [*terram suam fecit jurari*] to his brother Thibaut in the event that he did not return from across the sea."[26] Eight surviving barons and officials, by then mature men (*senes*) who had survived both the Third and Fourth Crusades, gave sworn testimony. Guy of Chappes

---

23. *Feoda* 1, no. 2012, ca. 1190. *Willelmus de Ruez* (a late scribal transcription of *Willelmus Rex* [of Provins]), replaced around 1190 by *Galfridus marescallus*. One century later the income attached to the marshal's office was called a *feudum marescalli* (Longnon, *Documents*, 2:10).

24. *Cartulary of Countess Blanche*, 294–95, no. 333, 1208/9, letter of the marshal and Milo Breban to Countess Blanche.

25. Gislebert of Mons, *Chronique*, 122–24 (*Chronicle*, 122–23), §84.

26. *PL*, 216:980–81, no. 1, October 1213, report of Robert, the papal legate, who sent a copy to Countess Blanche (Saint-Étienne, fols. 85v–86v).

was among several who said that they were present and swore to the succession, but Guy II of Dampierre, Oudard of Aulnay (marshal from 1203 to 1227), and Count William of Joigny said that although they heard about the swearing, they were not present, perhaps because they left for Acre in the summer of 1189 in the company of the king's uncles, Bishop Philip of Beauvais and Robert of Dreux.[27]

Like most crusaders, Count Henry made a number of last-minute benefactions and collected as much cash as possible for the expedition, both from the Saladin Tithe assessed to support the crusade and from the sale of privileges to the townsmen of Provins and Épernay.[28] Geoffroy might well have witnessed those acts, as well as the count's confirmation of sales by crusaders, but since the chancery ceased listing the names of witnesses in 1188, the marshal's presence at court was not recorded.[29] He did, however, witness several private transactions by crusaders preparing to leave, including one in which Guy of Chappes quitclaimed a field that a knight had held from him but alienated to support his mother and two sisters in a priory.[30]

Geoffroy also acted on his own account, selling part of the village of Vannes, just north of Troyes, to Bishop Manasses of Troyes, ostensibly for crusade expenses.[31] And he provided monastic endowments for the two daughters of his first marriage at aristocratic convents in Troyes where his two sisters were nuns. His oldest daughter Alice entered the wealthy Benedictine convent of Notre-Dame-aux-Nonnains, where his

---

27. Roger of Howden states that Count Robert of Dreux, his brother Bishop Philip of Beauvais, Count Erard II of Brienne, and "many other Christian pilgrims" arrived at Acre on 24 August 1189 (*Chronica*, 3:20). Howden mentions the "Franci et Campani cum gentibus regis" in that contingent at the siege of Acre in 1190 (*Chronica*, 3:22). According to Guy of Bazoches, that party included Count Erard II of Brienne and his brother André (of Ramerupt), the seneschal Geoffroy IV of Joinville, and Guy and Walter of Châtillon (*Chronosgraphie*, 6). See also Perry, *The Briennes*, 31, 35.

28. Henry commuted the *taille* he collected from the residents of Provins and its castellany for 600*l.* per annum; Countess Marie and young Thibaut swore to observe that privilege if Henry died overseas (*Layettes*, 1:164, no. 378, done in Provins, 1190). Henry granted Épernay a similar commutation for 120*l.* per annum (Nicaise, *Épernay*, 2:141, no. 15, 1190).

29. There was one exception: Geoffroy witnessed Henry II confirm his father's gifts to Boulancourt (Longnon, *Recherches*, 159–60, no. 23, March 1190).

30. Longnon, *Recherches*, 158, no. 19, 1187/88.

31. *Saint-Pierre*, 63–64, no. 51, 1188, letter of Bishop Manasses of Troyes recording his purchase of part of Vannes from "lord Geoffroy of Villehardouin." The bishop assigned life use of it to his nephew Walter (of Pougy), cathedral canon and archdeacon of Troyes (later bishop of Nevers), after which the property would pass to the cathedral chapter. The next bishop, Haice, quitclaimed his right to that property after initially claiming it (*Saint-Pierre*, 68–70, no. 58, 1191).

26   **CHAPTER 2**

sister Emeline was a nun and where Alice became abbess in 1234.[32] Geoffroy's endowment for Alice is the earliest extant letters patent drawn up in his name and validated with his seal. It was a family event, most likely held in the abbey in the presence of Geoffroy's brother, wife, sister, and his mayor, who was charged with rendering the revenue:

> Be it known to all, present and future, that I, Geoffroy of Villehardouin, marshal of Count Henry [II], have given to Notre-Dame [-aux-Nonnains] of Troyes and its nuns 20 *solidi* annually for my daughter Alice. They are assigned on my first annual revenues from Villy at Christmas. So that this be firmly observed, I have sealed [this letter] with my seal. These are the witnesses: the priests Felicius and Gonter [of the convent], my brother Walter, a knight, my [second] wife Chane, my sister Emeline [nun], my mayor Girard of Villy, and Walter of Lépine, Odo of Seleris, and Garnier Gener [the convent's servants].[33] Done in the year of Incarnation 1189.[34]

A round, yellow pendant seal is inscribed: "Seal of Geoffroy of Villehardouin" (fig. 2).[35] It is not an equestrian seal, which many of his fellow knights were acquiring at the time, nor does it mention his office. In fact, there is no evidence that Geoffroy possessed an earlier seal as a knight or even as marshal. At about the same time he placed his other daughter Dameron in the Fontevrist priory of Notre-Dame of Foissy, just beyond the walls of Troyes, where his sister Haye was a nun.[36] Marshal Geoffroy, then in his early forties, joined Count Henry and his officers on the Third Crusade, while his brother Jean stayed at home to serve as guardian of the lands of Guy II of Dampierre, who was unmarried.[37]

---

32. Longnon, *Recherches*, 121–23 (Alice) and 41–42 (Emeline).

33. The last three witnesses were *famuli* of the convent (*Notre-Dame-aux-Nonnains*, 13, no. 9, 1191).

34. AD Aube, 22 H 375 (formerly 22 H 40), 1189 (= *Notre-Dame-aux-Nonnains*, 8, no. 3 = Arbois de Jubainville, "Nouvelles recherches," 369, no. 1).

35. The slightly worn yellow seal reads *Sigillu[m] Gaufri[di] de Villa[Hardu]ini*. Photograph in Baudin, *Emblématique et pouvoir en Champagne*, CD-ROM: *Corpus des Sceaux*, 94, and "De la Champagne à la Morée," 111, fig. 4. On the significance of the heraldic device, the *croix recerclée* (or in modern terms the *croix ancrée*), as a regional/familial/feudal signifier, see Baudin, who speaks of "a clan network" (*réseau clanique*), "De la Champagne à la Morée," 102–6, esp. 105–6, and *Emblématique et pouvoir en Champagne*, 400–14.

36. Longnon, *Recherches*, 123–24, reasonably concluded that Geoffroy's letter recording his exchange of a field with the priory of Foissy, which is known only through a late abstract (Longnon, *Recherches*, 160, no. 24, 1190), was likely related to Dameron's entry into Foissy. For his sister Haye, see Longnon, *Recherches*, 42–43.

37. Guy II of Dampierre's mandate to Jean of Villehardouin and the "bailiffs of his land," asking them to protect the gift that Guy made to Clairvaux, probably occurred in July 1189

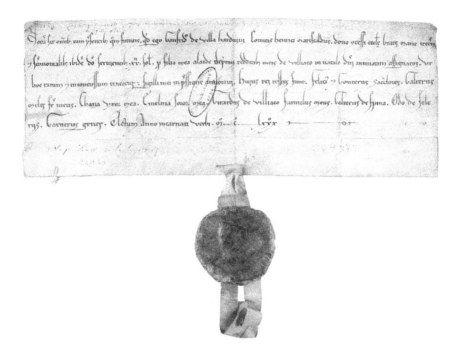

FIGURE 2. Geoffroy of Villehardouin's earliest extant letters patent with seal, 1189. Troyes, Archives Départementales de l'Aube, 22 H 375

The Expedition

The Third Crusade was widely popular in Champagne. The chronicler Robert of Auxerre noted that "illustrious men and worthy knights from France and Champagne set out for Jerusalem."[38] It is difficult to determine how many Champenois joined the crusade, since the chroniclers recorded the names only of the most prominent lords; many others are known from their benefactions and letters of sale mentioning their imminent departure.[39] Most of Count Henry's high officials accompanied him, including his chancellor Haice of Plancy and his treasurer Milo Breban, who later witnessed Henry's acts in Acre. Marshal

---

(*Clairvaux*, 546, no. 432, undated) since it was recorded in the cartulary right after Guy's own letter granting the monks permission to cut down five oak trees annually until he returned from overseas (*Clairvaux*, 303, no. 256, July 1189).

38. Robert of Auxerre, *Chronicon*, 254 (year 1190).

39. For example, those who announced their departures in their benefactions to Montiéramey included Clarembaud V of Chappes (Lalore, *Cartulaire de l'abbaye de Montiéramey*, 114–15, no. 83, ca. 1189), Giles of Plancy (118–19, no. 88, 1190), and Odo of Vendeuvre (no. 87, 1190).

CHAPTER 2

Geoffroy, however, is not mentioned in any of the documents issued during the expedition or during Count Henry's time in Acre. Nevertheless, he would have been expected to accompany the count overseas, just as the former marshal, William Rex of Provins, had traveled with the count's father in 1179. Geoffroy was still in Troyes in March 1190, when he witnessed Henry confirm his father's gifts to the monks of Boulancourt.[40] He likely set out with Count Henry in late May in the company of Henry's uncles, counts Thibaut V of Blois and Stephen of Sancerre, and a large contingent of barons and knights comprising an army of "greater Champagne." They headed south toward Burgundy and the Mediterranean. Within a few days they reached Vézelay, where Henry's chancellor drew up privileges for the Cistercians at Pontigny and Cheminon. "This was done at Vézelay while I am on the way to Jerusalem," said the count.[41] Passing through Vienne, they reached Marseille in early June.[42]

Philip left Paris on 24 June after observing a ninety-day mourning period for Queen Isabelle, who died in childbirth on 15 March. He met Richard at Vézelay on 4 July 1190, exactly three years after Hattin.[43] The two kings planned to travel together to Marseille and coordinate their journey to Palestine. Duke Hugh III of Burgundy and his son Odo joined them near Lyon with a large contingent of Burgundian barons and knights.[44] Count Henry, already in Marseille, made a number of benefactions, including a generous one for the Knights Hospitaller: enough land to construct a chapel in Bar-sur-Aube and a cemetery at one of the city gates. He instructed his mother to make the necessary arrangements.[45] The Champenois set sail as soon as ships were ready and landed at Acre in early July, the first sizable Western contingent to arrive. Henry brought new energy and innovative tactics to the stalled siege before the two kings arrived

---

40. Longnon, *Recherches*, 159–60, no. 23, March 1190.

41. *Pontigny*, 368–69, no. 382, 1190: license to sell wine annually in Troyes exempt from the entry tax and all other customary taxes, which Marie confirmed (Benton, "Recueil des actes," 1190o = AD Yonne, H 1405). In a second letter, Henry gave Pontigny a 10*l.* revenue, to be collected from the wardens of the fairs of Troyes for Masses for his safety while living and in his memory after death (*Pontigny*, 245–46, no. 200, 1190, Marie's confirmation). Still in Vézelay, Henry promised the monks of Cheminon all that he possessed in the village of Cheminon, effective after his death (Benton, "Recueil des actes," 1190m; AD Marne, 17 H 8, no. 8).

42. Mayer, *Die Kanzlei*, 2:908, no. 62, June 1190, done in Marseille, Henry's mandate to his bailiffs and agents to permit the poor from the Hôtel-Dieu of Provins, "which I founded by my own hand," to gather woods in his forests around Provins.

43. For Richard's expedition, see Gillingham, *Richard I*, 123–54.

44. Petit, *Histoire*, 3:37–54. Rhodes, *The Crown and the Cross*, 150–74, lists the Burgundians.

45. Delaville Le Roulx, *Cartulaire général*, 1:564, no. 888, done in Marseille.

MARSHAL OF COUNTESS MARIE AND COUNT HENRY II   29

nine months later.[46] The author of the *Itinerarium Peregrinorum* reports, perhaps from having seen them at the siege of Acre, that the knights from Champagne were known for their training in arms (*studiis armorum*).[47]

We know that Geoffroy of Villehardouin was at Acre because on 24 November 1190 he was captured by Saladin's forces. The *Itinerarium Peregrinorum* notes that the royal butler (Guy of Senlis) was captured and twenty others with him were captured or killed.[48] Roger of Howden reports that "the [royal] butler of Senlis was captured by the Turks, and the marshal of Count Henry was captured by the Turks."[49] They were among the revelers at the marriage of Conrad of Montferrat and Isabelle, heiress to the kingdom of Jerusalem after the death of her older sister Sybil. Inattentive, perhaps inebriated, the French were attacked at dawn by Saladin's archers, who were showering the crusader camp with arrows.[50] According to Bahā' al-Din Ibn Shaddād's biography of Saladin, the Franks were lured into an ambush, where many were killed; those who were captured were presented to Saladin, who treated them honorably and ordered them taken to Damascus, where they were allowed to write to their comrades in Acre for clothes and provisions.[51] Geoffroy would spend the next three years in captivity, until 1193 or early 1194, when he reappeared in Champagne.

Geoffroy consequently spent fewer than four months at the siege of Acre. The city capitulated on 12 July 1191 following the arrival of Philip II (20 April) and Richard I with his heavily armed and stocked flotilla (7 June). The staggering human losses on all sides at Acre became the defining event of the Third Crusade. Guiot of Provins, the poet who accompanied Richard I on that crusade, was so traumatized by what he saw that on

---

46. Hosler, *The Siege of Acre*, 72–85, credits Henry's leadership with reinvigorating the siege before the kings arrived. See *Itinerarium peregrinorum*, 92–93 (Nicholson, *Chronicle of the Third Crusade*, 97–99), bk 1, chaps. 42–43.

47. *Itinerarium Peregrinorum*, 67–68 (Nicholson, *Chronicle of the Third Crusade*, 76–77), bk.1, chap. 29.

48. *Itinerarium Peregrinorum*, 122–23 (Nicholson, *Chronicle of the Third Crusade*, 125), bk. 1, chap. 63.

49. Benedict of Peterborough (Roger of Howden is now identified as the author), *Gesta*, 2:148: "Pincera de Sain Liz captus est a paganis et marescallus comitis Henrici," which is expanded in Roger of Howden, *Chronica*, 3:88–89: "Pincera de Sainzliz captus a paganis et marescallus comitis Henrici captus a paganis." For the relationship between the *Gesta* and the *Chronica*, see Gillingham, "Roger of Howden." Ambroise, *History of the Holy War*, reports that the butler of Senlis was captured and twenty were killed or captured after the wedding (1:67, lines 4145–72).

50. Hosler, *The Siege of Acre*, recounts the event (96–98).

51. Ibn Shaddād, *The Rare and Excellent History of Saladin*, 139–40.

30   **CHAPTER 2**

his return he became a monk at Cluny and wrote a long lament naming the great barons who died at Acre. Of the eighty-nine names he mentions, nineteen (21 percent) were Champenois and another twenty-seven (30 percent) were related in some way to the counts or barons of Champagne, the only home region that he names.[52] Geoffroy's captivity spared him from witnessing the slaughter, notably the execution of several thousand Muslim prisoners during Richard's negotiations with Saladin. He also missed the assassination of Conrad of Montferrat on 28 April 1192 and the marriage of Conrad's pregnant widow to Count Henry of Champagne.[53]

In Champagne, two property transactions involving Geoffroy were relitigated in his absence by the new bishop of Troyes, Haice of Plancy, whom he had known as a cathedral canon since 1170. Haice first claimed the revenues at Vannes that his predecessor, Bishop Manasses, had purchased in 1188 "at his own expense" from "lord Geoffroy of Villehardouin, marshal of Count Henry [II]." The bishop ultimately accepted the original conditions of sale and quit his claim, but the next year he revisited the grant made by Geoffroy's father forty years earlier to the cathedral chapter. As Haice recounted it, Vilain of Villehardouin's gift of the tithe of Villehardouin for his son Roscelin's lifetime support as a cathedral canon should have passed to the bishop after Roscelin's death (ca. 1182). But instead, Roscelin's brothers, identified as knights and no doubt including Geoffroy, claimed the tithe; only after the bishop's court ruled against them did they cede possession. The issue resurfaced after Geoffroy's brother Vilain, subdeacon of Saint-Étienne, seized the tithe, only to relinquish it in 1192 after being excommunicated.[54] Had Geoffroy returned to Champagne by 1192 he surely would have participated in those suits. Whether news of his captivity and the possibility that he might not return prompted Bishop Haice's claims is an open question.

Return to Champagne

We know nothing about the circumstances of the marshal's release from captivity, but one intriguing bit of evidence suggests that he was

---

52. "Oh Champagne! How many barons / have you lost in such a brief time" (Guiot de Provins, *La Bible*, in his *Oeuvres*, 19–24, lines 324–479, composed in 1208). For an analysis of the names, see Grossel, *Le milieu littéraire en Champagne*, 1:132–49.

53. Evergates, *Marie of France*, 77–78.

54. *Saint-Pierre*, 68–70, no. 56, 1191. Bishop Bartholomew recounts how after Roscelin's death, his unnamed brothers seized the revenue. Later, Vilain II, subdeacon of Saint-Étienne, seized the tithe but released it after several cathedral canons intervened (Roserot, "Deux chartes," 282–84, no. 2, 1192, letter of the bishop of Troyes). See Longnon, *Recherches*, 35.

MARSHAL OF COUNTESS MARIE AND COUNT HENRY II 31

ransomed by the Templars, perhaps through the good offices of Count Henry, who remained the principal leader of the overseas Western forces after Richard's departure on 11 October 1192. Henry had sworn on Richard's behalf to the Treaty of Jaffa with Saladin on 2 September 1192 and developed a cordial relationship with Saladin after receiving several "robes of honor," which he sported in Acre.[55] It is possible that Henry arranged for the ransom of his marshal in the months prior to Saladin's death on 4 March 1193 or shortly thereafter during the troubled succession of Saladin's son al-Afdal.[56] If so, Geoffroy might have been accompanied home in 1193 by the four Templars who purchased two buildings and five chambers (*thalamos*) in adjacent buildings in Provins.[57] Witnesses to that transaction included "Brother William, almoner (of the count)" and "Brother Geoffroy marshal [*frater Gaufridus marescallus*]," raising the possibility that Geoffroy might have joined the Templars on temporary service (*ad terminum*) in thanks for being redeemed from captivity.[58] Brother William, almoner of Count Henry I, had accompanied Henry to Jerusalem in 1179, returned in 1181, and appeared with Geoffroy at Marie's court in 1185; he likely accompanied Henry II on the Third Crusade and perhaps was captured with Geoffroy on the same occasion at Acre in 1190 and returned with him in 1193. [59]

It is impossible to determine how Geoffroy was affected by his captivity. But if he did return in 1193, he did not resume his public role as marshal for at least another year, until sometime between 10 April 1194 and 1 April 1195, when he witnessed Count Walter III of Brienne present

---

55. Evergates, *Marie of France*, 78–79.

56. Humphreys, *From Saladin to the Mongols*, 75–76, 87–102.

57. Henry Bristaud, viscount of Provins, and his mother, Heloise of Nangis, both sealed a letter of sale for 300*l.* cash from the Templars (Carrière, *Histoire et cartulaire des Templiers de Provins*, 105–6, no. 84, 1193). Countess Marie confirmed the transaction with the same list of Templar witnesses (Carrière, 46–47, no. 7, 1193).

58. Four crusaders who were captured in Syria made similar commitments to the Hospitallers who redeemed them, becoming *confratri* of the Order, according to their charters, after being freed in 1207. Riley-Smith prints the charter of appreciation of 6 January 1208 (new style) of Jean of Villers ("The Hospitaller Commandery of Éterpigny," 392–93, no. 3). Villehardouin, *La conquête*, §231, mentions his capture. See also Longnon, *Les compagnons de Villehardouin*, 126–27. Villehardouin would have shared a respect for the knight-monks with William Marshal in England, who became a Templar on his deathbed (Holden, *History of William Marshal*, 2:420–21, lines 8352–66).

59. *Actes*, 1:439–40, no. 353, 1173: "Brother William, my almoner"; *Actes*, no. 527, 1179–80, done in Sebastia: "Brother William, knight of the Temple." Brother William, almoner, and Geoffroy, marshal, had witnessed Countess Marie's acts in 1185 and 1186 ("Léproserie," 531, 532). The fact that Countess Marie had her own almoner ("Brother Radulpus, my almoner") in 1192 (Benton, "Recueil des actes," 1192d), suggests that Henry II's almoner, Brother William, returned from the East only in 1193, after being captured with Villehardouin at Acre in late 1190.

32   CHAPTER 2

a grange and pastures to the Cistercian monks of Boulancourt.[60] Two distinguished persons were present: Jean of Possesse, a Cistercian monk who had resigned his castle lordship in the mid-1160s, and Geoffroy V of Joinville, seneschal of Champagne, who returned to France after the death of his father at Acre.[61] For the first time, the sources identify Geoffroy of Villehardouin not simply as marshal or as marshal of the count or countess, but as "marshal of Champagne" (*Campanie marescallus*), a title that reflected his anomalous position as marshal of both Count Henry II, who continued to involve himself in affairs at home while overseas, and Countess Marie, who ruled the county in his absence.[62]

On 16 March 1196 Geoffroy and Milo Breban appeared at Marie's court to witness the resolution of a dispute between the Cistercians at Pontigny and the knight Engobrand of Saint-Chéron.[63] But if the extant documents are indicative, neither Geoffroy nor Milo Breban regularly attended Marie's court during the next two years. Geoffroy did, however, witness a number of private transactions and sealed letters patent on his own account. He was pledge for 40*l.* that Clarembaud V of Chappes would deliver to the monks of Montiéramey the property he had purchased from a knight.[64] He witnessed as Peter of Magnant acknowledged the fealty he had given to Abbot Thibaut of Montiéramey as a dependent of the abbey.[65] And in a joint letter, Geoffroy and Abbot Peter II of Montier-la-Celle redeemed the mortgaged property of a knight who wished to give it to the leper house in

---

60. Longnon, *Recherches*, 165, no. 34, 1194. For Count Walter III of Brienne, see Perry, *The Briennes*, 33–47.

61. For Geoffroy V of Joinville, see Longnon, *Les compagnons de Villehardouin*, 18–19; for Jean of Possesse, see Evergates, *Aristocracy*, 240.

62. "Marshal of Champagne," which became conventional usage thereafter, identifies the office with the principality, rather than with a count or countess. Longnon notes that shift in the last decades of the twelfth century, as "marshal of France" and "marshal of Burgundy" likewise came to represent polities rather than rulers (*Recherches*, 55–56).

63. Longnon, *Recherches*, 166–67, no. 36, 16 March 1196. Milo Breban was still with Count Henry in Tyre on 30 October 1194 (Strehlke, *Tabulae Ordinis Theutonici*, 26, no. 30): the count exempted the Teutonic Knights from taxes on goods they purchased for their own use. Milo was at the siege of Acre in 1191 when the knight Manasses of Villegruis licensed him to acquire property from his fiefs in augmentation of the fief that Milo already held from him (Mayer, *Die Kanzlei*, 2:214–16, no. 15). In 1193 Milo witnessed as the count granted property at the city wall of Acre to the Teutonic Knights (Strehlke, *Tabulae Ordinis Theutonici*, 24–25, no. 28). In January 1193 at Jaffa both Milo *Brebanz* and "Milo of Provins" (son of Marshal William Rex) witnessed as Henry gave the Hospitallers property next to his *castellum* there (Delaville Le Roulx, *Cartulaire général*, 1:603, no. 954).

64. Lalore, *Cartulaire de l'abbaye de Montiéramey*, 147, no. 119, 1197, incomplete copy of Geoffroy's letter; the missing text is furnished by Longnon, *Recherches*, 167–68, no. 38. This Clarembaud is now numbered Clarembaud V; see Saint-Phalle, "Les seigneurs de Chappes," 51–58.

65. Lalore, *Cartulaire de l'abbaye de Montiéramey*, 250, no. 245, July 1208. The original fealty occurred before the marshal left on crusade; the second one, to Abbot Roland in 1208, occurred in the marshal's absence overseas.

MARSHAL OF COUNTESS MARIE AND COUNT HENRY II   33

Troyes as an entry gift for his daughter.[66] These were routine, unremarkable transactions conducted before any thought of another crusade had arisen.

Geoffroy last appeared at court with Countess Marie in the fall of 1197, when he and Milo Breban witnessed her confirmation of the sale of woods by Abbot Joscelin of La Charmoye to the Benedictine convent of Avenay.[67] Joscelin had just returned from Hungary after delivering Marie's letter of condolence to her half-sister, Margaret of France, on the death of her husband, King Bela III.[68] Margaret had stayed with Marie after the death of her first husband, Henry the Young King of England, before leaving in 1186 to marry Bela.[69] The abbot must have reported that Margaret planned to end her days in the Holy Land, and indeed she died in Tyre shortly after being welcomed there by Count Henry II and just days before he died in Acre on 10 September 1197. Countess Marie received news of those deaths in late September or early October 1197. Disconsolate, she made her last public appearance in October, most likely as she prepared to enter at the Fontevrist priory of Fontaines-les-Nonnes, just outside Meaux.[70]

Bishop Garnier of Troyes, too, was deeply moved by "an immense sadness" at the news of Henry's death, so much so that he took the cross for a personal journey to the Holy Land. But on reaching Piacenza he received a letter from Innocent informing him that the archbishop of Sens had complained about his absence from Troyes and therefore the pope dispensed Garnier from his vow and asked him to return home.[71] Countess Marie died in that same month, March 1198.[72] She was fifty-three. She had ruled the county almost continuously for two decades since Henry I's expedition to Jerusalem in May 1179.

---

66. "Léproserie," 537–38, 1197.

67. AD Marne, 67 H 1, fol. 6, 1197 (Cartulary of Avenay) = Benton, "Recueil des actes," 1197f. Count Henry the Liberal had given the woods to La Charmoye and therefore his license was required to alienate them.

68. AD Marne, 16 H 13, 1197 = Benton, "Recueil des actes," 1197e.

69. Evergates, *Marie of France*, 48–51, 56–57.

70. *Paraclet*, 117–18, no. 93, October 1197. Marie confirmed the deathbed testament of Helie of Villemaur, likely at the Paraclete; the fact that only Marie's chancellor and notary were present suggests that a small traveling party accompanied her to Fontaines-les-Nonnes; see Evergates, *Marie of France*, 153n114.

71. *Register*, 1:100–103, no. 69, 15 March 1198. The pope referred to Garnier's advanced age. For Bishop Garnier's life on the Fourth Crusade, see Longnon, *Les compagnons de Ville-hardouin*, 13–18.

72. Evergates, *Marie of France*, 89–90.

CHAPTER 3

Marshal of Count Thibaut III

Geoffroy was about fifty when Countess Marie died. As a civil servant embodying three decades of institutional memory and expertise, he would prove an invaluable, trusted mentor to eighteen-year-old Thibaut, whom he had known since birth. In light of subsequent events, it is likely that he played a key but discreet role in the six-month transition between Countess Marie's last appearance in October 1197 and Thibaut's homage to the king in April 1198. Of immediate concern was Thibaut's collateral succession. In 1190 the barons had sworn to accept an eleven-year-old boy as count in the event that his unmarried brother did not return from the crusade, but it was not anticipated that Henry might remain overseas, marry, and sire children who might claim his inheritance.[1] In fact, Henry had two daughters with Queen Isabelle of Jerusalem, and among aristocratic families in Champagne a younger brother did not preempt the rights of an older brother's living children. Although Thibaut was still a minor in terms of the comital office in March 1198, Count Henry's two daughters were much younger—and overseas. Ultimately what mattered was Philip II's acceptance of Thibaut's homage within weeks of Countess Marie's

---

1. For Thibaut II's life, see Arbois de Jubainville, *Histoire*, 4:73–100.

death. Although Philip's relations with Henry II during the Third Crusade were not cordial, the king had esteemed Henry the Liberal and readily accepted young Thibaut as his father's legitimate successor.

Geoffroy of Villehardouin and Milo Breban were among the eleven important men who accompanied Thibaut to Melun in April 1198 to do liege homage to the king. They swore on the Gospels that they wished the count to observe his homage and promised that if he did not, they would place themselves in captivity in Paris until he did so. They were allowed to leave the city during the day on their promise to return by nightfall, but if their captivity lasted for more than one month, the archbishop of Reims would interdict Thibaut's lands.[2] "Geoffroy, marshal of Champagne," was listed third among those who swore on Thibaut's behalf, after Guy II of Dampierre and Walter of Châtillon, and before the chancellor Walter, his brother Guy of Chappes, and Milo (Breban) of Provins—all veterans of the Third Crusade.

The substance of Thibaut's homage was artfully phrased to preclude future challenge. Philip stated that he received his nephew Thibaut in liege homage "for all the land [de tota terra] that my uncle Count Henry [I] held from my father [King Louis VII], and that Count Henry [II], Thibaut's brother, held from me." It would be an orderly succession, from father to son to brother. The term feudum was not mentioned, however, since much of Champagne was in fact held in fief from other lords, primarily the duke of Burgundy (Thibaut's cousin Odo), the archbishop of Reims (Thibaut's uncle William), and the bishop of Langres (Hulduin of Vendeuvre), a fact that the king was not about to recognize. It is not clear whether Geoffroy accompanied Thibaut to Paris in the summer of 1198 to join Philip's forces against Richard I of England, who was supported by a coalition of northern French barons, including Thibaut's cousin Louis, count of Blois, and brother-in-law Baldwin, count of Flanders.[3] But when Louis made peace with Philip on 1 September, swearing not to wage war against

---

2. Philip II's act: *Cartulary of Countess Blanche*, 51–53, no. 23, April 1198 = Delaborde, *Receuil des actes de Philippe Auguste*, 2:129–30, no. 581 = Longnon, *Documents*, 1:467–68, no. 3 = *Layettes*, 1:195–96, no. 473. Thibaut's act: Longnon, *Documents*, 1:468, no. 4, April 1198 = Evergates, *Littere Baronum*, 159–60, no. 1.

3. Thibaut was likely in Paris when he granted the canons of Saint-Victor a perpetual rent from his mill at Montereau for his and his ancestors' souls; photograph of the charter with pendent seal (AN, S 2107A, no. 38, 1198) in Villela-Petit, *1204*, 197, no. 6 (catalogue) and 198, cat. 6 (photograph). The charter, without witnesses, was presented by the count's chancellor, Walter of Chappes, who appears to have written it, which suggests that Thibaut was traveling with a small party. For a brief account of the war, see Gillingham, *Richard I*, 309–20.

36 **CHAPTER 3**

the king as long as he would do justice in his court, it was Thibaut who guaranteed Louis's oath.[4]

Five months after Count Thibaut's succession, in the midst of war between the two kings, the new pope, Innocent III (8 January 1198–1216), issued his encyclical *Post miserabile* (15 August 1198), which called for a new crusade to recover Jerusalem.[5] Those who took the cross were promised the remission of sins, while kings, cities, counts, and barons were asked to finance them. Crusaders were to meet the following March, but Innocent failed to mention a place of muster, or the leadership and logistics of the expedition. He sent Cardinal Peter Capuano to France to make peace between the two kings and to promulgate the papal bull granting indulgences for the remission of sins to those who took the cross, confessed, and committed themselves "to serve God" for one year in military service.[6] Cardinal Soffredo was sent to Venice to discuss support for the expedition.[7]

Marshal Villehardouin, reminiscing in 1207, prefaces his memoirs with the preaching of Fulk of Neuilly, a charismatic parish priest who called for moral reform and performed many miracles, riveting crowds even before Innocent called for a new crusade.[8] When in mid-September 1198 Fulk took the cross at the Chapter General meeting of Cistercian abbots and asked them to do the same, they declined, as it was contrary to their monastic vows. But on 5 November the pope authorized Fulk to recruit Benedictine and Cistercian monks and regular canons as his assistants (*coadiutores*) in preaching "to aid the province of Jerusalem."[9] Cardinal Capuano, who was sent to announce the papal indulgence, may have briefed Count Thibaut and the marshal while passing through Troyes on his way to Paris in the fall of 1198. It was

---

4. *Layettes*, 1:197, no. 478, 1 September 1198, at Vernon Castle, on the border between Normandy and the French royal domain: Count Thibaut's letters patent attesting that Louis, in the presence of many unnamed witnesses, swore not to make war against Philip and authorized Thibaut to present his letter to the king.

5. *Register*, 1:495–505, no. 336, 15 August 1198; translated in Andrea, *Contemporary Sources*, 9–19. Addressed to all towns, counts, and barons, it asked that they fund crusaders for two years; churchmen also were asked to contribute. The bull included indulgences for sins, papal protection of those who took the cross and their property, and suspension of the repayment of debts.

6. Maleczek, *Petrus Capuanus*, 95–116, discusses Peter Capuano's role in preparing the crusade.

7. Madden, *Enrico Dandolo*, 119–21.

8. Villehardouin, *La conquête*, §1. In a major reassessment of Fulk's life, Jones places Fulk's preaching of crusade within the larger context of Innocent's program of moral reform ("Fulk of Neuilly," 131–32).

9. *Register*, 1:597, no. 398, 5 November 1198; translated in Andrea, *Contemporary Sources*, 19–21. For Innocent's role in promoting the crusade, see Park, *Papal Protection*, 91–102.

that exceptionally generous (*si granz*) indulgence that induced so many to take the cross, said the marshal, implicitly commenting on the less than admirable conduct of some crusaders in the years since then.[10] As Villehardouin presents it, the groundswell of enthusiasm for the crusade generated by Fulk and his team of preachers set the stage for the cross-taking by the counts of Champagne and Blois one year later.

While war and crusade hung in the air, Villehardouin was busy with practical matters at home. Two of his letters patent from 1198 dealt with the village of Magnant, not far from Troyes. In one, he certified that the knight Hugh Curebois had mortgaged his share of the village to the monks of Montiéramy for 40*l.* cash and "promised faith" in the marshal's hand (*in manu mea fidem dedit*).[11] In the second charter he confirmed the resolution of a dispute between the bakers of Magnant and the monks over the use of certain dead wood for their oven. In both instances the monks asked the marshal, rather than the young count or the bishop, to confirm their rights. More consequential was his mediation of Count Thibaut's dispute with the cathedral canons of Troyes. The marshal, representing the count, and the archbishop of Sens, representing the canons, devised a compromise by which Thibaut was allowed to summon the chapter's men to military service only if he came in person to lead them or if he notified the chapter "by his letters patent or authorized messenger," and then only for the count's own business. Otherwise, the count's provost had to respect the immunity of the canons' cloister and related buildings and their officials living there.[12] That the new count, only nineteen, entrusted Geoffroy to represent him in binding arbitration reflected his trust in the marshal. For that loyal service, he gave Villehardouin the protection tax (*salvamentum*) owed by one of the cathedral chapter's villages, but on learning that the canons had charters from Count Henry I, Countess Marie, and Count Henry II granting them an annual grain revenue assigned from that tax, the marshal ordered his agents not to collect it.[13]

---

10. Villehardouin, *La conquête*, §2.

11. AD Aube, 6 H 20 = Lalore, *Cartulaire de l'abbaye de Montiéramey*, 156–57, no. 135, 1198. Hugh's brother retained the other half of the village.

12. AN, J 195, no. 2, 1198 = *Cartulary of Countess Blanche*, 270–72, no. 303, 1198 = *Layettes*, 1:198–99, no. 484, letter of John, dean of the cathedral. The count's military service was specified as being "in exercitum vel in expeditionem in propria persona pro negotio proprio" and was to be announced "per litteras suas vel per credibilem nuntium." Count Thibaut sealed a reciprocal letter (GC 12: *instr.* 282, no. 53 = Geary, "Saint Helen of Athyra," 152–53n10, 1198).

13. Longnon, *Recherches*, 173, no. 50, undated, but shortly after the mediation.

CHAPTER 3

Indirect evidence suggests that Villehardouin, as the count's closest adviser, had a hand in developing Thibaut's new policies regarding castle lordships within the county. In the brief time he was count, Thibaut acquired the castellanies of Nogent-sur-Seine (June 1199) and Sainte-Menehould (September 1200), he imposed liege homage on the younger sons of barons who were accustomed to hold their inheritances in fief from their older brothers, and he required that private castles be rendered to him at his need.[14] Those policies represented a dramatic expansion of comital rights over the castle lords, who had enjoyed virtual independence under Thibaut's predecessors. Thibaut's widow Countess Blanche implemented those policies, which ultimately contributed to a civil war in Champagne.[15]

The year 1199 was a critical one for the fifty-year-old marshal and twenty-year-old count. The pope expected the crusade would be led by the kings of France and England, who agreed to cooperate, but the death of Richard I (6 April) changed that calculus.[16] King John was preoccupied with Philip II's designs on Normandy and western France, while Philip, mindful of his experience on the Third Crusade, was not eager to lead a new crusade to Jerusalem. It is not clear when or how Count Thibaut emerged as first among the princely leaders of the northern French armies, but he was a natural choice to succeed his brother Henry II, who had earned high praise as leader of the overseas Franks in the 1190s. Thibaut also was close to his cousin Philip II, having done liege homage the previous year and having served in the king's forces against the English. Thibaut's uncle William, archbishop of Reims, and his aunt Adele, the queen mother, were still alive and might well have had a hand in promoting their attractive young nephew, of whom the marshal later said, "no man at that time had more true friends."[17]

On 1 July the marshal attended Thibaut's wedding in Chartres cathedral to Blanche of Navarre, youngest sister of King Sancho VII. Thibaut's cousin Bishop Renaud of Chartres officiated. Following the ceremony, Thibaut presented Blanche with her dower properties in a document he read aloud before the distinguished witnesses (*presentibus et audientibus*): the bride's older sister and Richard I's widow Berengaria; Thibaut's aunt Adele, dowager queen of France; his cousin Rotrou of Perche, bishop of

---

14. Evergates, *Aristocracy*, 34–36.
15. Evergates, "Countess Blanche."
16. See Ryan, "Richard I and the Early Evolution of the Fourth Crusade."
17. Villehardouin, *La conquête*, §36.

Châlons; Bishop Garnier of Troyes, a long-time friend of the comital family; counts William I of Joigny and Walter III of Brienne; Thibaut's seneschal Geoffroy V of Joinville and butler Walter of Châtillon—and "Geoffroy, my marshal."[18]

It is likely that Count Louis of Blois also attended the wedding celebrated in his land.[19] He and Thibaut had multiple common ancestors and had become close after Thibaut vouched for his loyalty to Philip the previous September. Their fathers were brothers, sons of Count Thibaut V of Blois. Their mothers were sisters, daughters of Louis VII and Eleanor of Aquitaine, who had served as regents while Louis and Thibaut were coming of age. Both counts had been touched by the Third Crusade. Louis, eighteen in 1190, had been at Acre with his father, who died there.[20] Although Thibaut was only eleven when Count Henry II left on that crusade, he must have heard stories of his older brother's exploits overseas. And so, even before Thibaut's wedding, the two young counts shared a close familial relationship, recent allegiances to the king of France, and experiences of the Third Crusade.

It is not hard to imagine that the pope's call for a new crusade prompted discussion during the wedding festivities of the unfinished business of the Third Crusade. Thibaut's uncles, counts Thibaut of Blois and Stephen of Sancerre, died on that expedition. Geoffroy V of Joinville and Walter III of Brienne witnessed the death of their fathers at Acre, and Bishop Renaud saw his brother, Count Henry I of Bar-le-Duc, die there. Marshal Geoffroy returned after three years of captivity, and Milo Breban returned after spending four years with Henry II. Although Villehardouin in 1207 did not see fit to disclose any of the conversation at the wedding, informal talk among the relatives and veterans of the Third Crusade must have convinced Thibaut, as his brother's successor, to lead an army from Champagne to redeem the failure of the Third Crusade. If Count Louis were present, as seems likely, the plan would have been to take a grand army of Champagne and Blois to the Holy Land.

---

18. *Layettes*, 1:204, no. 497, 1 July 1199: "Galfrido marescalco meo"; Evergates, *Feudal Society*, 58–59, no. 40. The sealed document that the chancellor presented (*per manum*) to Blanche contains the name of the scribe (*nota Petri*) who recorded Thibaut's reading of the dower letter.

19. Louis is not mentioned in Thibaut's dower letter because he was not directly connected to Blanche's dower lands in Champagne.

20. Brief biographies of Count Louis are in Longnon, *Les compagnons de Villehardouin*, 79–85, and Crépin-Leblond, "Louis, comte de Blois."

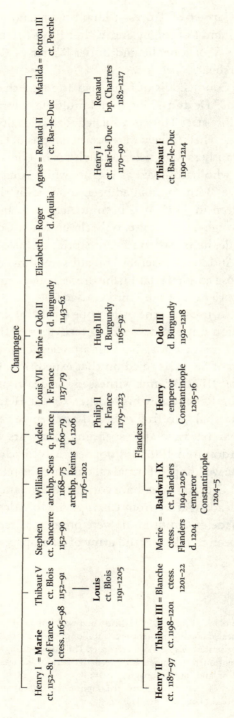

GENEALOGY 2. The counts of Champagne, Blois, and Flanders

Écry

Villehardouin states that on 28 November 1199, five months after Thibaut's wedding, Thibaut and Louis took the cross with their barons "at a tournament in Champagne at a castle called Écry" (ot un tornoi en Champaigne a un chastel qui ot nom Aicris).[21] Located in the valley of the Aisne River south of Château-Porcien, the flat land between Écry (today Asfeld) and Balham was an ideal site for a tournament. Villehardouin does not say that Fulk was present or that crusade was preached on that occasion, nor does he identify the sponsor of the event at an otherwise unknown tournament site. Ralph II, lord (*dominus castri*) of Écry, does not appear among the cross-takers in 1199, and there is no evidence that he joined the crusade.[22]

Young Thibaut was following what was becoming a family tradition. Fifty years earlier his father Henry I, then nineteen, took the cross at Vézelay after hearing Bernard of Clairvaux preach crusade, and in 1188 his twenty-two-year-old brother Henry II took the cross at Gisors after the kings of France and England made peace and his uncle, Archbishop William of Reims, preached crusade. The roster of those who took the cross with Thibaut and Villehardouin at Écry included Bishop Garnier of Troyes and twenty-two named barons and knights, of whom nine were related in some way to the marshal: his nephew Geoffroy and cousin Henry of Arzillières; his neighbors Vilain and William of Nully, Oger of Saint-Chéron, and Renaud II of Dampierre; his colleague Milo Breban; and the knights Manessier of l'Isle-Adam and Macaire of Sainte-Menehould.[23] Nine (41 percent) of those named are known to have been veterans of the Third Crusade.[24]

---

21. Villehardouin, *La conquête*, §3. Villehardouin is alone in identifying Ècry both as a tournament site and the place where Thibaut took the cross. Robert of Clari does not mention either Écry or a tournament. Manuscript O (Faral) reads *Aicris*, B (Dufournet) reads *Eris*. Manuscript G (BnF, fr. 15460) reads "between Écri and Baleham," that is to say between present-day Asfeld (département Ardennes, arrondissement Rethel) and Balham.

22. Ralph II owed castle-guard at Fismes in 1200–1201 (*Feoda* 2, no. 2271). In 1197 he sealed letters patent in which he called himself "Radulphus, dominus de Erchi"; he died in 1211. For a brief history of the Écry lords, see Newman, *Les seigneurs de Nesle*, 1:145–48, which does not mention Ralph I, who witnessed several acts of Count Henry I (*Actes*, nos. 24 (1152), 35 (1153), and was listed for a fief at Écry in 1178 (*Feoda* 1, Châtillon and Fismes, no. 763.

23. Villehardouin, *La conquête*, §5.

24. Longnon (*Recherches*, 64) names six veterans of the Third Crusade; in fact, there were nine: Henry of Arzillières, Oger of Saint-Chéron, Geoffroy V of Joinville, Manessier of l'Isle-Adam, Milo Breban, Guy of Chappes, Vilain of Nully, Walter of Vignory, and Villehardouin himself.

CHAPTER 3

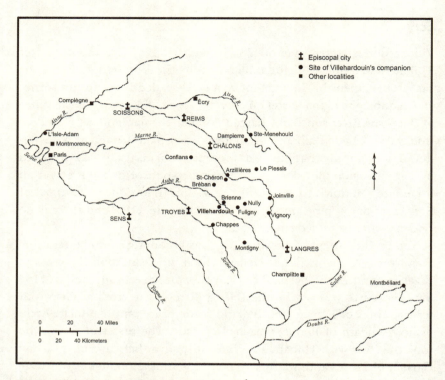

MAP 2. Villehardouin's Champenois companions at Écry

Events moved rapidly after the July wedding and November cross-taking. In letters to the prelates and lay leaders of Western Europe on 31 December, the pope announced the imposition of a one-fortieth (2.5 percent) tax on all ecclesiastical revenues to support the expedition to "the province of Jerusalem," and the appointment of a Hospitaller and a Templar to oversee the collection and disbursement of the funds.[25] On 4 January 1200 Innocent asked all Christians to aid the Holy Land and some "to fight the Lord's war" (*ad bellandum bellum Domini*).[26] In those same winter months Bishop Nivelon of Soissons took the cross with men from the royal domain, notably Mathieu of Montmorency and Guy, castellan of Coucy.[27] On 23 February 1200 Thibaut's sister

---

25. *Register*, 2:490–97, no. 258: "Graves orientalis terrae," 31 December 1199; translated in Andrea, *Contemporary Sources*, 24–32. Cistercians, Premonstratensians, and Carthusians were exempted.

26. *Register*, 2:497–501, no. 259, 4 January 1200.

27. The roster of oath-takers with Bishop Nivelon of Soissons clearly states (Villehardouin, *La conquête*, §7) that they took the cross *en France*, not at Écry.

MARSHAL OF COUNT THIBAUT III 43

Marie and brother-in-law Count Baldwin of Flanders took the cross in Bruges, followed shortly afterward by Count Hugh IV of Saint-Pol, who was married to Baldwin's paternal aunt Yolande of Hainaut.[28] By early spring 1200 the counts of Champagne, Blois, and Flanders and their barons and knights had taken the cross to reconquer Jerusalem.

For Geoffroy of Villehardouin, then in his early fifties, the cross-taking at Écry began a venture that would consume the rest of his life. With thirty years of service to the comital family, he had become the most prominent official in Champagne, closer to the count than even the chancellor, who formally presented the count's sealed documents to their beneficiaries. The marshal had survived the Third Crusade, had sworn to Thibaut's good-faith homage to the king, attended Thibaut's wedding in Chartres with the highest barons of Champagne, and was among the important Champenois who accompanied Thibaut to Écry. In view of his lament at Thibaut's death and his remembrance of the count's character, Geoffroy appears to have been more than a mentor, perhaps even a surrogate father to Thibaut, who was only an infant when Henry I died.[29]

The three organizing counts were relatively young—Thibaut was twenty, Louis and Baldwin were about twenty-seven—and closely related, Thibaut and Louis as cousins, and Thibaut and Baldwin as brothers-in-law.[30] They were joined by Hugh of Saint-Pol, the oldest at about forty-two and like Count Louis a veteran of the Third Crusade; Villehardouin would have known both Hugh and Louis at the siege of Acre.[31] One issue, however, divided the counts: Baldwin, Louis, and Hugh had sided with Richard of England in his war against Philip, while Thibaut had joined the French king in the field. Of the four counts, Baldwin possessed the most extensive recent military experience while still in his twenties; he avoided pitched battles whenever possible, and by destroying

---

28. Several barons took the cross with Baldwin at Bruges (Villehardouin, *La conquête*, §8). Hugh of Saint-Pol and Geoffroy of Perche followed later (§§9–10). The *Chronique* of Ernoul and Bernard, 337, states that Baldwin and his company took the cross at a tournament held near Péronne, between Bray-sur-Somme and Encre (today Albert), which is difficult to reconcile with Villehardouin's statement that Baldwin and Marie took the cross at Bruges.

29. Villehardouin, *La conquête*, §37.

30. Villehardouin remembers Thibaut (born May 1179) as being "no more than twenty-two," and Louis as "about twenty-seven" (Villehardouin, *La conquête*, §3).

31. For Hugh of Saint-Pol, see Longnon, *Les compagnons de Villehardouin*, 195–97, and Nieus, *Un pouvoir comtal entre Flandre et France*, 102–15. Hugh was born around 1158; he married Yolande, sister of Count Baldwin V of Hainaut and widow of Count Ivo II of Soissons, in 1178; he was knighted at about twenty-one in 1179. He would have been in his early thirties on the Third Crusade and about forty-two on the Fourth Crusade.

44   CHAPTER 3

bridges and blocking roads, he denied the royal army its supply wagons and siege engines.[32] After concluding a three-year war with the Treaty of Péronne in January 1200, which Philip signed in response to the papal legate's moral suasion, Baldwin emerged triumphant, a skillful politician and military leader free to pursue an overseas venture.[33]

In March 1200 an organizational meeting (*parlement*) of counts and barons was convened in Soissons to decide when the crusade would leave and by which route, which suggests that they expected to march together as a grand army. Soissons was a convenient venue for the meeting. Located between Flanders and Champagne, it was the episcopal seat of Bishop Nivelon, a royal bishop installed by Count Thibaut's uncle Archbishop William and an enthusiastic promoter of the crusade.[34] Marshal Geoffroy, representing Count Thibaut and acting de facto as chief of staff, does not name those in attendance or divulge any details of the deliberations, nor does he reveal whether he, as marshal, offered any advice. He admits only that the participants could not agree "because it seemed to them that there were not enough crusaders [*genz croisies*] yet."[35] Insufficient manpower would become Villehardouin's persistent concern throughout the expedition and post-conquest settlement.

About the same time, in April or May, the pope informed the prelates of France that he had established a commission to collect a one-fortieth tax from all ecclesiastical revenues to support the knights and other combatants who had taken the cross and promised to remain at least one year in the Holy Land. The pope prescribed the food and clothing of the crusaders and expanded the commission authorized to collect and disburse the funds to include Mathieu of Montmorency (representing both Philip II and Bishop Nivelon of Soissons), Walter of Godonville (representing Count Louis), the Champenois Milo Breban, the Flemish Conon of Béthune, and a Templar and Hospitaller.[36]

---

32. For Baldwin, the "science" of warfare was a mix of combat skills, weaponry, and maneuver around fortified sites; see Gillingham, "Richard I and the Science of War," 222.

33. Moore, "Count Baldwin IX of Flanders," stresses Baldwin's ingenuity in outmaneuvering the king's "ecclesiastical advantage" by using episcopal and papal resources for political ends. For Baldwin's life before the crusade, see Wolff, "Baldwin of Flanders and Hainaut," 281–88. Longnon, *Les compagnons de Villehardouin*, 37–40, summarizes Baldwin's crusade experience.

34. For Nivelon's life and career, see Claverie, "Un *Illustris amicus Venetorum*."

35. Villehardouin, *La conquête*, §11. Longnon (Villehardouin, *Histoire de la conquête de Constantinople*), 26, agrees in calling Villehardouin a *chef d'état-major*.

36. *Gesta Innocentii*, no. 133 (Powell, *The Deeds of Innocent*, 133–39), no. 84, April–May 1200, letter of Innocent to the prelates of France. The compiler of *Gesta* states that this letter was

MARSHAL OF COUNT THIBAUT III

Two months after Soissons, most likely in late May or June, "all the counts and barons who were crossed" reconvened at Compiègne in the royal domain. "Many opinions were voiced," Villehardouin recalled, suggesting a lively debate. He does not mention the issues at hand, but they must have included the location of the grand army's muster and whether it would march overland or sail from a southern port. Since that conference, too, failed to reach a consensus, it was agreed that the best course was for each of the three principal counts to appoint plenipotentiaries to make binding decisions regarding the logistics of the expedition. Given his reputation as a mediator, Geoffroy himself might have suggested that procedure as a way to expedite matters and obviate personal conflicts among the commanders. The three principal counts—Thibaut, Louis, and Baldwin—each selected two envoys (*messages*) and provided sealed letters of credence (*cartes pendanz*) stating that the principals would be bound by any agreement (*convenances*) reached by their envoys.[37] As his envoys, Count Thibaut appointed Geoffroy of Villehardouin and Milo Breban, his two most trusted officials, who had long served his father, mother, and brother.[38]

Geoffroy and Milo already knew one of Count Baldwin's envoys, the poet Conon of Béthune, also a veteran of the Third Crusade, whose father died at Acre. They may have met Conon earlier in Meaux, where Countess Marie often held court and where Conon visited Hugh II of Oisy, viscount of Meaux, his relative and mentor in the lyric arts.[39] Count Thibaut, who was in his early teens when he accompanied his mother on those occasions, must have esteemed Conan, for he later granted him a fief in Champagne.[40] Geoffroy, Milo Breban, and Conon, all in their fifties, would remain close throughout the next

---

representative of the many sent on that subject. Verdier, *L'aristocratie de Provins*, 182, identifies one of the tax collectors, "Milonis de Bramont," as Milo Breban.

37. When Villehardouin speaks of the counts entrusting their envoys with "fine charters pendant" (les bailleroient bones chartes pendanz) declaring that the counts would be bound by any agreements made by the envoys, he was referring to letters of credence that were presented to the doge on their arrival in Venice (*La conquête*, §13).

38. Villehardouin, *La conquête*, §§12–13. Manuscripts B, C, D, and E identify Villehardouin simply as "marshal," whereas A and O (copied in Venice) add "of Champagne."

39. For brief biographies of Conon, see Conon of Béthune, *Les chansons*, iii–vii, and Longnon, *Les compagnons de Villehardouin*, 146–48.

40. *Feoda* 3, no. 2594, of ca. 1201: "Cuno de Betuna, de feodo quod est apud Monasterium in Poeseia" (Moutiers-Yonne), entry added at the end of the roll of fiefs for Nogent-sur-Seine, the castellany acquired by Count Thibaut III from its heiress in 1198 (Evergates, *Aristocracy*, 239, 285n8). Thibaut must have granted the fief between April 1198 and May 1201.

46   **CHAPTER 3**

decade, from the initial planning of the crusade in the spring of 1200 through the post-conquest years as battlefield commanders in Constantinople's hinterland.

Venice

We know nothing further about Villehardouin's activities in 1200 beyond the three extant letters patent he sealed concerning matters in Champagne. In April he and Milo of Saint-Quentin, a garrison knight in Chantemerle, jointly announced the sale of property by a knight's son to Reclus Abbey.[41] In July, he resolved a dispute between a knight's widow and the Templars residing in the village of Fresnay by dividing the village and its revenues equally between them.[42] In October he confirmed a transaction between his mayor in Villy and the leper house in Troyes.[43] That was the last mention of Geoffroy before he arrived in Venice with his fellow envoys three months later, at the beginning of Lent (7 February 1201), to contract for transport of the northern French armies.

It is not clear when in the late summer or fall of 1200 the six envoys decided to visit the southern ports (*les porz de mer*). As veterans of the Third Crusade, they recognized the naval expertise of Pisa and especially of Genoa, which had established a dominant presence in the eastern Mediterranean after transporting Philip II's army in 1190.[44] But according to Villehardouin, the envoys concluded that Venice had the greatest capacity to supply the many ships necessary for what was expected to be a large force. It appears that the envoys knew that Venice was outfitting a fleet at the pope's direction, making it the obvious choice as the port of departure.[45] If Geoffroy's later trips to and from Italy are any indication, the envoys met in Champagne in late 1200, most likely in Troyes, before heading southward to Dijon and crossing the Alps at the Mont Cenis Pass on the way to Montferrat, Piacenza, and Venice.

---

41. Longnon, *Recherches*, 174, no. 52, 1199 (or 1 January–8 April 1200 [new style]); Villehardouin's brother Jean witnessed. Milo of Saint-Quentin, a garrison knight at Chantemerle (*Feoda* 1, no. 1288: liege and *estagium*) also held a fief in Sézanne (*Feoda*, no. 1779).

42. AD, Haute-Marne, 61 H 9, July 1200 = Longnon, *Recherches*, 174–75, no. 53.

43. "Léproserie," 541–42, 1200.

44. See Mack, "A Genoese Perspective of the Third Crusade."

45. As noted by Angold, *The Fourth Crusade*, 80–81. See also Madden, *Enrico Dandolo*, 119–21.

MARSHAL OF COUNT THIBAUT III

47

Villehardouin reports a warm reception in Venice when the envoys presented the doge, Enrico Dandolo, with their letters of credence attesting that the counts would accept whatever their envoys decided.[46] The Venetians expressed a "curiosity" about their mission, he recalled, clearly a politesse, since they were well informed about the crusade that had been actively promoted by Innocent III over the previous two years. The envoys requested a meeting of the Small Council and four days later were received in the doge's palace, where they presented the plan of the "high barons of France" (*les hals barons de France*) who had taken the cross to reconquer Jerusalem and avenge the "humiliation" (*hont*) of Christ. They asked for Venetian support. Villehardouin reports the gist of the speeches (*en tel maniere*) exchanged between the doge and the envoys but could not recall all that was said.[47] From his subsequent remarks it is clear that either he or Conon spoke for the delegation, for they represented Counts Thibaut and Baldwin, the two most important princes. Although Villehardouin portrays the negotiations as a joint undertaking by the six envoys, his detailed recounting of the negotiation suggests that he, as Count Thibaut's marshal, was lead negotiator. Given the magnitude of their project, the doge set a council meeting one week hence to discuss the matter.[48]

The doge announced that Venice offered to build a fleet of sailing ships (*nes*) to transport 4,500 knights and 20,000 "well-armed" foot soldiers, horse transports (*uissiers*) for 4,500 horses and 9,000 squires (two per knight), and provisions for horses and personnel for one year to support the expedition to the Holy Land and "to serve God and Christendom wherever we might go." The Venetians charged 85,000 marks, payable in advance at four terms, with the entire sum due before embarkment in June 1202.[49] To sweeten the deal, they offered in a separate commercial transaction (*compaigne*) to furnish fifty armed galleys (*galees*)

---

46. Villehardouin, *La conquête*, §§15–16. The letters of credence that Villehardouin describes in §13 were not the blank, sealed charters of the counts that the Venetian chancery filled in, stating that the envoys had accepted the contract for transport (§31). The negotiations with the doge and the Venetians are well described by Madden, *Enrico Dandolo*, 121–41.

47. Villehardouin, *La conquête*, §20. Jacquin, "Geoffroy de Villehardouin," analyzes the speeches.

48. Villehardouin, *La conquête*, §§14–20.

49. Villehardouin, *La conquête*, §§21–22. Tafel and Thomas, *Urkunden*, 1:362–68, no. 92, April 1201 = Longnon, *Recherches*, 177–81, no. 59. Both original copies of the contract state that the agreed price was 85,000 marks, as in manuscripts B, C, and D. Manuscripts A and O read 94,000 marks, either a copyist's error (Hendrickx, "A propos du nombre des troupes," 32) or Venice's initial asking price before it was negotiated to 85,000 marks (Queller and Madden, *The Fourth Crusade*, 11), which made the final price not much more expensive than the

48   **CHAPTER 3**

at their own expense in return for half of anything captured "at sea or on land."[50] After an evening's deliberation, the envoys accepted those terms.

The doge presented the proposal at the Great Council, which approved, then at several larger meetings, and finally at an open meeting in Saint Mark's Basilica. After Mass, the doge invited the envoys to address the people of Venice. Villehardouin recalls the scene in which he spoke on behalf of the envoys in that "most beautiful church" before an audience he estimated at 10,000, who heard of the proposal for the first time:

> Lords, the most distinguished and powerful barons of France have sent us to you. They implore you to take pity on Jerusalem, which is enslaved by the Turks, and they ask you, in God's name, to join them in avenging the dishonor [*honte*] of Jesus Christ. And for this, they have chosen you because they know that no other people have as great a mastery of the seas as you. They ordered us to fall at your feet and not rise until you have agreed to take pity on the [Holy] Land overseas.[51]

It was an emotional public performance, with the six envoys kneeling before the doge, to the acclamation of all: "We agree! We agree!" The doge then ascended the pulpit and made an impassioned speech praising the envoys and asking the Venetians to join the venture, but, said Villehardouin, "I cannot recall all the fine words that the doge said." For the marshal, whose official duties required discretion in council and deference to noble lords and princes, that moment in Saint Mark's was an exhilarating experience and a vivid memory recalled with relish six years later.[52]

The next day the contracts were drawn up without, however, revealing the crusade's true destination, which was Egypt, according to a plan discussed earlier to destroy the Ayyubid regime.[53] As Villehard-

---

contracts Genoa made in 1184 and 1190 for the Third Crusade. Bell, "Unintended Consumption," analyzes the numbers.

50. Villehardouin, *La conquête*, §§22–23. Villehardouin remembered that the doge spoke of sharing equally "all conquests that we make, on sea and on land" (§23), but the treaty states that the two parties would share "anything that is acquired by conquest or treaty," which Queller and Madden, *The Fourth Crusade*, 12–13, interpret as the "spoils of war," not land.

51. Villehardouin, *La conquête*, §§24–27.

52. Villehardouin, *La conquête*, §§25–30. Jacquin, "Geoffroy de Villehardouin," 132, reads the event, with its ceremonial discourses and oath-taking, as a highly charged emotional experience, one of several artful performances occasioned by the negotiations in Venice.

53. Villehardouin speaks of "Babylon," understood as "Cairo." As noted by Queller and Madden, *The Fourth Crusade*, 14–16, an attack on Egypt had been broached a half-century earlier. For the military thinking on sailing to Egypt rather than to Syria, which most crusaders

ouin later admitted, the decision to sail to Egypt was kept secret from the knights and commoners.[54] There was another reason for going to Egypt: the Venetians and the papacy surely knew that the overseas Franks had signed a truce with the Muslims on 1 July 1198 to last five years and eight months, effectively prohibiting any military offensive against Jerusalem until 1 March 1204. Since Egypt was not party to that agreement, it was vulnerable to attack, but in order not to upset the army, it was announced simply that they would be going "overseas."

At a meeting of the Venetian council with the six plenipotentiaries in April 1201, the doge presented the contract drawn up by the Venetian chancellor in the name of counts Baldwin, Thibaut, and Louis. The doge and the forty-six members of the council swore "on scripture" (*sor sainz*) to observe the contract, as did the six envoys.[55] It was a dramatic beginning to a momentous undertaking. The Venetians kept Thibaut's blank, pre-sealed charter (*pagamentum hoc vacuum*), which the Venetian chancery had filled in to state that Marshal Geoffroy and Milo Breban, acting as his fiduciaries, had accepted the contract (*instrumentum pactionis*) they had negotiated with Enrico Dandolo for transport to "the land of Jerusalem."[56] Villehardouin and Milo Breban were presented with a copy of the contract.[57] The fleet would be ready for "the barons and pilgrims" by the next feast of Saint John (24 June) and would set sail on 29 June 1202. The envoys then borrowed 2,000 marks to serve as down payment on the contracted sum. The contract also stipulated that the envoys obtain the approval of the pope and the king of France "if they are able to," but six years later the marshal, perhaps misremembering,

---

took as the goal of the expedition, see Murray, "The Place of Egypt in the Military Strategy," 127–28.

54. Villehardouin, *La conquête*, §30.

55. As Faral notes (Villehardouin, *La conquête*), 1:32–33n1, when Villehardouin speaks of oaths sworn *sor sains*, he means "on scripture," not "on relics," as it is usually translated. That reading is confirmed by Villehardouin's statement that he and the envoys *jura sor sainz* to observe their treaty with Venice (§31), whereas the treaty, written in Latin, states that the envoys "ad Evangelia sancta Dei juraverunt" (Tafel and Thomas, *Urkunden*, 1:362–68, no. 92, at 367 = Longnon, *Recherches*, 177–81, no. 59).

56. Longnon, *Recherches*, 181–83, no. 60, dated April 1201 = Tafel and Thomas, *Urkunden*, 1:359–60, no. 90 = Faral (Villehardouin, *La conquête*), 1:217–18, appendix 1, no. 2: "pagamenum hoc vacuum suo [Thibaut's] sigillo munitum." Queller finds these diplomatic blank charters the only extant copies for which there is clear evidence ("Diplomatic 'Blanks,'" 477–78).

57. The contract was drawn up in several copies for the envoys (Longnon, *Recherches*, 177–81, no. 59, April 1201 = Tafel and Thomas, *Urkunden*, 1:362–73, nos. 92–93). The contracts were carried by the crusaders to Constantinople, where they were copied in a chancery register known as "the Book."

50   CHAPTER 3

stated that both parties sent messengers announcing the plan only to Innocent III, who confirmed it "most willingly" (*mult volentiers*).[58]

That the envoys contracted for the transport of what would have been the largest sea-borne force at the time was a surprising miscalculation, since four of the envoys—Villehardouin, Milo Breban, Conon de Béthune, and Jean of Friaize—as veterans of the Third Crusade, should have had a more realistic expectation.[59] In 1190 Philip II contracted with Genoa for the transport of 650 knights, each with two mounts and two squires, for a total force of about 1,950, while Richard I had perhaps 900 knights.[60] Villehardouin does not explain why the envoys anticipated a considerable force of 4,500 knights, seven times greater than Philip's a decade earlier, since it was clear by the spring of 1200 that fewer combatants than expected had taken the cross. Possibly he was misled by his own familiarity with the registers of fiefs from Champagne which, he later reported, listed 2,200 knights of the count, of whom 1,800 performed castle-guard.[61] If the knights from Flanders, Blois, and the royal domain were added to those, the contracted number of 4,500 knights might have seemed entirely reasonable. A conventional calculation of two squires per knight (9,000) and twice as many common soldiers (20,000) would have brought the total number to about 35,000, not counting their mounts and support personnel.

It is also possible that the Venetians, after learning the actual destination, inflated the numbers and built a fleet to land in Egypt.[62] If the estimated number of crusaders had materialized, the main expedition would have projected a major armed force into the eastern Mediterranean; together with the fifty Venetian war ships, it would have sufficed to capture Cairo and establish Venice as the dominant commercial presence in Egypt and beyond.[63] As it was, only half the expected number

---

58. Villehardouin, *La conquête*, §§31–32. Whether Villehardouin or the *Gesta Innocentii* misrepresents the pope's reaction is not clear; see Faral, "Geoffroy de Villehardouin," 537–39, and Queller and Madden, *The Fourth Crusade*, 18–20.

59. Riley-Smith, "Toward an Understanding of the Fourth Crusade," 73–75.

60. Mack, "A Genoese Perspective of the Third Crusade," 50.

61. *Cartulary of Countess Blanche*, 294–95, no. 333, ca. 1208–9, report of Villehardouin and Milo Breban to the countess.

62. Pryor, "The Venetian Fleet," 121–22, concludes that the fleet of shallow-draft horse transports (*uissiers*) was perfectly adapted for an amphibious assault on Egypt, but not against Acre.

63. Villehardouin, *La conquête*, §30. This is the persuasive argument of Madden, *Enrico Dandolo*, 123–25. Riley-Smith, "Toward an Understanding of the Fourth Crusade," 77–79, likewise argues that the size and composition of the Venetian fleet meant that it was built for an amphibious landing in Alexandria, which Innocent had planned.

of crusaders arrived in Venice, still a sizable force of perhaps 18,000, of whom 12,000 to 13,000 were combatants. While Villehardouin later deplored the failure of many crusaders to muster in Venice, he made no attempt to explain a miscalculation that jeopardized the expedition. As he admits, the Venetians outfitted a fleet that could have transported three times the number of those who arrived in Venice and who became liable for the entire sum owed to the Venetians. It has been estimated that only 1,500 knights and 3,000 mounted sergeants ultimately embarked on 1 October 1202 and that by the time of the first assault on Constantinople in July 1203 only about 500 knights and as many sergeants remained in the main army, or about 11 percent of the number contracted by the envoys two years earlier.[64]

Villehardouin returned to Champagne after almost two months in Venice. It is highly likely that that he stopped at Montferrat to meet with Boniface, marquis of Montferrat, a prominent prince whose family was well known in the eastern Mediterranean.[65] Boniface's younger brother Renier had married the daughter of Emperor Manuel Komnenos, while the elder Conrad was known for having mounted a vigorous defense of Tyre against Saladin and for being with Count Henry II of Champagne at the siege of Acre.[66] Villehardouin had attended Conrad's wedding to Queen Isabelle of Jerusalem on 24 November 1190 before being captured by Saladin's troops, and he was still captive in Damascus when Conrad died under mysterious circumstances on 28 April 1192.[67] Boniface would have been keenly interested in a grand new crusade to retake Jerusalem and to avenge his brother's murder.

There was another, more pressing reason for Villehardouin to meet Boniface. The marquis was the same age, about fifty, and an experienced military leader, having served with Frederick Barbarossa against the Italian communes in the 1180s and in Sicily in the 1190s. Known

---

64. Riley-Smith, "Toward an Understanding of the Fourth Crusade," 81, estimates the eventual numbers of combatants in the first assault on Constantinople.

65. Queller and Madden, *The Fourth Crusade*, 9, suggest that Villehardouin met with Boniface on the way to Venice, but I concur with Longnon, *Recherches*, 71–72, who considers a meeting on Villehardouin's return from Venice, after the contract had been sealed, as more probable.

66. It is not clear whether Renier actually took possession of Thessalonika; see Barker, "Late Byzantine Thessalonike," 10. For Conrad's life overseas, see Jacoby, "Conrad, Marquis of Montferrat."

67. Harari, "The Assassination of King Conrad," reviews the evidence pertaining to the assassins.

52   CHAPTER 3

as a literate prince with a taste for lyric poetry, he attracted several of the best Provençal poets to Montferrat, notably Raimbaut of Vaqueiras, who served him loyally on the battlefield and at court.[68] The marshal certainly must have discussed his business in Venice and may well have shown Boniface the sealed contract he was carrying to Count Thibaut. In light of the lagging recruitment of crusaders to date, Boniface's military forces would add heft to the crusader army, and his funds would help defray the cost of the fleet being built in Venice.

If Villehardouin does not mention meeting Boniface, he does note that while crossing the Mont Cenis Pass in the Alps he encountered Count Walter III of Brienne, one of the most prominent barons in Champagne, who had attended Count Thibaut's wedding and was listed first among the barons who took the cross at Écry. Walter was on his way to claim his new wife's lands in Apulia, with the pope's active support.[69] In order to finance his journey, he sold several of his properties and mortgaged his county of Brienne to Count Thibaut for 700*l*.[70] Villehardouin notes that Brienne was accompanied by "many good men [*bone gent*] from Champagne who had taken the cross" with Brienne, notably Walter of Montbéliard, Eustace of Conflans, and Robert of Joinville. On being informed of the plan to sail from Venice a year hence, Walter promised that he and his men would arrive before the sailing. But, as Villehardouin noted regretfully in 1207, they failed to join the main army: "it was a great pity, since they were very worthy and courageous men" (*mult estoient preu et vaillant*). Knowing that Walter had died in Apulia two years earlier (June 1205), Villehardouin commented only that "events turn out as it pleases God."[71] That was Villehardouin's first encounter with Champenois knights who failed to muster in Venice. What he knew, but did not say, was that Brienne's troop included sixty knights and forty sergeants, a force of one hundred mounted combatants, together with the support personnel of his household, clerics, equipment, and multiple mounts.[72] He must have been painfully aware that the main army had been deprived of an entire tactical unit which, in retrospect, might have averted the defeat of the army at the battle of

---

68. See Raimbaut de Vaqueiras, *The Poems*.

69. Innocent sent letters to "the counts and barons, castellans and citizens" of Apulia asking them to support Walter (*Gesta Innocentii*, 53–54, 61–62; Powell, *The Deeds of Innocent*, 36–37, 45–46), nos. 30, 34. For a biography of Walter III of Brienne, see Perry, *The Briennes*, 33–47.

70. *Cartulary of Countess Blanche*, 292, no. 329, April 1201, at Sèzanne, act of Walter III.

71. Villehardouin, *La conquête*, §§33–34.

72. Perry, *The Briennes*, 42.

MARSHAL OF COUNT THIBAUT III

Adrianople (April 1205) that marked the end of the initial Frankish occupation of Byzantine lands.

The Death of Count Thibaut

Villehardouin recalled his return to Champagne in late April or early May: "I rode day after day until I arrived in Troyes and found my lord Count Thibaut ill and exhausted; he was happy to see me, and when I told him my news"—and presented him a copy of the contract with Venice— "he celebrated by taking a ride, which he had not done for a long time."[73] But his condition worsened, and anticipating his end, Thibaut made his testament and distributed the money he had collected for the crusade among his men and companions, "of whom he had many of the best—no man at that time had more of them." Eustace of Conflans, for one, received the considerable sum of 500*l.*, to be collected from the Templars, who were entrusted with the distribution of the funds.[74] Each recipient was required to swear on scripture to join the expedition in Venice. But, noted Villehardouin, many failed to keep their oaths, for which they were much blamed.[75]

Villehardouin was deeply moved by Thibaut's death on 24 May 1201 at the age of twenty-two. "It was a good death," he said. The count was mourned by a large gathering of his family and great men, "for no one of his age was more loved [*amés*] by his own men and by others."[76] He was buried in the chapel next to the resplendent tomb of his father Henry the Liberal, which Geoffroy had seen under construction by Mosan metal workers and enamalists in the 1170s while on garrison duty. The chapel's necrology records Thibaut's death on 25 May as "Thibaut the young count."[77] His widow, Countess Blanche, later had a magnificent "tomb of kinship" constructed, in which the recumbent Thibaut was

---

73. Villehardouin, *La conquête*, §35. Villehardouin carried a copy of the contract with him.

74. Thibaut was unaware that Eustace of Conflans left Champagne only weeks earlier for Italy in the company of Count Walter of Brienne, the very party that Villehardouin encountered at the Mont Cenis Pass on his return from Venice (Villehardouin, *La conquête*, §§33–34). In August 1201 the seneschal Geoffroy of Joinville asked Countess Blanche to authorize the Templars to release the monies to Eustace's brother Guy of Plessis, on Joinville's pledge that the transaction was legitimate (Delisle, *Mémoire sur les opérations financières des Templiers*, 95–96, no. 1). The fates of Eustace and Guy are unknown; see Longnon, *Les compagnons de Villehardouin*, 21–22.

75. Villehardouin, *La conquête*, §36.

76. Villehardouin, *La conquête*, §37.

77. *Obituaires*, 4 (1923): 461: "Obit Theobaldus comes juvenis, filius comitis Henrici hujus ecclesie [Saint-Étienne] fundatoris, VII libras in camera partitionis."

54   CHAPTER 3

surrounded by sculpted images of his father and mother, his sister and brother, his wife and her father, his daughter and son, and the kings of England (Richard I) and France (Philip II).[78]

It must have been a poignant moment for the marshal. Thibaut's death, following those of his father Henry I (1181), brother Henry II (1197), and his mother Marie (1198), did not augur well for the comital line, for the count left an infant daughter and a young, foreign-born wife who was nine months pregnant. Following Thibaut's interment, Countess Blanche sent a letter with her chancellor, Walter of Chappes, to the king who was in Sens, proposing the conditions under which she would be regent for her husband's lands. She promised to do liege homage to Philip whenever he asked for it and she was able to (after her confinement). She informed him that she had already done homage to the archbishop of Reims (Thibaut's uncle William) and the duke of Burgundy (Thibaut's cousin Odo III), and that Count Louis of Blois would do homage to her as regent (*sicut de ballio*). She named nine prominent barons of Champagne who would swear to her good faith in the matter.[79]

In his letter confirming Blanche's proffer, Philip added several clauses, including a provision that her infant daughter be raised at the royal court until she attained the canonical age of twelve for marriage, when she would be married in consultation with his mother (Dowager Queen Adele, the girl's great aunt) and ten prominent lords: Count Thibaut's uncle Archbishop William of Reims, his cousins Duke Odo III of Burgundy and Count Louis of Blois, his great barons William of Joigny, Guy II of Dampierre, Walter of Châtillon, Geoffroy V of Joinville (seneschal), Jean of Montmirail, Clarembaud V of Chappes—and "Geoffroy, marshal of Champagne."[80] The birth of Thibaut IV on 30 May 1201 ended an exceptionally charged six days following the count's death. Villehardouin had served three lords as marshal—Marie, Henry II, Thibaut III—and in Blanche he acquired a fourth.

---

78. Thibaut's tomb was constructed ca. 1208; see Evergates, "Countess Blanche," 83–84; Morganstern, *Gothic Tombs of Kinship*, 13–17; and Dectot, "Les tombeaux de comtes de Champagne," 32–41, 53–56, which identifies the "king of France" and "king of England" as Philip II and Richard I, rather than Louis VII and Stephen, as earlier believed (39, fig. 28).

79. *Cartulary of Countess Blanche*, 405–7, no. 449, May 1201. For details, see Evergates, "Countess Blanche."

80. Delaborde, *Recueil des actes de Philippe Auguste*, 2:235–38, no. 678, 1201, done in Sens. In a separate letter Philip confirmed Blanche's dower assigned at the time of her marriage (2:238–39, no. 679, 1201, done at Sens, a *vidimus* of Thibaut's dower letter of 1199). Rigord writes that since Thibaut III did not have a male heir at the time, Philip placed Thibaut's lands "under his tutelage and custody" (Rigord, *Gesta*, 368; Field, *Deeds of Philip Augustus*, 151, §141).

MARSHAL OF COUNT THIBAUT III   55

Villehardouin does not mention either his presence in Sens or his conversation with Philip, which he surely had, since the contract with Venice specified that the envoys obtain the king's approval "if they can." While in Sens, Villehardouin and the seneschal Geoffroy V of Joinville joined two of the king's barons, Mathieu of Montmorency (also a veteran of the Third Crusade) and his nephew Simon V of Montfort, in asking the count's cousin Duke Odo III of Burgundy to take the cross and lead the expedition overseas in Thibaut's place. Acting on behalf of the king, who had custody of Champagne and its regent countess, the marshal and seneschal addressed the duke: "Lord, you know the dire conditions overseas. . . . For God's sake, we ask you to take the cross and aid the land overseas in place of the count. We will give you the funds he collected and will swear on scripture to serve you as we would have served him."[81] In Villehardouin's telling, their offer was for Odo to lead the combined forces "in place of the count," meaning that Thibaut had been regarded as the first among the organizing counts, effectively the supreme commander. But Duke Odo, who saw his father die at Acre, had not taken the cross for the new crusade and declined the offer.[82] In fact, Odo already had indicated that he would not go on crusade when he took Thibaut's homage in Provins in 1200 and promised not to entertain any suit by a "man or woman" regarding the fief that Thibaut "and his heirs" held from him, because the count had taken the cross.[83] Even so, the marshal took Odo's rejection personally as an abdication of duty, and in his first open criticism of a great baron, he addressed his home audience: "You should know that he could have done much better."[84]

Geoffroy of Joinville was charged with taking the same offer to Count Thibaut I of Bar-le-Duc (1190–1214), then in his forties, who

---

81. Villehardouin, *La conquête*, §38. The fact that Villehardouin acted with two of the king's barons who were at Sens with Philip II indicates that he, too, was in Sens as part of the delegation of high officers acting on behalf of Countess Blanche. Duke Odo III of Burgundy, Simon V of Montfort, and Mathieu of Montmorency were among the king's ten barons at Sens who swore to the king's good faith in the matter with Blanche. For brief biographies, see Longnon, *Les compagnons de Villehardouin*, 113–14 (Simon of Montfort) and 116–18 (Mathieu of Montmorency); and Petit, *Histoire*, 3:87–251 (Odo III of Burgundy).

82. Petit, *Histoire*, 3:127–40, suggests that Odo was committed to Philip II in the affair of the king's divorce, and that the ecclesiastical council convened by Peter Capuano, the papal legate, in Dijon on 6 December 1199 was a contentious meeting regarding an interdict on royal lands, which constrained the duke to remain at home.

83. *Layettes*, 1:224, no. 605 = *Cartulary of Countess Blanche*, 95–96, no. 72 (Thibaut's homage); *Layettes*, 1:224, no. 606, 1200, "done in Provins" = Evergates, *Littere Baronum*, 50n2 (Odo's promise).

84. Villehardouin, *La conquête*, §39.

56   CHAPTER 3

also was a cousin of the deceased count but not present at the interment. Since Joinville and the count of Bar-le-Duc were neighbors in the eastern border zone of Champagne, it was expected that his appeal would be persuasive. But the count also declined and, like the duke of Burgundy, did not go on the crusade. Villehardouin surely knew that the count of Bar-le-Duc had lost both his father and older brother on crusade.[85] The staggering losses at Acre were not easily forgotten; neither the count nor the duke had any desire to return to the eastern Mediterranean. Nor, as allies of the king, could they join a crusade being led by Louis of Blois and Baldwin of Flanders, the king's recent foes.

Those refusals were a troubling turn of events (*mult fu granz desconforz*), the marshal said. The Champenois lost the opportunity of returning to Acre with the younger brother of Count Henry II, whose overseas exploits were still a fresh memory. For Villehardouin, Thibaut's death raised the critical problem of leadership. The treaty with Venice rested on the successful muster of three regional armies under the command of their princes. In the absence of a princely leader, the barons of Champagne, who were not bound by the treaty with Venice, would have to arrange their own travel to the Holy Land; that they largely bypassed Venice in favor of following the French Road to southern Italian ports is not surprising. The fracturing of a regional army from Champagne ultimately accounted for the limited role played by the Champenois in the conquest of Constantinople.

In late June 1201, one month after Thibaut's death, counts Baldwin, Louis, Hugh, and Geoffroy III of Perche (also a veteran of the Third Crusade and cousin of the deceased count) met in Soissons with many worthy barons (*preudome*) to decide on a course of action.[86] Bishop Nivelon hosted the meeting, as he had the meeting a year earlier to organize the

---

85. Villehardouin, *La conquête*, §39. Poull, *La maison souveraine et ducale de Bar*, 143, suggests that Thibaut of Bar-le-Duc, about forty-three at the time, declined because both his brother (on the Third Crusade) and his father (on the Second Crusade) had died overseas. Since he recently had terminated a war with counts Baldwin of Flanders and his brother Philip of Namur over the succession to the county of Luxembourg and the borders between Bar and Namur (*Oorkonden*, 2:253-58, no. 14, 16 July 1199), Thibaut also might not have relished the prospect of serving with Baldwin on the crusade.

86. Geoffroy III of Perche, grandson of Count Thibaut II of Champagne, died just before mustering in Venice. His brother Stephen succeeded him but became ill in Venice and stayed behind after the sailing on 1 October 1202. He later traveled to Italy and took passage to Syria. In the fall of 1204 he arrived in Constantinople and received Philadelphia in fief from Emperor Baldwin. He died at Adrianople in April 1205. See Thompson, *Power and Border Lordship*, 115-44.

expedition. Villehardouin took the floor to report on the offers declined by the duke of Burgundy and count of Bar-le-Duc, then addressed the barons: "My lords, listen to me. I will advise one thing, if you permit me. The marquis Boniface of Montferrat is an excellent *prodom* and one of the most esteemed men alive. If you were to ask him to come here and take the cross and the place of the count of Champagne, and if you were to grant him the command of the army [*la seignorie de l'ost*], he surely would accept it."[87] It was the need to recruit a leader of sufficient stature, experience, and resources to take Count Thibaut's place that prompted the marshal to propose inviting Boniface. Like the duke of Burgundy and the count of Bar-le-Duc, Boniface had not taken the cross, but he did have extensive military experience and was well informed about events in the eastern Mediterranean.[88] He was the ideal leader of a grand army to complete the work of the Third Crusade.

The marshal's certainty about Boniface's acceptance points to a prior discussion of Boniface's terms, no doubt broached during his return trip from Venice only weeks earlier, which Villehardouin failed to acknowledge (at least in recollection). The fact that Villehardouin knew Conrad of Montferrat from the Third Crusade might well have weighed in his esteem for the Montferrat brothers as successful military leaders.[89] Boniface apparently had agreed to join the expedition on the condition that he, as the oldest and most experienced of the self-appointed leaders, was made supreme commander of the army. Having witnessed the indecisive decision-making of the young counts, Geoffroy might have thought that Boniface would simplify the command structure and make it more effective under wartime conditions. As Count Thibaut's marshal and principal adviser, Villehardouin's recommendation carried weight. Yet the prospect of a foreign supreme commander did not sit well with

---

87. Villehardouin, *La conquête*, §41. Villehardouin later states that Boniface took the place of Count Thibaut *and* the supreme command of the army (Villehardouin, *La conquête*, §43). Clari, *La conquête*, §2, and Ernoul and Bernard, *Chronique*, 339–40, report that the *haut home* met at Corbie after the French envoys returned from Venice, agreed that there should be a supreme commander (*signor*), and chose Count Thibaut; see Gaggero, "Western Eyes in the Latin East," 93–95. Villehardouin, Clari, and Ernoul and Bernard distinguish between two distinct roles for Thibaut and Boniface, one as leader of the Champenois, the other as supreme leader of the combined armies. It was that second role that caused so much discussion among the barons.

88. For Boniface's life before the crusade, see Brader, *Bonifaz von Montferrat*. On the reasons for inviting Boniface, see Faral, "Geoffroy de Villehardouin," 570–72, and Queller and Madden, *The Fourth Crusade*, 25–28.

89. Queller and Madden, *The Fourth Crusade*, 28–39, review the roles of the Montferrat brothers in the eastern Mediterranean.

58   CHAPTER 3

the counts and barons, who chafed at the idea of a hierarchical command structure. A spirited discussion followed the marshal's speech, with "many words for and against." But with few alternatives, they all, "the great lords and the lesser ones," agreed to follow Villehardouin's advice. Letters were drawn up for envoys to take to Boniface, inviting him to join them. Hugh of Saint-Pol, who was close in age to Boniface and Villehardouin, later admitted in a letter to Robert of Boisleux, his seneschal at home, that Robert had been right to warn him of undertaking a venture "with such men who were young in age and maturity and did not know how to give advice for such an arduous affair."[90]

Boniface arrived in France in late August or early September. Passing through Champagne and the royal domain, he was received with "much honor" by his cousin Philip II, said Villehardouin, in effect revealing that he witnessed Boniface's reception in Paris.[91] It is likely, given the marshal's advocacy, that he accompanied Boniface from Troyes to Paris to meet the king, and then to Soissons, where he presented Boniface to the waiting barons. Villehardouin remembered how Bishop Nivelon, Fulk of Neuilly, and two unnamed Cistercian abbots with Boniface—one being Peter of Lucedio—pinned a cross on Boniface's shoulder in the orchard of Notre-Dame of Soissons.[92] Boniface then "received the command of the army" (reçoive la seignorie de l'ost), and in taking "the place of Count Thibaut of Champagne" (soit el leu le conte Thibaut de Champaigne), he received the monies Thibaut had collected for the crusader army.[93] The next day, after promising to meet in Venice, Boniface left "to attend his affairs" (por atorner son afaire), as Villehardouin put it.[94]

---

90. Pokornky, "Zwei unedierte Briefe," 203–9, no. 2 (July–August 1203); translated in Andrea, *Contemporary Sources*, 186–201. Nieus, *Les chartes des comtes de Saint-Pol*, 224–25, no. 143, identifies the recipient of Hugh's letter as Robert of Boisleux, his *cura terra mee*.

91. Villehardouin, *La conquête*, §42. Boniface's grandmother Constance of Savoy was the aunt of Louis VI's wife Adelaide of Savoy; Boniface therefore was a distant relative of both Philip II and counts Henry II and Thibaut III of Champagne.

92. Moore, "Peter of Lucedio," 242–43.

93. Villehardouin, *La conquête*, §43. Kittell, "Was Thibaut of Champagne the Leader of the Fourth Crusade?," argued that Villehardouin never called Thibaut the commander-in-chief and that Thibaut was not "formally elected" as commander-in-chief. In fact, Villehardouin states that Boniface was selected to replace Thibaut both as a regional leader and as supreme commander of combined armies (Villehardouin, *La conquête*, §44), and he continued to speak of Boniface as commander-in-chief, although in reality decision-making remained with the council of regional princes and leading barons; on this point, see Riley-Smith, "Toward an Understanding of the Fourth Crusade," 85–86.

94. Villehardouin, *La conquête*, §§43–44. Villehardouin noted earlier (§36) that Thibaut had reserved monies for the army separate from his grants to individual barons.

MARSHAL OF COUNT THIBAUT III

Villehardouin is silent about Philip's role in the selection of a supreme commander. Innocent had recruited Philip and Richard I to lead the new crusade, and although Philip declined the offer after Richard's death, circumstantial evidence suggests that he closely followed the preparations for the crusade and had a hand in choosing the crusade leader. According to the *Gesta* of Innocent III, the counts and barons elected the supreme commander of the crusade army on the advice (*cum consilio*) of Philip, who would have vetoed any suggestion that Baldwin replace Thibaut.[95] Aubri of Trois-Fontaines reported what was widely known, that Baldwin, Louis, Hugh, and Geoffroy of Perche had deserted Philip for Richard.[96] It is notable that Nivelon of Soissons, a royal bishop, hosted the planning conferences, and that the Venetians asked the envoys to obtain Philip's confirmation of the contract for transport. All of which suggests that in failing to mention his own presence in Sens after Thibaut's death and later in Paris, Villehardouin obscured his own consultations with Philip in offering the leadership of the crusade first to Thibaut's cousins, then to Boniface.

It appears that Villehardouin did not accompany Boniface to Cîteaux, where the Cistercian Chapter General met on 14 September 1201.[97] Counts Louis and Baldwin and many barons as well as abbots were in attendance, and Fulk preached crusade as he had in 1198 when the abbots refused to serve as military chaplains, finding it inconsonant with a Cistercian calling.[98] This time Fulk came armed with a letter from the pope authorizing a Cistercian presence on the crusade. Boniface and the counts of Flanders and Blois spoke in favor of the expedition, and Fulk, acting as liaison between the papal legate Peter Capuano, the crusade leaders, and the abbots, brought the Cistercians on board to support Innocent's crusade project.[99] Four well-known abbots (of Vaux-de-Cernay, Perseigne, Loos, and Cercanceaux) were authorized to take the cross and

---

95. Tafel and Thomas, *Urkunden*, 1:367, April 1201 = Longnon, *Recherches*, 181; and *Gesta Innocentii*, 131–32 (Powell, *The Deeds of Innocent*, 131–33); no. 83.

96. Aubri of Trois-Fontaines, *Chronica*, 877.

97. Villehardouin's brief description of the meeting (*La conquête*, §45) suggests that he heard about it and consulted the roster of Burgundian barons who took the cross there but did not attend.

98. Andrea reviews the reactions of the Cistercians to preparations for the Fourth Crusade ("Adam of Perseigne," 26–29).

99. Grasso, "Folco di Neuilly," 744–45, agrees with Jones, "Fulk of Neuilly," on Fulk's critical role in bringing the three parties together, especially the reluctant Cistercian abbots.

60   **CHAPTER 3**

join the crusade.[100] The meeting concluded with a regional cross-taking by prominent Burgundians, including William and Odo of Champlitte (grandsons of Count Hugh of Troyes), Guy of Conflans, Bishop Walter II of Autun, Count Guy of Forez, and Hugh of Berzé and his son Hugh (the poet).[101] The meeting at Cîteaux capped four anxious months following Thibaut's death. A new leadership had been selected, in great part due to the marshal's efforts, and the Cistercians (and the Burgundians) had been induced to join the crusade, two years after Écry and only months before the armies were to muster in Venice.

Final Preparations

Villehardouin is silent about the months between mid-September 1201 and Easter (14 April) 1202, when crusaders began to leave for Venice, three years after the pope initially had scheduled a general muster. But he was busy dealing with practical matters in the event that he did not return from overseas. He had become a substantial property owner, not of great estates but a patchwork of small, scattered properties and revenues obtained by inheritance, grant, marriage, and seemingly though his own purchases.[102] In December 1201 he gave the hospital of Saint-Étienne in Troyes a grain rent that Count Thibaut had granted him in consideration of his service and a tithe, which his daughter Alice would enjoy for her life as a nun in Notre-Dame-aux-Nonnains.[103] In February 1202 he confirmed that his nephews Geoffroy and Dreux of Villemaur sold a tithe rent held from them in fief by the wife of a knight.[104] In April he approved the gift that his brother Jean gave to the chapel in the church of Saint-Nicholas of Brandonvillers, which was held from him in fief, and added a 10*l.* revenue on his own

---

100. Statute 37 of the Chapter General states that, in response to the entreaties of Boniface and the counts of Flanders and Blois, the pope allowed four Cistercian abbots to take the cross and join the crusade; see Brown, "The Cistercians in the Latin Empire," 67–69; Andrea, "Adam of Perseigne," 21–23; and Longnon, *Les compagnons de Villehardouin*, 165 (Simon of Loos).

101. Villehardouin, *La conquête*, §45. Villehardouin mentions "many other fine Burgundians whose names are not written down," referring to a roster of oath-takers at Cîteaux that was recorded after the earlier rosters recorded in "the Book."

102. Map 3 is based on Longnon, *Recherches*, 6–13.

103. Arbois de Jubainville, "Nouvelles recherches," 371, no. 4, December 1201: 15 *modii* of oats at Jasseines.

104. Arbois de Jubainville, "Nouvelles recherches," 371, no. 5, February 1202.

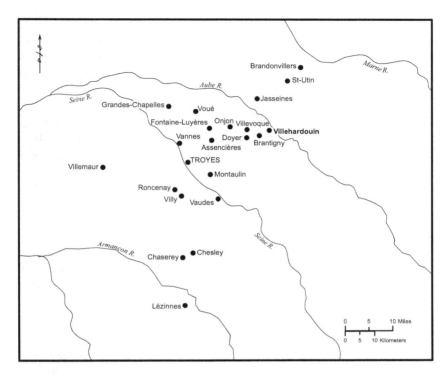

MAP 3. Villehardouin's properties in Champagne

account.[105] And he sealed a charter with his new seal consenting to his younger brother Guy la Grive's gift of a grain rent to the Cistercians at Larrivour.[106]

On the eve of his departure in late April or early May, Geoffroy sealed two related letters at his wife's inherited property at Lézinnes.

---

105. Robert, "Fondation d'une chapellenie," 133–34, no. 2, April 1202. This charter confirmed his brother's charter of 1197 (Robert, "Fondation d'une chapellenie," 132–33, no. 1). In that same month Jean enjoyed a revenue paid by Saint-Martin of Troyes, which he held *de feodo* from Geoffroy (Longnon, *Recherches*, 187, no. 67, April 1202).

106. Arbois de Jubainville, "Nouvelles recherches," 372–73, no. 7, 1202. The grain rent belonged to Geoffroy's *casamentum*. Baudin suggests that Geoffroy acquired his second seal, with a modified *croix ancrée*, just before departing on crusade, and that the heraldic *brisé* represented a new style developed in the 1190s by which younger sons acknowledged their junior lineal status (Baudin, "De la Champagne à la Morée," 99). A relatively intact seal of this type survives from 1208; see Baudin, *Emblématique et pouvoir en Champagne*, CD-ROM: *Corpus des Sceaux*, 95, and Chassel, *Sceaux et usages de sceaux*, 110, fig. 12.

62   **CHAPTER 3**

One charter simply states, without explanation and witnesses, that he gave land at the well of Chaserey to the Cistercian monks at Quincy.[107] The second, which the monks may have requested after obtaining the consent of his wife and sons, explains the circumstances of the gift:

> Be it known to all, present and future, that I, Geoffroy, marshal of Champagne, about to take the road to Jerusalem, have given the land that I have next to the well at Chaserey to the church of Quincy for the sake of my soul and those of my wife and children. My wife Chane and my sons Erard and Geoffroy consented to this. So that this be observed in perpetuity, I, Geoffroy, marshal of Champagne, have affixed my seal to this document. Done in the year of Incarnation 1202.[108]

This letter, providing for the salvation of his soul and those of his wife and children, is the last he is known to have sealed in Champagne. Milo Breban made similar provisions for anniversary Masses in the comital chapels of Provins and Troyes after his death.[109]

Geoffroy was in his mid-fifties. He had been a professional soldier since the 1170s and marshal for the last seventeen years, during which he assumed a high profile in Champagne. It is likely that he resided in Troyes, but little is known about his family beyond the names of his wife and children. If the extant records are indicative, he was active in local affairs, witnessing and confirming the acts of others and managing his own extensive portfolio of properties and revenues. Neither a count nor a castle lord, the "marshal of Champagne" had become Count Thibaut's most trusted official, and by his own account he played a critical role in planning the new crusade. After Thibaut's death, in the absence of an authentic regional leader, it was the marshal who embodied the identity of the Champenois overseas. Whether he formally relinquished his office before leaving for Venice is not clear, for "marshal of Champagne" remained part of his identity for the rest

---

107. AD Aube, 35 H 1, 1202 (after Easter, 14 April) = Arbois de Jubainville, "Nouvelles recherches," 372, no. 6.2, done at Lézinnes. Chaserey was a grange of Quincy, the sixth daughter house of Pontigny, founded in 1133 (Roserot, *Dictionnaire*, 1:346–47).

108. AD Aube, 35 H 1, 1202 (after Easter, 14 April) = Arbois de Jubainville, "Nouvelles recherches," 372, no. 6.1.

109. Verdier, *L'aristocratie de Provins*, 260n656, done in Provins, and 229n199, done in Troyes, both dated June 1202.

of his life. But after he left for Venice, never to return to Champagne, Countess Blanche appointed a new marshal, his nephew Oudard of Aulnay, younger brother of the former marshal Erard whom Geoffroy had replaced in 1185.[110]

110. In November 1203 the dean of Saint-Étienne confirmed that Oudard of Aulnay, "marshal of Champagne" (1203–27), was acting as guardian for Vilain, who had left on the crusade (Cartulary of Saint-Étienne of Troyes, fol. 131v). See genealogy 1.

CHAPTER 4

Sailing to Byzantium

Villehardouin set out for Venice after Easter, most likely in early May 1202 from Lézinnes, in the company of Odo and William of Champlitte, his neighbors at Pacy-sur-Armançon.[1] He does not say by which route he traveled, but most likely it was the same one he had followed earlier through Burgundy, across the Alps at the Mont Cenis Pass to Montferrat, and on to Pavia, Piacenza, and Venice. The three organizing counts were expected to arrive by June with their armies from Champagne, Blois, and Flanders, but Villehardouin is vague about the existence of a regional army from Champagne exactly one year after the death of Count Thibaut. At some point Mathieu of Montmorency had assumed the leadership of the Champenois, most likely on appointment by Philip II in his capacity as guardian of Countess Blanche and the county of Champagne. Although Montmorency held a fief in Champagne at Marly-le-Roi near the border town of Lagny, he was a royal baron who took the cross with the bishop of Soissons "in France."[2] Since he lacked the

---

1. As suggested by Petit, *Les sires de Villehardouin*, 11–12, and in his *Histoire*, 4:468–69.

2. Villehardouin, *La conquête*, §71. Montmorency was listed first among the barons "of France" with the bishop of Soissons. In Champagne, he held a "great fief" (*Feoda* 2, no. 2463, ca. 1190), but it is not clear when he acquired it. He was with Philip II on the Third Crusade

SAILING TO BYZANTIUM

requisite standing as a regional prince, he failed to forge an army of Champagne under his command. Instead, independent companies of barons and knights, who were not obliged to muster in Venice, traveled overland to Piacenza, where they took the French Road to Rome and the southern ports. It was precisely the lack of princely leadership and the failure to organize a unified force from Champagne that accounted for the dispersal of the Champenois and their limited role in the crusade and conquest of Constantinople.

Count Baldwin's Flemish army was the first to arrive in Venice.[3] He had mustered his men in Valenciennes in April 1202, two years after taking the cross. With him were Conon of Béthune and Renier of Trith, who appear prominently in Villehardouin's memoirs. Countess Marie of Flanders witnessed the muster and planned to accompany Baldwin, but since she was pregnant with her second child, she delayed her trip. After outfitting a fleet with provisions for his army overseas, Baldwin led his troops—knights, archers, and engineers—overland to Venice. Passing Clairvaux in the last week of April, he visited the tomb of his maternal uncle Count Philip, who died on the Third Crusade at Acre.[4] Noting that he "was going to Jerusalem," Baldwin gave the monks a 10*l.* revenue for his and Marie's souls and in memory of his uncle, "the most illustrious prince on earth," and further exempted them from all tolls and taxes in his lands on goods purchased for their own use.[5] He granted the same exemption to the monks at Cîteaux, as did Hugh of Saint-Pol, who was traveling with him, "following the example of Count Baldwin."[6] Several weeks later Count Louis granted Cîteaux the same exemption in his lands in recognition of the Cistercian support for the crusade.[7]

---

and served in the war against Richard I. Villehardouin later remembered him as one of the best knights "in the kingdom of France," that is, the royal domain (Villehardouin, *La conquête*, §200). Longnon, *Les compagnons de Villehardouin*, 116–18, provides a brief biography.

3. Angold, *The Fourth Crusade*, 75–108, traces the complicated relations between Venetians, French, Germans, and Byzantines from the muster in Venice through the installation of Emperor Baldwin in Constantinople.

4. Count Philip (r. 1168–91) confirmed that he and his wife Mathilda had chosen to be buried at Clairvaux (*Clairvaux*, 359, no. 289, 1191), with the consent of the monks (*Clairvaux*, 336, no. 276, 2 January 1190).

5. *Oorkonden*, 2:509–12, no. 243, and 2:514–15, no. 246, both April 1202.

6. Baldwin's grants: *Oorkonden*, 2:513–15, nos. 245–46, at Cîteaux, April 1202. Hugh's grants: Nieus, *Les chartes des comtes de Saint-Pol*, 221–22, no. 138, and 222–23, no. 140, both at Cîteaux, April 1202.

7. Petit, *Histoire*, 3:385, no. 1051, May 1202.

66   **CHAPTER 4**

Venice

Villehardouin arrived in Venice in late May or early June 1202. His first concern was the failure of the general muster. Count Baldwin's land forces had arrived, but his fleet, commanded by Jean of Nesle and carrying provisions and reinforcements, did not appear after hearing of "the great danger" (*le grant peril*) awaiting them in Venice. Villehardouin does not explain the danger but implies that many crusaders, hearing rumors of conditions in Venice, traveled to other ports for transport directly to Syria. The Venetians feared that an insufficient number of crusaders had arrived to pay for the fleet, which they had built on credit, since the full payment, due by the end of April, had not been rendered.[8] They were especially disturbed by reports that Count Louis, who was still en route, planned to bypass Venice, despite the contract his envoys had made in his name. They asked Villehardouin, whom they knew well from their negotiations the previous year, to go with Hugh of Saint-Pol to Pavia and persuade Louis to bring his men to Venice.[9]

Villehardouin and Hugh were ideal emissaries. They were mature men who had known young Louis and his father a decade earlier at the siege of Acre and more recently had encountered him during the lead-up to the crusade. "We rode out to Pavia in Lombardy," said Villehardouin, "where we found Louis with many good knights and good men. Through our reassurances and persuasion, many of those who had been heading to other ports by other roads turned instead to Venice."[10] By Villehardouin's discreet recounting, he and Hugh succeeded in convincing Louis to muster his men in Venice. We can only imagine how the distinguished marshal in his mid-fifties reminded the thirty-year-old count of his responsibility. Had Louis not altered course, he would have been the most prominent leader to circumvent Venice, and the most culpable, as he was bound by his sealed contract. The marshal was quite aware that the failure of the army of Blois to muster in Venice would have left the Flemish as the only regional army (in the absence of the Champenois) to pay for the newly built fleet, making it highly unlikely that the Venetians would have launched the ships.

On returning from Pavia, Villehardouin remembered, he encountered a "very large number" (*mult plenté*) of knights and sergeants in Piacenza

---

8. Madden, *Enrico Dandolo*, 131–32.
9. Villehardouin, *La conquête*, §§49–51.
10. Villehardouin, *La conquête*, §§52–53.

SAILING TO BYZANTIUM   67

intending to sail to Syria from Apulia. They included his cousin Henry of Arzillières and neighbors Vilain of Nully and Renaud II of Dampierre, castellan of Vitry; all three had taken the cross with him at Écry. He knew in 1207 that all eighty knights in that company had been killed or captured by Turks in Syria, and that Dampierre, who had received a sum of money from the dying Count Thibaut in order to fulfill Thibaut's crusade vow, was still being held captive.[11] Adam of Perseigne, one of the four Cistercian abbots authorized to accompany the crusade, likely was in that party but managed to return home, greatly disillusioned by the experience.[12] Villehardouin does not mention that his own nephew Geoffroy, who held a fief from Henry of Arzillières and later returned from Syria to conquer the Peloponnese, may have been in that same company.[13]

The Champenois were drawn to Acre by the "cluster" of their compatriots who stayed with Count Henry II after the Third Crusade.[14] Henry of Arzillières had been at the siege of Acre with his two brothers: Walter died there, but William stayed and became marshal of the Templars in Acre.[15] Villehardouin's nephew Vilain of Aulnay also remained in Acre until his death in 1207.[16] Guy of Chappes, who had witnessed Count Henry II's marriage in May 1192, returned home sometime before 1197 and appeared at Écry in November 1199.[17] Milo Breban stayed with

---

11. Villehardouin, *La conquête*, §231. Aubri of Trois-Fontaines, *Chronica*, 878, states that Thibaut, gravely ill, gave Dampierre money to fulfill his vow.

12. Andrea, "Adam of Perseigne," 24–25, 30–32, concludes that Adam probably accompanied Renaud of Dampierre to Piacenza and Apulia in the summer of 1202, then sailed with him to Syria, and returned to France in the spring or summer of 1203. In January 1204, as papal legate, he oversaw the disputed election of the archbishop of Reims.

13. Buchon, *Recherches et matériaux*, 1, pt. 2:26, no. 2, 1200. "I, Geoffroy [son of Jean] of Villehardouin," announces that he gave his share of the tithe of Longeville-sur-Laines to the chaplain of Brandonvillers, with the approval of Henry of Arzillières, from whom he held it in fief. His father Jean of Villehardouin witnessed. Henry of Arzillières sealed a separate letter in confirmation (cited by Longnon, *Recherches*, 177, no. 58, 1200).

14. Perry, *John of Brienne*, 43, on the "Champenois cluster," and Donnachie, "Crown and Baronage," especially 123, for those who witnessed acts of Count Henry II between 1192 and 1197.

15. For William of Arzillières (marshal of the Templars in Acre, 1203–13), see Burgtorf, *The Central Convent*, 671, and Longnon, *Les compagnons de Villehardouin*, 22–23. While in Acre, Henry and William of Arzillières granted the Templars revenues near Paris and in Champagne (Mayer, *Die Kanzlei*, 2:911–13, no. 14, ca. 1190).

16. Vilain of Aulnay remained with Count Henry II in Acre after the Third Crusade (Strehlke, *Tabulae Ordinis Theutonici*, 29–34, nos. 36–41, August 1200–May 1206). His brother Oudard of Aulnay, marshal of Champagne, acted as guardian of his lands in Champagne (Cartulary of Saint-Étienne of Troyes, fol. 131v, November 1203).

17. Saint-Phalle, "Les seigneurs de Chappes," 60.

68   CHAPTER 4

Henry II until October 1194 and returned shortly after Villehardouin was released from Damascus.[18] In the summer of 1202 Clarembaud of Broyes, master of the school of the comital chapel in Troyes, traveled to Syria with the papal legate Soffrendo and the next year was elected archbishop of Tyre.[19]

The stream of armed contingents passing through Italy via the French Road to the southern ports became in effect a "second front" of the crusade; one-quarter of all those mentioned by Villehardouin at Évry bypassed Venice to sail directly to Syria.[20] Among his own companions that percentage was even higher: of the twenty Champenois at Écry whose histories are known, three followed Count Walter of Brienne to Apulia (in May 1201) and eight others sailed to Syria from southern Italian ports (in the summer of 1202); only nine (45 percent) mustered in Venice.[21] It was that reduction in the main army, Villehardouin lamented, and the inability of those who did muster to pay for the fleet that led to the "great misfortune" (*granz mesaventure*) of the expedition.[22] He did not say it, but the absence of a regional army under the leadership of Count Thibaut accounted in large part for the failure of the muster in Venice, and ultimately of the crusade itself.

Villehardouin rejoiced at the sight of the Venetian fleet of sailing ships, galleys, and horse transports. But he was troubled by the continual desertion from the army because the Venetians had built a fleet for "three times as many" passengers as had arrived by 29 June, the date set for the sailing. It was a sizable fleet—150 sailing ships, 50 war galleys, and 150 horse transports built to land on the shallow shores of Egypt.[23] He recalled the anger of those who had paid their way but were not

---

18. Milo Breban was still in Acre in October 1194 when Count Henry II exempted the Teutonic Knights from taxes on the goods they purchased for their own use (Strehlke, *Tabulae Ordinis Theutonici*, 26, no. 30).

19. Clarembaud witnessed acts by Count Henry the Liberal in the 1170s (*Actes*, nos. 336, 345, 456), was master of the school of Saint-Étienne of Troyes ("Léproserie," 532–33, 1186), and was elected archbishop of Tyre (1203–13); see Mayer, *Die Kanzlei*, 2:300–302. He was remembered in Saint-Étienne's obituary (*Obituaires*, 4:465, 16 July).

20. Kedar, "The Fourth Crusade's Second Front," 95–96, calculates that of ninety-four crusaders named by Villehardouin as having taken the cross, two died before muster; of the remaining ninety-two, between twenty-one and twenty-four (23 and 26 percent) went directly to Acre.

21. Grossel, *Le milieu littéraire en Champagne*, 1:165 (table of the Champenois and their destinations). Longnon, *Les compagnons des Villehardouin*, 64, provides slightly different figures. See also Dufournet, "Villehardouin et les Champenois," 61.

22. Villehardouin, *La conquête*, §55. Queller, Compton, and Campbell, "The Fourth Crusade," review the many reasons for not mustering in Venice.

23. Pryor, "The Venetian Fleet," 118, and Queller and Madden, *The Fourth Crusade*, 69–71.

allowed to embark before the entire payment was rendered. To counter the widespread talk, even among the barons, of abandoning the expedition, counts Baldwin, Louis, and Hugh set an example by contributing from their own funds and offering even their fine dishware of gold and silver for the common good, but even that fell far short of what was owed. Many, especially the poor, returned home in the summer due to lack of money to pay for food.[24] By the fall of 1202 only about 12,000 to 13,000 crusaders remained.[25] Villehardouin sympathized with the Venetians, who had completed their part of the contract, and instead blamed those who failed to join the army in Venice.[26] The second consequence of Thibaut's death, beyond the fragmentation of the regional army from Champagne, was the failure to render the four pre-payments for the fleet—due on 1 August and 1 November 1201, and 20 February and late April 1202. Thibaut had collected funds specifically for the expedition, apart from the funds he granted to individuals, and would have been a major contributor to its general expenses.[27]

To forestall a complete collapse of the project, the doge Enrico Dandolo offered to delay—not cancel—payment of the 34,000 marks still owed in return for help in capturing the port city of Zara, a commercial rival on the opposite shore of the Adriatic that King Bela III of Hungary (r. 1173–96) had occupied since 1181.[28] Villehardouin quotes the Venetians, who claimed that Zara had been taken from them unjustly; after failing to retake it in 1187, they saw the arrival of a crusader army in Venice as a unique opportunity to conquer the city.[29] Informed of that proposal, Pope Innocent III sent Cardinal Peter Capuano to Venice to prohibit, under pain of excommunication, any attack against Christians, specifically at Zara, a Christian city then under King Emeric of Hungary (r. 1196–1204), who had taken the cross. Villehardouin does

---

24. Madden, "Food and the Fourth Crusade," emphasizes the persistent lack of provisions, both in Venice and during the expedition to Constantinople, as a major factor in the conduct of the crusade.

25. Bell, "Unintended Consumption," 79–93, confirms Villehardouin's estimate (Villehardouin, *La conquête*, §56) of about 12,000 combatants sailing from Venice.

26. Villehardouin, *La conquête*, §§56–61.

27. Villehardouin, *La conquête*, §36. Villehardouin states that Boniface took the funds (§43), but it is not known what became of them. Clari (*La conquête*, §8) states that Venetian envoys were paid 25,000 marks at Corbie at an undetermined date; the only other mention of the Corbie meeting is in Ernoul and Bernard, *Chronique*, 338–39, which may have taken it from Clari. It is not clear why such a large payment would be made at Corbie; the fairs of Champagne would have been a more appropriate place for international financial transfers.

28. Stephenson, *Byzantium's Balkan Frontier*, 281–84.

29. Villehardouin, *La conquête*, §§62–63.

70   **CHAPTER 4**

not mention the doge's objection to the cardinal's intrusion in what for the Venetians was strictly a business transaction. On the cardinal's return to Rome after his unsuccessful mission, the pope sent letters directly to the crusade leaders, informing them personally of his prohibition, and he directed Abbot Peter of Lucedio, Boniface's confidant, to remind them of his threat to excommunicate.[30]

Villehardouin recalls the serious split within the army over whether to accept the doge's proposal, but the barons, having exhausted their personal resources and with the expedition at risk of dissolution, agreed in the end to conquer Zara for the Venetians. Robert of Clari, who was in the army, later reported that only the leaders knew of that plan.[31] To build support among Venetians for the enterprise, the doge gave a stirring speech in Saint Mark's. The marshal admired the elderly, blind doge who took the cross in an emotional performance before the altar, thus demonstrating his commitment to the project. Villehardouin remembered that moment as critical to preserving the army, and he quotes the substance of the doge's speech, which induced perhaps 15,000 Venetians to join the expedition, either by choice or by selection through lottery.[32]

Boniface, "commander of the army" (qui sires ere de l'ost), arrived in Venice on 15 August, six weeks after the original date set for embarkation and an entire year after he had accepted the supreme command of the army at Soissons.[33] It is not clear how much Villehardouin knew at the time of Boniface's movements and his plan to use the crusader army to restore Prince Alexios IV to the throne in Constantinople after his father Isaac had been deposed, blinded, and imprisoned by his own brother. The pope already had rebuffed the request of Boniface and Alexios to divert the crusader army from its announced mission.[34] Villehardouin did not comment on the coincidence of a messenger from Prince Alexios arriving in Venice with a letter addressed to Boniface within days of

---

30. According to the *Gesta Innocentii*, 138–39 (Powell, *The Deeds of Innocent*, 139–40), no. 85, after the pope personally prohibited Boniface, as the supreme commander, from attacking Zara, Boniface "prudently absented himself" from the expedition before the attack. For the date (May–June 1202) and interpretation of Innocent's letter, see Queller and Madden, *The Fourth Crusade*, 102–3. See also Moore, "Peter of Lucedio," 242.

31. Clari, *La conquête*, §13.

32. Villehardouin, *La conquête*, §§64–69. Madden, *Enrico Dandolo*, 129–30 (on the lottery).

33. Brader, *Bonifaz von Montferrat*, 171–79, reviews what little is known about Boniface's movements between August 1201 and August 1202.

34. As reported in the *Gesta Innocentii*, 131–32 (Powell, *The Deeds of Innocent*, 131–33), no. 83. For a fuller account of this subplot, see Maleczek, *Petrus Capuanus*, 136–39, and Queller and Madden, *The Fourth Crusade*, 63–69.

SAILING TO BYZANTIUM 71

Boniface's own arrival, but he did recall the essence of the letter read aloud to the commanders: young Alexios had escaped from prison in September 1201 (at the very moment that Boniface took the cross in Soissons) and had joined his brother-in-law Philip in Swabia.[35] In recounting his misfortunes, Alexios explained that when he landed in Verona, he was advised to contact the great army forming in Venice. The barons were moved by his story, said Villehardouin, and sent envoys to Alexios and Philip offering to help the prince reclaim the throne of Constantinople, if he would help them recover the land overseas.[36] Well-informed clerics, who would have heard of the recent usurpations of the imperial crown in Constantinople, could vouch for young Alexios's quest to regain his rightful inheritance.[37] Villehardouin does not explain why the barons agreed so readily to employ a crusader army for an entirely political purpose, but the understanding must have been that Alexios would relieve the crusade of its debt to Venice.

Two weeks after arriving in Venice, Boniface left with Abbot Peter of Lucedio, ostensibly to consult with the pope about the recent turn of events but perhaps, as the papal chancery claimed, to retain an unsullied reputation in the face of the impending destruction of Zara, a Christian city that the pope, viva voce, had expressly prohibited Boniface and his army from attacking.[38] Soon afterward a company of German barons and knights arrived in Venice with the bishop of Halberstadt and several prominent nobles. Villehardouin does not hint at any machination behind Alexios's letter to Boniface, nor does he explain the arrival of German ambassadors just days before the embarkment.[39] An astute observer like Villehardouin would have sensed that the diversion of the army to Zara would lead inevitably to Constantinople. As a practical matter for the marshal, however, there was no viable alternative to moving large numbers of men, horses, and supplies onto the ships for a voyage to wherever it might lead, as the treaty put it. But he clearly understood in retrospect that the first diversion of the expedition from its

---

35. Alexios fled Constantinople in late September or October 1201 (Brand, *Byzantium Confronts the West*, 275–76). Boniface was in Hagenau by 5 December 1201, when he witnessed Philip of Swabia's act (Rzihacek et al., *Die Urkunden Philipps von Schwaben*, 2:139–41, no. 61).

36. Villehardouin, *La conquête*, §§70–73.

37. Angold, *The Fourth Crusade*, 61–69, reviews what Western authors had written about the imperial usurpations in Constantinople.

38. *Gesta Innocentii*, 138–39 (Powell, *The Deeds of Innocent*, 139–40), no. 85.

39. Villehardouin, *La conquête*, §74.

72   CHAPTER 4

goal of sailing to the Holy Land was the beginning, in modern parlance, of mission creep.

Zara

Villehardouin vividly recalled the scene of the fleet's departure during the week of 1 October, "1202 years after the incarnation of Jesus Christ."[40] Large sailing ships with knights' shields hanging from the sides, horse transports, and war galleys carried in total about 11,000 crusaders, 21,000 Venetian sailors and other Italians, and more than 300 stone-throwing machines. Villehardouin observed: "Never did a finer fleet set sail from any port."[41] Robert of Clari remembered the doge's impressive galley and the emotion of the crusaders as they left port.[42] The voyage lasted more than a month while the fleet with its captive army visited several ports along the Adriatic coast in pursuit of Venice's interests before it arrived at Zara on 10 November.[43] The marshal was impressed by the city's walls and high towers: "you could not have asked for a more beautiful, wealthier, or more strongly defended city." After the harbor chain was broken, the port was easily taken. The knights and sergeants disembarked, the war horses were led off the transports, and a tent city was constructed in preparation for the siege. Villehardouin noted for the record that Boniface was absent, having stayed behind to attend to some of his "affairs" ("por affaire que il avoit"), a remarkable comment about a supreme commander before the army's first major operation. Boniface did not arrive until mid-December, an entire month after the conquest of Zara.[44]

Villehardouin is reticent about his own role in the capture, occupation, and destruction of Zara, as if he took no part in it or wished to forget it. Yet as the de facto leader of the Champenois in the absence of Montmorency, who stayed behind in Venice because of illness,

---

40. Queller and Madden, *The Fourth Crusade*, 55–99, present a rounded account of the voyage from Venice to Constantinople.

41. Villehardouin, *La conquête*, §§75–76. Madden, "Food and the Fourth Crusade," 217, calculates the number of personnel. See also Pryor, "The Venetian Fleet," 114–18, and Riley-Smith, "Toward an Understanding of the Fourth Crusade," 81.

42. Clari, *La conquête*, §§13–14.

43. For a map of the voyage from Venice to Constantinople, see Pryor, "The Venetian Fleet," 104, and for the ports visited between Venice and Zara, see Queller and Madden, *The Fourth Crusade*, 71–72. Madden, *Enrico Dandolo*, 133–54, describes Venice's role in the diversion to Zara and beyond.

44. Villehardouin, *La conquête*, §§77–79.

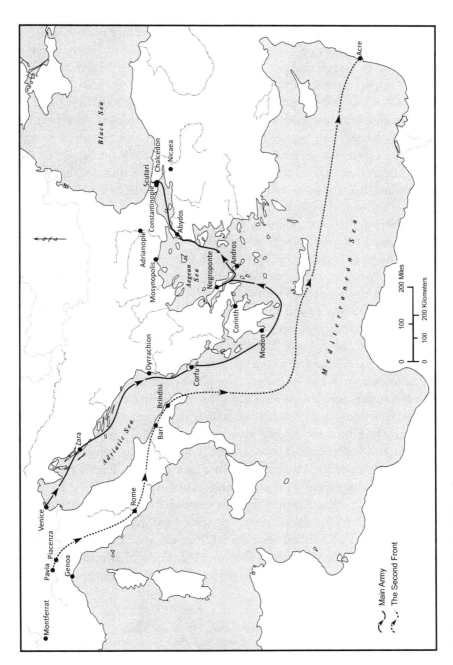

MAP 4. Itineraries of the Fourth Crusade

74   CHAPTER 4

Villehardouin would have attended the discussions between the crusade leaders and the doge. On 12 November the city agreed to surrender on terms, but negotiations were undermined by a party within the army that sought to disband, while the commanders deliberated on whether to attack the city. At that point Guy, the Cistercian abbot of Vaux-de-Cernay, stood up and addressed the council: "Lords, on behalf of the pope, I prohibit you from attacking this city, for it is a Christian city and you are pilgrims."[45] The doge was greatly irritated, Villehardouin recalled, and replied that since the army had sabotaged a peaceful surrender of the city, he would hold the Franks to their agreement to take the city by force. The counts and barons were divided, but those wishing to attack the city supported the doge, for to do otherwise, they said, would be shameful (*honi*) for not fulfilling their agreement made in Venice. Villehardouin does not reveal whether he supported the doge, whom he admired, or those who heeded the pope's directive. But he did acknowledge the deep discontent in the army, with many wanting to abandon an expedition having little to do with liberating Jerusalem. On the morning of 13 November, the sappers and catapulters attacked the walls and towers of the city, and five days later Zara fell.[46]

Since winter was at hand, the doge counseled that they should stay in that well-provisioned city until spring. The city and its spoils were divided in half, with the Venetians taking the port. But the occupation was not a happy one. Three days after the conquest a melee broke out between Venetians and French that quickly degenerated into a violent conflict lasting into the night. The outclassed sailors suffered many wounded and killed, and it took an entire week for the doge and the barons to restore order. The marshal must have been involved in the ongoing deliberations among the commanders but divulges nothing about them. He says only that "two weeks later [in mid-December] Boniface of Montferrat, who had not yet arrived, appeared," as if to note (again) that the commander-in-chief had been absent from the attack on a Christian city against an explicit papal prohibition. Mathieu of Montmorency, who arrived with Boniface, assumed leadership of the Champenois, and

---

45. Villehardouin, *La conquête*, §83. *Gesta Innocentii*, 139 (Powell, *The Deeds of Innocent*, 140–46), no. 86. It appears that Cardinal Peter Capuano took the pope's letter to Venice but left after giving it to Abbot Guy of Vaux, who read it to the council just before the assault on Zara; see Andrea, "Essay on Primary Sources," in Queller and Madden, *The Fourth Crusade*, 244n105.

46. Villehardouin, *La conquête*, §§80–85.

the marshal reverted to his role as chief of staff and observer of the expedition's course.[47]

On 1 January 1203 messengers arrived with a letter from Philip of Swabia announcing Prince Alexios's imminent arrival. Villehardouin remembered the letter, which was read aloud to the assembled barons in the doge's quarters. Philip proposed a treaty between Alexios and the crusaders. If the army restored him to the throne in Constantinople, Alexios would place the Byzantine church under the pope's authority; he would pay and provision the crusader army, and he would lead 10,000 of his own troops to Egypt for one year and maintain 500 knights outre-mer for the rest of his life.[48] Villehardouin was present the next day at a heated discussion (*ot parlé en maint endroit*) between the counts, barons, and prelates. Abbot Guy of Vaux-de-Cernay spoke against the offer since the crusaders expected to go to Syria and had not consented to fight (yet again) against Christians. Those who spoke in favor of the treaty argued that the army was useless in Syria and that the recovery of the Holy Land passed "through either Egypt or Greece" (par la terre de Babilone ou par Grece); moreover they "would forever incur shame" if they abandoned the expedition. If Villehardouin remembered correctly, that was the first open recognition that the original goal of the expedition had been Egypt, with Constantinople now presented as an alternative route to the Holy Land.

Villehardouin does not mention a key factor in the discussion: that Alexios's promise of fielding an army of 10,000 men for one year would almost double the size of the crusader army, and 200,000 marks of silver would pay off the debt owed to the Venetians. The Cistercian abbots were just as divided as the army, he said, and were preaching both for and against going to Constantinople. He singles out Abbot Guy who preached "very often" that it was wrong (*mals*) to go to Constantinople when they should go to Syria. The abbot of Cercanceaux also was opposed. But Abbot Simon of Loos, who was "very holy and a *prodom*," together with certain other Cistercian abbots, urged the army to stay together in order to recover the Holy Land. "You should not be surprised

---

47. Villehardouin, *La conquête*, §§86–91. For Boniface's possible motives, see Faral, "Geoffroy de Villehardouin," 571–72.

48. Villehardouin, *La conquête*, §93. Manuscripts B and O read "en la terre de Babillone" (Egypt); manuscript D reads "en la terre d'outremer," while manuscript C omits the entire phrase.

76   **CHAPTER 4**

if the laymen disagreed," Villehardouin observed, "for the White Monks of the Cistercian Order in the army were equally divided."[49]

At that point Boniface and counts Baldwin, Louis, and Hugh intervened. They reaffirmed their agreement with the Venetians because they would be dishonored (*il seroient honi*) if they did not. And so, in the doge's tent they "and those who agreed with them" formalized a second diversion; together with Alexios's envoys, they swore oaths and sealed letters patent agreeing to sail from Zara to Constantinople in support of Alexios. But, added Villehardouin, "the Book" reports that "only twelve" of the French barons swore to it, that is, Boniface, the counts of Flanders, Blois, and Saint-Pol, and eight unnamed others: "No more could be found."[50] He does not say whether he was among the unnamed "others." But Hugh of Saint-Pol, writing three months later, named "the marshal of Champagne" among the eleven who spoke in favor of going to Constantinople: five Champenois—Villehardouin, Mathieu of Montmorency, Milo Breban, Macaire of Sainte-Menehould, and Manessier of l'Isle-Adam—and six others—Count Baldwin, Conon of Béthune, Renier of Trith, Jean of Foisnon, Anselm of Cayeux, and Hugh himself. All eleven went on to play prominent roles in the conquest of Constantinople.[51]

Villehardouin is brutally honest in admitting to the widespread opposition to another diversion and the simmering discontent within the army that led soldiers to leave in merchant ships. "And so," he observed, "the army was severely diminished each day." He mentions one notable desertion: Renaud of Montmirail, "a very high baron of France," sought permission from Count Louis to take a ship with his men to Syria to deliver an unspecified message. "He swore on scripture with his right hand raised," as did all of his knights, to return within two weeks of landing there. But, said the marshal, "they did not keep their oaths, for they did not return to the army."[52] The desertion of a prominent baron with his

---

49. Villehardouin, *La conquête*, §§94–97.

50. Villehardouin, *La conquête*, §§98–99. For "the Book," a chancery register in Constantinople, see chap. 8 ("The Book").

51. Pokorny, "Zwei unedierte Briefe," 204; translated in Andrea, *Contemporary Sources*, 188. Hugh of Saint-Pol, perhaps wishing to forget Zara, places this swearing on Corfu rather than Zara, but Hendrickx, "Les Chartes de Baudouin de Flandre," 68–71, locates it firmly at Zara.

52. Villehardouin, *La conquête*, §§101–2. Villehardouin earlier had regarded Renaud of Montmirail as "a very high baron" (§4). Renaud arrived in Constantinople from Syria after the second siege of Constantinople and died at the battle of Adrianople in April 1205; see Longnon, *Les compagnons des Villehardouin*, 114–15.

company not only reduced the size of the army, it also set a bad example for those who remained.

With low morale and continuing desertions jeopardizing the army's cohesion, a baronial council (without the Venetians) decided in February 1203 to send a four-member delegation to Rome to seek the pope's absolution for attacking a Christian city: Bishop Nivelon, Count Baldwin's chancellor Master Jean of Noyon, and two barons, Robert of Boves representing Montmorency and Jean of Friaize representing Count Louis. The fact that they swore on scripture to return to the army after presenting their case to the pope suggests that the commanders were aware of the "optics" of four high-ranking men leaving the army, perhaps not to return. They carried a letter from Baldwin, Louis, Hugh, and the Burgundian brothers Odo and William of Champlitte stating that they feared excommunication for what had occurred at Zara and were ready to submit to the pope.[53]

Villehardouin quotes the envoys on their return as having justified their acts to the pope on the grounds that they had been compelled to renegotiate the initial contract for transport because so many crusaders had embarked at ports other than Venice, and those who did arrive in Venice were unable to pay what was owed for the newly built fleet. They put themselves at the pope's mercy. In his response, they reported, the pope said that he understood why they had been compelled to go to Zara, but they must return all stolen property and swear to obey him henceforth before the cardinal legate Peter Capuano would absolve them of their sin.[54] The mission was successful, except that Robert of Boves failed to return; by traveling instead to Syria, he "perjured himself" (*s'en perjura*), commented the marshal.[55]

Villehardouin undoubtedly witnessed all the high deliberations at Zara, and while he reports the deep division within the army as well as among the commanders and even among the Cistercian abbots, he neither betrays the confidential discussions within the leadership councils nor openly states his own views. Mindful as he was of the poor morale among the troops, that is, the knights and support personnel, he as marshal was deeply offended by the "departers," many

---

53. *Oorkonden*, 2:530–32, no. 256, (1–20) April 1203, done at Zara.

54. *Register*, 5:318–20, no. 161, February 1203; translated in Andrea, *Contemporary Sources*, 45–48. Innocent's letter gives details not supplied by Villehardouin.

55. Villehardouin, *La conquête*, §§106–7. Robert of Boves arrived in Constantinople at an undetermined date and later fought with Emperor Henry in the Lombard war; see Longnon, *Les compagnons de Villehardouin*, 124.

CHAPTER 4

of whom left Zara in merchant ships. Some of them paid dearly, he moralized, five hundred drowning on one occasion, while others who took the land route were massacred in Slavonia. If he did not openly express his deep misgivings about mission creep, he was troubled by the continuing drain of troops and their leaders from the main force that sapped the army's morale and undermined its cohesion as a fighting force.

On the day after Easter, 7 April 1203, the crusaders left the city of Zara and the Venetians razed it to the ground and prepared the fleet to sail. At that point Simon V of Montfort left with his brother Guy and several companions whom Villehardouin names, including "the abbot [Guy] of Vaux-de-Cernay, a monk of the Cistercian order, and many others" who opposed the diversion to Constantinople.[56] Shortly afterward, Enguerrand of Boves, one of the "high barons," and his brother Hugh left "with as many men as he could from his lands [*païs*]." Those desertions were a great loss to the army and shameful [*honte*] for those who left, Villehardouin remarked.[57] The departure of the barons with their knights, in effect, entire tactical units, worried the marshal. It was a reminder that the army was an aggregate of independent companies whose primary loyalties were to their barons and compatriots.

Corfu

The fleet left for Corfu on 20 April. The marshal stayed behind with Boniface and the doge to wait for prince Alexios, who arrived from Germany five days later. They sailed first to Dyrrachion (Durazzo), which was, as the marshal noted, part of the Byzantine Empire (and a terminus of the Via Egnatia, which extended across Thrace to Constantinople); the residents swore loyalty to Alexios as their future emperor. On arriving at Corfu, Boniface pitched his tent next to Alexios's at the center of the tent city, since Philip of Swabia had asked him to look after the young prince. That symbolic act, viewed by the entire encamped army, confirmed Boniface's reputation in the ranks as a supreme commander who was pursuing a personal agenda. Villehardouin

---

56. Lippiatt, "Duty and Desertion," argues that it was not so much the destruction of Zara that prompted Simon to leave as the prospect of another diversion having nothing to do with the Holy Land. Villehardouin (*La conquête*, §109) places Simon's departure just before the sailing to Corfu.

57. Villehardouin, *La conquête*, §§108–10.

remembered the three weeks on that rich and fertile island as enjoyable, except for "an unfortunate event which was difficult and hard." A "large part" of those who at Zara had been against the diversion to Constantinople again spoke against a long, perilous venture without end; they planned to stay on Corfu after the fleet left for Constantinople and would ask Count Walter of Brienne to send ships from Brindisi to take them to Syria.[58]

For Villehardouin, the disaffection within the ranks on Corfu was the most serious threat yet to the integrity of the main army. "I cannot name all those who were stirring up trouble in this matter," he observed, "but I will name several of the principal leaders" who openly advocated abandoning the expedition; he made special note of those from Champagne—Oger of Saint-Chéron, Guy of Chappes and his nephew Clarembaud of Chappes, and William of Aulnay. "More than half of the army" agreed with them, according to "the Book," he said, but were ashamed (*por la honte*) to speak out.[59] It must have pained him to name his fellow Champenois. Oger had sworn with him for Helvide of Aulnay in 1185 in the cathedral of Châlons, Guy was among the eleven barons who swore with him to Philip on behalf of Count Thibaut in 1198, and both Oger and Guy had been with him on the Third Crusade. As Villehardouin knew well in 1207 when dictating his memoirs, Oger, Guy, and Clarembaud were among the many who left for home in April 1205, just before the critical battle at Adrianople. Here he is expressing his own disapproval of the conduct of his closest companions from Champagne, at the same time informing his audience that these returnees had displayed less than admirable behavior on the crusade.

The four senior commanders—Boniface, Baldwin, Louis, and Hugh—convened a council of like-minded barons to address the morale of the army. In one of his rare revelations of council deliberations, and perhaps quoting himself, Villehardouin captured the collective sentiment: "Lords, we are in a bad spot. If these men leave us, after so many have left along the way, our army will be lost, and we will not be able to conquer anything. So let us ask them to take pity on themselves and on us, and not dishonor themselves by preventing us from aiding the land

---

58. Villehardouin, *La conquête*, §§111–13.
59. Villehardouin, *La conquête*, §114.

80 CHAPTER 4

of outre-mer."[60] The council then took Alexios and all the bishops and abbots in the army to the valley outside the city where a *parlement* was being held by those who planned to leave.

As Villehardouin describes the scene, the barons dismounted, approached the disaffected men, and in an emotional display of humility fell to their knees in tears; reprising the marshal's own performance in Saint Mark's, they vowed not to rise until the men promised to stay. The disaffected withdrew to discuss the matter among themselves. Taking pity "on their lords and relatives and friends" who had abased themselves, they agreed to stay until the Feast of Saint Michael (29 September 1203), that is, until the treaty with the Venetians expired four months hence, one full year after leaving Venice. The barons were required to "swear on scripture in good faith" to abide by their promise to provide ships for those who still wished at that time to sail directly to Syria.[61] As the highest military officer, who claimed that he was "present" at all the senior councils, Villehardouin must have sworn with them on that occasion. That ended what had been the most concerted challenge to the commanders, who were determined to take an intact army to Constantinople.

It was the first time, according to Villehardouin, that the senior commanders sought, indeed were compelled to seek, the army's consent to a course of action. Ultimately the disaffected remained with the army for another two years, until April 1205, when they returned home with the bulk of the crusader army. For the marshal, disaffection in the ranks and by the "high men" had represented a recurring threat to the army. Four years later he still remembered the relief he felt at the sight of the fleet leaving Corfu: "The day was clear and beautiful, with a light, mild wind," and "never have I seen such a beautiful sight, of sailing ships, horse transports, and war galleys as far as the eye could see, and it lifted up the hearts of the men." He noted the date: "on the eve of Pentecost [24 May], 1203 years after the incarnation of our lord Jesus Christ."[62]

As they passed Cape Malea, they met a ship of crusaders and pilgrims returning from Syria who at first refused from shame (*honte*), he said, to identify themselves to the fleet heading in the opposite direction. A sergeant who jumped ship was taken on board and cheered by

---

60. Villehardouin, *La conquête*, §115. On the moral dilemma of the just war, see Schmandt, "The Fourth Crusade and Just-War Theory," 208–13.

61. Villehardouin, *La conquête*, §§116–18. Hugh of Saint-Pol states that the commanders promised to stay only one month in Constantinople (Pokorny, "Zwei unedierte Briefe," 204; translated in Andrea, *Contemporary Sources*, 189).

62. Villehardouin, *La conquête*, §§119–20.

SAILING TO BYZANTIUM 81

the men. Villehardouin speaks as if he had been in the advance party with Boniface, Baldwin, the doge, and young Alexios that landed at the island of Negroponte (Euboea). After holding a council meeting, they set out for the island of Andros, where they presented Alexios to the residents.[63] From Andros they proceeded to Abydos on the Hellespont (1 June 1203). They were well received, Villehardouin remembered, and stayed a week until they were joined by the main flotilla. From Abydos they sailed to the monastery of Saint Stephen, where they landed in full sight of the walls of Constantinople. The only misadventure on the way was the death of Guy of Coucy, a "high man of the army" (and a poet of some repute), who was buried at sea.[64] Out of respect for the dead, Villehardouin passed over in silence the fact that just weeks earlier Guy had been one of the leaders of the "depart" faction.

Villehardouin's admission that the envoys and Venetian negotiators deceived the army as to its ultimate destination has been read as a disingenuous justification of the fleet's subsequent diversions to Zara and Constantinople. But for the marshal, those diversions were improvisations made in the face of changing circumstances. New contingencies arose at each stage of the journey, and the sheer momentum of the expeditionary force in transit—of thousands of personnel with horses, weapons, assault machines, and provisions in hundreds of vessels—necessitated timely decisions. For him, the diversion to Zara was justified on purely practical terms (feeding the army) and military necessity (launching the ships in Venice and keeping the army intact). At Zara the commanders accepted Alexios's promises of military and financial support as justification for another diversion, although the public argument to the army was based on shame and honor, not practical needs. Neither the commanders at the time nor Villehardouin in retrospect admitted that the primary reason for sailing to Constantinople, as to Zara earlier, was to repay the debt still owed to Venice.[65] The marshal understood that once the fleet set sail, the Venetians, as creditors, became more than equal partners in determining its destination. Absent the failed muster and the consequent debt owed to Venice, the course of events would have been quite different.

---

63. Polemis, "Andros on the Eve of the Fourth Crusade," summarizes all that is known about Andros in the twelfth century.

64. Villehardouin, *La conquête*, §§121-26. For Guy of Coucy as a poet, see Lerond, *Chansons attribuée au chastelain de Couci*.

65. Neocleous, "Financial, Chivalric or Religious," makes a strong case for debt—not conspiratorial, chivalric, or religious motives—as the driving force behind the diversions.

CHAPTER 5

Constantinople

On 23 June 1203, the fleet sailed from Abydos to the monastery of Saint Stephen, just southwest of the sea walls of Constantinople, from where they could see the city in all its splendor.[1] "It was a wondrous sight to behold," said Villehardouin, addressing his listeners. "You should know that those who had not seen Constantinople stared in disbelief that such a magnificent city existed, with its high walls, strong towers encircling the entire city, superb palaces and majestic churches, so many that none believed it possible without seeing them in person. . . . There was not a man so bold whose skin did not shiver from the sight, for never was such a great enterprise undertaken by so few men since the creation of the world."[2]

The counts, barons, and the doge held a *parlement* in the abbey church to discuss the next course of action. A spirited exchange ensued, Villehardouin recalled, perhaps because Innocent's letter to the commanders prohibiting the diversion to Constantinople had arrived.[3] Finally the

---

1. Queller and Madden, *The Fourth Crusade*, 101–203, provide a detailed account of events leading up to the coronation of Baldwin as emperor.

2. Villehardouin, *La conquête*, §§127–28.

3. *Register*, 6:163–65, no. 101 (a letter), and 6:164–68, no. 102 (a draft of a letter without address), both dated to ca. 20 June 1203; translated in Andrea, *Contemporary Sources*, 59–69. See also Schmandt, "The Fourth Crusade and Just-War Theory," 212–13.

doge rose to address the council. The gist of his speech was that, based on his earlier experience in Constantinople, it would be perilous for an army in need of provisions to control such a densely populated city and its vast hinterland; he counseled caution and suggested that the fleet anchor at nearby islands to replenish their supplies before attacking the city. The barons accepted his advice, said the marshal. But the next day they ignored it—"as if no one had ever heard of it"—and sailed past the high walls of Constantinople full of onlookers before landing on the opposite shore in front of the imperial palace at Chalcedon, where the entire army and its support personnel came ashore. Villehardouin vividly recalled the scene of horses being led off the transports and knights and sergeants disembarking with their arms, leaving only the Venetian sailors on board. For three days the men and their mounts refreshed themselves in that exceptionally beautiful and bountiful countryside. Then the Venetians sailed to the imperial palace at Scutari, a short distance from Constantinople, while the army marched overland from Chalcedon. For nine days they encamped at Scutari facing the emperor's troops, who had set up camp to prevent a landing on the opposite shore.[4]

From this point through the first assault on Constantinople, Villehardouin furnishes a detailed description of the army's movements and the baronial deliberations in which he participated as chief of staff, but without revealing his opinions.[5] He recalled one dramatic incident at Scutari on 1 July, when a company of eighty knights under the command of the brothers Odo and William of Champlitte, Oger of Saint-Chéron, and Manessier of l'Isle-Adam set out on a foraging mission. Encountering a Greek cavalry force "of about five hundred" arrayed for battle, the French fell into four units of twenty knights each, charged, and "with the help of our lord God" destroyed the Greek formation. They gathered much booty, which they shared, "as they should have."[6]

The next day, 2 July, a messenger arrived with a letter from Emperor Alexios III addressed to the counts and barons. A Lombard by the name of Nicholò Rosso presented his letter of credence to Boniface, who had the emperor's letter read aloud in council in the Scutari palace. Rosso then addressed the barons. Villehardouin quotes the essence of his

---

4. Villehardouin, *La conquête*, §§129–37.

5. For a close reading and comparison of three eyewitness accounts of these events (by Villehardouin, Clari, and Choniates), see Noble, "Eyewitnesses of the Fourth Crusade." For the Venetian actions through the final conquest, see Madden, *Enrico Dandolo*, 158–72.

6. Villehardouin, *La conquête*, §§138–40.

84   **CHAPTER 5**

speech: The emperor asked, why did the fleet come to Constantinople, since they, too, were Christians and were headed to the Holy Land? "If you need supplies and money, they will be provided so that you can leave. But you cannot harm us even if you had twenty times the number of men."[7] The barons and the doge asked Conon of Béthune, "a fine knight, wise, and very eloquent," to reply for all. As the marshal describes the scene, Conon rose to deliver a threat, to the effect that Alexios was an illegitimate emperor; they had come to restore his nephew Alexios as the rightful emperor, who would pardon him and provide him a comfortable retirement.[8] After the envoy left, Villehardouin continued, it was decided that the doge and Boniface of Montferrat would take the Byzantine prince to sail along the city walls to present him to the people of Constantinople as their true emperor. A second galley of barons and knights shouted up to the crowd lining the walls, "here is your rightful lord," and reminded the onlookers that the prince's father had been unjustly blinded and imprisoned. But, said the marshal, "not one person gave the slightest sign of support" for the imperial claimant out of fear of the emperor, or perhaps because they did not understand the language of the soldiers.[9]

The next day after Mass, a *parlement* was held on horseback (*li parlemenz a cheval*) in the middle of a field to form the battalions (*batailles*) of knights, archers, and foot soldiers for combat.[10] It was an open meeting staged to build esprit in the face of the coming battle,

---

7. Villehardouin states that he did not include details of the letter, suggesting that his scribe consulted the letter preserved in the chancery archive; see chap. 8 ("the Book").

8. Villehardouin, *La conquête*, §§141–44.

9. Villehardouin, *La conquête*, §§145–46.

10. Villehardouin uses *bataille* (*corps de bataille* in modern French) seventy-one times (Naïs, *Index complet*, 41) in referring to a combat unit rather than to a fixed number of combatants. I have translated *bataille* as a "battalion" when it refers to a regional army but "company" when it refers to a smaller tactical unit of mounted knights ranging between 80 to 140 knights and most often estimated at around 100 knights (appendix 2, table 1). Verbruggen, *The Art of Warfare*, 77, translates *bataille* as "battle," a unit of twenty knights, on the basis of Valenciennes's observation that *batailles* at the battle of Philippopolis consisted of twenty knights (*Histoire*, §543); but Valenciennes said that the *batailles* consisted of "*only* twenty knights," that is, they were below full strength. Villehardouin states that the knights landing at Scutari "formed into companies" (*La conquête*, §139), and 200 knights who had lost their horses "made up a company [*firent bataille*] of knights on foot" (§178). At Adrianople the troops of Villehardouin and Macaire of Sainte-Menehould together formed "a very large company" (plus grant bataille, §362), and during the retreat from Rodosto the Venetian and French survivors "formed into companies" (ordenerent lor batailles) of indeterminate size for the march to Constantinople (§386). In short, a *bataille* was a combat unit of varying size, a *corps de troupes*, as Natalis de Wailly, 541, comments in his edition of the memoirs (Villehardouin, *Geoffroi de Ville-Hardouin*).

"and you could see many knights mounted on fine war horses."[11] After a heated back-and-forth discussion as to the order of battle (*bestance i ot d'unes choses et d'autres*), the council decided that Count Baldwin would take the vanguard because he had the largest number of experienced knights, archers, and crossbowmen. The Second Battalion would be led by Baldwin's brother Henry, the Third by Count Hugh of Saint-Pol, and the Fourth by Count Louis of Blois, who also had a great number of knights, said the marshal. The Champenois formed the Fifth Battalion under Mathieu of Montmorency, with Marshal Geoffroy seemingly second-in-command and including Manessier of l'Isle-Adam, Milo Breban, and Macaire of Sainte-Menehould (all three had sworn at Zara), as well as Guy of Chappes, his nephew Clarembaud, and Oger of Saint-Chéron (who were among the mutinous faction on Corfu). The Sixth Battalion of Burgundians was commanded by Odo "the Champenois" of Champlitte, who was among the disaffected on Corfu, while the "very large" Seventh Battalion of Lombards and Germans, commanded by Boniface of Montferrat, would take up the rear guard.[12] Each battalion was made up of "many good knights from their lands and regions [*lor païs*]." Villehardouin does not state the obvious, that each regional battalion consisted of relatives, neighbors, companions in military service and, not least, those who spoke the same dialect. But in noting that Baldwin, Louis, and Boniface had the largest forces, Villehardouin reveals that the Champenois and Burgundians were among the smaller contingents; neither was led by a regional prince who might have attracted a larger following, and both battalions served initially in reserve.[13]

If each battalion was comprised of seventy to one hundred knights, with about as many mounted sergeants, the entire assault force would have numbered about a thousand mounted combatants, not counting

---

11. Villehardouin, *La conquête*, §147. Harari, "Knowledge, Power, and the Medieval Soldier," suggests that the soldiers were kept apprised of the commanders' intentions by their demeanor and their conversations overheard at open assemblies.

12. Verbruggen, *The Art of Warfare*, 217–18, notes that the supreme commander usually stayed in the rear. But here it appears that the senior commanders were deliberately denying Boniface the honor of leading the assault, or perhaps, as a practical matter, wished to keep the northern French-speaking forces together.

13. Villehardouin, *La conquête*, §§148–53. Rhodes, *The Crown and the Cross*, 187, compared the fifteen crusaders from Burgundy on the Fourth Crusade to the fifty on the Third Crusade, a reduction that reflects the absence of Duke Odo and his followers. Longnon lists the thirty-seven from Champagne mentioned by Villehardouin (*Les compagnons de Villehardouin*, 11–27).

86   **CHAPTER 5**

archers and foot soldiers.[14] "Be assured," Villehardouin reminded his listeners, "that this was one of the most dangerous ventures ever attempted." The bishops and clergy attached to the army counseled all to make their confessions and draw up their wills, since they knew not when God might call them. And they did so "most willingly and most piously." Hugh of Saint-Pol later wrote home that the city was conquered by only 500 knights together with an equal number of mounted sergeants and 2,000 foot soldiers, which he regarded a stunning feat.[15]

The First Assault

Villehardouin observed the landing of troops and horses in front of the Tower of Galata shortly after sunrise on 5 July (fig. 3).[16] The fully armed knights accompanied their saddled mounts in the horse transports (*uissiers*), while the rest of the attack force followed in the sailing ships (*nefs*). Each galley towed a horse transport facing backward, then cast it off so that it landed with its rear ramps open to the shore. "The knights disembarked fully armed, with helmets laced and lances in hand as they jumped into the water up to their belts." The archers, sergeants, and crossbowmen followed from their vessels. Once on shore, the knights extended lances to face down a Greek force. With the beachhead secured, the horses were led down the gangplanks from the transports, and the knights mounted and drew up in formation. Villehardouin remembered that amphibious landing as an extraordinary event: "No one ever had made such an audacious landing."[17]

He was impressed by how Baldwin led the army inland past the Tower of Galata to the Estanor, a "very fine and wealthy" Jewish quarter, where they encamped for the night.[18] The next day, after a murderous fight, they captured the Galata fortress and breached the chain

---

14. Riley-Smith, "Toward an Understanding of the Fourth Crusade," 82.

15. Hugh of Saint-Pol, letter, in *MGH SS*, 18:203–8; translated in Andrea, *Contemporary Sources*, 177–201, at 197.

16. Queller and Madden, *The Fourth Crusade*, 119–34, narrate the first conquest. Angold, *The Fourth Crusade*, xx (map 4), diagrams the first assault. Kolias, "Military Aspects of the Conquest," analyzes the respective forces, leadership, and outcome of the battle.

17. Villehardouin, *La conquête*, §§156–57. Pryor, "The Chain of the Golden Horn," 372–74, finds Villehardouin's account of the amphibious landing improbable. However, I have accepted it as the strong visual memory of an experienced military officer who witnessed an unusual amphibious landing in the face of an armed force.

18. Jacoby, "Les quartiers juifs de Constantinople," 175–79, describes the Estanor suburb.

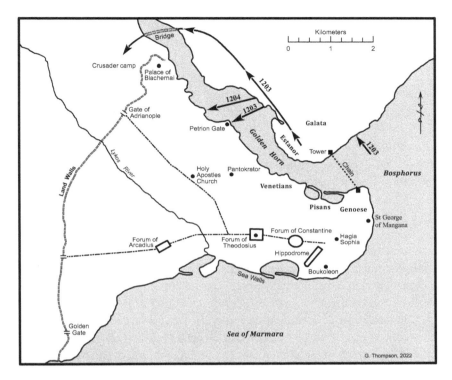

FIGURE 3. Plan of Constantinople, 1204

across the Golden Horn, allowing the fleet to enter the port.[19] A joint French-Venetian council then planned the assault. The Venetians advocated for a naval attack, with knights ascending ladders that extended from the ships to the walls, but the French preferred to attack from land "with their horses and arms." So the council agreed to a joint attack, the Venetians by sea and the French by land. Five days later, on 10 July, Villehardouin watched the army march in formation from the camp to a position above the port opposite the Blachernai palace, where they waited while engineers worked through the night to repair the stone bridge destroyed by the Greeks. The next morning they traversed the restored bridge and made camp along the city's great land walls facing the palace.[20]

It took ten days to construct a large, semi-permanent camp surrounded by palisades, during which Villehardouin was unable to frame

---

19. Pryor, "The Chain of the Golden Horn," 380, fig. 3, a photograph of the chain.
20. Villehardouin, *La conquête*, §§158–64.

CHAPTER 5

a running narrative of events across the broad front line. Instead, he offers vignettes of individual bravery in the many skirmishes between the Byzantines and the French, for which the entire army was summoned "six or seven times a day" to defend the camp: "I cannot tell you how many blows, how many wounded, how many dead there were." He laments that William of Champlitte of the Sixth Battalion had his arm fractured by a stone thrown from the city wall. And he remembers that the soldiers were constantly short of food. After ten days of skirmishing, the attack began on Thursday morning, 17 July. Baldwin led the ground assault with his brother Henry, Hugh of Saint-Pol, and Louis of Blois, while three battalions—the Champenois Fifth, the Burgundian Sixth, and Boniface's Seventh—defended the camp against sorties from the city gates.[21] The attack forces were the same that had fought together against Philip II in France. Villehardouin does not say who decided the plan of attack, but it appears to have been devised by the commanders in council rather than by Boniface, the nominal supreme commander of the joint forces.

Villehardouin does not explain how the land forces coordinated with the navy, but he was well informed about the Venetian success in scaling the walls at the Petrion Gate defended by English and Danish mercenaries (the Varangian Guard). He attributes the success of the naval assault to the doge, who although old and blind, had his men land him on the beach with the banner of Saint Mark. "Forty witnesses" later told him that they had seen the banner flying from one of the towers, although no one knew how it had gotten there. At that point, as the Venetians were entering the city from the towers, the emperor mounted a three-pronged attack against the crusader camp. The six French battalions (without Boniface's Italians and Germans) drew up in ranks in front of the camp's palisades, with archers and crossbowmen in front, mounted knights and foot soldiers behind. Villehardouin noted that two hundred knights who had lost their horses (perhaps at sea) fought on foot as a

---

21. Villehardouin, *La conquête*, §§166–70. Andrea, *Contemporary Sources*, 182–84, argues that Villehardouin misremembered that event of four years earlier, and that Hugh of Saint-Pol's letter to his bailiff written in August 1203, only two months after the event, is more reliable in stating that the assault was led by Boniface and counts Baldwin and Louis; see Pokorny, "Zwei unedierte Briefe," 207; translated in Andrea, *Contemporary Sources*, 195–96. Yet the marshal states that Boniface's forces defended the camp "on the side of the fields" (par devers les chans, §170), that is, on the right side facing the walls, next to the Champenois and Burgundian battalions, a detail that Villehardouin, who was there with the Champenois, would have remembered.

separate unit. The disciplined French refused to give ground despite being vastly outnumbered, he said, and the Greeks finally withdrew. The Venetians, for their part, moved out from their captured towers into the city, but meeting fierce resistance, they set fires to cover their retreat back to the towers.[22]

During the night of 17 July the emperor fled—it was a miracle, said Villehardouin—leaving the city to the French and Venetians and to the "astounded" residents. The imperial guard escorted the blind emperor Isaac II Angelos from prison to the throne in the Blachernai palace (18 July), then informed the French army.[23] The success of the attackers has been attributed to their courage, fighting skill, and leadership, and the defeat of the Byzantine forces to a "total lack of leadership."[24] Niketas Choniates, who witnessed these events from inside the walls, called Emperor Alexios a "spectator," not a military leader who could rise to the occasion, and someone who had planned his escape even before the assault.[25]

Only at this point in the narrative does Villehardouin refer to his own acts. At a joint council of barons and counts with the Venetians it was decided that before allowing young Alexios to enter Constantinople, they would send a delegation to verify conditions in the city and obtain the old emperor's confirmation of his son's promises made at Zara to support the crusaders financially and materially. As Villehardouin describes it, he and Mathieu of Montmorency, leaders of the Champenois battalion, and two Venetians representing the doge, were sent to confront the emperor. The four envoys rode to the city gate, dismounted, and walked under the watchful eye of English and Danish mercenaries to the Blachernai, where they met Emperor Isaac and a crowd of well-dressed men and women, including the emperor's "very beautiful" wife Margaret, sister of King Emeric of Hungary. After being honorably greeted, said Villehardouin, the envoys requested a private audience, and so they entered a side room with the emperor, his wife, the imperial chancellor, and an interpreter. Speaking for the envoys, Villehardouin presented the terms, which he quotes at length.[26] As a staff officer, not a commander,

---

22. Villehardouin, *La conquête*, §§173–74. For the first fire of 17–18 July 1203, see Madden, "The Fires of the Fourth Crusade," 73–74, 93 (map).

23. Villehardouin, *La conquête*, §§175–83.

24. Noble, "Eyewitnesses of the Fourth Crusade," 85.

25. Choniates, *O City of Byzantium*, 297–300, §§543–48.

26. Villehardouin, *La conquête*, §§184–86.

90   CHAPTER 5

he could address the emperor more forcefully than protocol allowed the generals:

> My lord, you [*tu*] see how we have served your son, and how we observed our agreement with him. But he may not enter the city until he has guaranteed the agreement he has with us. As your son, he asks you to confirm it on the same terms he agreed to. [The emperor asks: "What are those terms?"] I will tell you the terms: first, to place the Roman Empire under obedience to Rome, from which it has been separated. Then to pay 200,000 marks of silver to the army and a year's provisions for both the soldiers and the barons. Third, to furnish 10,000 men on his own ships and maintain them at his expense for one year. Fourth, to maintain 500 knights at his expense for the rest of his life for defending the land overseas. Such is the agreement [*convenance*] your son made with us, as he confirmed by his oath and letters patent [*chartes pendenz*] and approved by King Philip of Germany, who is married to your daughter. We wish that you, too, confirm that agreement.[27]

Villehardouin in all likelihood presented the document that Alexios had sealed at Zara. The emperor initially demurred at the onerous provisions, but after much discussion he swore to accept them and sealed a charter with golden seals (*chartes pendanz bulles d'or*). Villehardouin, as lead envoy, returned with it to the camp.[28] Like his earlier speeches, this one had its intended effect, a reminder of the force of speech. The barons then escorted young Alexios into the city.

The Coronation of Alexios IV

The next day the old emperor and his son asked the counts to relocate the army's tents across the Horn next to Estanor in order to avoid incidents between the army and the people of Constantinople; the barons and Venetians readily agreed. Villehardouin would live in that tent city for the next ten months, until May 1204, enjoying "peace and quiet and the abundance of good food."[29] He does not speak of any interaction with the Jewish community of Estanor, but he frequently visited the city, marveling at but not describing the fine residences and the

---

27. Villehardouin, *La conquête*, §§187–88.
28. Villehardouin, *La conquête*, §§189–90.
29. Villehardouin, *La conquête*, §191.

many magnificent churches. He notes the wealth of the city and its innumerable relics, "as many as in the entire rest of the world," and he remembers that Greeks and Franks were in accord and traded all manner of goods, no doubt including relics, which were more abundant here than in any other city, he said. It was agreed that the new emperor would be crowned on 1 August. Shortly thereafter, Alexios began to pay what he had promised as compensation to those who had paid Venice for their passage.[30] According to Niketas Choniates, Alexios had relics and icons melted down in order to pay the crusader army.[31]

Marshal Geoffroy attended the coronation of Alexios IV but does not describe what must have been an impressive ceremony in Hagia Sophia; he says only that Alexios was crowned according to the Greek custom. Nor does he mention the fact that later that month the four senior commanders—Baldwin, Boniface, Louis, and Hugh—informed Pope Innocent and several others of the recent turn of events in a carefully worded justification for conquering Constantinople against Innocent's express prohibition.[32] They passed over the events at Zara and Corfu to describe the assault on Constantinople as a restoration of the legitimate emperor. Similar letters were addressed to Otto IV of Germany and "to all the faithful in Christ, archbishops, bishops, prelates and clerics, barons, and knights."[33] Alexios, for his part, informed the pope that, on the advice of the prelates in the crusade, he accepted the supremacy of the pope, as he had promised earlier when asking the crusaders to restore him to the Byzantine throne.[34]

At about the same time Hugh of Saint-Pol wrote to Robert of Boisleux, his "faithful friend" and custodian of his lands, describing his adventures since Corfu (but omitting the destruction of Zara).[35] If his report is correct, Constantinople was conquered by 500 knights and as many mounted sergeants and 2,000 foot soldiers; they represented about

---

30. Villehardouin, *La conquête*, §§191–93.

31. Choniates, *O City of Byzantium*, 302, §552.

32. *Register*, 6:358–61, no. 210 (211), ca. 25 August 1203 = *Oorkonden*, 2:534–38, no. 258; translated in Andrea, *Contemporary Sources*, 79–84.

33. *Oorkonden*, 2:542–45, no. 260, early August 1203.

34. *Register*, 6:355–56, no. 209 (210), 25 August 1203; translated in Andrea, *Contemporary Sources*, 77–79.

35. Pokorny, "Zwei unedierte Briefe," 203–9, no. 2, undated; translated in Andrea, *Contemporary Sources*, 186–201. Pokorny dates the letter to late July or early August, as does Nieus, *Les chartes des comtes de Saint-Pol*, 224–25, no. 143, whereas Andrea, *Contemporary Sources*, 180n16, suggests 25 August. Since the letter refers to "our new emperor," it clearly was written after the coronation of Alexios on 1 August. Nieus identifies the recipient as Robert of Boisleux.

92   CHAPTER 5

one-third of the knights who sailed from Venice one year earlier but only about 11 percent of the number anticipated by the treaty with Venice.[36] At the end of his letter Hugh names the great barons who abandoned the crusade at Zara so that the home audience would know: Stephen of Perche, Renaud of Montmirail, Enguerrand and his brother Hugh of Boves, Simon of Montfort, and the abbot (Guy) of Vaux; they had placed the crusade in great danger, he said, meaning that they took their men with them, thus reducing the size of the army and weakening its morale. He concluded by saying that he planned to proceed to Jerusalem in the spring of 1204. If Villehardouin sent a similar letter to his family, there is no record of it.

The rest of the year, August through December 1203, was marked by increasingly difficult relations between the Greeks and the Franks encamped across the Horn. Shortly after his coronation, Alexios IV visited the crusader camp, where he was received with great respect (*mult honor*), said Villehardouin. But one day, at a secret meeting with the barons in Baldwin's tent, Alexios pleaded—Villehardouin, who was present, quotes his speech—that he could not possibly pay what he had promised, and that many Greeks regarded him as a puppet of the foreigners. He reminded the barons that their agreement with Venice regarding the fleet expired on 29 September 1203, but he promised that if the army stayed until next March, he would have time to collect the rest of the monies owed them. The barons agreed among themselves that the proposal would benefit both sides, but they needed the army's consent to amend what they had promised on Corfu.[37]

A general meeting (*parlement*) of barons, captains, and most of the knights was called to consider the emperor's proposal. A heated discussion (*ot mult grant descorde*) ensued, since the barons on Corfu had sworn on scripture to provide transport to Syria for those who wished to leave on 29 September. The same dissenters, said the marshal without naming them, threatened to leave the never-ending expedition that still lacked definite plans to sail to Syria, the announced goal set by Innocent five years earlier in calling for a crusade to recover Jerusalem. "Give us the ships you promised us," they demanded, "because we want to go to Syria." But "others," said Villehardouin, meaning the barons, argued that it would be better to wait for the spring sailing, because the sailors would not leave during the winter months, and both the monies

---

36. Riley-Smith, "Toward an Understanding of the Fourth Crusade," 81.
37. Villehardouin, *La conquête*, §§194–96.

and provisions promised by Alexios would aid the expedition sailing "to Syria by way of Egypt." After a vigorous debate, all agreed to remain an additional six months, until 29 March 1204, almost two years after the great army had mustered in Venice. The Venetians, too, promised to stay, and the emperor gave additional financial support. "And so, peace was restored to the army." Once again the army had been preserved, this time on the promise, without the oaths of the commanders, that the spring sailing would take them to Syria.[38]

At about the same time in August, Mathieu of Montmorency, leader of the Champenois, died and was buried in the Hospitaller church in Constantinople. It was "a great misfortune," said the marshal, without specifying the circumstances of his death, for he was "one of the best knights in the kingdom of France, and one of the most esteemed and most loved."[39] Villehardouin passes over the fact that, in the absence of any other distinguished baron from Champagne, he assumed command of the Champenois as de facto successor of Montmorency and, by extension, of Count Thibaut. For the next four years, through the rest of his memoirs, he would act as leader of the Champenois forces.

Immediately after the army agreed to stay, Emperor Alexios took a combined force of Greeks and French to present himself beyond Constantinople and to counter the Bulgarian king Kalojan (r. 1197–1207), who had taken over "almost half of the empire" west of the capital, said Villehardouin. That was the marshal's first mention of Kalojan as posing an immediate threat to the capital, a threat that would overshadow the rest of his memoirs.[40] For the next three months Boniface of Montferrat, Hugh of Saint-Pol, Henry of Flanders, and William of Champlitte and their battalions (the Second, Third, Sixth, and Seventh) accompanied Alexios and his Greek forces beyond the capital.

Marshal Geoffroy stayed in the camp with counts Baldwin and Louis, who was still ill, along with the rest of the army (the First, Fourth, and Fifth Battalions), and thus was a witness from across the Horn to events in the city. He saw how a brawl between the Greeks and Latins led to a fire on 19–20 August that quickly engulfed churches, palaces, and

---

38. Villehardouin, *La conquête*, §§197–99.

39. Villehardouin, *La conquête*, §200.

40. Villehardouin, *La conquête*, §§201–2. Gjuzelev, "La Quatrième croisade et ses conséquences pour la Bulgarie médiévale," provides a convenient summary of Byzantine-Bulgarian relations from this point to the end of Villehardouin's memoirs in 1207. For a biography of Kalojan, see Madgearu, *The Asanids*, 114–74.

94   **CHAPTER 5**

merchant shops, spreading all the way to the port.[41] "I do not know who maliciously set the fire," he said, but it continued for a week, causing incalculable losses of men, women, and children, and of material goods. It must have reminded him of the great fire in Troyes fifteen years earlier (23 July 1188) during preparations for the Third Crusade. The Latins who resided in Constantinople—at least 15,000, he estimated—fearing for their lives, crossed over the Golden Horn with their families and possessions seeking refuge in the crusaders' tent city. Villehardouin remembered the exodus of the Latins as causing a lasting separation of Greeks and Latins, and a permanent resentment on both sides. He also noted the death of Abbot Simon of Loos, one of the strongest supporters of the diversion to Constantinople.[42]

The joint Greek-French expedition returned to a warm welcome on 11 November. Alexios retreated to the Blachernai, while Boniface and the barons returned to their tent city. Thereafter Alexios kept his distance, ending his visits to the barons, withholding his promised payments, and even avoiding his protector Boniface; he felt more secure, said Villehardouin, having established his authority beyond the capital. The marshal did not mention another factor: large quarters of Constantinople had been destroyed by fire in Alexios's absence. Boniface and the French counts, for their part, felt betrayed. Recognizing the danger of maintaining an encamped army without a clear purpose, a council of barons and the doge decided to send a delegation of three Venetians and three French—Geoffroy of Villehardouin and his colleagues Milo Breban and Conon of Béthune—to confront the emperor.

Villehardouin recalls how they mounted their horses, with swords at the side, and rode to the Blachernai palace. They found the old emperor and his son the new emperor sitting side-by-side on thrones surrounded by distinguished men and women. Conon, who was "most wise and well-spoken," presented their demands. Villehardouin remembered Conon's tough words: "My lord, we came to you [*a toi*, he used the familiar *tu*] because you both swore to uphold your agreement—and we have your charters in proof of that—yet you have not fulfilled its conditions despite our frequent requests. We will take whatever measure necessary to obtain what is our due, but we will not initiate any act before announcing our plans, because it is not the custom in our lands to commit

---

41. Madden, "The Fires of the Fourth Crusade," 74–84, 93 (map) provides a detailed description of the three fires. See also Van Tricht, *The Latin Renovatio*, 23–24.

42. Villehardouin, *La conquête*, §§201–5.

treason [*traïson*]." The Greeks, not accustomed to such harsh words spoken in the emperor's presence, were outraged, said Villehardouin, who was relieved to have escaped retribution before leaving the palace. "And so the war began" between the Greeks and the Franks.[43]

The Second Assault

Villehardouin skipped over the December riots in the city and the clashes between Greeks and Franks except to say that they lasted through the winter months. He resumed his narrative with the spectacular naval attack by the Greeks, who sent seventeen large burning ships against the Venetian ships at anchor on 1 January 1204. Viewing the attack from across the Horn, he admired the skill of the sailors in deflecting the burning ships and was relieved that only one Pisan ship was lost that night. He noted the gravity of the event: if the fleet had been destroyed, the army would have been stranded, unable to leave by land or by sea. But it was the coup d'état by the emperor's chamberlain, Mourtzouphlos Doukas, who imprisoned then executed Alexios IV (8 February) and declared himself emperor, that prompted the barons to act.[44] A *parlement* of Venetians and barons attended by the bishops and clergy decided that such an evil person had no right to rule; moreover, since the Greeks had withdrawn obedience to Rome, they violated the first clause in the treaty sealed by Alexios at Zara and accepted by his father in Constantinople. Beyond the moral and religious objections to Mourtzouphlos, it might be said that his usurpation, the culmination of two decades of coups, represented the end point in "the disintegration of a political system."[45]

For Villehardouin, the murder of the young emperor and the death of his father shortly afterward was a turning point. Even the Latin clergy, hitherto ambivalent about the diversion of the expedition, agreed that

---

43. Villehardouin, *La conquête*, §§207–16. Villehardouin contracts the time between the challenge to Alexios and the 1 January 1204 attack on the Venetian fleet. He fails to note conditions within Constantinople, especially the bloody clashes between Greeks and Franks in December, as described in the *Devastatio Constantinopolitana* (translated in Andrea, *Contemporary Sources*, 218), and in Queller and Madden, *The Fourth Crusade*, 144–47, 157–58.

44. Villehardouin, *La conquête*, §§217–22. Villehardouin makes no mention of the popular discontent with Alexios and the mob's attack on Hagia Sophia (15 January 1204). Nor does he mention Boniface's cooperation with Alexios in these weeks; see a detailed analysis in Madden, "Vows and Contracts," 452–61. For the reign of Alexios V (Mourtzouphlos), February–March 1204, see Noble, "Eyewitnesses of the Fourth Crusade."

45. Angold, "Byzantine Politics," 67.

96   CHAPTER 5

war was "right and just."[46] It was "a great comfort" to the army, he said, that the "clergy," meaning the senior prelates, granted a papal indulgence to those who, after making confession, died in order to subject the city to the Roman Church.[47] In fact, the pope reprimanded bishops Nivelon and Garnier for absolving those who had destroyed Zara, a Christian city, without papal authorization, and warned, under threat of excommunication, against occupying the lands of the Greeks.[48]

January and February 1204 were marked by interminable skirmishes between Franks and Greeks. One notable event was Count Henry's raiding party at Philia that captured a much-revered icon and the imperial standard of Mourtzouphlos, who barely escaped capture. Villehardouin's vivid account of that clash must have come from Henry himself on his return to Constantinople.[49] At this point Villehardouin was reminded of those who had bypassed Venice to sail directly to Syria: there were many more crusaders in those crossings than the army besieging Constantinople, he claimed. He exaggerated only slightly. If between 500 and 700 knights assaulted the city, and if a total of 300 knights had left the main army to cross to Acre, the crusade's "second front" represented about half of those attacking Constantinople. But it still was a substantial number.[50] They suffered severely, he observed, for almost all were either captured or killed, as he must have heard later from the knights returning from Acre. Among those killed were Vilain of Nully, one of Villehardouin's neighbors in Champagne and "one of the best knights of the world," and Giles of Trazegnies, the constable of Flanders. Geoffroy's countrymen Renaud of Dampierre, William of Nully, and Jean of Villers were taken prisoner. Jean of Villers was redeemed by the Hospitallers around the time Villehardouin was dictating his memoirs, but Dampierre would remain captive for thirty years.[51] The marshal had encountered them in Piacenza in the summer of 1202; he could not

---

46. For the clergy's rationale, see Schmandt, "The Fourth Crusade and Just-War Theory," 214–18.

47. Villehardouin, *La conquête*, §§224–25.

48. *Register*, 6:389–93, nos. 230 (231) and 231 (230), early February 1204; translated in Andrea, *Contemporary Sources*, 90–95.

49. Villehardouin, *La conquête*, §§226–28.

50. Villehardouin, *La conquête*, §229. See Kedar, "The Fourth Crusade's Second Front," 96–97.

51. Riley-Smith, "The Hospitaller Commandery of Éterpigny," 392–93, no. 3, charter of 6 January 1207 (old style), by which Jean of Villers becomes a *confrater* of the Hospitallers in thanks for obtaining his release. William of Nully's fate is unknown; see Longnon, *Les compagnons de Villehardouin*, 25–26. Renaud of Dampierre returned home after a thirty-year captivity; see Longnon, *Les compagnons de Villehardouin*, 60–63; Evergates, *Feudal Society*, 120–22, no. 95,

help but observe: "No one who abandoned the army at Venice escaped shame and misfortune."[52]

Both the crusader army and the Byzantines spent March 1204 preparing for the inevitable attack on the city. The marshal surely must have understood the significance of the moment, as a crusade for the liberation of Jerusalem was turning into a war of conquest of the capital of Byzantium. Mission creep finally yielded a new mission for the army. To plan for the post-conquest settlement, a *parlement* of the army and the Venetians decided on the division of future spoils, the election of a Latin emperor, and the partition of imperial lands.[53] Villehardouin witnessed what he called a lively exchange of opinions (*assez i ot parlé et avant et arriera*) before a formal agreement (*convenance*) was reached and written up as a *concordia* between the crusade leaders and the Venetians. It would serve as a template for regime change and an empire reorganized under a Latin emperor and foreign rulers.[54] It did not deal with governance or succession, issues that were left to the future emperor.

Villehardouin recalled the principal clauses of the agreement.[55] Booty taken within Constantinople was to be collected for the payment of debts owed to the Venetians; anything remaining would be divided equitably between the parties. A new emperor would be elected "from the army" by a twelve-member commission, six from each party, while the Venetian clergy would assume control of Hagia Sophia and elect the next patriarch. The new emperor would receive the Blachernai and Boukoleon palaces

---

1233; Barthélemy, "Chartes de départ et de retour"; and in greater detail, Pippenger, "Lives on Hold."

52. Villehardouin, *La conquête*, §§230–31. Henry of Arzillières had returned home by 1205, when he confirmed a gift made in his absence by "Geoffroy, son of Jean, lord of Brandonvillers" (Longnon, *Recherches*, 196–97, no. 77). Henry is listed in the feudal register for Vitry (*Feoda 5*, no. 3179) of 1210–14. More than a dozen knights from Picardy escaped from captivity; see Riley-Smith, "The Hospitaller Commandery of Éterpigny."

53. Hendrickx, "Les *parlements*," 214, rightly terms the *parlement* as a necessary open meeting to determine the post-conquest order.

54. Neither of the two copies of the *concordia* survives. Later copies are: one drawn up in the name of Boniface of Montferrat (whose name appears first) and counts Baldwin of Flanders, Louis of Blois, and Henry of Saint-Pol, which the Venetians retained (*Oorkonden*, 2:553–59, no. 267, March 1204 = Tafel and Thomas, *Urkundnen*, 1:449–52, no. 120); and a second one, drawn up in the name of the doge (Tafel and Thomas, *Urkunden*, 1:444–49, no. 119, March 1204). For detailed analyses, see Carile, "Partitio Terrarum Imperii Romanie," and Van Tricht, *The Latin Renovatio*, 41–53. Queller and Madden, *The Fourth Crusade*, 175–76, provide a convenient summary. Madden, *Enrico Dandolo*, 169–89, represents the Venetian side of the March *concordia*, with a map (189, fig. 9) of Venice's share of the empire.

55. Villehardouin states the clauses as if he were reciting from memory; it is possible that he consulted, or had his scribe consult, the written *concordia* or a copy of it retained in the chancery; see chap. 8 ("The Book").

98   **CHAPTER 5**

and one-quarter of the imperial lands within the city and beyond; the remaining three-quarters were to be divided equally (three-eighths each) between Venetians and crusaders. A commission of twenty-four, twelve from each party, would distribute fiefs and titles (*les fies et les honors*) with their attached military service owed to the emperor.[56] Finally, all combatants were to remain in service for one year, until the end of March 1205, in the third extension of obligatory service since the muster in Venice almost three years earlier. Those who wished to leave at that time would be free to do so; those who remained would be in the new emperor's service in an army of occupation. Both parties, meaning the Venetians and the barons, swore to the pact.[57] Villehardouin does not remark the audacity of the *concordia* plan, in which the army was effectively transformed into a force of occupation. A well-informed cleric might have noticed the irony in the fact that the crusaders planned to attack a Christian capital and dismantle its provinces in the very month that the truce prohibiting an attack on Turkish-occupied Jerusalem expired.

The assault began on Friday, 9 April 1204. The ground forces of men and horses formed into battalions and were transported across the Golden Horn from their encampment to the walls along the port (fig. 3). They suffered heavy losses at first, he admits. After the failure of the initial assault, the barons and the doge held a *parlement* with the army in a church near the encampment; they agreed to resume the attack on Monday, 12 April, and to capture the city towers from flying bridges on the ships. The largest ships, *Pilgrim* and *Paradise*, were bound together so as to encircle a tower so tightly that the soldiers on board could climb ladders and cross the bridges from opposite sides to dislodge the defenders.[58] Villehardouin fails to identify bishops Nivelon and Garnier as the commanders of *Pilgrim* and *Paradise*, but his detailed account of the naval maneuvers and the beachhead established by the knights in front of the city walls suggests that he was an eyewitness to the attack from across the Horn.[59] After fierce fighting, the Venetians captured several

---

56. The *concordia* states that *feuda et honorificentias* would be distributed (*Oorkonden*, 3:558, no. 267).

57. Villehardouin, *La conquête*, §§234–35. Villehardouin fails to mention what might have seemed in retrospect a relatively minor provision, that the new fiefs were to be inherited by women as well as men. Baldwin and Marie of Champagne had only an infant daughter at the time, and he might well have been thinking about the future of his lands in the event he did not return home.

58. Villehardouin, *La conquête*, §§236–42.

59. Baldwin's letter of late May 1204 to the pope identified the bishops. Madden, *Enrico Dandolo*, 129, notes that the round ship *Paradise* joined the fleet after returning from the East.

towers and opened the city gates, while the knights, who fought their way up ladders set against the walls, captured four other towers. The rest of the knights quickly entered the city and routed the Greeks.

Mourtzouphlos took flight by night, while Boniface's men, fearing a Greek counterattack, set a fire that "consumed more houses than in three of the largest cities in France," as Villehardouin put it. "That was the third fire in Constantinople since the French arrived."[60] By Tuesday, 13 April, Constantinople was an open city. It appears that Villehardouin had stayed in the rear at the command center until this point, when he entered the city. He remembered that Boniface "raced" (*chevaucha*) to the Boukoleon palace, where he found the sisters of the kings of France and Hungary (Agnes and Margaret), former empresses who had fled their private residences for the safety of the Boukoleon.[61] Count Henry occupied the Blachernai on behalf of Baldwin. Villehardouin noted for the record that Count Louis, who had suffered from quartan fever through the winter, remained bedridden on a transport during the assault.

The marshal had become familiar with Constantinople after the first conquest, but he marveled anew at the city's wealth, even after the destructive fires of the previous August. He noted the extraordinary range of valuable objects that passed to the victors as spoils of war: gold and silver tableware, silk and clothing, precious stones, "and all the finest objects ever found on earth." He still remembered the amount of booty as more than had been found in any city "since the creation of the world," but he provided no details as to the treatment of the residents and their properties during the three days of looting and violence unleashed by the conquering soldiers.[62]

Two residents of Constantinople left moving accounts of the army's conduct after the city's fall. Nicholas Mesarites, a church official, wrote of the destruction of his house and the violence of the Franks, their arrogance and crudeness. "Sword-brandishing warriors breathing murder, men in armour with spears, swords, and lances, archers and horsemen with terrifying glances" perpetrated unspeakable indignities on women.

---

60. Madden, "The Fires of the Fourth Crusade," 98, maps the three fires.

61. Villehardouin, *La conquête*, §249. Clari, *La conquête*, §53, states that the French barons, on entering the Boukoleon, asked whether Agnes (of France) was still alive; on being told that she had married the Greek commander Theodore Branas and lived in a nearby palace, they visited her. But they were badly received, said Clari, because she could not speak French (she had left France two decades earlier at nine years of age). For her subsequent role in the principality of Adrianople, see Short, "Agency and Authority."

62. Villehardouin, *La conquête*, §250.

100   **CHAPTER 5**

His was a long lamentation for those who suffered at the hands of the barbarian conquerors.[63] Niketas Choniates, a government official, provided an even more detailed description of the conquerors, who committed "outrageous crimes" in stripping the altars and icons, smashing and melting down reliquaries and religious objects, and violating women, even nuns. Most culpable were those who had a cross pinned to their shoulders.[64] Choniates and his family were saved by a Venetian friend, and five days later he and his pregnant wife were among the many leading families that left the city, traveling first to Selymbria, then returning to Constantinople before settling in Nicaea five months later.[65]

The sack of the city lasted three days before the commanders restored a semblance of order.[66] Boniface, "who was commander of the army" (qui sires ere de l'ost), and the doge and barons sent a crier through the city announcing that all the booty was to be collected, on pain of excommunication, at three churches and then distributed by a joint French-Venetian commission. The Venetians were paid 50,000 marks; the remaining 100,000 marks were distributed within the army: a knight received as much as two mounted sergeants, each of whom received as much as two foot soldiers. But, Villehardouin recalled, despite the threat of excommunication, there were those who did not comply, to the loss of those who did, and a good number (assez en i ot) who kept their booty were hanged for theft. He remembered one instance in which a knight of Hugh of Saint-Pol was hanged with his shield around his neck for having kept his booty. "Greed is the root of all evil," he observed.[67] Despite those incidents of war, the marshal found it extraordinary that a total force of 20,000 combatants (French and Venetian) could conquer the most heavily fortified city in the world.[68]

---

63. Nicholas Mesarites, "*Epitaphios* for His Brother John," in *Nicholas Mesarites*, 168–71; Villehardouin, *La conquête*, §§33–35. Phillips, *The Fourth Crusade*, 258–70, collects the eyewitness reports of looting and violence in the city immediately after its fall. Queller and Madden, *The Fourth Crusade*, 193–203, provide a succinct account of the "devastation" of Constantinople.

64. Choniates, *O City of Byzantium*, 314–20, §§573–82.

65. Choniates, *O City of Byzantium*, 322–26, §§586–94. For his reaction to the conquest, see also Page, *Being Byzantine*, 72–93. For estimates of property damage and number of displaced persons, see Madden, "The Fires in Constantinople," 88–89. For the immediate fates of the Greeks and Italians, some leaving, others staying, see Jacoby, "The Greeks of Constantinople," 53–59.

66. Angold, *The Fourth Crusade*, 111–13, concludes that the sack of the city caused less material damage than the fires of the previous August.

67. Villehardouin, *La conquête*, §§252–55.

68. Villehardouin, *La conquête*, §251.

Regime Change

Villehardouin is discreet in describing the lead-up to the election of a Latin emperor after the fall of the city. He was present at a preliminary meeting (*parlement*) of the entire army held on Sunday, 18 April, which revealed a serious disagreement (*la grant discorde*) as to whether Boniface of Montferrat, still the nominal supreme commander, or Baldwin of Flanders, whose troops had been in the vanguard of the attack, should be emperor.[69] It was decided to continue the discussion two weeks hence on 2 May, in what would be the fourth *parlement* since March.[70] In the meantime, the senior leaders (*li preudome de l'ost*), meeting in private, feared that "if we elect one of those two distinguished men, the other will be so envious that he will leave with all his men." The loss of either of the two largest battalions, the First (Flemish) or Seventh (Lombard), would seriously jeopardize the post-conquest settlement. The barons, or their clerics, recalled the rivalries among the princes of the First Crusade, one century earlier, when Godfrey of Bouillon was chosen king of Jerusalem. Since it was imperative that both Boniface and Baldwin remain with their forces to install the new regime, it was decided that the new emperor would retain the capital and the lands in the west, primarily Thrace, and the one not chosen as emperor would receive in consolation "the land across the Straits toward the land of the Turks" and "the island of Crete" to be held in homage; that is, he would be the emperor's "man" (*en sera ses home*).[71] The two candidates agreed "most graciously" (*mult debonairement*) to that arrangement, said the marshal.[72] Villehardouin does not mention what Clari reports, that Boniface, who

---

69. I have accepted the 18 April date proposed by Saint-Guillain, "Comment les Vénitiens," 719–20, against Faral (Villehardouin, *La conquête*), 2:61n2. Saint-Guillain concludes that the four post-conquest meetings were held on Sundays: 18 April for deciding the procedure for an election; 2 May for choosing electors; 9 May for the election of Baldwin; and 16 May for the coronation.

70. Villehardouin, *La conquête*, §§256–57. Hendrickx, "Les *parlements*," 214–15, notes the continuing importance of *parlements* as general consultative meetings until Baldwin's coronation.

71. Villehardouin, *La conquête*, §258. Saint-Guillain, "Comment les Vénitiens," 720–32, has shown how manuscripts A and O read *l'isle de Crete*, whereas manuscripts B, C, and D, by error, read some form of *Grece*. Faral, following Natalis de Wailly, rendered it as "l'isle de Grece" (Villehardouin, *La conquête*, §264), which modern translators and commentators have understood as the Peloponnese. Saint-Guillain found it curious that Faral, in his meticulous edition of manuscript O, preferred the erroneous reading of C and D.

72. Villehardouin, *La conquête*, §258.

102   CHAPTER 5

had occupied the Boukoleon palace, was forced to vacate it before the election.[73]

At the reconvened general *parlement* on Sunday, 2 May, Villehardouin witnessed the selection of twelve electors, six Venetians and six French, who swore on scripture to select the best man as emperor. He does not name the electors, but Baldwin, in his letter to the pope after the election, named the army's six electors, all prelates: the bishops of Soissons (Nivelon), Troyes (Garnier), and Halberstadt (Conrad), the bishops-elect of Bethlehem (Peter) and Acre (Baldwin's cleric Jean of Noyon), and the Cistercian abbot of Lucedio (Peter).[74] The twelve electors were locked in the chapel of the patriarch's palace adjoining Hagia Sophia, where they remained for one week "until they reached an agreement," which is to say after an extended discussion. Villehardouin does not mention the role played by the Venetian electors, who distrusted Boniface for his deep ties to the Byzantine imperial family and to Venice's trade rival Genoa. An Emperor Boniface would be inimical to Venetian commercial interests in Constantinople.[75] At midnight on Sunday, 9 May, Bishop Nivelon of Soissons, the senior French prelate, announced the election of Baldwin, the thirty-two-year-old count of Flanders, instead of Boniface, an international figure in his early fifties who had been recruited to lead the crusade. The crowd waiting in the palace erupted in celebration, said the marshal. The coronation was set for Sunday, 16 May 1204.[76]

Villehardouin remembered the coronation in Hagia Sophia as a festive affair, with Boniface and Louis displaying suitable deference to the new emperor, but he omits details furnished by Clari, that Louis carried the imperial standard, Hugh the imperial sword, and Boniface the crown.[77] A long procession accompanied Baldwin to the Boukoleon for a sumptuous feast. Only two events marred the occasion. Odo the Champenois of Champlitte, commander of the Sixth (Burgundian) Battalion,

---

73. Clari, *La conquête*, §§93–94

74. *Oorkonden*, 2:564–83, no. 271, late May 1204; translated in Andrea, *Contemporary Sources*, 98–112.

75. Faral, "Geoffroy de Villehardouin," 574, notes Choniates's observation that the doge, fearing the Montferrat as a powerful Italian family, preferred the younger and more malleable Baldwin. For the Venetian electors, see Madden, *Enrico Dandolo*, 175–77.

76. Villehardouin, *La conquête*, §§259–61.

77. Clari, *La conquête*, §§96–97. Clari's text describes in great detail Baldwin's coronation vestments and his robing in a side room of Hagia Sophia, but it is unclear whether that text was in his oral report. It was unlikely that a spectator knight like Robert of Clari would have had access to Baldwin's dressing room and been able to describe Baldwin's elaborate vestments with such precision.

died before the coronation and was buried in the Church of the Apostles. More ominous, and a portent, was Boniface's marriage on the day before the coronation to "the empress," that is, Margaret of Hungary, sister of King Emeric and widow of Emperor Isaac III, who had been murdered only a month earlier. Margaret was, as Villehardouin noted twice before, "a most beautiful woman."[78] An attentive reader or listener of the marshal's narrative would have sensed a looming confrontation between Boniface and Baldwin. All this occurred "in the year of the Incarnation of Jesus Christ, 1204."[79]

---

78. Villehardouin, *La conquête*, §§185, 212. For Margaret's important political role as Boniface's wife, see Short, "Agency and Authority," 33–35.

79. Villehardouin, *La conquête*, §§262–63.

Chapter 6

Marshal of Emperor Baldwin

The first order of business after Baldwin's coronation was to reward Boniface with the fief promised to the losing party in the election, the land across the straits on the Turkish side and the island of Crete. Baldwin "well knew that he was obliged to grant it," said Villehardouin, "and would do so most willingly." Seeing that Baldwin was amenable, Boniface then asked whether he could exchange the land across the straits for the kingdom of Thessalonika, ostensibly to be closer to the ancestral lands of his new wife Margaret, sister of King Emeric of Hungary, whom he had married the day before Baldwin's coronation.[1]

A council of commanders discussed Boniface's request at length ("assez en fu parlé en maintes manieres"), said the marshal, without mentioning the troubling issue that Boniface might create an independent state in Thessalonika, reviving the one his brother Renier had received two decades earlier under the Byzantine emperors.[2] A king of Thessalonika married to the widow of the last Byzantine emperor and supported

---

1. Villehardouin, *La conquête*, §264. Saint-Guillain, "Comment des Vénitiens," 731–32, reminds us that the property exchanged for Thessalonika was in Asia Minor; it did not include Crete.

2. On Renier of Montferrat, see Haberstumpf, *Dinastie Europee nel Mediterraneo Orientale*, 43–76, and "Bonifacio di Montferrato."

by the large Seventh Battalion posed an existential threat to the Latin settlement. Ultimately "the emperor granted it, and he [Boniface] did homage for it" (li empereres li otroia et cil en fist homage) in the presence of the council, which Villehardouin attended. "There was much rejoicing throughout the army," he said, "because the marquis was one of the most esteemed knights and one of the best loved, for no one was more generous to them. And so, as you have heard, the marquis remained in the land" to aid in the conquest of Constantinople's hinterland.[3] The kingdom of Thessalonika was the first fief established in the new Latin empire, months before fiefs were distributed to the other barons and knights. In writing to Pope Innocent, Boniface identified himself as "marquis of Montferrat, and by the grace of God king of Thessalonika and lord of Crete."[4]

Baldwin acted immediately to embed the new Latin regime. He adopted a new seal, effective on the day of his coronation, 16 May 1204. On the obverse, a figure sits on a throne holding the scepter and orb in the Byzantine manner, with his new title in Greek, "Baldwin, emperor" (*Baldovinos despotis*); on the reverse a Western-style mounted knight holds a shield and upright sword with the inscription in Latin: "Baldwin, by the grace of God, emperor of Romania" and "count of Flanders and Hainaut."[5] The chancery adopted his full title in official documents: "Baldwin, by the grace of God, king of the Romans and *augustus*, count of Flanders and Hainaut," and replaced Baldwin's comital "I" with the imperial "we."[6]

Shortly after his coronation, Baldwin sent a long, carefully crafted letter to the pope recounting the seemingly improbable sequence of events

---

3. Villehardouin, *La conquête*, §265. Clari, *La conquête*, §99, states that Baldwin initially demurred because Thessalonika was not his to give (it had been assigned to Venice by the *concordia* of March 1204), but Villehardouin later reiterated that Boniface had done homage to Baldwin for Thessalonika and assured Boniface that the doge, Count Louis, Conon of Béthune, Manessier of l'Isle-Adam, and Geoffroy himself "well knew of the agreement [*convenance*] made between the two" (Villehardouin, *La conquête*, §286).

4. *Register*, 8:100–101, no. 59 (58), undated: "marchio Montisferr(ati), Dei gratia regni Thessalonicensis et Crete dominus." The editors date this letter to before 12 August 1204, which seems likely if Boniface were announcing to Innocent that he was king of Thessalonika as well as lord of Crete, for which he had done homage to the new Latin emperor of Constantinople. Andrea, *Contemporary Sources*, 160–61, translates and dates the letter to ca. 15 April 1205.

5. *Oorkonden*, 2:604–5, no. 275, June 1204. A photograph of his golden bull is in Villela-Petit, *1204*, 190, plate 6, catalogue 47a and b, 234. On the significance of Baldwin's titles, especially of *Rom(anie)*, see Van Tricht, *The Latin Renovatio*, 62–66.

6. Prevenier, "La chancellerie de l'empire latin."

CHAPTER 6

that led to his election as emperor of Constantinople.[7] It justifies in detail the violence done to the city and its people, and it depicts the storming of the city walls as a triumph of Western Christianity. In appealing to the pope, who had prohibited violence against fellow Christians, Baldwin referred to "the entire Latin people" (*omni Latinorum gente*) and "all Latins" (*Latinos omnes*), as if to remind Innocent that the conquest of Constantinople was a triumph of Latin Christianity over the Greek. But Baldwin also called for a council of Greeks and Latins in order to reach a modus vivendi under the new regime and to reconnect Rome and Constantinople, the new Rome, over which the pope could assert his authority. The chancery drew up copies of the letter for the archbishop of Cologne, the abbot of Cîteaux and Cistercian monasteries, and "all Christians," namely prelates and barons, knights, sergeants, and "the entire [Latin] Christian people."[8] The letter not only justified the conquest of Constantinople, it forced Innocent to change his position, from prohibiting war against Christians to justifying the subjugation of Orthodox Christians.[9] Thereafter both the conquerors and the papacy turned to the task of ruling Byzantine lands and Greek-speaking Eastern Christians. Neither Baldwin nor Villehardouin mentioned the status of the new patriarch of Constantinople, which the *concordia* of March had awarded to the Venetians, nor the status of the Greek church and clergy.[10] In recalling the transitional month of May 1204, Villehardouin failed to reflect on the significance of the conquest, the election of a Latin emperor, and the imminent dismantling of a Christian empire.

Garrison Commander of Constantinople

Collegial decision-making among the commanders, a hallmark of the organization and conduct of the expeditionary force, ended with Baldwin's spectacular coronation as emperor in Hagia Sophia. Villehardouin

---

7. *Register*, 7:253–62, no. 152, dated by the editors to shortly after 16 March 1204 = *Oorkonden*, 2:564–77, no. 271; translated in Andrea, *Contemporary Sources*, 98–112.

8. *Oorkonden*, 2:577–603, nos. 272–74, after 16 May 1204. Those letters had wide circulation in France. Robert of Auxerre copied one letter into his chronicle (*Chronicon*, 267–69), and Rigord claims that he saw and read Baldwin's letter (*Gesta*, 382–83 [Rigord, *Deeds*, 156–57], §147). Aubri of Trois-Fontaines, the Cistercian author of a universal chronicle, also cites Baldwin's letter (*Chronica*, 882).

9. *Register*, 7:264–70, no. 154, 13 November 1204; translated in Andrea, *Contemporary Sources*, 115–26. Chrissis, *Crusading in Frankish Greece*, 2–12, analyzes the significance of the letter.

10. See Angold, "Thomas Morosini."

indirectly notes how the war council of peers became in effect an advisory council to Baldwin, who accepted its advice, or not, during his year as emperor (16 May 1204–15 April 1205). The shift was abrupt. When news arrived that Mourtzouphlos had captured Tchorlu, Baldwin's council and the doge advised him to leave a garrison (*garnie*) in the capital, since it was inhabited by Greeks, and to lead an army to "conquer the land" beyond the capital. Count Louis, who was still ill, would remain in Constantinople with the doge. Conon of Béthune would assume custody of the Boukoleon and Blachernai palaces for Baldwin. "And for defending the city [*garder la ville*], Geoffroy, the marshal of Champagne, would stay with Milo Breban of Provins, Manessier of l'Isle-Adam, and their men [*lor genz*]." In effect, Villehardouin became garrison commander of the capital with his Champenois of the Fifth Battalion.[11]

The chancery was explicit in distinguishing Baldwin's "men of Flanders" from his "men of Romania," who were identified as "the marshal of Champagne," Conon of Béthune, Milo Breban, Manessier of l'Isle-Adam, and Macaire of Sainte-Menehould.[12] No longer did the old war council of peers make executive decisions collectively; it had been displaced by Baldwin's council consisting of his brother Henry of Hainaut, his relative Hugh of Saint-Pol, and the Flemish barons who had served him at home in the war against the king of France. Villehardouin's reticence about his relationship with Baldwin reflects the fact that he was excluded from Baldwin's inner circle, most likely due to his good relations with Boniface. As de facto garrison commander of the capital, his expertise was called on only in extraordinary circumstances.

Villehardouin tells us nothing about his life in Constantinople, about how he acquired the residence where he lived for the next four years, or his interactions with local Greeks and Italians beyond the fact that the wealthiest Greeks continued to leave the city for Asia Minor.[13] Nor does he recall his relations with his own colleagues. And he ignores

---

11. Villehardouin, *La conquête*, §§267–68. Manuscript D, fol. 91v, corrects an ambiguous punctuation to read that Conon of Béthune took custody of the imperial palaces and the Champenois were responsible for protecting the capital: "et pour garder la ville demoura Joffrois li mareschaus de Champaigne, Miles li Braibans de Prouvins, et Menessiers de Lille et lor gens."

12. *Oorkonden*, 2:612–17, nos. 280–81, done in the Blachernai palace, February 1205, "coram hominibus nostris de Flandria and coram hominibus nostris de Romania."

13. For the Venetians in Constantinople after May 1204, see Jacoby, "The Venetian Government and Administration." See also Jacoby, "The Greeks of Constantinople."

108   **CHAPTER 6**

entirely the presence of bishops Nivelon and Garnier, the leading prelates of the crusade who were openly acquiring relics in what even Villehardouin admitted was the relic capital of the world.[14] He recalls only military activities beyond the capital reported by official couriers, returning commanders, travelers, survivors, refugees, and "news" of uncertain provenance. Whereas earlier in his memoirs he focused on speeches, deliberations, and the conduct of those who left the main army, now he dwells on the size of military units, troop movements, and the distance of cities from Constantinople in terms of days traveled (appendix 2, tables 1–3). It was a purview and responsibility not available to ordinary knights like Robert of Clari, who reported only what he saw and heard, or later to Henry of Valenciennes, the canon whose reportage of Emperor Henry's deeds includes memorable speeches and character portraits but displays little understanding of military issues. In a sense the marshal assumed a position analogous to the one he had held in Champagne, whose compass extended beyond Troyes to the walled towns in the county and the network of roads and rivers that connected them to the capital. But unlike the tranquil interior of Champagne, the hinterland of Constantinople was an active war zone, a land still to be conquered and occupied.

Baldwin versus Boniface

Villehardouin recounts in detail the four months between Baldwin's coronation in mid-May and the resolution of his conflict with Boniface over the status of Thessalonika in September. Like young Alexios IV the previous August, Baldwin set out in June with a large force of knights to display his authority as the new emperor and to search for Mourtzouphlos. He sent his brother Henry ahead with one hundred knights (of the Second Battalion) to Adrianople, an almost impregnable city located on the Via Militaris and ranking in size and importance with Constantinople and Thessalonika. Then, leaving Count Louis and the doge in charge of Constantinople and Villehardouin in command of the garrison, Baldwin followed Henry with the bulk of the army (the First, Third, and Sixth Battalions) to Adrianople. He promised the Greeks that he would rule their city according to the customs (*as us et as costumes*) it had enjoyed under the Greek emperors, and at their request

---

14. Villehardouin, *La conquête*, §192. For the transfer of relics from Constantinople to the West, see Lester, "What Remains," and Lester, "Translation and Appropriation."

MARSHAL OF EMPEROR BALDWIN   109

he installed a garrison of forty knights and one hundred mounted sergeants under the command of Eustace of Salperwick, a "most worthy and valiant knight," for they feared Kalojan, who often attacked them.[15] Baldwin then marched to Mosynopolis in search of Alexios III, who was reported to be occupying the city but had left after capturing and blinding Mourtzouphlos, an act that shocked the marshal.[16]

Boniface and Margaret left Constantinople with the Seventh Battalion shortly after Baldwin's departure. They took the Via Egnatia, the main highway to Thessalonika, usually a twelve-day journey, but on the way they learned that Baldwin was in Mosynopolis and that he planned to continue on to Thessalonika (map 5). On reaching Mosynopolis, Boniface asked Baldwin not to go to Thessalonika, the fief for which he had done homage. Villehardouin quotes his plea, which he must have heard later from Boniface himself: "My lord," he said, "I have heard news from Thessalonika that the people there will gladly accept me as their lord; I am your man [*hom*] and hold Thessalonika from you, so I ask that you allow me to go there." "I do not know by whose advice" it was, Villehardouin remarked, but Baldwin replied that he would go anyway, then left with a large force for Thessalonika in a transparent attempt to prevent the restoration of a kingdom of Thessalonika within the newly constituted empire. The two parted on bad terms (*par mal*), said the marshal, who blamed Baldwin's council for giving bad advice (*malvais conseil*).[17] Boniface's poet-companion Raimbaut de Vaqueiras even penned a poem criticizing Baldwin for listening to his barons rather than being generous, as befitted an emperor.[18]

Baldwin continued on the Via Egnatia past Christopolis, La Blanche, and Serres to Thessalonika, which surrendered after he gave assurances that he would respect the city's customs. Meanwhile, Boniface parried Baldwin's move by taking his forces to Didymoteichon, which the marshal remembered as "a very fine, strongly fortified, and very wealthy" hilltop castle. The Greeks accepted Boniface, he said, because of their high regard for his wife Margaret, the former empress.[19] Leaving Margaret and a garrison at Didymoteichon, Boniface led a joint French-Greek

---

15. Villehardouin, *La conquête*, §273. *Oorkonden*, 2:608-9, no. 277, ca. 12 August 1204, Baldwin's privileges to Thessalonika.

16. Villehardouin, *La conquête*, §§269-71.

17. Villehardouin, *La conquête*, §§276-78.

18. Raimbaut de Vaqueiras, "Conseil don a l'emperador," in his *Poems*, 225-28, no. 20.

19. Short, "Agency and Authority," 33-36, emphasizes Margaret's role in helping Boniface secure his lands. Asdracha, *La région des Rhodopes*, 134-36, describes Didymoteichon as a

110   **CHAPTER 6**

force to Adrianople, which he besieged. The gravity of the moment was not lost on Eustace of Salperwick, Baldwin's garrison commander, who dispatched two couriers to Constantinople; they rode "day and night" on the Via Militaris, normally five days distance from the capital, with news of an impending clash between two powerful commanders that threatened to become a full-scale war.[20]

On hearing that news in Constantinople, the doge and Count Louis were greatly disturbed, said Villehardouin. They convened the barons still in the city to the Blachernai palace, where they asked Villehardouin to go to Adrianople and persuade Boniface, "if he could," to lift the siege. They chose him, he admitted, because he "was highly regarded by Boniface and would be more influential than anyone else." He took Manessier of l'Isle-Adam, "one of the best knights of the army and one of the most respected," with him to Adrianople, where they were warmly received by Boniface and his counsellors, including William of Champlitte. In a rare moment of self-revelation, Villehardouin recounts how, after those formalities, he forcefully (*mult durement*) rebuked Boniface for besieging Adrianople without informing the council in Constantinople, which certainly would have resolved the matter. It must have been an awkward moment for the marshal to speak so directly to the former supreme commander of the expeditionary force whom he personally had recruited to the crusade. Boniface protested that Baldwin had unjustly entered his fief, for which he had done homage.[21]

With much effort, said Villehardouin, he succeeded in persuading Boniface to lift the siege of Adrianople and to submit his dispute with Baldwin to a council made up of the doge, Count Louis, Conon of Béthune, and Villehardouin himself, all who "well knew the accord [*convenance*] between the two," that is, they had witnessed Boniface's homage to Baldwin for Thessalonika. The marshal was proud of his role in the affair. It was his reputation, he said, that allowed him to convince Boniface, who commanded a virtually private army, to accept mediation and return to Didymoteichon.[22] By his own account, Villehardouin had

---

hilltop fortress, surrounded by double walls, in which a garrison, administrative personnel, and wealthy families lived; the unfortified lower town was inhabited by laborers.

20. Villehardouin, *La conquête*, §§279–82.

21. Villehardouin, *La conquête*, §§283–85.

22. Villehardouin does not mention, and apparently was unaware of, the document sealed by Boniface on 12 August 1204 with the two Venetian envoys who accompanied the marshal to Adrianople. This may have factored in Boniface's willingness to accept arbitration (Tafel and Thomas, *Urkunden*, 1:512–15, no. 123 = Saint-Guillain, "Comment les Vénitiens," 756–57,

averted war through his own perseverance and through the influence of Boniface's personal advisers, particularly William of Champlitte and Odo de la Roche, whose families had ties to Champagne and who had welcomed him with "great honor." He also recalled with satisfaction that both the Greek residents of Adrianople and Boniface's besieging army thanked him and Manessier for defusing a potentially explosive conflict between two strong-willed commanders.[23]

On returning to Constantinople, Villehardouin reported on his successful mission to Boniface. The doge, Louis, and the council then drafted a letter inviting Baldwin likewise to accept their mediation. Trusted couriers (*bons messages*) met Baldwin, who was on his way to Adrianople after leaving Renier of Mons in charge of Thessalonika. On hearing the letter read aloud, Baldwin at first was not amenable, but after a contentious meeting with his barons (*assez i ot grosses paroles dites*), he reluctantly agreed to return to the capital because, said Villehardouin, he did not wish to alienate the doge and Count Louis.[24] Another factor must have weighed in his decision: his army was stricken by a severe illness and forty men had died, including his chancellor Jean of Noyon. Villehardouin remembered Jean as a very fine cleric who had comforted the army with his inspiring speeches on the word of God.[25]

Then Villehardouin (representing the Champenois) was dispatched to Didymoteichon with Renier of Trith (representing the Flemish), Gervase of Châteauneuf (representing Count Louis), and two Venetians in order to accompany Boniface and Margaret with due ceremony back to Constantinople. As the designated go-between, Villehardouin asked Boniface to keep his promise to accept mediation, which he did. It may have been at this point that Raimbaut of Vaqueiras, poet and Boniface's close companion, penned a poem of advice to Emperor Baldwin ("Conseil don a l'emperador"). He advised Baldwin that if he wished to be a worthy man (*pros*), he should give richly for his honor and reputation, and that if he wished to rescue the Sepulcher, he needed support to fight their common enemies. The poet also had words for Villehardouin:

I want to give my advice to the marshal,
who is loyal and true, that

---

appendix). None of Boniface's barons witnessed Boniface seal the document. For its significance, see Madden, "The Latin Empire," and *Enrico Dandolo*, 186.

23. Villehardouin, *La conquête*, §§286–87.

24. Villehardouin, *La conquête*, §§288–96.

25. Villehardouin, *La conquête*, §290.

CHAPTER 6

I will blame him and Milo Breban
if the emperor is not most worthy,
and generous, and honest.[26]

Villehardouin and the envoys accompanied Boniface, Margaret, and one hundred knights to Constantinople, where Count Louis, the doge, Conon of Béthune, and the marshal held a *parlement*. They reaffirmed the agreement (*convenance*) of May by which Baldwin granted Thessalonika to Boniface, who did homage for it.[27] The *parlement* was a face-saving occasion for Baldwin, who certainly knew that he was in the wrong, to repair his relations with Enrico Dandolo and Count Louis. Villehardouin again acted as the trusted agent of execution: he would take custody of Didymoteichon, releasing it to Baldwin only after Boniface sent an official courier (*creant message*) or sealed letters patent (*letres pendanz*) stating that he had entered Thessalonika. Boniface "and his wife" were accompanied to Thessalonika by Baldwin's envoys, who formally transferred Baldwin's lordship over the cities along the way that only months earlier had accepted him as their ruler. The marshal appreciated the fact that Boniface's new wife, the former empress, who had converted to the Latin rite on their marriage, facilitated his becoming, if not emperor, at least king of Thessalonika.[28]

Villehardouin dwells at length on the conflict between the victor and the loser of the imperial election because it threatened the very foundation of the new empire. If his role earlier in council had been purely advisory, in this matter he took full credit for assuring the survival of the Frankish occupation. Indeed, Niketas Choniates credits the marshal—"one of the most powerful figures among the Latin host"—with

---

26.

Al marescal voil retraire
mon cosseil, q'es leials e bos.
mas lui, e Miles de Burban,
blasmarai se non es fort pros
e larcs e francs l'emperaire.
    Vaqueiras, "Conseil don a l'emperador," in *Poems*, 227, no. 20.

27. I think that *la convenance fu retraite* means that the original agreement "was reaffirmed," in the sense that the original homage rendered after Baldwin's coronation was still valid, as Villehardouin reported here (*La conquête*, §286) and earlier in May (§265).

28. Villehardouin, *La conquête*, §§297–300. At about the same time, Innocent recognized that Margaret, on marrying Boniface, had converted to the Latin rite (*Register*, 8:248–50, no. 135, 1205, ca. 15 August–10 September).

MARSHAL OF EMPEROR BALDWIN

facilitating the mediation between Boniface and Baldwin.[29] By the end of September 1204, four months after Baldwin's coronation, peace was finally established between Baldwin and Boniface. "The land from Constantinople to Thessalonika was so peaceful," said the marshal, "that anyone could safely travel the road [the Via Egnatia] between the two cities in twelve days."[30]

The Distribution of Fiefs

Baldwin had spent the first four months of his rule in the field searching for Mourtzouphlos and then clashing with Boniface over Thessalonika. The Greek cities not involved in the military maneuvers between Baldwin and Boniface were untouched by the regime change in Constantinople, and there is no evidence that any fiefs had been granted as envisioned by the *concordia* of March. Only in October, after the status of Thessalonika was resolved, did the formal dismemberment of the Byzantine Empire begin.[31] Villehardouin speaks as if he were part of the twenty-four-member commission that allocated fiefs to the senior commanders as recorded in a document known as the "Partitio Terrarum Imperii Romanie."[32] He states that Emperor Baldwin granted (*dona*) the fiefs with titles (*haltes honors*), without mentioning whether homage was done, as would have been expected.[33] Count Louis received the duchy of Nicaea—"one of the most prestigious lands of the empire"—but since he was still ill, he sent Peter of Bracheux and Payen of Orléans with 120 knights to occupy it. Hugh of Saint-Pol received Didymoteichon, but he, too, stayed in the capital, afflicted with gout.[34] Renier of Trith received Philippopolis, one of the largest, richest, and most

---

29. Choniates, *O City of Byzantium*, 329–30; Villehardouin, *La conquête*, §600.

30. Villehardouin, *La conquête*, §§301–2.

31. Angold, "Turning Points in History," reviews the long-term consequences of the dismantling of the imperial system.

32. The "Partitio Terrarum Imperii Romanie" is undated. Oikonomedes, "La décomposition de l'Empire Byzantin," dates it to before the imperial election of 9 March 1204. Carile, "Partitio Terrarum Imperii Romanie," 155, dates it to mid-September 1204, following the reconciliation between Boniface and Baldwin. The mid-September date seems preferable, since Villehardouin mentions it only after the resolution of the conflict between Baldwin and Boniface. See also Lock, *The Franks in the Aegean*, 45–51, and Van Tricht, *The Latin Renovatio*, 47–53.

33. Hendrickx, "Le contrat féodal et le fief," 235–36, points out that the titles or "high honors" distributed in October 1204 carried quasi-official status, placing them in the same category as the emperor's marshal, constable, and seneschal.

34. Villehardouin, *La conquête*, §304. Longnon, *Les compagnons de Villehardouin*, 91, identifies Peter as of "Bracheux," not "Brachieux," as he is usually identified.

114   **CHAPTER 6**

strongly fortified cities on the Via Militaris; he and his 120 knights were well received by the Greeks, said Villehardouin, because they had been maltreated by Kalojan.[35] On 11 November Baldwin's brother Henry left with 120 knights to take possession of Abydos and Adramyttion. Stephen of Perche received the duchy of Philadelphia, while Macaire of Sainte-Menehould took 100 knights to Nicomedia, a city two days' journey from Constantinople that the Greeks abandoned just before he arrived. Except for Philippopolis and Didymoteichon in Thrace, all the major fiefs were in lands yet to be conquered in Asia Minor, lands that Boniface had exchanged for Thessalonika.[36]

Although he does not mention it, Villehardouin received a fief in Thrace consisting of Makri, Trajanopolis, and the monastic compound of Bera, all located strategically at the western border with the kingdom of Thessalonika and just south of the Via Egnatia (see map 5).[37] The small fortified port town of Makri on the Aegean Sea, together with the walled town of Trajanopolis and the walled monastery of Bera with its enclosed town and outlying properties constituted a block of land standing strategically and symbolically between Baldwin's imperial lands and Boniface's kingdom.[38] They represented the marshal's stature perfectly, as a high officer who stood between the two most powerful leaders of the Latin settlement. Since the marshal's duties kept him in the capital, he sent his nephew Anselm of Courcelles with eighty knights to take possession of his fief.[39]

---

35. Villehardouin, *La conquête*, §§304, 311. Asdracha, *La région des Rhodopes*, 154–62, describes Philippopolis as it would have been at the time. For the subsequent history of Philippopolis, see Van Tricht, "The Duchy of Philippopolis."

36. Villehardouin, *La conquête*, §§304 (Nicaea), 310 (Abydos), 312 (Nicomedia), 316 (Philadelphia).

37. According to the *partitio*, Villehardouin received the "Pertinentia Macri et Trianopoli cum casali de Brachon" (Tafel and Thomas, *Urkunden*, 1:482; and Carile, "Partitio Terrarum Imperii Romanie," 220, line 82; 270). Asdracha, *Le région des Rhodopes*, describes Makri (117–18), Trajanopolis (118–19), and Bera (124–26) as Villehardouin would have known them. Alanièce and Gilet, "Les fiefs de Geoffroy de Villehardouin en Thrace," describe the state of Villehardouin's lands in Thrace in the early twenty-first century. The monastic compound of Bera contained a church (which survives), a mill, a library, a dormitory for seventy-four monks, and a guest house, an altogether substantial community around which a town developed; see Kazhdan et al., *The Oxford Dictionary of Byzantium*, 1:282–83.

38. *Bullarium Hellenicum*, 255–64, no. 87, at 260, 2 May 1210. Innocent's letter announcing the decision of the second *parlement* of Ravennika identified Makri as marking the eastern limit of the kingdom of Thessalonika. On Villehardouin's fief as a border lordship, see Van Tricht, *The Latin Renovatio*, 197–98.

39. Villehardouin later states (*La conquête*, §382) that on his way to the battle of Adrianople (April 1205), he sent word to his nephew Anselm of Courcelles to bring knights from his lands to reinforce the French facing the Bulgarians. Anselm may not have survived the

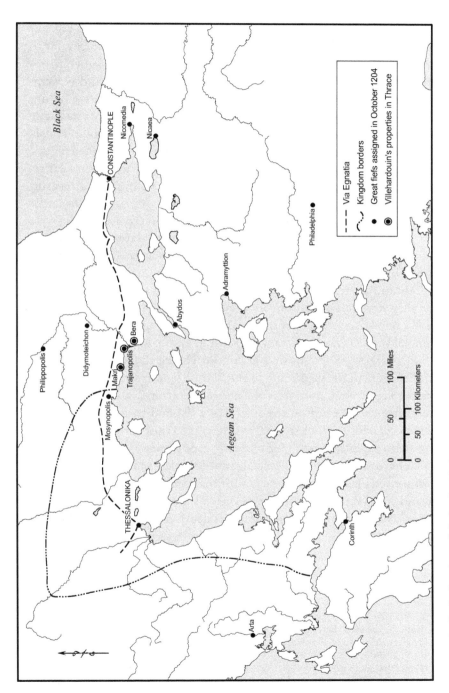

MAP 5. The distribution of great fiefs, October 1204

116   **CHAPTER 6**

The precision of the figures that Villehardouin recalled in 1207, three years after the distribution of fiefs, suggests that he consulted a register listing the number of knights available to serve the emperor, similar to the registers of fiefs with which he was familiar in Champagne.[40] Altogether about 460 knights left Constantinople in October and November to occupy the key walled cities beyond the capital. Even if he undercounted, there would have been fewer than 1,000 knights available to meet the Bulgarian forces in Thrace and the Greek revolts in Asia Minor. Of his fifteen references to unit size, nine are for 100 knights, three for 120, and two for 140 (appendix 2, table 1). Those were relative, not exact, numbers, convenient tranches of twenty knights for measuring approximate unit size. The actual number of combatants was larger and included mounted sergeants, turcopoles, and mercenaries who were mentioned in other contexts. Whether non-combatants accompanied them is an open question; the marshal was concerned with knights trained in mounted combat. Units of 100 to 140 mounted knights were a potent mobile force, but Villehardouin was always sensitive to the fact that they were vastly outnumbered by Kalojan's army. The enormity of the feudalization project, of imperial lands being awarded as lordships to be held in fief from a distant emperor at a time when massive armies of Bulgarians and Cumans were at large in Thrace, did not escape him. If October marked the beginning of the Frankish occupation of the Greek cities and the fragmentation of the occupying army, it also set in motion forces that would erupt in the spring of 1205 and consume the rest of his memoirs. He attributed the Greek revolts to the conduct of their new lords, who exploited their lands harshly, "some more so, some less."[41]

Villehardouin interrupts his narrative to describe a spectacular event he witnessed in Constantinople "about that time" (between late September and 11 November): the execution of Mourtzouphlos, the blinded former usurper, who was pushed to his death from the top of the Column of Theodosius, "high justice" being done, said Villehardouin.[42] According to Clari, it was the doge who suggested "for a high man, high

---

battle; in November 1205 his wife Beatrice acted in his stead in exchanging rights with Notre-Dame-aux-Nonnains as his uncle Gui la Grive witnessed (*Notre-Dame-aux-Nonnains*, 89–90).

40. Hendrickx, "Le contrat féodal et le fief," 238, also postulates such a register.

41. Villehardouin, *La conquête*, §§303–4.

42. Villehardouin, *La conquête*, §§306–8. Jacquin, *Le style historique*, 72–73, notes that when Villehardouin speaks of *en cel termine*, he was marking a relatively exact date, in this context an almost contemporary event.

justice," a phrase that must have resonated on the street.[43] Villehardouin remarked that a scene still visible on the column depicted an old prophecy of the fall of an emperor.[44] He may have recalled the prophecies he had heard earlier predicting the fall of Constantinople at the hand of foreigners, and the virulent anti-Greek views of Bishop Geoffroy of Langres, a close associate of Bernard of Clairvaux, who tried to convince crusaders encamped outside Constantinople in 1147 to conquer the city because it was Christian in name only, and could be easily taken.[45]

Villehardouin notes that in the same autumn months of 1204 a wave (*uns granz passages*) of knights, turcopoles, and mounted sergeants arrived in Constantinople.[46] They were part of the "second front" of the crusade that had bypassed Venice in 1202 and sailed directly to Syria, but after the fall of Constantinople, they sought fiefs in the Latin empire, in the process emptying Syria of crusaders. The pope wrote to the bishops of France of the dire need for new recruits.[47] It was through those arrivals from Acre that Baldwin heard about the death of his wife Marie. Villehardouin had known her since her birth in Troyes in 1171 and had witnessed her marriage in 1186 to young Baldwin of Flanders. Baldwin had developed such an attachment to her, according to Gislebert of Mons, that it was said he sought no other woman but her.[48] She was twenty-three when she became countess of Flanders in 1194, and during the next seven years she and Baldwin appeared together in many charters.[49] In February 1200 she took the cross with Baldwin, expecting to accompany him overseas, but by the time he left in the spring of 1202 she was pregnant, and so she stayed behind until her daughter Marguerite was born. Unaware that the crusade had landed in Constantinople, she sailed to Marseille and Acre, where she received a message from Baldwin that he was in Constantinople. But before she could leave, she

---

43. Clari, *La conquête*, §109.

44. Jacquin, *Le style historique*, 339, notes that Villehardouin was the only contemporary author to note the prophecy.

45. Magdalino, "Prophecies on the Fall of Constantinople," 50–53.

46. Villehardouin, *La conquête*, §§315–16. The turcopoles were local troops of mixed parentage, in this case mostly likely of Turkish and Eastern Christian background, who made up the light cavalry; Villehardouin had a company of them in his expedition to liberate Renier of Trith at Didymoteichon (Villehardouin, *La conquête*, §438).

47. Kedar, "The Fourth Crusade's Second Front," 106–7, points out that the diversion of manpower to Constantinople weakened the Frankish presence in the Levant. Innocent's letter of July 1205 (*Register*, 8:227–29, no. 126) reflected the need to replenish the manpower in both the Byzantine lands and the Levant.

48. See Joris, "Un seul amour."

49. For a brief biography, see Nicholas, "Countesses as Rulers in Flanders," 127–29.

118   **CHAPTER 6**

contracted the plague and died on 9 August 1204 at the age of thirty-three. Villehardouin remembered her as a much-loved countess who had been expected to share the throne with Baldwin in Constantinople. The marshal was touched by her death, as he had been by the death of her brother Thibaut three years earlier: "she was greatly mourned by all Christians, for she was a very fine lady and much honored."[50]

At this point Villehardouin interrupts his narrative to relate three concurrent developments beyond the capital. One was in Asia Minor, where Theodore Lascaris was about to besiege Adramyttion, which Count Henry's knights had occupied. Refusing to be isolated within the city, Henry led his knights beyond the city walls to defeat a large Greek force.[51] The second front was at Nauplion and Corinth, both occupied by Leo Sgouros and besieged by Boniface. The third, which Villehardouin describes in greater detail, was in the Peloponnese, where a company of knights sailing from Syria to Constantinople in search of fiefs encountered "contrary winds," as he put it, and landed at the port of Modon, where they wintered while their ship was being repaired. As the marshal relates it in 1207, this company was led by his brother Jean's son Geoffroy, who was invited by a local Greek magnate to join in conquering the Peloponnese in the absence of imperial government after the fall of Constantinople. But after his Greek partner died and was succeeded by an uncooperative son, the marshal's nephew and his companions rode from Modon along the western coast to Patras and then along the Gulf of Corinth to Nauplion to seek Boniface's help. Young Geoffroy declined Boniface's offer of a fief and instead invited one of Boniface's barons, William "the Champenois" of Champlitte, grandson of Count Hugh of Troyes and a "good friend" (*mult ere ses amis*), to join him in conquering the fertile land of the northwestern Peloponnese, "what is called the Morea."[52]

As Villehardouin describes it, in the spring of 1205 his nephew Geoffroy and William of Champlitte led a company of one hundred knights plus a detail of mounted sergeants from Corinth along the northern coast of the Peloponnese to Morea, then south along the western coast to the southern ports of Modon and Coron; by summer they had

---

50. Villehardouin, *La conquête*, §§317–18.

51. Villehardouin, *La conquête*, §§321–23 (19 March 1205). Villehardouin here compresses the chronology of evolving events in three theaters of operation during the winter and early spring of 1204–5.

52. Villehardouin, *La conquête*, §325.

captured Kalamata.[53] Villehardouin knew that the pope had recognized William "the Champenois" as "prince of all Achaia."[54] But he could not have imagined that two years after dictating his memoirs, his nephew Geoffroy, whom he regarded as "very honorable, very valiant, and a fine knight," would become prince of Achaia, encompassing most of the Peloponnese, and found a dynasty that would survive through the thirteenth century, long after the marshal's own descendants at home had shed the Villehardouin surname. For the marshal, the events in Asia Minor, at Corinth and Nauplion, and in the Peloponnese were part of the general imposition of French rule over Byzantine cities and provinces following the collapse of the Byzantine imperial government in April 1204.

The Battle of Adrianople

Constantinople was relatively tranquil during the winter months of 1204–5 after being emptied of the tactical commanders and their troops. Only Baldwin and the doge, along with counts Louis and Hugh, both too ill to travel, remained with a skeleton force of troops. The Champenois patrolled the city and defended the walls, while the Venetians and Pisans occupied the port. Baldwin held court in the Blachernai palace, solicited combatants ("volunteers") from Flanders for an expedition to the Holy Land in the spring, and sent relics to Philip of France with a letter stating that they came from the Boukoleon palace.[55] None of those acts directly touched the marshal or drew his comment. The status of the Greek church was uncertain until December, when the pope directed the installation of Latin clerics in churches abandoned by Greek prelates.[56]

The new year began inauspiciously with the death of Hugh of Saint-Pol, who after long suffering with gout was buried in the Saint George of Mangana monastery in Constantinople.[57] Nicholas Mesarites, whose

---

53. Villehardouin, *La conquête*, §§326–30.

54. *Register*, 8:269–71, no. 154 (153), 19 November 1205, letter to Patriarch Thomas Morosini of Constantinople.

55. *Oorkonden*, 2:631–32, no. 290, undated but likely before April 1205, letter to the bishops of Cambrai, Artois, Thérouanne, and Tournai, seeking recruits; and 2:633, no. 291, undated letter to Philip II of France.

56. *Register*, 7:290–91, no. 164, 7 December 1204, letter from Innocent to "the bishops and abbots in the Christian army in Constantinople."

57. Villehardouin, *La conquête*, §§314, 334. An obituary from Arras puts Hugh's death on 21/25 January (Nieus, *Un pouvoir comtal entre Flandre et France*, 146n21).

120   **CHAPTER 6**

brother was a monk there, recalled how the monks had been maltreated after the conquest by soldiers who cut off their beards. But after the initial violence ended, the monks were summoned by the crusade commander in charge of the monastic grounds, who on hearing about that incident made symbolic amends by insisting that Mesarites's brother sit on the seat of honor as they conversed through an interpreter. After "intelligent conversation," said Mesarites, the foreigner—Hugh of Saint-Pol—declared that "if the people of Byzantium had been led by such leader, we [the crusaders] might even have submitted and taken an oath of fealty."[58] For that expression of good will, the monks accepted his burial on their grounds.

In February 1205 the Greek cities in Thrace, encouraged by the Bulgarian king Kalojan, rose in rebellion against the Frankish occupation. They swore loyalty to Kalojan out of fear, said Villehardouin, and were expelling or killing their newly installed French garrisons. At Didymoteichon most of Count Hugh's garrison was captured or killed. Venetians and Franks were expelled even from Adrianople, and the garrisons at Arcadiopolis and Tchorlu abandoned their posts and returned to the capital.[59] Villehardouin describes what he calls an extraordinary event (*une grante mervoille*) at Philippopolis, nine days distant from the capital, which he learned about later from "the Book."[60] Renier of Trith was occupying the city with 120 knights, but morale was so bad that most of the garrison—Renier's own son, brother, son-in-law, and nephew, plus thirty knights—abandoned the city, intending to return to Constantinople. Intercepted by the Greeks, however, they were turned over to the Bulgarians and beheaded. A just reward for their disloyalty, remarked the marshal. Then eighty more knights left Philippopolis, fearing shame (*honte*) less, as he put it, than their fate at the hands of the Bulgarians.[61] But if fear motivated them to abandon their relatives and comrades, Villehardouin knew that it was within their right to return home at the expiration of their year of obligatory service at the end of March, as provided by the *concordia* of March 1204.

Baldwin, Louis, and the doge were deeply troubled by the bad news (*novelles malvaises*) that arrived daily (*de jor en jor*), said Villehardouin, who attended their discussions. They feared that with so few men left

---

58. Nicholas Mesarites, "*Epitaphios* for His Brother John," in *Nicholas Mesarites*, 171.
59. Villehardouin, *La conquête*, §§333–40.
60. See chap. 8 ("The Book").
61. Villehardouin, *La conquête*, §§345–46.

MARSHAL OF EMPEROR BALDWIN

in the capital after the distribution of fiefs, and the loss of cities so close to Constantinople, the entire countryside would be lost. Baldwin decided to recall his military captains from across the Turkish Straits in order to mount a concerted offensive against the Bulgarians in Thrace. He ordered his brother Henry to return from Adramyttion and Macaire of Sainte-Menehould to return from Nicomedia, while Louis instructed Payen of Orléans and Peter of Bracheux, who were holding Nicaea for him, to abandon all those lands except Espigal on the coast.[62] Villehardouin summoned his nephew Anselm of Courcelles to bring his men from Makri and Trajanopolis.[63]

Baldwin ordered Villehardouin to gather as many men as possible and lead an advance force to Adrianople. But few remained in the city, he recalled, because many knights were returning home, three years after setting out to muster in Venice. It is the first time that the marshal, then in his late fifties, is known to have commanded a detachment of knights in the field. He recalled in detail the lead-up, the decisive moments, and the aftermath of the battle in which he played a leading role. With Manessier of l'Isle-Adam as second-in-command, he led a small contingent along the Via Militaris, the old Roman highway between Constantinople and Adrianople, to Tchorlu, where they stayed for four days waiting for reinforcements from the capital (map 6). The combined force of eighty knights then rode on to Arcadiopolis, and from there to Bulgarophygon and Nikitza, both abandoned by the Greeks for the more heavily fortified Adrianople, which was already flooded with refugees. Villehardouin remembered the abandoned cities and the movement of displaced Greeks that portended a great battle between Kalojan's massive armies and the Franks.[64]

Although few knights remained in Constantinople after the distribution of fiefs the previous October, Baldwin and Louis decided to leave Conan of Béthune, Milo Breban, and the papal legate Peter Capuano in charge of the capital while they followed Villehardouin to Nikitza with the 140 knights who had returned with Macaire of Sainte-Menehould from Nicomedia plus 40 others; together with the marshal's troops they made up a small but not inconsequential force of about 220 knights plus several hundred mounted sergeants. On arriving at Adrianople, with Kalojan's banners flying from the towers, they set up their siege

---

62. Villehardouin, *La conquête*, §§340–43.
63. Villehardouin, *La conquête*, §382.
64. Villehardouin, *La conquête*, §§343–44.

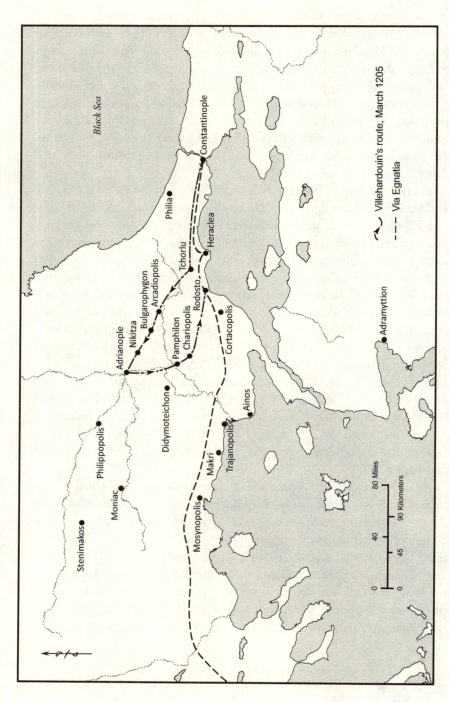

MAP 6. Villehardouin's march to and retreat from Adrianople, April 1205

engines and blocked the gates. On 29 March, just as they were about to attack the well-garrisoned city, the doge arrived with 140 Venetian troops, making for about 360 mounted combatants in all, not counting archers, crossbowmen, and turcopoles. For the next two weeks the army prepared for battle: siege engines were constructed from any wood they could find, while the sappers began to undermine the city walls. Villehardouin remembered that there was little food on Easter (10 April). On hearing that Kalojan was approaching with a large force intent on breaking the siege, they took up their positions; the main army under Baldwin would confront the Bulgarians and Cumans, while Villehardouin and Manessier, in reserve, each guarded a city gate, and the Venetians guarded a third.[65]

The battle of Adrianople lasted two days, Wednesday and Thursday, 13–14 April. As Villehardouin describes it, Cuman horse archers— "about 14,000, who were not baptized"—tested the unprepared Franks, who rushed out in disarray (*a desroi*) and "very foolishly" (*molt folement*) pursued the lightly armed horsemen, who suddenly turned, killing and wounding many of the Franks and their horses.[66] That evening Baldwin gathered the barons in his tent to discuss a course of action. It was decided to issue strict orders for the army to stand in line motionless in front of the camp, and not pursue the attackers under any circumstance. Criers announced the order throughout the camp.

The next day, Thursday, 14 April, shortly after Mass and a meal, they were met by a wave of Cuman mounted archers who again drew the Franks from their defensive position. Count Louis, in his first battlefield experience since his long convalescence in Constantinople, led his men in pursuing the attackers, who executed the same feigned retreat of the previous day, disrupting his forces and causing large losses of men and horses. Compounding his rash move, Louis called to Baldwin to follow him. Abandoning his position behind the front line, and against all odds, Baldwin tried to rescue Louis but was himself captured. Villehardouin does not blame Louis for disobeying the order to stand back.

---

65. Villehardouin, *La conquête*, §§347–54. Madgearu, *The Asanids*, 146–56, recounts the battle from the Bulgarian perspective.

66. Villehardouin, *La conquête*, §355. For a detailed description of the weapons and tactics of the Cuman horse archers, with an analysis of the main stages of the battle based primarily on Villehardouin's account, see Mitchell, "Light Cavalry, Heavy Cavalry," 114–18. Stoyanov, "The Size of Bulgaria's Medieval Field Armies," 738, estimates the number of Bulgarian combatants at Adrianople at about 4,000 plus 4,000 Cumans. For the critical military role of the Cumans in the Second Bulgarian Empire, see Vásáry, *Cumans and Tatars*, 13–56.

124 **CHAPTER 6**

Instead, he faulted Louis's men who "were not knights and did not know the skill of arms" (they were mounted sergeants, *serjanz a cheval*); losing courage, they broke formation and left Louis fatally wounded on the field. Villehardouin praised Baldwin's battlefield valor, as reported to him by witnesses "who were there." In fact, Baldwin's initiative ultimately may have bought time for the defeated army to retreat to safety behind the front lines.[67] But with Baldwin's capture and the death of Louis and so many barons—Jean of Friaize, Stephen of Perche, Renaud of Montmirail, Mathieu of Walincourt—and Bishop Peter of Bethlehem, among many others, the crusader army was effectively destroyed.[68]

As Villehardouin relates it, he managed to prevent a complete rout. When he saw what was happening at the front, he gathered as many men as he had at the gate and ordered Manessier, who was stationed at the second gate, to join him. With their combined forces making up a "very large company," he rode out to the front as fast as possible to establish a defensive shield wall, which stood motionless facing the enemy. The retreating soldiers passed through to the rear, leaving the dead, including Count Louis, on the field of battle. The line held firm against the charging Cumans, Vlachs, and Greeks, who withdrew as darkness fell. The marshal took credit for halting the chaotic retreat and restoring discipline in the demoralized army.[69]

Villehardouin asked the doge to meet him at the front line, where in private he reported the army's defeat, Louis's death, and Baldwin's capture. He counseled an orderly retreat at night. His own men would remain in full battle array at the front while the doge kept the survivors in their tents with campfires burning until late in the night. Then, with the doge's forces in the lead and Villehardouin's in the rear, the defeated army proceeded to the port of Rodosto, three days distant. He was proud of the fact that he commanded the rear guard, protecting the retreating army so that "no one was left behind," not even the wounded. In his telling, he had saved what was left of the army from its first loss in the field since it arrived in Constantinople.[70] Clari ascribed the defeat to the arrogance and "disloyalty" of the commanders, who had betrayed the common soldiers, and to their "horrible sins" committed after the

---

67. Villehardouin, *La conquête*, §360. Mitchell, "Light Cavalry, Heavy Cavalry," 115, credits Baldwin's act with giving time for the fleeing soldiers to pass safely though Villehardouin's defensive line.
68. Villehardouin, *La conquête*, §361.
69. Villehardouin, *La conquête*, §§362–63.
70. Villehardouin, *La conquête*, §§364–66.

MARSHAL OF EMPEROR BALDWIN

fall of Constantinople.[71] For Villehardouin, the defeat was due to inferior mounted troops (perhaps mercenaries) and, implicitly, to bad leadership; but in the end, he conceded that "God allows misfortunes" (*mesaventures*).[72]

On the way to Rodosto, the retreating army stopped at Pamphilon, where they met a newly arrived detachment of 100 knights and 140 mounted sergeants from Count Louis's fief in Nicaea heading to Adrianople under the command of Peter of Bracheux and Payen of Orléans. Riding past the column of dejected soldiers, they approached the marshal in the rear and asked: "Sir, what do you want us to do?" "You can see what state we are in," he replied. "Since you and your horses are fresh, you take up the rear guard and I will move forward to calm our men, who are very demoralized and need encouragement."[73] Villehardouin remembered that "they took up the rear guard exactly as they should, for they were good and honorable knights," meaning disciplined, well-trained, and courageous, in contrast to the retreating army. The marshal then led the army to Chariopolis on Friday 15 April. There they rested their horses, just ahead of the king of Bulgaria, who was in hot pursuit. From Chariopolis, once it was dark, he led the army through the night and arrived the next evening, Saturday, 16 April, at Rodosto, a wealthy and strongly fortified city of Greeks, where they found lodging.[74] The strategic retreat to Rodosto, concludes the military historian J. F. Verbruggen, was "most remarkable: they covered more than eighty-three miles [ordinarily three days travel, according to the marshal] in less than forty-eight hours."[75]

On arriving at Rodosto the surviving commanders, fearing that Constantinople itself was at risk of attack, dispatched messengers by sea with the news that the doge and the marshal and their men had escaped from Adrianople and would return shortly to the capital. At that very moment in Constantinople, five large Venetian ships fully laden with pilgrims and knights—about 7,000 combatants (*homes a armes*),

---

71. Clari, *La conquête*, §112.

72. Villehardouin, *La conquête*, §360.

73. Villehardouin, *La conquête*, §372. The scribe had been relating Villehardouin's account of the battle in the third person, but here, instead of writing "the marshal said that," the scribe transcribed the marshal's speech verbatim. For the transformation of Villehardouin's account in the first person into the third person, see "Geoffroy of Villehardouin as Author" in chap. 8.

74. Villehardouin, *La conquête*, §§373–74.

75. Verbruggen, *Art of Warfare*, 222.

126   **CHAPTER 6**

Villehardouin estimated—who had completed their obligatory year of service at the end of March, were about to set sail for home.[76] Robert of Clari, the Picard knight who later dictated his own oral history, may have been among them.[77] The cardinal-legate Peter Capuano, Conon of Béthune, and Milo Breban, who had stayed in the capital, appealed for them to remain, but to no avail. When the ships laid in at Rodosto the day after the defeated army arrived from Adrianople, Villehardouin and the survivors implored them to remain with the depleted Frankish forces, but the ships slipped away early the next morning. Villehardouin notes that one of the ships was boarded by men from Blois and Chartres, in effect marking the departure of Count Louis's forces after his death.[78]

Villehardouin had saved the defeated army from annihilation, and possibly the Frankish settlement itself from collapse. But the disaffected knights as well as the non-combatant pilgrims finally chose to leave after three years of deprivation and deception, with little prospect of fulfilling their vows to go to Jerusalem. Even knights in the field were deserting their posts to return home. For Villehardouin, it was a desperate time. It seemed unlikely that the remnants of the defeated army could be re-formed into a credible field army when most of the countryside beyond the capital had fallen to Kalojan. Count Louis was dead, Baldwin was captive, Bishop Garnier of Troyes had died, most likely on the field of battle, and Count Hugh of Saint-Pol had died in Constantinople. Except for Boniface, who was in Thessalonika, and Count Henry, who was still on his way to Adrianople, the entire first generation of commanders had disappeared. The defeat at Adrianople and the departure of most of the crusader army brought an abrupt end to Baldwin's rule and the first phase of the Latin settlement.

It must have been especially bitter for the marshal that several of his close companions had returned to Champagne even before the battle as part of a general abandonment of the occupied cities by their French garrisons. Oger of Saint-Chéron and Guy of Chappes had been with him on the Third Crusade and ever since Écry. But in April 1205 they appeared in Countess Blanche's court to witness Clarembaud VI of Chappes confirm his father's gift made in his absence to the Cistercians

---

76. Villehardouin, *La conquête*, §375–76. The English translation reading "70,000 men-at-arms" should read "7,000" (vii. mile home a armes).

77. Robert of Clari seems to have left at this time, as suggested by Noble (Clari, *La conquête*, 14n165).

78. Villehardouin, *La conquête*, §§377–79.

MARSHAL OF EMPEROR BALDWIN

at Larrivour.[79] Then Guy and Clarembaud witnessed as Oger sealed a letter from Vilain of Aulnay, who was still in Acre, stating that he had given the Templars a village in Champagne in the presence of William of Arzillières, marshal of the Temple in Acre.[80] Of the twenty-two Champenois named by Villehardouin at Écry and the nine who mustered with him in Venice, only three—Macaire of Sainte-Menehould, Manessier of l'Ile-Adam, and Milo Breban—remained with him in Constantinople in May 1205, three years after leaving home.[81]

Baldwin's rule had been a transitional year in which a crusader army recruited to liberate Jerusalem had become an army of occupation of Christian Constantinople and, very briefly, of its provinces. Villehardouin had played a major role in what were for him, in retrospect, the three critical events in that year. By force of his reputation he resolved the conflict between Baldwin and Boniface that threatened to destabilize the Latin settlement. As marshal, with oversight of the military disposition of the empire, he was a member of the commission that assigned the major fiefs of the new regime. And as a field commander at Adrianople, he saved a defeated army after the capture of Baldwin and death of Louis and many of the barons.

---

79. AD Aube, 4H31 = Larrivour, fol. 13r, done in Troyes, April (after Easter, 10 April) 1205. Elizabeth of Chappes earlier had approved of her husband's gift (Larrivour, fol. 13v., August 1203). Brief biographies are in Longnon, *Les compagnons de Villehardouin*, 23 (Oger of Saint-Chéron), 57–58 (Guy of Chappes), and 58–60 (Clarembaud of Chappes). For details on Clarembaud (now designated Clarembaud VI, d. 1246), see Saint-Phalle, "Les seigneurs de Chappes," 57–59 and 59–63 (on Guy of Chappes, d. 1221).

80. Vilain asked Oger of Saint-Cheron to seal his letter in the presence of witnesses authenticating his gift of the village of Sancey (today Saint-Julien) to the Templars, which he made in the presence of William of Arzillières and Robert of Camville, who were "at that time" (*tunc*) marshal and preceptor of the Templars in Acre (between 1200 and 1204); see Burgtorf, *The Central Convent*, 645–46, 671. Vilain's letter is known only through a *vidimus* by the official of Troyes in 1256 (AN, S 4956, no. 6), which dates it "MCCJ." The "j" has been read either as an elongated "i" and therefore 1201 (as in Longnon, *Recherches*, 29n1), or as an incomplete "v," *quinto*, as it appears in a fifteenth-century Templar cartulary (Petit, *Histoire*, 3:481–82, no. 1455) and therefore 1205. Since Oger, Guy, and Clarembaud had returned from Constantinople by April 1205, the most likely date of Vilain's letter is 1205. Oudard of Aulnay, marshal of Champagne, confirmed his brother Vilain's letter in February 1206 at Vitry (Petit, *Histoire*, 3:481, no. 1456).

81. Longnon, *Les compagnons de Villehardouin*, 64.

Chapter 7

Marshal of Emperor Henry

As Villehardouin relates it, Count Henry was still on his way from Adramyttion in April 1205 when he learned of the army's defeat from Greeks who had escaped Adrianople. So, instead of traveling north from the port of Ainos to Adrianople, he took the Via Egnatia to Cortacopolis, where his men spent the night (map 6). He was joined by Villehardouin's nephew Anselm of Courcelles and the marshal's knights from Makri and Trajanopolis, along with a company of knights who had deserted Renier of Trith at Philippopolis, for a combined force of one hundred knights and five hundred mounted sergeants.[1] They arrived the next day in Rodosto, where the defeated army was resting. Villehardouin and Enrico Dandolo briefed Henry about conditions in the field; they reported that the entire hinterland except Rodosto and Selymbria had fallen to Kalojan, and Cumans had appeared at the very gates of the capital. Without blaming Count Louis,

---

1. Villehardouin, *La conquête*, §382. Anselm of Courcelles likely traveled with Villehardouin to Venice. He was in the Fifth Battalion during the assault on Constantinople, and remained with the Champenois garrison until October 1204, when he took custody of Villehardouin's fief. It is not known whether he survived the battle of Adrianople, but he seems not to have returned home, for in November 1205 his wife Beatrice, acting in his stead, authorized the marriage of one of his dependents (*Notre-Dame-aux-Nonnains*, 89–90). See also Longnon, *Les compagnons de Villehardouin*, 65–66.

MARSHAL OF EMPEROR HENRY

Villehardouin regretted Baldwin's failure to wait for reinforcements from the scattered fiefs before proceeding to Adrianople, for if those had been present at the battle, he said in retrospect, the army would not have been defeated.

With the doge's, and no doubt the marshal's, tacit consent, twenty-eight-year-old Count Henry assumed the regency of the empire for his captured brother.[2] Leaving the doge in Rodosto, Henry and Villehardouin led the remnants of the army back to Constantinople, three days distant, by way of Selymbria, where Henry installed a garrison of knights. The frightened people of Constantinople gave them a warm welcome, said the marshal, for "except for Rodosto and Selybria, all the land [beyond Constantinople] was held by Kalojan, and beyond the strait all the land except Espigal was held by Theodore Lascaris."[3]

Henry faced the formidable task of rebuilding a field army and creating a new chain of command from men of modest backgrounds. The marshal, a mature diplomat and military officer in his late fifties, assumed the same close advisory role with Henry, still unmarried at twenty-eight, that he had with Count Thibaut seven years earlier. His companions Manessier of l'Isle-Adam and Macaire of Sainte-Menehould, who survived Adrianople, together with Milo Breban and Conon of Béthune, who had remained in Constantinople, became Henry's leadership team, displacing Baldwin's privileged "men of Flanders," many of whom must have perished in Baldwin's company at Adrianople. Villehardouin, Milo Breban, Macaire, and Manessier were of knightly families and had served together in the main Champenois contingent since Écry four years earlier.[4] All in their fifties and, except for Manessier, veterans of the Third

---

2. Villehardouin, *La conquête*, §§380–85. Villehardouin is vague as to how Henry "was received" (*fu receüz*) as regent. We might assume that the marshal and the doge, the highest-ranking survivors of Adrianople, accepted Henry, an experienced military leader in his own right, as regent for his brother. For Henry's likely birth on 20 August 1177 at Valenciennes, see Van Tricht, "De jongelingenjaren," 189–90. For Henry's rule, see Van Tricht, "La gloire de l'empire" and the relevant passages in *The Latin Renovatio*.

3. Villehardouin, *La conquête*, §387.

4. Van Tricht, *The Latin Renovatio*, 251–55, 261–68, classifies Macaire of Sainte-Menehould, Manessier of l'Isle-Adam, Milo Breban, and Conon of Béthune as members of "the central elite" of the conquest who survived Adrianople, but he misclassifies their social origins as baronial (266–67, tables 8, 9); they are more accurately classified as being from knightly families. Although Vilain's grandfather Odo was lord of Arzillières, Villehardouin's father Vilain was only of knightly standing, as were the marshal's brothers Guy and Walter. Milo Breban and his brother Jean entered Count Henry I's service as *servientes*, indicating that they were not from baronial families. Manessier of L'Isle-Adam, a fifth son, was of *moyenne noblesse* (Civel, *La fleur de France*, 181). Longnon, *Les compagnons de Villehardouin*, 45, claims without evidence that Macaire was the son of the castellan of Sainte-Menehould, but he seems more likely to

130   **CHAPTER 7**

Crusade, they replaced an entire cohort of senior commanders and the doge, who died shortly after Adrianople.[5] Their daunting task was to preserve the Latin settlement.

Henry was advised to send Bishop Nivelon to Rome, France, and Flanders to seek aid in the aftermath of Adrianople and the departure of so many combatants. In his letter to Pope Innocent, Henry explained how he and the other barons recalled from Asia Minor were too dispersed and too few to face the large armies of Kalojan and his Greek allies. He reported the capture of Baldwin, listed the prominent barons who fell at Adrianople, and mentioned the retreat to Rodosto.[6] And he announced that Bishop Nivelon would come to Rome to seek the pope's counsel and aid. The bishop carried an identical letter from Henry addressed to archbishops, bishops, abbots, deans, counts, barons, knights, and all "sons of the universal church," appealing for aid and combatants to stabilize the occupation and to serve in the eventual expedition to the Holy Land. On arriving in Soissons, Nivelon forwarded copies of Henry's letter with his own postscript, asking for pilgrims to take the cross and join the Christian army.[7] Unlike Baldwin's encyclical of May 1204 celebrating the conquest of Constantinople and the election of a Latin emperor, Henry's letter painted a somber picture of conditions after the defeat at Adrianople.

The Devastations of 1205–6

The summer months of 1205 were trying ones for the regent emperor and his marshal. Once again the mission changed, from a crusade to recover Jerusalem, to the restoration of a Byzantine imperial claimant, to the foundation of a Latin empire with a new ruling class, and finally to the defense of Constantinople and the cities in Thrace and Asia Minor with a severely reduced military capability. Villehardouin remembers the months after Adrianople as a time of unrelenting attacks on all fronts, with depleted units struggling to stave off Kalojan's far larger

---

have been the son of Aubert, who owed six weeks castle-guard in Vitry (*Feoda*, no. 385), where Macaire himself was listed (no. 515).

5. Madden, *Enrico Dandolo*, 266n144, accepts Villehardouin's statement that Dandolo died before Pentecost (29 May) 1205 and was buried in Hagia Sophia (Villehardouin, *La conquête*, §388).

6. *Register*, 8:239–43, no. 132 (131), done in the Blachernai, 5 June 1205.

7. Pokorny, "Zwei unedierte Briefe," 199–202, no. 1, done in the Blachernai, 15 June 1205, embedded in Nivelon's undated letter addressed to all Christians.

Bulgarian forces, which were savaging the countryside and attacking cities beyond the capital, creating in the process a stream of refugees caught between the Bulgarian and French forces. Henry tried to check Kalojan in Thrace, while Boniface abandoned the siege of Nauplion in order to defend Thessalonika. Villehardouin resumed his position as garrison commander in Constantinople, where he assessed reports of distant, synchronous events. His third-person narrative is so detailed and compressed that it is impossible to determine when he is recounting what he heard at the time and when his scribe is expanding his testimony with relevant information.

Leaving Villehardouin in Constantinople, Henry set out on the Via Militaris to Tchorlu and Arcadiopolis, which had been abandoned, and Bizoë, which surrendered, but at Apros his men were so brutal and destructive that the horrified Greeks from the surrounding towns fled to Adrianople and Didymoteichon (map 7). Villehardouin wanted his listeners to know that those atrocities solidified Greek animosity toward the Franks. While Henry besieged Adrianople, Kalojan captured Serres, razed the city and its fortress to the ground, and killed or deported its garrison and residents, who had surrendered on terms. Survivors brought grim stories of brutality and beheadings to the capital. Henry passed the rest of the summer at the strategically located city of Pamphilon, alert to any advance by Kalojan toward the capital but without engaging the Bulgarians.[8]

Villehardouin relates the fate of Philippopolis, "one of the finest cities of the empire," which Renier of Trith had received in fief. In the aftermath of Adrianople, the entire garrison abandoned the city, leaving the Greeks no choice but to surrender to Kalojan, he said. Renier retreated to the hilltop fortress of Stenimakos, where he remained with a small detachment for the next thirteen months under such dire conditions that they were reduced to eating their horses.[9] In Philippopolis, Kalojan's forces murdered the archbishop and committed all manner of atrocities before razing the entire city, including its walls and towers, and burning down the fine homes of those who had surrendered. And so, Villehardouin remarked, the noble city of Philippopolis, "the third finest in the empire" (after Constantinople and Adrianople), was destroyed.[10]

---

8. Villehardouin, *La conquête*, §§390–97. Madgearu, *The Asanids*, 156–60, follows Kalojan's attacks in Thrace after the battle of Adrianople.

9. Asdracha, *La région des Rhodopes*, 162–64, describes Stenimakos.

10. Villehardouin, *La conquête*, §§399–401.

132   **CHAPTER 7**

After an indecisive summer parrying Kalojan, Henry returned to Constantinople in October. In consultation with his barons, he decided to reinforce Rhousion with 140 knights and a detachment of mounted sergeants, and to install a garrison of 120 knights with mounted sergeants in Bizoë. Making amends for the atrocities at Apros, he granted the city to Theodore Branas, the former governor of the theme of Adrianople-Didymoteichon-Apros, "who was married to the sister [Agnes] of the king of France." Branas, said Villehardouin, who was residing in Constantinople, was "the only Greek who supported the Franks."[11]

In that same month of October, Henry delegated Villehardouin, by that time known as "marshal of the empire," to work with Marino Zeno, Venice's new podesta in the empire, to devise a new constitution of governance based on a review of the *concordia* of March and the *partitio* of October 1204. The resultant document, framed as a confirmation of the *concordia*, formalized a "mixed council" (*consilium*) of Frankish barons (*magnates*) and Venetians, whose advice the emperor was bound to heed in military affairs. It was a recognition of the fact that the crusade, conquest, and settlement had been a joint Frankish-Venetian project from the start. The "constitution" (*pactum scriptum*) also reaffirmed the obligation of all fiefholders to be available for annual military service from 1 June to 29 September, whenever requested by the emperor and his council "for defending the empire." At the formal presentation of the document in the Blachernai palace, Henry swore to its enumerated clauses in the presence of the French (*Francigenis*) witnesses: Geoffroy (*marescalcus imperii*), Conon of Béthune (*protovestiarius imperii*), Manessier of l'Isle-Adam (*major coco*), Macaire of Sainte-Menehould (*panetarius*), and Milo Breban (*buticularius*). Villehardouin does not mention his role in drafting the document, but the fact that he and Marino Zeno swore to uphold its provisions and both sealed the document along with the emperor attests to the old marshal's close relationship with Henry.[12] The constitution of October 1205 not only redefined the emperor's advisory council and limited his authority, it marked the ascension of the

---

11. Villehardouin, *La conquête*, §403. Agnes (b. 1171), daughter of Louis VII, married Alexios II (r. 1182–83), then Alexios II Komnenos (r. 1183–85), and finally Theodore Branas sometime before 1204; see Short, "Agency and Authority."

12. Longnon, *Recherches*, 191–94, no. 74, October 1205, done in Constantinople in the Blachernai = Tafel and Thomas, *Urkunden*, 1:571–74, no. 160. The original document does not survive; a thirteenth-century copy records the existence of the three seals (Longnon, *Recherches*, 191n4). For an analysis, see Van Tricht, *The Latin Renovatio*, 53–59.

Champenois, and especially of Villehardouin, to the highest level of imperial governance.[13]

Villehardouin remained in Constantinople through the winter of 1205 and spring of 1206 receiving reports and "news" of events beyond the city. It was an especially fraught period in which Kalojan and Theodore Lascaris together overran virtually the entire empire beyond the capital. The marshal was particularly concerned about Kalojan, who in mid-January began to destroy the walled Greek towns along the Via Egnatia between Rhousion and Athyra.[14] For Villehardouin, the fall of Rhousion (31 January 1206), not far from his fief at Makri, marked a major reversal of Frankish efforts to control the Greek cities.

The "sad news" (*doloruse novele*) of Rhousion's fate reached the capital on 2 February 1206, brought by survivors who fled first to Rodosto, then to Constantinople. They reported that Thierry of Tenremonde, a Flemish knight who commanded a garrison of 140 knights and a large number of mounted sergeants, had raided an encampment of Cumans and Vlachs on 30 January. On returning to Rhousion, just before reentering the city walls, his company was ambushed and all but destroyed by an overwhelming force of Cumans, Vlachs, and Greeks. Ten knights who survived fled by night to Rodosto.[15] The other Greeks cities quickly submitted to Kalojan, who consequently amassed a great army, said Villehardouin, according to the firsthand reports he received. The fear in Constantinople, he recalled, was that the Latin occupation had ended. To counter a defeatist spirit, Henry sent Macaire of Sainte-Menehould with fifty knights to strengthen the garrison at Selymbria.[16] About the same time he sent a dolorous report to Innocent recounting the loss of Rhousion and death of Thierry of Tenremonde.[17]

---

13. Shortly afterward, Geoffroy, "marshal of the entire empire of Romania," and Milo Breban conducted an inquest with two Venetian representatives to determine which *casalia* in Thrace belonged to the Venetians and which to the French. After taking testimony from local residents, they listed the villages that fell into each zone (Longnon, *Recherches*, 201–2, no. 83, without date, but clearly related to the sorting out of zones of authority during the early settlement).

14. Madgearu, *The Asanids*, 160–64, describes Kalojan's campaign in Thrace, with a map (161) of the route of destruction along the Via Egnatia.

15. Stoyanov, "The Size of Bulgaria's Medieval Field Armies," 738–39, confirms the size of Kalojan's forces as reported by Villehardouin on the basis of survivor reports (Villehardouin, *La conquête*, §406). Thierry of Tenremonde, who spent the 1190s in Syria, came to Constantinople in September or October 1204, when Emperor Henry appointed him garrison commander of Rhousion; see Kedar, "The Fourth Crusade's Second Front," 107–8.

16. Villehardouin, *La conquête*, §§402–14.

17. *Gesta Innocentii*, 146–47 (Powell, *Deeds of Innocent*, 199–200), no. 106.

134   **CHAPTER 7**

With the fall of Rhousion, the trunk road between Constantinople and Thessalonika was severed, as city after city was destroyed along the Via Egnatia. Apros, which was held by Theodore Branas and garrisoned by Franks and Greeks, was razed to the ground and its residents taken away as prisoners after the local leaders were executed. Even the port city of Rodosto, despite its strong walls, was torn down after it was abandoned by the Venetians, Franks, and Greeks who fled into the countryside. Villehardouin does not note but surely knew that the Venetian port, a critical nexus for provisioning the inland cities, was a major loss.[18]

The catalogue continued: Panedon, Heraclea, Daïn, Tchorlu, Athyra, all victims of the Cumans. "They destroyed cities and fortresses and caused so great a devastation that nothing like it has ever been heard," recalled the marshal. Even Athyra, close to the capital and full of refugees, was taken and subjected to a great slaughter. "Know that every fortress and city that surrendered to Kalojan was completely razed and destroyed, and its residents taken into captivity."[19] Villehardouin repeats his memory of the dire conditions in the early months of 1206: "Nothing within five days travel from Constantinople escaped devastation except Bizöe and Selymbria." Beyond Bizöe, where Anseau of Cayeux commanded a garrison of one hundred twenty knights, and Selymbria, where Macaire of Sainte-Menehould had fifty knights, nothing stood between Kalojan's forces and Constantinople.[20] Villehardouin does not mention the fate of his own lands at Makri, Trajanopolis, and Bera, which also were destroyed, according to the Byzantine historian George Akropolites.[21]

Only in the late spring of 1206 did the tide of events begin to turn for the Franks. The Greeks in Kalojan's service, seeing the wanton destruction of their cities, sent messengers to Theodore Branas, who was still in Constantinople. They begged him to ask Henry for the return of Adrianople and Didymoteichon and promised their loyalty. Since Adrianople had lacked a ruler since the death of Hugh of Saint-Pol (January 1205), Henry's council advised that he grant the two cities "to Branas and to the empress, his wife" in return for "service"

---

18. Villehardouin, *La conquête*, §§413–16.
19. Villehardouin, *La conquête*, §420. Akropolites, *History*, 139–40, confirms Kalojan's systematic devastations and includes Villehardouin's lands at Trajanopolis and Makri among those destroyed. Asdracha, *La région des Rhodopes*, 117–20, concludes that Makri apparently survived after being sacked, whereas Trajanopolis was practically destroyed in 1206.
20. Villehardouin, *La conquête*, §421.
21. Akropolites, *History*, 143n16.

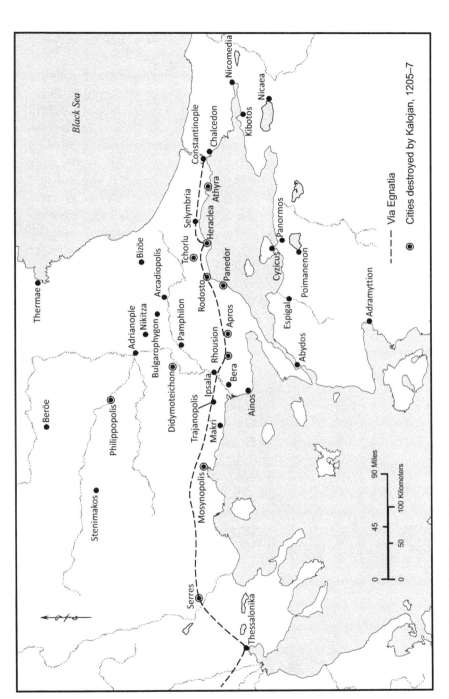

MAP 7. Cities destroyed by Kalojan, 1205–7

136   **CHAPTER 7**

to the emperor.[22] That was the first great fief granted to a Greek. "And thus peace was made between the Greeks and the Franks," said Villehardouin.[23]

Villehardouin was with Henry in Constantinople shortly after Easter (2 April 1206) when couriers arriving daily (*de jor an jor*) from Didymoteichon and Adrianople pleaded with Henry and Branas for help against Kalojan. The Greeks had refused Kalojan entry into Adrianople, telling him—Villehardouin quotes their defiant speech, as reported by couriers—"Sir, when we surrendered to you and revolted against the Franks, you swore to us that you would protect us; but you did not, and instead you have devastated Romania. We know well that you will do to us what you have done to the others." On the advice of his council, Henry decided to relieve Adrianople. He and the marshal took 400 knights, turcopoles, and mounted crossbowmen to Bizoë, where on 23 June they received a desperate appeal warning of the imminent fall of Didymoteichon. Despite the reluctance of some of the barons to venture that far beyond the capital, said Villehardouin, Henry decided that they would be shamed (*honi*) if they did not go.[24]

On the morning of 24 June, after the men made confession and received communion, Henry proceeded with his troops to Adrianople while Villehardouin, with Macaire of Sainte-Menehould as second in command, led a column of eight companies from Bizöe to Didymoteichon. Conon of Béthune and Milo Breban commanded the second company. Uncertain as to whether they had sufficient troops to engage the Bulgarians, and whether the Greeks could be trusted, they nevertheless marched to Didymoteichon. On hearing of their approach, Kalojan lifted the siege, burned his siege engines, and decamped, which was thought a "great miracle," given the disparity in their forces. After a brief respite, Villehardouin and his men rejoined Henry in Adrianople, and together they pursued the retreating Bulgarians for five days before stopping to rest. At that point fifty knights left because of a disagreement (*discorde*) with Emperor Henry, as Villehardouin puts it discreetly, no doubt over venturing so far from the capital. In consultation with

---

22. Short, "Agency and Authority," 36, points out the importance of Agnes, as both a Frank and an assimilated Byzantine, in facilitating this arrangement. Branas soon resolved the ambiguous status of Adrianople by establishing a formal relationship with Venice (Tafel and Thomas, *Urkunden*, 2:17–19, no. 169, 1206). For the subsequent history of Adrianople and Didymoteichon, see Van Tricht, "The Byzantino-Latin Principality of Adrianople."

23. Villehardouin, *La conquête*, §§422–24.

24. Villehardouin, *La conquête*, §§425–29.

his barons, however, Henry decided to continue for another two days to Moniac, where they rested for five days (map 6).[25]

It may have been Villehardouin himself who suggested going still further to rescue Renier of Trith, who had been besieged for thirteen months deep in enemy territory at Stenimakos. While Henry and most of the army stayed at Moniac, Villehardouin, again in the vanguard, as he reminds the listener, led a strike force far to the west of Adrianople to Stenimakos. For three days the marshal, Conon of Béthune, Macaire of Sainte-Menehould, and Milo Breban, together with a company of Venetians and a troop of turcopoles and mounted crossbowmen, rode through enemy territory further than they previously had ventured. "Know that those who went on this mission went at great peril, and I know of few missions as dangerous," remarked Villehardouin. He noted again that he was in the vanguard (*l'avangarde*) and that he was the first to meet Renier at Stenimakos on 26 July 1206. The relief force spent the night in the "very fine town" below the fortress. For the marshal, it was an exuberant, daring adventure and a distinct personal achievement. It was his second major success as a battlefield commander, a year after saving the defeated army at Adrianople. The only sad note was that Renier confirmed rumors (*oï dire*) that Emperor Baldwin had died in Kalojan's prison.[26]

The marshal and his troops returned to Moniac with the news of Baldwin's death, then accompanied Henry back to Adrianople. Leaving forty knights under the command of Theodore Branas, they returned to Constantinople to prepare for Henry's coronation. At a preliminary ceremony on 12 August, in the presence of the Venetian podesta Marino Zeno, the papal legate Benedict of Santa Susanna, and Patriarch Thomas Morosini, Henry swore on the altar of Hagia Sophia to observe the foundational documents of the new regime: the *pactum* of March 1204, the distribution of fiefs in October 1204 (*particiones*), and the constitution (*pactum scriptum*) of October 1205.[27] The coronation was celebrated with great joy and dignity on 20 August, said Villehardouin, without mentioning any details.

---

25. Villehardouin, *La conquête*, §§430–35.

26. Villehardouin, *La conquête*, §§436–40. Rumors of Baldwin's escape and the return of a "false Baldwin" to Flanders circulated twenty years later; see Wolf, "Baldwin of Flanders and Hainaut," 294–301.

27. Tafel and Thomas, *Urkunden*, 2:34–35, no. 174 (dated 12 August 1206).

138   **CHAPTER 7**

The celebration was short-lived. Within days, news arrived that Kalojan again was besieging Adrianople. Leaving the marshal in charge of Constantinople, Henry led a force to break the siege, but Kalojan, learning of his arrival, abandoned it.[28] While in Adrianople, Henry wrote to his brother Geoffroy, canon of Saint-Amé of Douai, reporting on events since the capture of Baldwin, particularly the destruction of Rhousion and Philippopolis; he asked Geoffroy to plead with their brother Count Philip of Hainaut to send as much aid as possible, for there were only 600 knights and 10,000 sergeants available in the entire empire.[29] At the same time he wrote to King Philip II confirming the death of Baldwin.[30]

After retreating from Adrianople, Kalojan besieged and captured Didymoteichon, razed its walls "to the ground" (fondi les murs trosque en terre), and sent all its residents into captivity. Henry organized two companies of knights and local Greeks under the command of his brother Eustace of Hainaut and Macaire of Sainte-Menehould to rescue the men, women, and children taken captive, together with their possessions and livestock. On returning to the destroyed city and seeing that its walls could not be rebuilt, Henry pursued Kalojan into Bulgarian territory. All these events Villehardouin heard about later from Henry, who returned to Constantinople with the approach of winter in early November after two months in the field.[31]

Henry and his council decided to rebuild the towns destroyed by Kalojan in Thrace and by Lascaris in Asia Minor. Peter of Bracheux took 140 knights to Espigal and Cyzicus, where he had the walls and fortifications rebuilt, while Dietrich of Looz returned to Nicomedia, whose fortress had been torn down, and Boniface of Montferrat began to refortify Serres.[32] Shortly after Christmas an envoy arrived from Thessalonika to announce that Boniface's daughter Agnes had arrived in Ainos for her marriage to Henry. Villehardouin and Milo Breban were dispatched to escort her to Constantinople. They returned in early January for the wedding held in Hagia Sophia on 4 February 1207. It was a joyous occasion, said Villehardouin, implicitly noting its significance in finally

---

28. Villehardouin, *La conquête*, §§441–43.

29. Tafel and Thomas, *Urkunden*, 2:37–42, no. 176, September 1206, Henry's letter to his brother, "done with the army at Adrianople."

30. Hendrickx, "Recherches," 149–50, no. 29, 1206, after 20 August.

31. Villehardouin, *La conquête*, §§444–50.

32. Villehardouin, *La conquête*, §§454, 456, 495.

MARSHAL OF EMPEROR HENRY 139

ending the long-running rivalry between Boniface and the house of Flanders. A line of Latin emperors now seemed possible.[33]

The Two-Front War

In those winter months of 1206–7 Emperor Henry faced his greatest challenge yet—a two-front war led by Kalojan in the west and Theodore Lascaris in the east. Villehardouin understood that a secure Frankish settlement still hung in the balance due to a lack of manpower. "At no time have any people been so burdened by war," he said, as if reminding his home audience, "for they were scattered in so many places."[34] Kalojan again besieged Adrianople, which was garrisoned by only eleven knights, while his Cuman allies rode right up to the gates of Constantinople. Across the straits, Lascaris launched a general attack against the towns and fortresses garrisoned by the French. At the end of March 1207, a desperate call came from the castle of Kibotos, which Macaire of Sainte-Menehould was defending with forty knights.

Villehardouin recalled the scene in the Boukoleon on a Saturday morning when he and Conon of Béthune, Milo Breban, and a few others were having a meal with Henry. A messenger rushed in from Kibotos: Lascaris had launched an assault on the fortress by land and sea. A quick decision was made to send a rescue force of seventeen Venetian and Pisan ships. Villehardouin, who had remained in Constantinople since returning from Stenimakos in August, remembered how the sailors ran down to their ships and set sail as soon as the knights boarded with their arms. A forced rowing through the night, with Henry in the lead ship and Villehardouin and Milo Breban behind, brought them to Kibotos by sunrise. They immediately engaged a fleet of sixty Greek ships. Since the battle was inconclusive, plans were made to resume the attack the next day at dawn. But at midnight the Greeks hauled their ships to shore, burned them, and abandoned the siege. Because the city was in such a state of disrepair that it was not defensible, it was decided to abandon it and transport its residents to Constantinople.[35]

The marshal returned to the capital while Henry spent the spring months leading troops from one place to another, relieving besieged castles and trying unsuccessfully to engage Kalojan in battle. In April

33. Villehardouin, *La conquête*, §§457–58.
34. Villehardouin, *La conquête*, §460.
35. Villehardouin, *La conquête*, §§459–71.

140   **CHAPTER 7**

Kalojan once again besieged Adrianople, and for the entire month his siege engines and miners attacked the towers and city walls, which were razed to the ground, but hand-to-hand combat prevented his forces from entering the city. Since the Cumans, on whom he had depended in the past, decided to return home, he abandoned the siege. It was taken as a miracle, observed Villehardouin, that Kalojan abandoned the siege of a city that was so close to defeat.[36]

In May an urgent call came from Cyzicus on the coast of Asia Minor, which was being attacked by naval and ground forces. After consulting with his knights and barons and the Venetians, Henry dispatched a relief force of fourteen galleys. Villehardouin, Conon of Béthune, Milo Breban, and Macaire of Sainte-Menehould each commanded a vessel. It was the marshal's second successful sea battle, for the Greek ships withdrew before engaging. Cyzicus was saved, the fleet returned to Constantinople, and the army prepared to go to Adrianople. Almost immediately, however, word came that Lascaris had sent a force to Nicomedia, and so Henry again postponed his march to Adrianople and instead took a relief force to Nicomedia and forced Lascaris to retreat.[37]

At that point, while Henry and Villehardouin were still in Nicomedia, Lascaris proposed a two-year truce: he would release all prisoners taken at Nicomedia if Henry would dismantle the fortresses at Cyzicus and Nicomedia. It was clear that the Franks lacked the manpower to defend both Thrace and Asia Minor, and so on the advice of his barons, who pointed out that a two-front war was not winnable, Henry agreed to a truce. We can almost hear Villehardouin speaking when he says that the emperor's council concluded that "it was not possible to fight two wars at the same time . . . it was better to lose Asia Minor than Adrianople and the rest of his lands [in Thrace]." A truce with Lascaris would break the Bulgarian-Greek alliance. Henry accepted their advice. That strategic decision, to save the lands west of Constantinople, marked the end of the Latin occupation of Asia Minor. The Latin empire was reduced to the city of Constantinople and its immediate environs in Thrace.[38]

In late June Villehardouin accompanied Henry to Adrianople, where they were warmly welcomed by the Greeks in procession from the city. Henry surveyed the destroyed walls and reassured the residents of his support against the Bulgarians. Meanwhile Boniface, who had arrived

---

36. Villehardouin, *La conquête*, §§473–75.
37. Villehardouin, *La conquête*, §§476–79.
38. Villehardouin, *La conquête*, §§485–89.

at Mosynopolis after rebuilding Serres, sent a courier inviting Henry to meet in Ipsala, since they had not met for many months on account of the insecurity of the countryside.[39] Leaving Conon of Béthune in charge of Adrianople with one hundred knights, Henry and Villehardouin traveled to Ipsala, where the Via Egnatia meets the Hebros River, at the border between the emperor's lands and the kingdom of Thessalonika. They stayed with Boniface for two days. After Henry informed Boniface that his daughter Agnes, then about fifteen, was pregnant, Boniface did homage to Henry, just as he had done to Baldwin.[40] Boniface then offered Villehardouin a fief within the kingdom of Thessalonika, either Mosynopolis or Serres, whichever he preferred, to hold in liege homage (*fu ses home liges*), saving of course the marshal's primary loyalty (*fealte*) to Emperor Henry. Villehardouin does not say which city he chose, but it must have been Mosynopolis, a major city on the Via Egnatia that Kalojan had only partially destroyed and that was closer to his lands in Makri and Trajanopolis.[41]

Boniface and Henry agreed to meet again in Adrianople in late October to wage war together against Kalojan. But shortly after Villehardouin and Henry returned to Constantinople, they heard that Boniface had died in a skirmish with a large Bulgarian force just beyond Mosynopolis on 4 September. It was reported that he was decapitated and his head sent to a jubilant Kalojan. "What a grievous loss," said Villehardouin, "for Emperor Henry and for all the Latins in Romania to lose such a man through such a misfortune [*per tel mesaventure*]. He was one of the best barons and most generous, and one of the best knights there ever was. This misfortune occurred in the year of the incarnation of Jesus Christ 1207."[42] With those words, the marshal ended his memoirs. They were especially freighted in that he had personally recruited Boniface as supreme commander of the expeditionary forces and had witnessed Bishop Nivelon pin the cross on Boniface in Soissons exactly six years earlier. On other occasions Villehardouin ascribed misfortune to the will

---

39. Villehardouin, *La conquête*, §§494–95.

40. Villehardouin, *La conquête*, §496.

41. Longnon, *Recherches*, 95, concludes that Villehardouin, in mentioning Mosynopolis first, intimated that he chose it. Longnon, in Valenciennes, *Histoire*, 59–60n5, explains further why Villehardouin probably chose Mosynopolis. Asdracha, *La région des Rhodopes*, 105–6, notes that despite Akropolites's statement, it appears that Mosynopolis remained habitable and quickly recovered.

42. Villehardouin, *La conquête*, §§498–500. Manuscripts B, C, and D read "1207." Manuscripts A and O erroneously give "1206." Raimbaut of Vaqueiras also probably died in that clash; see his *Poems*, 35–36.

142   **CHAPTER 7**

of God, who sometimes allowed bad things to happen, as he reminded his listeners. This time, God did not intervene, for or against. It was a fitting comment on the fate of the crusade, and a sober comment on the last decade of the marshal's life.

A Time for Memoirs

The marshal stayed in Constantinople with Milo Breban from September 1207 to May 1208, before they returned to the field against the Bulgarians at Philippopolis. It was during that nine-month interlude that Villehardouin appears to have dictated his memoirs.[43] He was about sixty. He does not say why he decided to record his memoirs, but the death of Boniface of Montferrat might have caused him to reflect on the dramatic events of his life since November 1199. All the senior leaders of the crusade had perished—Thibaut of Champagne, Baldwin of Flanders, Louis of Blois, Hugh of Saint-Pol, Boniface of Montferrat, Enrico Dandolo, Garnier of Troyes, and Nivelon of Soissons. Even their formidable adversary Kalojan was assassinated shortly after Boniface died in September 1207.[44] Having been privy to the leadership councils since 1199, the marshal alone remained to preserve the memory of the great seaborne expedition from its origin; only he could describe how a crusade to recover Jerusalem, to redeem the failure of the Third Crusade, had turned instead into the conquest of the greatest Christian city in the Mediterranean.

Two recently arrived Flemings may have encouraged Villehardouin, as the most knowledgeable survivor of the crusade, to record his memoirs. One was Henry of Valenciennes, a learned canon who arrived in Constantinople in September 1205 bearing letters of introduction from Innocent III addressed to the emperor and patriarch of Constantinople.[45] The pope praised Valenciennes "for his knowledge and character"

---

43. Faral (Villehardouin, *La conquête*), 1:xviii, suggests a date of 1208 at the earliest, seemingly in order to place the memoirs after the July battle of Philippopolis. If that were the case, one would expect the marshal to have signaled his deeds at Philippopolis, the first pitched battle won by the Franks since the conquest, an event that he surely would have celebrated as comparable to his saving the army at Adrianople three years earlier. I agree with Longnon, *Recherches*, 97, that Villehardouin more likely dictated his memoirs in the months between Boniface's death in September 1207 and May 1208.

44. Madgearu, *The Asanids*, 167–73, describes Kalojan's last months and the recent attempts to identify his assassin and to locate the site of his burial.

45. *Register*, 8:243–51, nos. 133–37. Longnon, "Le chroniqueur Henri de Valenciennes," 143, suggests that Valenciennes carried the letters from Rome.

MARSHAL OF EMPEROR HENRY 143

and requested that he be made a canon of Hagia Sophia and assigned a prebend.[46] Valenciennes joined the emperor's entourage and from May 1208 recorded his deeds in the field, in effect extending the marshal's memoirs as a record of the overseas experiences of the brother-counts of Flanders for a home audience. It is also possible that the impetus for the memoirs came from Peter of Douai, a knight and familiar of Count Baldwin who arrived in Constantinople with a company of reinforcements in late 1207 or early 1208 in response to Bishop Nivelon's call for combatants to defend Constantinople.[47] Whether or not Villehardouin was influenced by either Valenciennes or Douai, he must have completed his memoirs before he led the advance guard to the battle of Philippopolis on 31 July 1208.

By the spring of 1208 the view from Constantinople was profoundly different from what it had been after the conquest four years earlier. In September 1204, after the resolution of the conflict between Boniface and Baldwin, Villehardouin could look ahead to the foundation of a new Latin state ruled by the great lords of the crusade. Seven months later, however, in April 1205, his view was shattered. The main army had been virtually destroyed at Adrianople, an entire cohort of commanders had been killed, and most of the knights were returning home after three years of ever-changing missions that never led to Acre. The years following Adrianople were dominated by incessant rescue missions in response to Bulgarian invasions in Thrace and to the Greeks in Asia Minor. Villehardouin's narrative is imbued with a sense of impending collapse in the face of devastation throughout the former Byzantine provinces, now an active war zone devolving into largely independent polities: the principality of Achaia, the duchies of Athens and Philippopolis, the kingdom of Thessalonika, the despotate of Epirus, the empire of Nicaea, and Venetian naval bases. After the abandonment of Asia Minor in May 1207, the emperor and his marshal embarked on a frantic defense just to hold on to the ravaged lands in Thrace. Of Villehardouin's closest

---

46. *Register*, 8:251, no. 137, 7 September 1205, letter to Thomas Morosini, Venetian patriarch of Constantinople, in support of "Master Henry," whom Longnon, in "Le chroniqueur Henri de Valenciennes," 143, identifies as Henry of Valenciennes.

47. Peter of Douai witnessed a number of Count Baldwin's acts in Flanders (1195–1200) and remained in the count's service there until the fall of 1207 or early 1208. He fought in the battle of Philippopolis, returned to Flanders in late 1209, served as bailiff of Douai for several years, and died in 1221. For his life, see Longnon, *Les compagnons de Villehardouin*, 182–83.

144 **CHAPTER 7**

companions from Champagne, only Milo Breban remained.[48] It was in that fraught environment that Villehardouin recalled the extraordinary events that marked his life after he took the cross at Écry.

Villehardouin's Last Years

In March 1208, before embarking on another summer campaign, Villehardouin made a final provision for his daughters and his elderly sisters who were nuns in two prestigious convents in Champagne. In identical letters he endowed lifetime incomes for his sister Emeline and his daughter Alice in the Fontevrist priory of Foissy, and for his sister Haye and his daughter Dameron in the Benedictine convent of Notre-Dame-aux-Nonnains in Troyes. In the first document he granted one-half of two tithe revenues to each convent:

> I, Geoffroy of Villehardouin, marshal of Romania and Champagne, make known to all, present and future, who read this document that I gave one-half of my tithe revenue at Brantigny and Doyer to Notre-Dame of Foissy and the other half to Notre-Dame [-aux-Nonnains] of Troyes in perpetuity, on the condition that my daughter Alice and my sister Emeline [in Nonnains] will collect half of that tithe annually for their lifetimes; my daughter Dameron and my sister Haye [in Foissy] will collect the other half for as long as they live. After their deaths, the above-named convents will possess those revenues in perpetuity. So that what is written here be permanently observed, I have sealed it with my seal. Done in the month of March in the year of the Lord 1208.[49]

The second document provides equal shares of the tithe at Voué.[50] Both documents identify Villehardouin as "marshal of Romania and Champagne," but the extant seal is his old seal that reads "Geoffroy, marshal of Champagne."[51] Those are his last known transactional

---

48. In September 1205 Milo Breban's wife Isabelle still expected him to return when she promised to obtain his approval for her exchange of tenants with Countess Blanche (Provins, Bibliothèque Municipale, ms. 85, no. 37). Manessier is last recorded in October 1205, while Macaire is last recorded in the spring of 1207; see Longnon, *Les compagnons de Villehardouin*, 43–45, 45–48.

49. *Notre-Dame-aux-Nonnains*, 90, no. 131, March 1208 (new style).

50. Longnon, *Recherches*, 204–5, no. 88, March 1208 (new style).

51. Photograph of the extant seal in Baudin, *Emblématique et pouvoir en Champagne*, CD-ROM, Corpus des Sceaux, 95: "Si[gillum] Gaufridi mar[escalli] Campanie"; and "De la Champagne à la Morée," 111, fig. 5. See also Chassel, *Sceaux et usages de sceaux*, 110, fig. 112.

MARSHAL OF EMPEROR HENRY

letters.[52] There is no evidence that he communicated with his wife Chane, who was sealing letters as *"marescalissa* of Champagne" with their younger son Geoffroy.[53] Their eldest son Erard assumed her inheritance as "lord of Lézinnes."[54]

At about the same time in 1208 or 1209 Countess Blanche, regent of Champagne, asked Villehardouin and Milo Breban about the status of the fiefs of counts Thibaut V of Blois and Stephen of Sancerre, who died at Acre in 1191. In their reply, Villehardouin ("marshal of Romania") and Milo Breban ("butler of Romania") noted that the counts of Blois and Sancerre were her liegemen for their fiefs, which she could verify by consulting the rolls of fiefs (*scripta feodorum*) deposited in the comital chapel of Saint-Étienne of Troyes.[55] Milo Breban added that he had witnessed the new rolls being drawn up on the eve of the Third Crusade and deposited in Saint-Étienne, and that Count Henry II took a codex copy with him overseas.[56]

Villehardouin's whereabouts during the rest of 1208 are known from Henry of Valenciennes's *Histoire*. For thirteen months, from 25 May 1208 to September 1209, Valenciennes accompanied the emperor as a war correspondent, reporting on his campaigns against the Bulgarians and the recalcitrant barons of Thessalonika after Boniface's death. His history of those campaigns features action portraits of Emperor Henry and his battlefield commanders—Villehardouin, Peter of Douai, and Conon of Béthune.[57] It was Marshal Geoffroy, said Valenciennes, who advised the emperor to do battle with the Bulgarians in the late spring of 1208, while Peter of Douai, who was in Henry's confidence, became Henry's bodyguard in the forthcoming hostilities. In July 1208 Villehardouin and Milo Breban, both about sixty, led the advance guard to engage the

---

52. Villehardouin sent another letter, now lost, consenting to his brother Jean's gift to the Maison-Dieu du Chêne; it is known only through the confirmation of the bishop of Troyes (Longnon, *Recherches*, 206, no. 91, 1208).

53. *Saint-Loup*, 211, no. 160, dated by Longnon, *Recherches*, 209, no. 98, to 1208–10.

54. Longnon, *Recherches*, 203–4, no. 86, 1207: Erard and his wife Mabile confirmed the sale to Quincy Abbey of the fief that Hugh Curebois held from them.

55. Counts Thibaut and Stephen are listed in the fief rolls of 1178 under *Feodi Magni* (*Feoda* 1, nos. 2034, 2035).

56. *Cartulary of Countess Blanche*, 294–95, no. 333, ca. 1208–9 = Longnon, *Documents*, 1:xiii, no. 2, letter of Geoffroy of Villehardouin and Milo Breban to Countess Blanche. In the new rolls of fiefs drawn up ca. 1209–10, the fiefs of the counts of Blois and Sancerre were described in language that seems borrowed from the marshal's letter (*Feoda* 2, nos. 2421, 2427).

57. Valenciennes's reportage, which lacks a title, is conventionally called a history; see Longnon, "Le chroniqueur Henri de Valenciennes" and "Sur l'histoire de l'empereur Henri."

146   **CHAPTER 7**

Bulgarians at Philippopolis.[58] As the battle was about to commence, the marshal gave a rousing speech to his troops, appealing both to the righteousness of their cause and to the examples of their predecessors:

> Men, for God's sake, make sure that you attack with force, to the point that we are not blamed or mocked by our enemies. Whoever loses his nerve should be banned from the glory of Our Lord. For God's sake, remember your worthy predecessors [*preudomes anciens*], who are still cited in the books of history [*es livres des estores*]. And know well that whoever dies for God in this battle, his soul will rise in all glory to God's paradise, and whoever survives will be honored for the rest of his life and will be praised in eulogy after his death.
>
> If we truly believe in Our Lord, the field of battle will be ours. If the enemy is more numerous than we are, what does it matter? That will simply mislead them, and tomorrow they will find us a little tired but still on the field of battle. For God's sake, men, do not wait for them to attack us. If I know one thing about war, it is that when one attacks an enemy forcefully at the start, they are more easily overcome and degraded. And whoever slacks off under these conditions, God will not reward with the honor of glory.[59]

If those were not the marshal's exact words, Valenciennes did capture Villehardouin's esprit as commander before the battle.[60] The six companies, each of twenty to twenty-five knights, were drawn up in echelon for the attack. Emperor Henry remained in the rear with fifty knights in reserve. It has been estimated that the French forces consisted of about 1,300 mounted troops and about 3,900 infantry and archers, for a total of about 5,200 combatants facing King Boril of Bulgaria's smaller forces, which lacked sufficient cavalry to attack the French in the field.[61] With Villehardouin and Milo Breban leading the attack from the wings, the French secured a decisive victory on 31 July. Shortly after the battle they returned to Pamphilon, where Emperor Henry dictated a letter to his chancellor Walter of Courtrai

---

58. Valenciennes, *Histoire*, §§528–30.

59. Valenciennes, *Histoire*, §§534–35. The first paragraph is translated in Chrissis, *Crusading in Frankish Greece*, 38.

60. Longnon, "Le chroniqueur Henri de Valenciennes," 147–49, notes Valenciennes's ability to portray the characters of the main actors in his drama.

61. Verbruggen, *The Art of Warfare*, 210, sketches the order of battle. Stoyanov, "The Size of Bulgaria's Medieval Field Armies," 739–40, estimates the size of the respective forces.

for the pope, explaining the significance of the victory—he called it a miracle—for the subjugation of the Roman *imperium* and for the future of Latin Christendom in the East.[62]

Since Pamphilon, a critical crossroads city, was in ruins, Henry left Villehardouin in charge of rebuilding it. According to Valenciennes, the marshal spared no expense in hiring masons to repair the walls, and after completing that task he returned to Constantinople for the winter.[63] Thereafter he remained in the capital while Henry traveled with Milo Breban to Thessalonika to obtain the homages of the rebelling barons. That is Valenciennes's last mention of the marshal. The rest of his *Histoire* is devoted to the Lombard War in Thessalonika and the negotiations with Michael of Epirus, two events in which Conon of Béthune and Peter of Douai played important roles.

In the autumn of 1209, after two years as a military commander for Emperor Henry, Peter of Douai returned home to resume his position as bailiff of Douai. Like Valenciennes, he had arrived in Constantinople after the conquest to find a shattered city occupied by a Frankish garrison and a Flemish emperor facing unceasing military threats in the countryside. They had witnessed firsthand the excruciating task of pacifying the lands beyond the capital, Valenciennes as a close observer and Douai as a battlefield commander and diplomatic envoy. It is highly likely that Douai left Constantinople with a copy of Villehardouin's memoirs and Valenciennes's history, which together provided a detailed narrative of the deeds of the brother-counts of Flanders since their departure from Flanders in the spring of 1202.[64] During the intervening seven years, the king of France had seriously weakened the independence of Flanders, and in September 1208 Baldwin's young daughters, heirs of the county, were placed in the king's custody.[65] A home audience would have been eager to hear "news" of their counts from a distant theater of war.[66] Villehardouin's memoirs and Valenciennes's history together provided detailed narratives from

---

62. *Register*, 11:333–34, no. 202 (207), September 1208, from Pamphilon. Valenciennes echoed that sentiment in calling the victory a miracle both for the expansion of the (Latin) empire and for the glorification of the Church of Rome (Valenciennes, *Histoire*, §544).

63. Valenciennes, *Histoire*, §§550, 554.

64. As Longnon, *Les compagnons de Villehardouin*, 183, suggests, it is the most likely explanation for the transfer of the texts to Flanders.

65. For a brief narrative of events in Flanders in the aftermath of the crusade, see Wolff, "Baldwin of Flanders and Hainaut," 288–94.

66. Longnon, "Sur l'histoire de l'empereur Henri," 210.

148   CHAPTER 7

the perspective of the commanders; written in vibrant vernacular prose and sprinkled with dramatic speeches, they offered an altogether gripping account of events in the East.

It is not known whether Villehardouin remained in Constantinople after he supervised the rebuilding of Pamphilon. He was about sixty and most likely retired from active military service, perhaps to rebuild Makri, Trajanopolis, or even Mosynopolis, as he did Pamphilon. There is no evidence that he visited his nephew Geoffroy, who as regent and then as prince of Achaia was in the process of establishing a principality in the Peloponnese, but it is highly likely, given the constant flow of news to Constantinople, that he was well informed of his nephew's exploits and must have felt some satisfaction that Henry appointed young Geoffroy seneschal of Romania in 1209.[67]

On 2 May 1210 Villehardouin appeared with Valenciennes at the second *parlement* of Ravennika, where in the presence of many bishops and barons, the "marshal of the entire empire of Romania," and "Henry [of Valenciennes], canon of the church of Hagia Sophia of Constantinople," witnessed as the patriarch of Constantinople confirmed the "resignation" by the barons of Thessalonika, who agreed to return all the churches, monasteries, and ecclesiastical property and revenues they had expropriated, and further to exempt the church from all taxes except the *akrostikon*, the Byzantine land tax owed by churchmen as well as laymen.[68] The resignation applied to all lands west of Villehardouin's port town of Makri, which marked the border between the emperor's lands and the kingdom of Thessalonika. It did not apply to the principality of Achaia, where Prince Geoffroy was in the process of distributing confiscated church lands as fiefs. It is entirely possible that at this point Villehardouin traveled from Ravennika to Corinth or perhaps as far as Andravida beyond Patras to meet his nephew, although there is no record of such a visit.

---

67. Henry of Valenciennes, *Histoire*, §670, reports that at the first *parlement* of Ravennika, the marshal's nephew became "a man" (*homo*) of the emperor and was appointed seneschal of the empire "in augmentation" of his fief.

68. Valenciennes, *Histoire*, §669. Innocent III's letter announcing the "resignation" at the second *parlement* of Ravennika is preserved in Honorius III's letter of 19 January 1219 (*Bullarium Hellenicum*, 255–64, no. 87). The editors (263n3) question whether "Henry *magister*" was Henry of Valenciennes, noting that the text should read "Henry, *magister* Boniface, canons of Hagia Sophia." The context of the event, however, does suggest that the emperor sent two high officers, Villehardouin and Valenciennes, to witness on his behalf.

MARSHAL OF EMPEROR HENRY   149

We lose sight of Marshal Geoffroy for the next two and a half years while Emperor Henry was in the field combating Bulgarians and Greeks. In all likelihood he remained in Constantinople, where he had lived since May 1204, for there is no evidence that he returned home or retired to Makri and Trajanopolis. On 11 December 1212 he appeared at Halmyros, where he witnessed the resolution of a dispute between the Hospitallers and the bishop of Gardiki. The bishop had complained to the pope that the Hospitallers had seized and refused to relinquish the castle of Gardiki and several villages (*casali*). [69] In the presence of many barons and churchmen, the archbishops of Thessalonika and Philippi settled the dispute; Conon of Béthune, Geoffroy of Villehardouin, and Milo Breban sealed the document of record.[70] That is the last mention of Geoffroy of Villehardouin. He would have been about sixty-five.

It is not known when or where Villehardouin died, or where he was buried.[71] He might have lived to hear that his son Erard served as a knight banneret in Philip II's forces at the battle of Bouvines on 27 July 1214.[72] News of the marshal's death may have reached Champagne in that same year, when his brother Jean, then about seventy years old, and his wife Celine took the cross, most likely in preparation for a journey to visit their son Geoffroy, prince of Achaia.[73] Jean was in Corinth in 1216, when he and Prince Geoffroy and his wife Elizabeth

---

69. The bishop first complained to Innocent on 15 July 1210 (*Register*, 13:187–88, no. 112 [114]). The pope initially delegated the archbishops of Athens and Thebes to resolve the matter, with the power to excommunicate if necessary, but because of the Hospitallers' "contumacy," he appointed Cardinal Benedict to adjudicate the matter (*Register*, 13:195–96, no. 118 [120], 14 August 1210).

70. *PL*, 216:910–13, no. 115, 27 September 1213 (= Delaville Le Roulx, *Cartulaire général*, 3:157–59, no. 1413), letter of Innocent III to the bishop and chapter of Gardiki: it quotes the letter of the archbishop of Philippi, dated 11 December 1212 at Halmyros, reporting the mediated settlement to the pope. On his way to Halmyros, Villehardouin might well have passed through Kalamata, located midway between Gardiki and Halmyros.

71. Longnon, *Recherches*, 104–10, concluded that Villehardouin died sometime between 1212 and 1218, but the fact that Honorius III's letter of 21 April 1217 does not include his name among the high officers of the empire suggests that he died before 1217 and perhaps as early as 1213, when his son Erard appeared as *dominus* of Villehardouin (Longnon, *Recherches*, 212–13, no. 104, January 1213).

72. Longnon, *Documents*, 1:437 (list of Champenois knights bearing banners): *Erardus de Villi*. Longnon (*Documents*, 1:xli) dates the list to 1214 and links it to the battle of Bouvines. Arbois de Jubainville, *Histoire*, 4:132–33, and Longnon, *Recherches*, 125, accept that date. The re-edition of that list (Baldwin et al., *Les registres de Philippe Auguste*, 1:308) dates it to 1204–7/8, but in reference to Erard of Villy's life, 1214 seems the more likely date.

73. Jean and Celine took the cross in 1214 (Longnon, *Recherches*, 215, no. 108), but in February 1215 Jean delegated the master of the Hôtel-Dieu of Chêne to collect the revenues in

150   CHAPTER 7

sealed a grant for Clairvaux.[74] There was no mention of the marshal. Nor did Pope Honorius III mention the marshal in his letter of 1217 addressed to the highest officials of the empire—the butler Milo Breban, the regent Conon of Béthune, the prince (Geoffroy) of Achaia, the seneschal of Thessalonika, and the patriarch of Constantinople.[75]

The marshal had died before March 1218, when Erard, "lord of Villehardouin" and son of "Geoffroy of Villehardouin, marshal of Champagne," renewed his father's grants to Notre-Dame of Foissy for Erard's sister Dameron and aunt Haye; the nuns would celebrate annual Masses for Erard's father and mother, and for himself and his wife Mabile.[76] In June Erard renewed his father's similar grants to Notre-Dame-aux-Nonnains for his sister Alice (his aunt Emeline apparently had died).[77] The next year, in May 1219, Erard established annual anniversaries for his parents and younger brother Geoffroy at the hospital at Chêne and at Larrivour, the Cistercian monastery near Villehardouin that became a kind of "family monastery" for the burial of Erard's descendants.[78] Those anniversaries are the only remembrances of Geoffroy of Villehardouin in Champagne.

In 1223 Erard of Villehardouin succeeded his cousin Oudard of Aulnay as marshal of Champagne, but he was the last of his father's line to carry the Villehardouin name in Champagne; he came to be known as Erard of Villy (later Villy-le-Maréchal) from the name of the fief that his

---

all his lands until he returned, suggesting that Celine died before he left (Longnon, *Recherches*, 217, no. 111).

74. AD Aube, 3 H 726, 1216, original charter with their seals = Mayer, *Die Kanzlei*, 2:921–22, no. 19. A photo of the charter and its three seals is in Baudin, Brunel, and Dohrmann, *The Knights Templar*, 234–35, no 16. Prince Geoffroy, with the consent of his wife Elizabeth and his eldest son Geoffroy (II, the future prince), gave the village of Harcourt in Champagne to Clairvaux.

75. *Bullarium Hellenicum*, 159–61, no. 20, 21 April 1217. Conon died at about seventy on 17 December 1219; see Longnon, *Les compagnons de Villehardouin*, 146–49, and Conon de Béthune, *Les chansons*, iii–vii. Milo Breban died in his mid-seventies in 1224; Verdier, *L'aristocratie de Provins*, 195–208, discusses the succession to his estate in Champagne. For Milo's possessions in Constantinople, see *Bullarium Hellenicum*, 518–20, nos. 241–42, 16 November 1224.

76. AD Aube 23H3 = Longnon, *Recherches*, 227, no. 128, March 1218 (old style). Longnon dated this hitherto unpublished document to March 1219 (new style), but in view of Erard's similar letter of June 1218, I have retained 1218.

77. *Notre-Dame-aux-Nonnains*, 92, no. 138, June 1218: three tithes for Alice's lifetime enjoyment. For a biography of Erard of Lézinnes/Villy/Villehardouin, see Longnon, *Recherches*, 124–30.

78. Longnon, *Recherches*, 228, no. 130, May 1219, for Chêne. AD Aube, 4H55 = Longnon, *Recherches*, 228, no. 129, May 1219, for Larrivour. Baudin, "Larrivour," 465, notes that their gifts to Larrivour and burials there made it effectively a "family monastery" for the rest of the century.

father Geoffroy had received from Count Henry I in the 1170s.[79] In 1231 Erard's son William of Villy succeeded him as marshal of Champagne.[80] Thereafter the Villehardouin name resonated only in the Peloponnese, where Prince Geoffroy and his sons ruled as princes of Achaia.

---

79. Erard adopted the Villy name in 1213 (Roserot, *Dictionnaire*, 3:1847). In May 1219 he exchanged all his revenues at Villemaur (from his mother's inheritance) for Countess Blanche's property at Villy, which became his primary property (*Cartulary of Countess Blanche*, 132–33, no. 119). In 1222 Erard of Chacenay identified him as Erard of Villy (*Cartulary of Countess Blanche*, 136–37, no. 124). See also Longnon, *Recherches*, 124–30.

80. Longnon, *Les compagnons de Villehardouin*, 54–55.

CHAPTER 8

The Marshal and His Scribe

If the memoirs can be reasonably dated to the eight months Villehardouin spent in Constantinople during the winter and spring of 1207–8, neither the scribe (or scribes) nor the conditions under which they were recorded are known, though it seems likely that he would have dictated to a cleric from Champagne who spoke his dialect. The marshal was familiar with the process of recording proceedings at court. Shortly after he became marshal, for example, he witnessed Countess Marie confirm the resolution of a property dispute involving the leper house in Troyes. A court notary, using shorthand or rapid writing (tachygraphy), transcribed the proceeding on a temporary surface, perhaps a wax tablet or pieces of parchment; from that transcription (*reportatio*) a chancery scribe made a fair copy on parchment for sealing and presentation.[1] The formal document contained the scribe's name (*nota Willermi*) to warrant the accuracy of what he had heard (in the vernacular) and transcribed (into Latin), with the names of those who witnessed, in this case including Andreas Capellanus and Milo Breban as well as the marshal.[2]

---

1. Parkes, "Tachygraphy in the Middle Ages," 27–32. For a modern test of the accuracy of listening to one language while simultaneously writing another, see Weijers, "Note sur une expérience de *reportatio*."

2. "Léproserie," 531, 1185, document prepared by the notary William (1181–87).

THE MARSHAL AND HIS SCRIBE   153

Although an initial court transcription does not survive in Champagne, a rare example of both a *reportatio* and its fair copy survives from a papal inquest of circa 1220. Erard of Brienne, a minor local baron, was deposed by a papal legate to explain why he had unleashed a war against Countess Blanche, regent of Champagne. A scribe first transcribed Erard's vernacular testimony into Latin, both verbatim and as the scribe reported it in the third person, on three pieces of parchment, then copied it word for word in a formal document as a dossier for the pope's consideration.[3] Villehardouin's scribe employed that same two-step process, first recording his dictation on a temporary surface, then making a fair copy on parchment; but unlike in court and inquest records, the scribe recorded the marshal's words directly in the vernacular. That decision, not to translate into Latin, is in itself a unique feature of the memoirs, which clearly were not intended as a chronicle or official record but as a highly personal account of the marshal's experiences, a testament in fact, to be read aloud to a lay audience at a time when vernacular texts, notably romances and translations from Latin, were becoming increasingly common. Villehardouin might even have heard Evrat, a canon in the comital chapel, read his fresh translations of Genesis to Countess Marie.[4]

Geoffroy of Villehardouin as Author

The marshal was an accomplished public speaker and understood the force of the spoken word as he addressed a distant audience in Champagne after a five-year absence overseas. His scribe, like the scribe of Erard of Brienne's deposition, quotes him at the very beginning as the author (*je*), who describes Fulk of Neuilly "of whom I speak" (dont je vos di). And the papal indulgence, "about which I will tell you" (tel con je vos dirai), was so generous that many took the cross because of it.[5] In a

---

3. AN, J 1024, no. 79, fragment of a roll of three pieces of parchment of different sizes and written in different hands (*Layettes*, 5:84, no. 248, of 1219/20), copied word for word in the legate's official report (AN, J 194, no. 64 = *Layettes*, 1:526–28, no. 1474). The scribe quoted Erard verbatim, reported his account of events in the third person, and extracted the contents of Countess Blanche's letter promising to petition the pope for Erard's release from excommunication.

4. The modern editor of Evrat's *Genèse* suggests that Erard read his translations of Genesis to Marie as he finished them in the 1190s; see Evergates, *Marie of France*, 85–87.

5. Villehardouin, *La conquête*, §§1–2. Villehardouin refers to himself as *je* eight times in manuscript O (Naïs, *Index complet*, 189–90): he does not know the names of those who took the cross (§§1, 2, 10); he quotes his advice to the barons at Soissons (§41); he names those in

154 **CHAPTER 8**

number of instances the authorial *je* is either implicit or omitted by his scribe or by later copyists, as in "[I] do not know by whose advice" ([je] ne sai per cui conseil) Baldwin occupied Thessalonika, for which Boniface had done homage, and "[I] do not know who [(Je) ne sai quex genz] maliciously set fire to the city [in August 1203] with flames so intense that no one could extinguish it."[6] In a few cases the appearance of *je* depends on the manuscript tradition, appearing in some copies, absent in others.[7]

The marshal also addresses his audience directly. His very first word is *sachiez*, "know (that)" or "you should know (that)," which he repeats sixty times in the course of his dictation, primarily to introduce an important event, to assert his veracity, or to criticize a decision.[8] Of Odo of Burgundy, who declined the offer to replace Thibaut after the count's death, "You should know that he could have done better" (Sachiez que il peust bien mielx faire). And of those who kept looted property after the conquest, "you should know" that justice was done and many were hanged. Villehardouin's "we" (*nos*) also functioned as an implicit *je*, as translators are aware, as in "we do not know the names" (nos ne savonz pas les nons) of the Burgundians who took the cross at Cîteaux. In each case, whether explicit or implicit, Villehardouin is quoted by his scribe as if speaking to a listening audience.[9]

More problematic are the cases where Villehardouin appears to refer to himself in the third person. "When Geoffroy, the marshal of Champagne, crossed the Mont Cenis pass, <u>he</u> met Count Walter of Brienne . . . and when <u>he</u> told them the news of what had been accomplished [in Venice], they told <u>him</u> that they would be there."[10] Is the scribe quoting the marshal verbatim, with Villehardouin referring to himself in the third person, as is generally interpreted? Or, as I think more plausible, is

---

Corfu who dissented with the decision to proceed to Constantinople (§114, twice); he quotes his response to Emperor Isaac (§187); and he orders the retreat from Adrianople (§372). Thirty-six other times he uses *je* in quoting speeches by Alexios (10 times), Boniface (9), the doge (7), the abbot of Vaux (3), the marshal's nephew Geoffroy (2), a sailor (2), Philip of Germany (1), a Greek lord (1), and Count Louis (1).

6. Villehardouin, *La conquête*, §§277, 203. Bull, *Eyewitness and Crusade Narrative*, 268–69, lists the instances in which Villehardouin claims not to know.

7. When Villehardouin states that he does not remember all that the doge said in Saint Mark's (*La conquête*, §30), manuscripts C and D have "ne vos puis je tout raconter," while A and O have "ne vos puis tout raconteur," and B has "ne vous puis toutes ranconter."

8. Beer, *Narrative Conventions of Truth*, 35–46. Naïs, *Index complet*, 336–37, lists sixty-one instances of *sachiez* in manuscript O, while *Index general*, 159, lists forty-nine in manuscript B and fifty-five in manuscript D.

9. Villehardouin, *La conquête*, §§39, 255, 45.

10. Villehardouin, *La conquête*, §§33–34.

THE MARSHAL AND HIS SCRIBE   155

the scribe reporting the marshal's words in the third person? Villehardouin would have said, of his return from Venice, "When I crossed the Mont Cenis pass, I met Count Walter of Brienne . . . and when I told him the news of what had been accomplished in Venice, he told me that they would be there." And when the text has "Geoffroy the marshal rode day after day until he arrived at Troyes in Champagne and found his lord, Count Thibaut, ill and exhausted but cheered by his arrival," Villehardouin more likely would have said, "I rode day after day until I arrived in Troyes and found my lord Count Thibaut ill and exhausted but cheered by my arrival."[11] Although the manuscript editors and translators after them have read similar statements as if the marshal were speaking of himself in the third person, the fifty-nine instances in which "Geoffroy the marshal" appears to recount his own acts are best read as the scribe's restatement of Villehardouin's words. Forty-two (71 percent) of those passages relate to the post-conquest period in which Villehardouin describes his own acts as military commander.[12]

On occasion the scribe enters the text to vouch for the accuracy of Villehardouin's hyperbolic statements. In reporting how the Venetian sailors saved their ships from the burning Greek ships launched against them, the scribe observed that "Geoffroy the marshal of Champagne, who dictated this work [qui ceste ovre dita], faithfully attests [bien tesmoigne] that no sailors ever defended themselves better." In like manner, "Geoffroy of Villehardouin, marshal of Champagne, faithfully attests [et bien tesmoigne] that, as far as he knows it to be true, never since the beginning of time was there so much booty in a city."[13] The scribe, much like a court notary, affirms the accuracy of his recording. Thus the text of the memoirs is a subtle blend of the marshal's own words recorded verbatim, his testimony recorded by the scribe in the third person, and the scribe's validation of Villehardouin's testimony.

The Elements of Narrative

Close readers of the memoirs are aware of their composite nature. In addition to the marshal's own observations and speeches, and his recall

---

11. Villehardouin, La conquête, §35.

12. Appendix 2, table 4. Beer, In Their Own Words, 40–41, makes a similar calculation from fifty-one references: forty (78 percent) occur between May 1204 (Villehardouin, La conquête, §268) and September 1207 (§496).

13. Villehardouin, La conquête, §§174, 218, 250.

156   **CHAPTER 8**

(or reconstruction) of the speeches of others, they include a variety of eyewitness reports, "news," rumors, and written records, as well as information contained in "the Book." From those diverse sources, essentially "texts" in themselves, he weaves a narrative of events related in some way to his own experiences.[14]

Time and Place

As if to preface his memoirs with appropriate gravity, Villehardouin begins with a date: "Know that 1198 years after the Incarnation of our lord Jesus Christ," Fulk of Neuilly began to preach the word of God in the Ile-de-France and neighboring lands.[15] After dating the tournament at Écry to "the year after Fulk's preaching," he locates six pivotal events by year: the sailing from Venice (1202), the fleet's departure from Corfu (1203), the coronation of Baldwin (1204), the battle of Adrianople (1205), the coronation of Henry (1206), and finally the death of Boniface of Montferrat at Mosynopolis (1207). To retain the attention of his audience while drawing them into a narrative ever shifting in time and place, he addresses them directly ("know that"), announces events to come ("as you will hear"), notes concurrent events ("at about the same time"), and reminds them of what he has already reported ("as you have heard").[16] He dates most events by the religious calendar—Lent, Ash Wednesday, Easter, Pentecost, the feast days of Saint John and Saint Michael, Holy Cross, All Saints, and Advent—which if not absolute chronological markers had the merit of being familiar to his listeners. When he does not remember an exact date, he recalls its relative chronology: the barons met in Compiègne in the spring of 1200 "less than two months after" their initial meeting in Soissons; the doge

---

14. Poirion, "Les paragraphes et le pré-texte," 53–54, views Villehardouin's narrative as consisting of preexisting materials, what he calls "pré-textes," including written records as well as eyewitness accounts and other oral reports. Jacquin, "Geoffroy de Villehardouin," 122, concurs in calling Villehardouin's direct speeches "veritable documents" embedded in the narrative. Andrea, "Essay on Primary Sources," 299–302, briefly assesses Villehardouin's sources.

15. Villehardouin dates Fulk's preaching to 1197, but as Faral notes (Villehardouin, *La conquête*, 1:30n2), the date should be 1198 (new style), that is, between the beginning of Innocent's pontificate (8 January 1198) and Easter (29 March 1198).

16. Bull, *Eyewitness and Crusade Narrative*, 272–73, captures the dynamic between speaker and audience in suggesting that *sachiez* was a narrative technique to slow the relentless flow of information, and to introduce the narrator's emphasis or guidance in understanding the events narrated.

THE MARSHAL AND HIS SCRIBE

promised to respond to the envoys' request in four days, and they in turn promised to reply in eight days.[17]

Within those chronological markers he grounds his narrative in a sequence of places. In the first half of the memoirs, devoted to the four years and five months between the cross-taking at Écry and Baldwin's coronation (§§1–263), he recalls events within a lineal succession of places at which he was present: Soissons, Compiègne, Venice, Troyes, Cîteaux, Venice, Pavia, Piacenza, Zara, Corfu, Negroponte, Andros, Chalcedon, Scutari, and finally Constantinople. Each site occasioned speeches, council meetings, or a *parlement*. He speaks of *parlement* twenty times, usually to denote a general assembly convened by the barons to obtain the army's consent to a course of action, often planned by the commanders in the face of opposition in the ranks to a continuing and uncertain campaign.[18] On Corfu a *parlement* of the army compelled the commanders to abase themselves and "swear on scripture in good faith" to transport them to Syria.[19] When the newly installed Alexios IV asked for an extension of the army's presence in Constantinople, the barons replied that "they could not do that without the consent of the army."[20]

He speaks of "council" (*conseil, conseils, consels*) more than one hundred times to describe meetings of varied composition.[21] A small council, essentially the "leadership team," consisted of the senior commanders—the counts, the doge, and a few others, notably the marshal, who claimed to have been "present" at all the meetings. A larger meeting of up to fifty persons included the tactical commanders (the "barons"), who were the key link between decision-making and its implementation. In Villehardouin's telling, speeches at councils and *parlements* set powerful visual scenes in places that served as linchpins of his narrative.[22] Those scenes also reveal the fundamental nature of the crusader

---

17. Villehardouin, *La conquête*, §§11, 17, 19.

18. In manuscript O, *parlement* appears twenty times, of which eighteen (90 percent) are before May 1204 (Naïs, *Index complet*, 281). Manuscript D lists *parlement* nineteen times (Naïs, *Index général*, 214).

19. Villehardouin, *La conquête*, §§115–17.

20. Villehardouin, *La conquête*, §196.

21. In manuscript O, *conseil* appears eighty-two times, *conseils* ten times, and *consels* sixteen times, for a total of 108 times (Naïs, *Index complet*, 81–82). *Conseil* and its related terms appear 119 times in manuscript B and 113 times in manuscript D (Naïs, *Index général*, 61–62). Riley-Smith, "Toward an Understanding of the Fourth Crusade," 84–86, classifies the three types of council.

22. Poirion, "Les paragraphes et le pré-texte," 53–54, explores the role of Villehardouin's visual memory in framing scenes of speeches as chronological markers of the expedition. Jacquin, *Le style historique*, 416–34, analyzes the role of direct discourse and its mise-en-scène

158   **CHAPTER 8**

army: it consisted of volunteers who had to be persuaded to follow the commanders.

The time-place continuum shifts in the second half of the memoirs, which deals with the post-conquest period and the marshal's recent experiences under emperors Baldwin and Henry (§§264–500). The linear view of events is displaced by a concentric view from Constantinople where Villehardouin, residing as garrison commander, interweaves simultaneous events beyond the city into his master narrative. No longer does he mention public speeches of persuasion or collegial decision-making by peers in council; those were supplanted by orders from the emperor, who consulted a small council of advisers.[23] The narrative now moves from walled city to walled city, almost randomly in response to external military threats: Thessalonika, Didymoteichon, Adrianople, Philippopolis, Rodosto, Rhousion, Stenimakos, Kibotos, Cyzicus, Ipsala, Mosynopolis. These were sites of military encounters that Villehardouin identifies by the size of their garrisons, the names of their commanders, and the number of days distant from the capital.[24] His challenge was to incorporate distant, concurrent events that he had not witnessed within his narrative line. "While" (*endementiers que*) Baldwin marched to Thessalonika, Boniface rode to Adrianople; Mourtzouphlos was captured "about the same time" (*en cel termine*) that fiefs were granted in Constantinople; Hugh of Saint-Pol died in Constantinople "about the same time" that the Greek cities were swearing allegiance to Kalojan.[25] It is that simultaneity of events that gives Villehardouin's post-conquest narrative its kinetic force.

---

in the memoirs. Jacquin offers the most extensive analysis of the memoirs as a written text, with pointed comparisons to Clari and Ernoul-Bernard.

23. Schon, *Studien zum Stil*, 190, calculates the declining frequency of direct discourse in the memoirs, from 19.5 percent (§§1–100) to 1.5 percent (§§401–500), for an average of 9 percent for the entire text, compared to about 50 percent for epics. Villehardouin mentions a *parlement* only twice after Baldwin's coronation, in both cases understood as private conversations among the senior commanders: in Constantinople when Baldwin and Boniface renewed the *convenance* they had reached after the election (Villehardouin, *La conquête*, §299), and at Ipsala where the two agreed to meet later to fight Kalojan (§497).

24. Appendix 2, tables 1–3.

25. Villehardouin, *La conquête*, §§281, 306, 334. Poirion, "Les paragraphes et le pré-texte," 46–48, gives examples of Villehardouin's relating of events that occurred after (*lors*), at the same time (*en cel termine*) or as a consequence of (*ensi*) another event. Jacquin, *Le style historique*, 71–73, provides additional examples.

Speeches

Speeches are a critical armature of Villehardouin's narrative, serving as mileposts, turning points, or simply dramatic moments at a time when "words ruled men."[26] He especially valued the well-crafted speech, the high art of persuasion, and begins with Fulk of Neuilly, whose forceful preaching—and miracles—were so well known, he says, that the pope enlisted him in recruiting crusaders. He quotes with evident satisfaction his own public speeches to the Venetians in Saint Mark's, to the barons in Soissons advocating for Boniface of Montferrat, and to Emperor Isaac II in Constantinople, persuading him to honor his son's treaty with the crusaders—all three scenes restaged in memory as performances.[27] But after the inauguration of Baldwin, he becomes a discreet staff officer, quoting only his private speeches: to the doge recommending an organized retreat from Adrianople, and to a newly arrived company of knights asking them to take up the rear of the retreating army.[28]

He quotes speeches of the doge, of the abbot of Vaux, and especially of Conon of Béthune, who was chosen to deliver hard words to the emperor's messenger at Scutari and later to the newly installed Emperor Alexios IV in the imperial palace. He also quotes letters read aloud as de facto speeches, the most notable being Emperor Alexios III's letter to the commanders on the fleet's arrival at Constantinople.[29] Those were public scenes at pivotal moments in the narrative. Whether the texts as we have them record the actual or reasonable approximations of spoken words, or are "literary representations" of oral speech, they nonetheless capture the essence of the spoken message and its reception.[30]

Villehardouin also recounts several dramatic scenes of "collective speech."[31] A faction of the army, resisting the extension of their compulsory service after Alexios IV's coronation, shouted: "Give us the ships you [the barons] swore to provide, because we want to go to Syria." When a *parlement* of the entire army could not agree as to whether Boniface

---

26. Poirion, "Les paragraphes et le pré-texte," 57. For the importance of direct speech in the memoirs, see Frappier, "Les discours dans la chronique de Villehardouin," 65n35, which lists nineteen instances of direct speech.

27. Villehardouin, *La conquête*, §§9, 41, 187.

28. Villehardouin, *La conquête*, §§364, 372.

29. Villehardouin, *La conquête*, §§65, 82–83, 213–16, 141–44.

30. For the importance of direct discourse even if written as "a literary representation of the oral," see Rodríguez Somolinos, "Variation et changement," 276–81.

31. For collective speech ("discours collectifs"), see Frappier, "Les discours dans la chronique de Villehardouin," 66–69, and his list (68n48) of sixteen examples (to which §372 should be added).

160   **CHAPTER 8**

or Baldwin should be emperor, the leading barons (the *prodomes* of the army), meeting in private, said: "Lords, if we select one of these two 'high men' [*halz hommes*], the other will be so disaffected that he will leave with all his men and the conquest will be for naught. Let us find a way to keep them both."[32] And the Greeks in Adrianople refused to open their gates to Kalojan in a defiant speech to the effect that they no longer trusted him after he had devastated their cities in Thrace.[33] Those unattributed speeches representing the collective view of the army, the barons (perhaps even the marshal himself) in council, and the residents of Adrianople reveal the deep undercurrents within the primary narrative line.

It has been claimed that Villehardouin's narrative was touched by epic style and romances.[34] Yet the speeches he quotes are not the speeches of epic.[35] They are reasonable representations of speeches that he had heard or were reported to him. They deal largely with the conduct of the crusade and the post-conquest settlement; they are not battlefield orations. Although he lived in the company of several poet-combatants, he neither mentions their works nor identifies them as poets, which is notable in someone so attuned to the art of speaking.[36] He praises Conon of Béthune, one of his closest companions, as a diplomatic emissary and battlefield commander, not for his excellence as a lyric poet but for his speech-making. He mentions Hugh of Berzé and his son Hugh (the poet) only at Cîteaux, where they took the cross with the Burgundians, and Guy, castellan of Coucy, only when he took the cross, was among those at Zara who opposed the diversion to Constantinople, and died at sea.[37] He fails even to mention Boniface's closest companion, the poet Raimbaut of Vaqueiras, whom he surely had met in Adrianople during

32. Villehardouin, *La conquête*, §§225, 196–98, 256–57.

33. Villehardouin, *La conquête*, §425.

34. Beer's *Villehardouin* (1968) has had an enormous influence on recent commentators in viewing the memoirs in terms of epic language, style, and structure. *In Their Own Words* extends her reading to conclude that Villehardouin's quotations of speech and his silences reflect a "personal conception of the Fourth Crusade as an epic *manqué*" (56). Dufournet, "La bataille d'Adrianople," similarly sees epic features in Villehardouin's account of the battle.

35. Marnette, "Narrateur et point de vue," shows how the narrative of an author-combatant focusing on witnessed events differs fundamentally from epic narrative, which features speech and direct discourse. Marnette effectively dismisses any attempt to ascribe epic influences to Villehardouin's memoirs. Noble reaches the same conclusion through an analysis of Villehardouin's terse descriptions of the crusade commanders and the absence of an "epic style combatant" ("Epic Heroes" and "1204," 103).

36. Grossel, *Le milieu littéraire en Champagne*, 1:162, finds no evidence that Villehardouin was touched by the lyrics of his poet-companions.

37. Villehardouin, *La conquête*, §§213, 45, 124.

THE MARSHAL AND HIS SCRIBE   161

his mediation between Boniface and Baldwin, and who addressed the marshal in one of his poems. Nor does he allude to any scene or character from an epic, romance, or even biblical text. He does praise several companions for their valor, and he remembers the deceased, but it can fairly be said that, for the marshal, the crusade was without epic heroes. His language is better seen as a reflection of the military culture in which he lived.

Eyewitness Reports

Villehardouin's narrative is driven primarily by what he personally experienced, witnessed, or heard from trusted sources. His recall of events, locating them by time and place, suggests an excellent visual memory, as one would expect from a senior military officer.[38] On occasion he may have misremembered or confounded events, but save evidence to the contrary, his recollections are sober and credible. His account of the battle of Adrianople, based on what he himself did and what he heard from others at the front line, is a gripping battlefield scene: soldiers fleeing from the collapsed front line informed him of the conditions at the front and of Baldwin's valorous conduct, which the marshal acted on because it was reported by "those who were there" (bien tesmoignent cil qui la furent).[39] He learned about Boniface's difficult siege of Nauplion and Corinth by "those who were there" (li portent tesmoig cil qui la furent).[40] In retelling events conveyed by credible witnesses, by "those who were there," he was practicing what Philip of Beaumanoir, bailiff of Beauvais, explained in his treatise on the customs of the Beauvaisis (circa 1280): "A person who wants to say: 'I know it for certain,' cannot say so unless he says: 'I was present and saw it.' And thus you can testify to knowing for certain what you are testifying."[41]

---

38. Poirion, "Les paragraphes et le pré-texte," 45, argues that the paragraph divisions and modern punctuation introduced by Natalis de Wailly in 1874, and retained ever since, distort the inherent structure of Villehardouin's narrative, which is composed of coherent visual scenes.

39. Villehardouin, La conquête, §360.

40. Villehardouin, La conquête, §332.

41. "Qui veut dire: 'Je le sais de certain,' il ne puet dir s'il ne dit: 'J'i fui presens et le vi.' Et ainsi puet on tesmoignier de savoir ce qu'on tesmoigne certainement" (Beaumanoir, Coutumes de Beauvaisis, 2:138–39 [Beaumanoir, The "Coutumes," 447–48], §1234).

162   **CHAPTER 8**

It is important to remember that Villehardouin spent at least six months in Constantinople, from September or October through March or April every year between 1203 and 1207. He received a constant stream of "news" (*noveles*) brought to the capital by travelers, survivors, envoys, and by official couriers, who must have been far more numerous than can be detected today and who account for how well-informed he was about troop movements and events beyond the capital.[42] Most news traveled by road, the lifeline connecting the capital to its hinterland, but it also traveled by sea. When the defeated army arrived in Rodosto from Adrianople, they sent "trustworthy couriers" (*bons messages*) by sea, which was faster than the three days required for travel by road, to report that they were safe and would return soon.[43] Against those credible reports, Villehardouin contrasts what was spread by rumor (*oï dire*). When he heard (*il en oï*) that a knight named Anselm of Remy was responsible for the defeat of the garrison at Nicomedia commanded by the seneschal Dietrich of Looz, he "did not know whether that was true or false" (ne seut s'il fu tort ou a droit).[44] He accepted, and repeated, eyewitness reports and "news" reported by credible witnesses, but he was skeptical of unverifiable rumors, especially when they pertained to military matters.[45]

Written Records

Eyewitness reports, by the marshal himself or by others, comprise only one source of information in the memoirs.[46] Edmond Faral, editor of the now standard edition of the memoirs, and most modern commentators find Villehardouin's chronology and detailed accounting of events so precise that he must have kept personal notes or "a sort of personal journal."[47] Such a reading rests on two assumptions: that

---

42. *Novels* are mentioned forty-one times in manuscript O (Naïs, *Index complet*, 265), forty-one times in manuscript B, and forty-two times in manuscript D (Naïs, *Index général*, 201).

43. Villehardouin, *La conquête*, §375.

44. Villehardouin, *La conquête*, §484.

45. For a review of how twelfth-century historians writing in Latin assessed oral information, see John, "Historical Truth."

46. After analyzing the narratives of the Second, Third, and Fourth Crusades, Bull, *Eyewitness and Crusade Narrative*, 292, concludes that "on a strict reading of the narrative, the *Conquête* is scarcely to be categorized as an 'eyewitness' text at all."

47. Faral (Villehardouin, *La conquête*), 1:xiii–xvi. Longnon, *L'histoire de la conquête*, 26, and Andrea, "Essay on Primary Sources," 300, both credit the marshal with an exceptional memory but allow that he may have kept a journal or notes. Courroux, *L'Écriture de l'histoire*, 83n4, 281, likewise assumes that Villehardouin kept notes that he later wove into his narrative.

THE MARSHAL AND HIS SCRIBE   163

Villehardouin could write in either Latin or vernacular, and that he kept a current record of his experiences. Neither seems likely. He must have developed a practical literacy honed through years of service as marshal that allowed him to decipher administrative records like the rolls of fiefs and transactional letters patent written in Latin, and he might have possessed as well a "phonetic literacy" in French, by which he sounded out written words one by one.[48] But it is difficult to imagine him making notes or writing a journal while exercising his duties as marshal; writing, after all, was the business of clerics.

Great lords, of course, traveled with clerics who drafted correspondence and transactional documents (charters) en route. Count Baldwin was accompanied on his way to Venice in 1202 by what could be called an "itinerant chancery," which produced his charters at Clairvaux and Cîteaux, drafted his letters patent in Constantinople, and accompanied him to Thessalonika in the summer of 1204.[49] Count Louis, too, traveled with his chancellor and a cleric.[50] But Villehardouin seems not to have had a secretary-cleric with him, either on his diplomatic missions or during his military campaigns. In one memorable scene he describes how he and three other envoys, on meeting Emperor Isaac in the Blachernai in July 1203, requested a private audience; the emperor took his wife, his chancellor, and an interpreter into a side room, where the envoys presented their request. The imperial chancellor drafted and sealed a charter, which Villehardouin took back to the camp. He makes no mention of a cleric accompanying the envoys; his account of that meeting four years earlier appears to have been entirely from memory.[51]

If Villehardouin's testimony was primarily a retrospective oral account, he did have access to documents available in the chancery archive to fact-check his memory. Baldwin's traveling chancery clerics most likely carried the rosters of oath-takers and the contracts with Venice and Alexios, as well as the letters received en route to Constantinople (from the pope, Philip of Swabia, and Emperor Alexios III). The new regime's internal records (the *concordia*, *partitio*, and *pacta*) also were available, as well as letters received from religious and political leaders. Less certain is whether the internal records between commanders were

48. Saenger, "Books of Hours and Reading Habits," 142, defines "phonetic literacy" as the ability to decode written texts "syllable by syllable, and to pronounce them orally."

49. Villehardouin, *La conquête*, §290. See Prevenier, "La chancellerie de l'empire latin," 63, 67.

50. Riley-Smith, "Toward an Understanding of the Fourth Crusade," 82.

51. Villehardouin, *La conquête*, §§185–90.

164   **CHAPTER 8**

preserved, although dispositive letters, like Boniface's letter sent by courier to Villehardouin in Didymoteichon, announcing that he had arrived in Thessalonika, may well have been deposited in the chancery.[52] All those records appear to have been destroyed, perhaps systematically, in 1261 in order to expunge all trace of the Latin regime after the Byzantine restoration.

"The Book"

Villehardouin cites a "Book" (*li livres*) eighteen times, referring to what it does or does not contain.[53] Editors, and translators after them, have taken those references to mean the marshal's own book-in-the-making, with English translators since Marzials (1907) rendering *li livres* as *"this* book." But Villehardouin never claims authorship of "the Book." His scribe specifically identifies his narrative as his "work" (*ouvre*), as in "he who composed this work." That understanding of "work" as a composition rather than a physical entity accords with earlier usage by vernacular writers.[54] "The Book" (*li livres*) is better understood here as an existing physical volume, an official record compiled from various documents preserved in the chancery. Villehardouin cites it primarily for details he does not know and for lists of names—of those who took the cross, who died in battle, and who deserted the main army.[55] "The Book does not name many of the high men" (li livres ne fait mention) who took the cross with counts Thibaut and Louis. It "is silent" (se taist) about the names of many barons who took the cross with the bishop of Soissons, and it "does not speak" (ne parole mie) of the many who did the same with Count Baldwin in Bruges.[56] "I do not know" (nous ne quenoissiens pas) the names of many who took the cross with Hugh of Saint-Pol, says Villehardouin, as if he were reading a roster of

---

52. Villehardouin, *La conquête*, §299.

53. Table 5. Eighteen instances are listed both in Naïs, *Index complet*, 222 (for manuscript O), and Naïs, *Index général* (for manuscripts B and D).

54. Early writers in Old French like Geoffroy Gaimar, Robert Wace, and Benoît of Sainte-Maure also understood *livre* to be a physical object; see Damian-Grint, *The New Historians*, 234–51.

55. "The Book" lists the names of those who took the cross (Villehardouin, *La conquête*, §§5, 6, 7, 8), who died in battle (§§231, 361, 409), and who did not join or who deserted the main army (§§54, 114, 345, 367, 376).

56. Villehardouin, *La conquête*, §§5, 6, 7. Both Faral and Natalis de Wailly translate *ore* as "ici," whereas Dufournet, 45, renders it "maintenant." English translations make it appear that Villehardouin is referring to his own testimony as a written record.

THE MARSHAL AND HIS SCRIBE 165

oath-takers or listening to it being read to him.[57] The lists of cross-takers in 1199 and 1200 were, in effect, rosters of those who had "signed up" for the crusade.[58] They remind us of the tournament rolls inscribed with the names of prominent participants as souvenirs, like the one that William Marshal's biographer consulted to great effect forty years after the memorable tournament at Lagny in November 1179.[59]

Villehardouin's regional lists of cross-takers (§§5–10), likely copied from "the Book," were inserted between his opening remarks on Fulk's preaching (§§1–4) and his account of the first organizational meeting in Soissons in the spring of 1200 (§11). He or his scribe cites the same lists, in the same order, when naming the notable members of the battalions formed at the *parlemenz a cheval* in preparation for the first assault on Constantinople.[60] Clearly those rosters had been taken to Venice and Constantinople as records of combatants in the grand army. Taking critical records overseas was not unusual. Count Henry II took a codex copy (*exemplum*) of the rolls of his fiefholders of Champagne with him on the Third Crusade as a record of the organization of his county with the names and location of his almost two thousand fiefholders.[61]

"The Book" also contained reports of events during the voyage. Villehardouin knew the barons from Champagne he encountered at Piacenza who were traveling to Apulia in June 1202, but not the many knights and mounted sergeants in their company "whose names are not written down" (dont li nom ne sunt mie en escrit), that is, recorded in a chancery register.[62] "The Book reports" (vos retrait li livres) that only twelve

---

57. Villehardouin, *La conquête*, §9.

58. Delisle, "Chroniques et annales diverses," 228, suggests that the similar lists of cross-takers in Villehardouin and the Anonymous of Béthune's *Chronique française des rois de France* were copied from an original compilation of cross-takers from northern France; omitted were the Burgundians who took the cross at Cîteaux in September 1200 (Villehardouin, *La conquête*, §45). See Delisle, "Extraits d'une chronique française," 760.

59. Holden, *History of William Marshal*, 1:230–31, lines 4538–40. On tournament rolls, see Crouch, *Tournament*, 37, and "Historical Introduction" to *History of William Marshal*, 3:36–37.

60. It is clear that Villehardouin was extracting from the rolls of cross-takers in 1199–1200 when he lists the names, in the same order, of the notables in the seven battalions at Scutari. Compare the two lists for Champagne (Villehardouin, *La conquête*, §§5, 151), and Saint-Pol (§§9, 19). The list for Burgundians (§§45, 150) who took the cross at Cîteaux in September 1200 must have been added to the earlier lists. Villehardouin failed to name the notables in Count Louis's Fourth Battalion because he knew that most of them had died with Louis at the battle of Adrianople (§§6, 150).

61. *Cartulary of Countess Blanche*, 294–95, no. 333, ca. 1208-9, letter of Geoffroy of Villehardouin and Milo Breban to Countess Blanche.

62. Villehardouin, *La conquête*, §54. Manuscripts C, D, and E read: "dont li nom ne fuert mis en escrit," which clearly means that the names had not been recorded in the record that

166   **CHAPTER 8**

barons swore to the treaty with Prince Alexios at Zara, he said, and "the Book clearly records" (li livre tesmoigne bien) that more than half of the army on Corfu was in agreement with the barons who wished to leave. After describing his march to Adrianople in April 1205, he breaks his narrative to relate a dramatic concurrent event, the desertion of Renier of Trith's garrison at Philippopolis, which he learned about later from an entry in "the Book" (or conte li livres une grant mervoille).[63] In each instance but one, Villehardouin cites "the Book" in the present tense—it speaks, it mentions, it names, it recounts, it reports, it is witness to—as if it were an existing record. In the single case of the future tense, Villehardouin states that "the Book will not tell you all the words" exchanged at the council held at Saint Stephen's monastery in June 1203, meaning that that it did not provide a complete transcript of the deliberations.[64]

Like other Old French authors, Villehardouin understood *li livres* to be a physical document, not his own own dictated oeuvre that he was in the process of composing. The diverse information cited from "the Book" suggests that it was a chancery register compiled as a document of record. The existence of such a register is expressly cited in August 1206. The priest and notary Odo recorded the ceremony he witnessed of Emperor Henry swearing on the altar of Hagia Sophia to observe the three foundational documents of the new regime. Like the court scribes in Champagne, Odo affirmed that he witnessed and verified what he had recorded. Then Vivianus, the emperor's chief *scriptor, notarius, et judex*, copied Odo's record, as he said, "neither adding nor omitting but faithfully copying it in the Book [*fideliter in libro*] by my own hand," in effect making an official copy in a chancery register.[65] Vivianus made similar

---

Villehardouin was consulting. Manuscript B reads: "li nom ne sunt mie ci escrit," which has been translated as "written here," as if the book referred to Villehardouin's transcription; but the copyist of B erred in reading *en* as *ci*, which translators have rendered "ici" or "here." When English translations render "speak," "recount," "tell," et cetera, in the future tense, they reinforce the interpretation that "the Book" refers to Villehardouin's own testimony; such a reading is not supported by the manuscript texts.

63. Villehardouin, *La conquête*, §§98–99, 114, 345. All the manuscripts read "the" book, not "this" book.

64. Villehardouin, *La conquête*, §129. Manuscripts A and O read: "Totes les paroles qui la furent dites ne vos conterai mie li livres." Manuscripts C and D read: "Totes les paroles qui la furent dites ne vous retraira li livres." Manuscript B omits all reference to the book.

65. Tafel and Thomas, *Urkunden*, 2:34–35, no. 174, 12 August 1206: "Ego Oto, sancti Yeremie presbiter et notarius, rogatus ut scriberem, interfuy, scripsi, compleui et roboraui. Ego Viuianus, scriptor, notarius et iudex domini Henrici imperatoris, autenticum huius uidi et legi, nec addidi nec minui, nisi quod in eo inueni, ideoque fideliter *in libro isto* exemplaui et propria manu mea firmaui atque subscripsi." For what is known about the notary Vivianus, who was active as late as 1211, see Van Tricht, *The Latin Renovatio*, 121–22n65.

THE MARSHAL AND HIS SCRIBE   167

copies of the April 1201 contracts with Venice, which had been carried to Constantinople, certifying in the same manner that he had copied them "faithfully in the Book," neither adding nor subtracting from the originals.[66] It is not known when Vivianus assumed his position, but it was likely in 1205 or 1206, when Emperor Henry tasked him with making an official codex copy of the chancery's vital documents. A codex was portable; in the event that the Cumans and Bulgarians captured Constantinople, which was a real possibility at the time, "the Book" could be saved as a copy of the essential records of the crusade. Villehardouin and his scribe certainly knew "the Book" as a chancery register and consulted it in 1207–8 to supplement and fact-check the marshal's memory.

The Scribe's Testimony

In a number of passages, especially in the second half of the memoirs, the scribe describes events that transpired in Villehardouin's absence. In one notable passage, the scribe sets the scene in the Blachernai, where the doge, Louis, and some barons in the summer of 1204 discuss a course of action regarding the hostilities between Baldwin and Boniface. The doge and Louis asked "Geoffroy of Villehardouin, marshal of Champagne," to go to the siege of Adrianople to defuse the conflict "if he could, for he was highly regarded by Boniface and it was believed that he would have more influence than anyone else; at their pleas, and considering the gravity of the situation, he said that he would go most willingly, and he took Manessier of l'Isle-Adam with him . . . and so they left Constantinople."[67] The scribe writes as a witness, and perhaps from minutes he took of the meeting. He continues in Villehardouin's absence to describe the return of Macaire of Sainte-Menehould and his men from Nicomedia: "the emperor was very happy to see them . . . and so they left Constantinople with about one hundred forty knights and rode day after day until they reached the fortress of Nikitza, where Marshal Geoffroy was quartered."[68] Those clearly were the scribe's words written in the marshal's absence.

The text of the memoirs embodies a complex interplay between the marshal and his scribe. The scribe quotes Villehardouin verbatim when describing his experiences, the speeches he gave or heard, and the

---

66. Tafel and Thomas, *Urkunden*, 1:362–73, nos. 92–93.
67. Villehardouin, *La conquête*, §§283–84.
68. Villehardouin, *La conquête*, §§347–49.

168   **CHAPTER 8**

eyewitness accounts of events reported to him. The scribe also reports Villehardouin's testimony in the third person, vouches for his veracity, and adds extracts from documents of record found in the chancery's "Book." He even inserts his own account of events occurring in Villehardouin's absence, in effect contextualizing the marshal's narrative. Yet if the marshal's scribe enters the text as a second narrative voice to enhance Villehardouin's oral testimony, he remains a discreet professional; he is not as intrusive as Marco Polo's scribe, Rustichello da Pisa, an accomplished writer of romances, who entered the text in a blatant attempt to share authorship with Polo.[69]

---

69. Gaunt, *Marco Polo's "Le Devisement du Monde,"* 41–62, draws some comparisons with Villehardouin and his scribe.

CHAPTER 9

The Memoirs of a *Preudomme*

Jean Longnon, who spent many years studying Villehardouin and his family and companions, described the marshal's character manifest in the memoirs: a sober and precise speaker, prudent and wise in council, a brave and hardy knight, confident and disciplined in the face of adversity, loyal to his lord, honest and a man of his word—all qualities that characterized what contemporaries regarded as making a *prud'homme*. "Villehardouin was in essence a *prud'homme*," wrote Longnon: "he lived his history; his memoirs are that of a *prud'homme*."[1] As Longnon knew from his edition of *The Chronique de Morée*, "Geoffroy of Villehardouin, marshal of Champagne" was remembered in early fourteenth-century Greece as a *vaillans et preudhomme*, a courageous and excellent man. It was the marshal, Count Thibaut's *maistre conseillier*, says the *Chronique*, who encouraged Thibaut to go on crusade and who, after the count's death, organized the Fourth Crusade.[2]

The marshal of course did not claim to be a *preudhomme*—that would have been unseemly—but he freely used the term and its cognates, which acquired increasing currency in the last decades of the twelfth

---

1. Longnon, *L'histoire de la croisade*, 23–24, and earlier in his *Recherches*, 110–14.
2. *Chronique de Morée*, §7.

170   **CHAPTER 9**

century.[3] What makes his memoirs unique is that they are spoken by the "marshal of the empire," an accomplished diplomat and battlefield commander in his sixties who was a close observer of the character and conduct of his companions; although he maintained an appropriate discretion with regard to his superiors (with one exception), he nevertheless assessed their qualities (often obliquely), their good deeds, and their moral lapses and failures. He offers a case study of a senior military officer viewing retrospectively the conduct of those around him and the core values they had acted upon, or not, within the context of a military organization that had been formed to liberate Jerusalem but had morphed into an army of conquest and occupation of the Byzantine empire. His comments on what he had witnessed during the previous eight years reflect his own values as a *preudomme*.

How to Be a *Preudomme*

Prescriptive texts on what made a *preudomme* were well known in the twelfth century. Often used to characterize particularly devoted hermits, monks, and other religious, the term came to be applied to laymen and even laywomen who possessed admirable character and exhibited exemplary conduct. Villehardouin was still a garrison soldier in Troyes in 1184 when Countess Marie attended a performance of *Eructavit* in the priory of Foissy, just beyond the walls of Troyes, where the poet reminded Marie and her royal guests—her half-sister Margaret, widow of Henry the Young King of England, and her sister-in-law Adele, dowager queen of France—that the prophets called holy men *prodome*; he quoted the words of King David who advised barons, kings, and counts to do good and be *prodome*, "as they should."[4] The *prodome* was modeled as someone in a leadership position who was expected to exhibit integrity and act responsibly.

It is not entirely clear what drove the diffusion of *preudomme* as a term of approbation among the laity during the last decades of the twelfth century, but the romances of Chrétien de Troyes in the 1170s and 1180s may well have contributed to its currency.[5] Chrétien's most extensive

---

3. Crouch, *The Chivalric Turn*, 56–82 ("The *Preudomme*"), provides a wide-ranging review of the references, primarily in literary works, depicting "an idealized *preudomme*."

4. Meliga, *L' "Eructavit*," lines 43–45, 1522–27. See Evergates, *Marie of France*, 48–52.

5. Köhler, *L'aventure chevaleresque*, 149–59, briefly reviews the use of *prodom* in *Erec et Enide* and *Yvain*. Crouch, "When Was Chivalry?," especially 293–95, poses the larger question of

THE MEMOIRS OF A *PREUDOMME*   171

use of *prodom* is in the *Roman de Perceval (Le Conte du Graal)*, where it appears eighty-one times, usually to characterize the ethical comportment of knights.[6] The poet makes a pointed distinction between worldly achievement and quality of character in dedicating his tale to Count Philip of Flanders, who was, he says, *lor plus prodome* of the Roman Empire, even more so than Alexander the Great, who had vices. The count will not listen to vulgarity nor hear ill spoken of anyone; he loves true justice, loyalty, and Holy Church; he hates base conduct ("villainy") and hypocrisy; and he is most generous but does not signal his charity and good works.[7] Therefore, boasts Chrétien, he will rhyme the best story ever told at court from a book that the count gave him.

Two scenes stand out in the education of young Perceval as a *prodome*. In the first, his mother recounts the fate of his father, a well-born and wealthy lord, who after suffering a crippling wound lost his wealth and lands but remained a *prodom*, like other *prodomes* who suffered reversals of fortune.[8] Although Perceval's mother claimed to be only of knightly lineage, she counseled: "Dear son, speak with *prodomes* and be with *prodomes*, for a *prodom* will never give bad advice to someone in his company"; protect maidens in distress; and pray in the Holy Church.[9] In the second scene, Gornemant, a mature *prodom*, instructs Perceval in how to be a good knight. He first clothes the boy in suitable attire, then ceremonially fastens his right spur and raises him on a war horse (*destrier*), thus making him a *chevalier*, and arms him with a sword. Then he counsels the new knight: be without base conduct (*vilenie*), hold your tongue and do not speak too freely, aid a maiden in distress, and go to church—"I heard my mother say the same thing!" cried Perceval.[10]

Villehardouin's *Prodomes*

Unlike the authors of romances and conduct literature, the marshal describes the actual conduct and moral failings of his companions,

---

the evolution of the concepts of chivalry and the *preudomme*, and their crossing in the years around 1200.

6. *Perceval: Concordancier*, 429–30.

7. *Perceval*, lines 21–35. Manuscripts A and O of the memoirs read *prodom*, as does Guiot de Provins's copy of *Perceval* (BnF, fr. 794).

8. *Perceval*, lines 411–42.

9. *Perceval*, lines 524–64.

10. *Perceval*, lines 1593–1672.

172   **CHAPTER 9**

dispensing judgments according to his own values and naming those he deemed worthy of being called *preux* or *prodome*. He remembers two religious and two laymen, all deceased, as *prodom*. He recalls Fulk of Neuilly as a charismatic preacher of the crusade, a *prodome/preudon* who even performed miracles.[11] Although Fulk died in May 1202 before the muster in Venice, the marshal remembers him as an effective preacher and supporter of Innocent's crusade project. Villehardouin also pays tribute to Abbot Simon of Loos, a Cistercian "holy man" and one of four abbots authorized at Cîteaux to accompany the crusade army. Villehardouin appreciated Simon's preaching at Zara urging the army to accept the diversion to Constantinople, so supporting the leadership's (and Villehardouin's own) position.[12] Simon "wished the best for the army," said the marshal, and was a *prodon*. For the marshal, Fulk and Simon were genuine supporters of the crusade mission.[13]

Of the two laymen he qualified as *prodon*, the more prominent was Boniface of Montferrat. At a *parlement* in Soissons in June 1201, after reporting that both the duke of Burgundy and the count of Bar-le-Duc had declined to replace Count Thibaut as leader of the crusade, Villehardouin addressed the barons in a speech that he quotes: "The marquis Boniface of Montferrat is a distinguished *prodom* and one of the most esteemed men alive today."[14] That is the only case in which he openly praised a living *prodom* in the presence of the counts and barons. Although he later had occasion to berate Boniface, he repeated his positive assessment after Boniface's death at the hand of Kalojan's forces: the marquis was "one of the best and most generous barons and one of the best knights on earth."[15]

Villehardouin's fourth named *prodome* was Renier of Mons, a knight left as garrison commander (*chevetain*) of Thessalonika in August 1204 while Baldwin led his army to confront Boniface at Adrianople. Villehardouin remembered Renier as a *mult ere prodom* who died in Baldwin's absence.[16] It was a great loss, said the marshal, who must have known

---

11. Villehardouin, *La conquête*, §2: *prodome* (A and O), *saint home* (C and D); §3: *preudon* (A and O), missing in C.

12. Villehardouin, *La conquête*, §§97, 206: "qui ere sainz hom et prodom" (A and O).

13. Clari, *La conquête*, §1, lines 10–11, 28–29, calls the same two prelates *molt preudons*.

14. Villehardouin, *La conquête*, §41: "est mult prodom et un des plus proisiez qui hui cest jor vive" (AOCD); B omits *prodom*.

15. Villehardouin, *La conquête*, §500.

16. Villehardouin, *La conquête*, §300: "mult ere prodon" (AOCD), "mult iert preudom" (B). Renier had been close to Baldwin before the crusade; see Longnon, *Les compagnons de Villehardouin*, 162. Earlier, Villehardouin called Renier "mult preuz et vaillanz" (§289).

THE MEMOIRS OF A *PREUDOMME*   173

Renier personally but does not report any deeds that made him worthy. Fulk, Simon, Boniface, and Renier were memorialized as exemplary individuals who had given their lives to the crusade project. In the marshal's lexicon, *prodom* commemorated an upstanding leader, whether spiritual or military.

Villehardouin also used *prodon* in a general sense to designate the barons collectively. Those who took the cross with the bishop of Soissons and with the count of Flanders were *prodomes*, as were those who met in *parlement* at Soissons in late June 1201 to select a replacement for Count Thibaut.[17] At Zara the *prodomes* of the army ended the melee between the French and the Venetians; in Constantinople the *prodome de l'ost* held a private meeting to discuss the election of an emperor before a *parlement* of the army met; the *prodoms* of Baldwin's army were greatly saddened by the death of the chancellor Jean of Noyon in Serres.[18] As second-level commanders, the barons were the backbone of the army, exercising leadership at the company level; their conduct and loyalty were critical to the army's cohesion, for they carried their men with them, whether choosing to remain in the army or to leave with all their equipment, mounts, and support personnel. For the marshal, the *prodom* was the critical link between the senior commanders and the combatants of the army.

Villehardouin spoke of others as "worthy and valiant" (*preuz et vaillaint*), a stock expression also used by his contemporary Guiot of Provins, whom Villehardouin may have known on the Third Crusade. Guiot's *Bible* (1206–8), written after he returned from Acre and entered Cluny, lamented those who died on that crusade: "the good princes, the good barons who held grand courts and gave fine gifts [*biaus avoirs*]; God! how they were *preu et valant*, and rich and wise and esteemed."[19] Raimbaut of Vaqueiras, the poet companion and beneficiary of Boniface's largesse, advised Emperor Baldwin in similar terms: an emperor should be worthy, generous, and honest.[20] But if Guiot and Raimbaut associated worthiness with status, wealth, and generosity (to one's followers), the only name on Villehardouin's list that would have qualified among the crusaders as a "high man" who held court and awarded gifts to his followers was Boniface of Montferrat.

---

17. Villehardouin, *La conquête*, §§7, 8, 40.
18. Villehardouin, *La conquête*, §§89, 257, 290.
19. Guiot de Provins, *La Bible*, lines 116–20.
20. Raimbaut de Vaqueiras, *Poems*, 237, no. 20: *pros, larcs*, and *franc*.

174   **CHAPTER 9**

For Villehardouin, *preux et vaillant* referred more broadly to the professional competence and moral rectitude of those in military service. He named four of those worthies. The first was William "the Champenois" of Champlitte, a grandson of Count Hugh of Troyes, who took the cross with the Burgundians at Cîteaux, served in the Sixth Battalion at Constantinople, joined Boniface after the fall of the city, and became prince of Achaia. Villehardouin hints that William was influential in convincing Boniface to accept mediation of his conflict with Baldwin and therefore was, in Villehardouin's eyes, *mult preuz et mult vaillant.*[21] If William, as prince of Achaia, distributed fiefs to those in his company, Villehardouin did not note that as an example of princely generosity to his followers. The marshal's second worthy was his own nephew Geoffroy, who had accompanied William in conquering the Peloponnese and received Kalamata in fief; he was "most worthy and courageous and a fine knight" (mult preuz et moult vaillainz et bons chevaliers).[22] The author of the *Chronique de Morée*, who had the memoirs at hand and knew the younger Geoffroy as the founder of a line of Villehardouin princes of Achaia, goes so far as to invent a speech for Prince William in which he praises young Geoffroy "for setting an example for all *prudhommes.*"[23]

The two other *preu et vaillaint* were knights, one in Baldwin's service, the other in Boniface's. In August 1204 Eustace of Salperwick took command of forty knights and one hundred mounted sergeants in Adrianople, while Baldwin led his army to Mosynopolis. It was Eustace who sent messengers to Constantinople warning of an imminent clash between Baldwin and Boniface that threatened the Frankish settlement.[24] Eustace appeared later in Constantinople, where he must have impressed the marshal, who deemed him "very worthy and very courageous."[25] Dreux of Etroeungt, who died in Boniface's service at the siege of Corinth, also was a *preuz* and *vaillanz* knight, but Villehardouin does not explain

---

21. Villehardouin, *La conquête*, §167. See Longnon, *Les compagnons de Villehardouin*, 210–12.

22. Villehardouin, *La conquête*, §326. See Longnon, *Les compagnons de Villehardouin*, 32–41, and *Recherches*, 28–34.

23. *Chronique de Morée*, §§109, 124.

24. Villehardouin, *La conquête*, §§281–82.

25. Villehardouin, *La conquête*, §273: "moult preux et moult vaillant." Eustace of Salperwick had been a close companion of Arnold II of Guines. After the defeat of Adrianople, he returned to Constantinople and was among the Flemish barons who witnessed Baldwin's act at the Blachernai in February 1205 (*Oorkonden*, 2:615–17, no. 281). He likely died two months later in Baldwin's company at Adrianople. See Longnon, *Les compagnons de Villehardouin*, 160–61.

THE MEMOIRS OF A *PREUDOMME*   175

why.[26] The marshal celebrated the four *preuz* and *vaillaint* for their conduct and leadership in military service.

The one political leader Villehardouin esteemed throughout was Enrico Dandolo, the doge of Venice. The marshal admired him from their first meeting. The aged doge rallied the Venetians to the crusade, which entailed building and manning a large fleet; he participated in all the senior leadership meetings; he led the Venetian assault on the walls of Constantinople; and then, despite his infirmities, he brought a contingent of Venetian troops to the battle of Adrianople and, after the defeat, led the remnants of the army to Rodosto.[27] Villehardouin remembered him as *mult sages et preuz*.[28]

Villehardouin deemed nine men in all as *preudom* or *preuz*: a charismatic preacher of the crusade, a holy Cistercian abbot who supported the diversions to Constantinople, an Italian marquis chosen as supreme commander of the crusade, the prince of Achaia, the marshal's nephew and baron of Kalamata, two knights serving as garrison commanders, a knight of indeterminate role at the siege of Corinth, and the doge of Venice. Of the nine honored for their exemplary character and deeds, six were in military service.

Notably missing from Villehardouin's list are the two original crusade leaders, counts Baldwin of Flanders and Louis of Blois, whom he had observed and closely interacted with over the course of several years. He knew Baldwin from the many council meetings since 1201 and had admired his military leadership during the conquest of Constantinople. But he had seen a less admirable side of Baldwin, who as emperor transgressed in entering Boniface's fief of Thessalonika and who had excluded the marshal from his inner council of Flemish barons. Villehardouin had known Louis since at least 1198, when he vouched for Louis's loyalty to Philip II, and in 1202 he brought Louis to his better senses to muster in Venice. But Louis, who had been sickly throughout the voyage and conquest and during Baldwin's year as emperor, gave Baldwin bad advice by suggesting he go to Adrianople before reinforcements arrived; he then disobeyed the order proclaimed throughout the camp not to pursue the Cumans, an act that led to the army's defeat and

---

26. Villehardouin, *La conquête*, §332. See Longnon, *Les compagnons de Villehardouin*, 167–68.

27. Madden, *Enrico Dandolo*, 117–94.

28. Villehardouin, *La conquête*, §§15, 25, 29, 364. Clari, too, recognized the doge as "molt ers preusdons et sages" (Clari, *La conquête*, §93, lines 11–12). The *Chronique de Morée* also cites the doge as *preudhomme* (§§35, 64, 67).

176   **CHAPTER 9**

the consequent conditions under which the marshal recorded his memoirs.[29] Villehardouin memorializes neither Baldwin nor Louis at their deaths; he says simply that Louis "was killed" at Adrianople, and "many were saddened" on hearing confirmation of Baldwin's death.[30]

Nor does Villehardouin honor the two senior religious leaders, Nivelon of Soissons and Garnier of Troyes. He knew both prelates well, Nivelon as host of the planning councils and Garnier as cathedral canon and later as bishop of Troyes. Both had been closely involved in every stage of the crusade: they sat on the leadership councils, they commanded ships during the voyage to and assault on Constantinople, they preached sermons to the troops and accompanied them in battle, they justified the shifting mission of the army, they served as envoys of the crusade, and they elected the new emperor. Yet Villehardouin does not mention either prelate during Baldwin's year as emperor, when they were deeply implicated in the frenzied quest for relics, conduct that he may have deemed unworthy of a principled prelate. He fails to note that Bishop Garnier died at Adrianople, although he does mention the death of Bishop Peter of Bethlehem.[31] He must have heard of Bishop Nivelon's death in Bari on 1 September 1207, but makes no mention of it.[32] In retrospect, Villehardouin found that neither the lay nor the spiritual leaders of the crusade were worthy of being remembered as *prodomes*.

Geoffroy of Villehardouin: *Prodom*

During more than three decades of military service Villehardouin and his comrades must have discussed among themselves a code of military conduct. He was not a count or baron—nor the son of one—nor was he still a knight when dictating his memoirs. His unique position as a senior staff officer, someone in between, was reflected in his assessment of the character and conduct of his social and military superiors and the knights he led in battle. If he qualified few individuals as *preux* or *prodom*, he recalled the many who failed to observe the requisite

---

29. Villehardouin, *La conquête*, §§246, 268, 341.

30. Villehardouin, *La conquête*, §§360, 439.

31. The obituary of the cathedral of Troyes states that Garnier died in Constantinople on 14 April 1205 (Longnon, *Les compagnons de Villehardouin*, 15n33), that is, shortly after he sent home a collection of relics.

32. Claverie, "Un *Illustris amicus Venetorum*," 506–14. For Nivelon's collection of relics, see Perry, *Sacred Plunder*, 80–81; Barber, "The Impact of the Fourth Crusade," 300–331; and Gaposchkin, "Nivelon of Quierzy."

THE MEMOIRS OF A *PREUDOMME* 177

qualities of someone in a leadership position: observing one's oath, being loyal to one's lord and companions, giving good counsel, and acting courageously in the face of adversity.

Villehardouin was especially attentive to the role of oaths as warrants to personal conduct. He is known to have taken three oaths before the crusade: in the cathedral of Châlons he swore on relics (*super sanctis reliquias*) to warrant Helvide of Aulnay, at Melun he swore on scripture (*super sanctum Evangelium*) to warrant Thibaut's homage to Philip II, and in Venice he swore on scripture (*evangelia sancta Dei*) to confirm the treaty for overseas transport on behalf of Count Thibaut.[33] On one occasion in the memoirs he speaks of warranting himself: when attempting to convince the duke of Burgundy to assume leadership of the crusade in Thibaut's place, he promised to swear on scripture (*sor sainz*) to serve him just as he would have served Thibaut.[34]

He was vexed by those who failed to observe their oaths.[35] Many who received money from Count Thibaut swore on scripture (*il jureroit sor sains*) to meet in Venice, he said, but they did not and were "much blamed." The commanders of the Flemish fleet swore to sail to Venice, but did not. Renaud of Montmirail and his men left Zara for Syria after "he swore on Scripture with his right hand" to return within two weeks, but "they did not keep their oaths [*sairemenz*]."[36] His harshest words were for Robert of Boves, who in the delegation sent from Zara to Rome swore on scripture to return but did not, and so he perjured himself (*s'en perjura*), said Villehardouin.[37] Those prominent departures became, in effect, desertions in the eyes of those who remained.

Villehardouin describes a dramatic moment on Corfu when the counts, bishops, and abbots headed off a potential mutiny by swearing oaths to provide ships to the disaffected to sail to Syria if they remained with the army for five more months. The barons were required to "swear on scripture in good faith" (*jureroient sor sainz loialment*), suggesting that the military chaplains carried copies of biblical texts on the march as much for oath-taking as for liturgical purposes.[38] But in Constantinople, one month before the expiration of that term of service, when

---

33. See Faral (Villehardouin, *La conquête*), 1:32–33n1.
34. Villehardouin, *La conquête*, §38.
35. Dufournet, *Les écrivains de la IVe croisade*, 2:282–320, notes how exceptional Villehardouin is in mentioning so many oaths, mostly not observed.
36. Villehardouin, *La conquête*, §§36, 48, 102.
37. Villehardouin, *La conquête*, §§105–6.
38. Villehardouin, *La conquête*, §117.

178   **CHAPTER 9**

the army agreed to extend its stay until March 1204, no mention was made of oaths, and in March the *concordia* between the crusaders and the Venetians extended the army's service for another year without its consent, again without the warranting oaths of the commanders.[39] Villehardouin last mentions oaths sworn on scripture in May 1204, when six prelates swore (*jurerent sor sainz*) to elect the best man as Latin emperor.[40] With the crusader army's transformation into an army of occupation, the sworn oath to one's conduct was displaced by loyalty to one's commander and companions.

Having been loyal to four lords in Champagne and two in Constantinople, Villehardouin understood the critical importance of loyalty to the good order of governance and the military. Disloyalty to one's lord and to one's companions was, for him, a grave personal offense. He severely rebuked (*mult durement*) Boniface for being disloyal to Baldwin in the dispute over the status of Thessalonika. Boniface objected that he had been injured by his lord, who aggressively entered the fief for which he had done homage, and therefore was justified in capturing Didymoteichon and besieging Adrianople, both in Baldwin's imperial lands. But for Villehardouin, loyalty to one's lord was paramount.[41]

Although the Champenois on crusade were bereft of a prince from whom they held fiefs and to whom they could be loyal, Villehardouin, as the count's surrogate, nevertheless regarded them as disloyal if they did not muster in Venice and remain with the main army through its diversions. He was so troubled by acts of disloyalty that he recorded the names of the disloyal for posterity: those who failed to muster with the army (the count of Brienne and his company, the knights at Piacenza), those who intended to bypass Venice (Count Louis of Blois), those who left the army at Zara (Montmirail, Boves), and those who threatened to leave at Corfu (his fellow Champenois Oger of Saint-Chéron, Guy of Chappes, and his nephew Clarembaud). He was astounded that Renier of Trith's own family abandoned him at Adrianople—his son, brother, nephew, and son-in-law, together with thirty knights—but they were justly rewarded, he said, by being captured and beheaded.[42] The marshal celebrated his own loyalty to the army during the retreat from

---

39. Villehardouin, *La conquête*, §§195, 234.
40. Villehardouin, *La conquête*, §258.
41. Villehardouin, *La conquête*, §§275–86.
42. Villehardouin, *La conquête*, §345.

THE MEMOIRS OF A *PREUDOMME*   179

Adrianople: "everyone, on foot or mounted, the wounded and the others, no one was left behind."[43] Loyalty passed in both directions.

Loyalty carried with it the obligation to give good counsel. Villehardouin mentions several occasions when he gave timely advice: to the planning council in advocating for Boniface's appointment as supreme commander, to the doge in advising a nighttime retreat from Adrianople, and to Emperor Henry in recommending withdrawal from Asia in order to defend the capital and Thrace. According to Valenciennes, Villehardouin advised Emperor Henry to do battle with the Bulgarians at Philippopolis, which was a great victory.[44] Against his own examples of giving good counsel, Villehardouin notes instances of bad counsel. "I do not know by whose advice" Baldwin ignored Boniface's plea not to invade his fief of Thessalonika, he said; for that bad advice (*malvais conseil*) he blamed Baldwin's council of Flemish barons rather than Baldwin's impulsive behavior.[45]

Honor, shame, and blame occupied a large place in Villehardouin's world view. Honor, for him, was a public act according respect to a prominent personage, typically at an arrival.[46] The doge "greatly honored" the six envoys on their arrival in Venice and, Villehardouin notes with evident satisfaction, he and Manessier of l'Isle-Adam were greatly honored (*les honora mult*) by Boniface's men on arriving in Adrianople.[47] Boniface had accorded Baldwin "all possible honor" after the election, thus demonstrating publicly his acceptance of the outcome, while Baldwin was received "with great honor" when he returned to Constantinople for the mediation of his right to Thessalonika.[48] Hugh of Saint-Pol, however, was "honored" only at his funeral, as he departed.[49] These were all cases of prominent individuals being accorded publicly the respect due to their standing.

Shame (*honte*) and blame (*blasme*) also were public acts, assigned for lapses in personal conduct. Villehardouin criticized the Burgundian barons who took the cross at Cîteaux, traveled to Marseille, and bypassed Venice; for that they incurred "great shame" (*grante honte*), were much

---

43. Villehardouin, *La conquête*, §366.
44. Villehardouin, *La conquête*, §§529–30.
45. Villehardouin, *La conquête*, §§277–78.
46. Hodgson, "Honour, Shame and the Fourth Crusade," reviews the usage of the terms in Villehardouin and Clari.
47. Villehardouin, *La conquête*, §§15, 284.
48. Villehardouin, *La conquête*, §§261, 295.
49. Villehardouin, *La conquête*, §334.

180   **CHAPTER 9**

blamed (*blasmé*), and suffered great misfortune (*grant mesaventure*). Others who avoided Venice to sail directly to Syria were killed and "no one escaped misfortune and shame."[50] If some barons opposed the conquest of Zara, others argued that they would be shamed if they did not abide by their agreement with Venice; on Corfu the leading barons argued that they would be "forever shamed" if they did not continue to Constantinople. Emperor Henry even confided to his council that he feared being shamed if he did not respond to a desperate appeal from the people of Didymoteichon for aid against Kalojan.[51] For the marshal, shame and blame were incurred by those who abandoned the main army, who did not honor their contracts, who lost courage in the face of the enemy, and who did not rise to the occasion to exercise their leadership responsibilities.

Like Chrétien de Troyes, Villehardouin envisions the *prodom* primarily as a man in military service who abides by a military code of conduct. But he knew that not all knights were *prodom*.[52] He was even more severe than Guiot of Provins in criticizing those who were unworthy. Guiot wrote in his satiric *Bible* that few men of his time were worthy of being called *prodom*; only the Hospitallers were *prodomes*—"and that is the truth."[53] Villehardouin echoes that assessment in his litany of unworthy conduct. Recalling the fall of Constantinople, he noted that knights were hanged for not surrendering their loot for an equitable distribution, and he moralized that "greed [*covoitise*] was the root of all evil."[54] He was blunt about the conduct of the French knights at Apros, whose indiscriminate killing and looting so appalled the Greeks in the neighboring villages that they fled to heavily fortified Adrianople, and he attributed the revolt of the Greek cities in the spring of 1205 to the great French lords, who after receiving fiefs in November 1204 maltreated their new subjects, some more so, some less, as he put it.[55] Those were not the acts of *prodomes*.

If Villehardouin did not know of Vegetius's prescriptions for a military code of conduct—honor, courage, loyalty, skill in arms—he nevertheless echoed them in his own observations of the acts of his comrades.[56]

---

50. Villehardouin, *La conquête*, §§50, 231.
51. Villehardouin, *La conquête*, §§84, 96, 429.
52. Köhler, *L'aventure chevaleresque*, 151.
53. Guiot de Provins, *La Bible*, lines 1849–50.
54. Villehardouin, *La conquête*, §§252, 255.
55. Villehardouin, *La conquête*, §§391, 303.
56. Allmand, *The "De Re Militari*,*"* 261–63, 269–72, 277–81.

His code of conduct was purely secular. He makes no mention of his own prayers or entering a church except in his official capacity—in Saint Mark's to give a speech of persuasion, in the abbey church of Saint-Stephen with the barons to plan the assault on Constantinople, twice in Hagia Sophia to attend the coronations of Baldwin and Henry, and perhaps once to witness the coronation of Alexios IV. Like Chrétien de Troyes, he makes no mention of an obligation to protect the church or the clergy. Nor does he represent the crusade as a holy war or part of a divine plan. Confession and Mass before battle were conventional acts of tending to one's own soul, not calls for divine intervention in battle. Even the clergy who told the army that it was "right and just" to capture Constantinople, and promised a papal indulgence to those who died in battle, did not appeal for divine intervention.[57]

For Villehardouin, God's will is inscrutable. He intervenes in human affairs only when, and as, he wishes. He prevented the breakup of the army in Venice and at Zara, and enacted four miracles—the retreat of Greek forces during the sieges of Constantinople, and Kalojan's abandonment of sieges at Didymoteichon and Adrianople despite his superior forces.[58] "If God did not love the army," said Villehardouin, it would not have held together at Zara, and leaving Corfu, "God gave them good wind."[59] But God did allow misfortune at the battle of Adrianople and at Rhousion, where most of the garrison was killed.[60] Other misfortunes not ascribed to God, like the deaths of Mathieu of Montmorency and Boniface of Montferrat, simply occurred. Since God's acts are unpredictable, and known only in retrospect, human affairs are governed by personal conduct, of which the *prodom* is the exemplar.

---

57. Villehardouin, *La conquête*, §225.

58. Villehardouin, *La conquête*, §§61, 104 (Venice and Zara); §§175, 182 (Constantinople); §432 (Didymoteichon); §475 (Adrianople). For the role of religion in the memoirs, see Milland-Bove, "Miracles et interventions divines."

59. Villehardouin, *La conquête*, §§104, 136.

60. Villehardouin, *La conquête*, §§360, 408.

Epilogue

Geoffroy of Villehardouin is remembered today primarily as a "chronicler" or "historian" of the Fourth Crusade and as the earliest prose "writer" in Old French. Yet only the first half (52 percent) of his memoirs—and they are war memoirs, not a history—deals with the crusade proper, the five years between his cross-taking at Évry and the installation of Count Baldwin of Flanders as emperor of Constantinople. To view Villehardouin through the prism of the crusade alone is to miss the context of the second half of the memoirs—which he dictated, not wrote—describing the fraught post-conquest years when he served as garrison commander of Constantinople, leader of the Fifth (Champenois) Battalion, and field commander defending the Latin occupation against superior Bulgarian and Greek forces.[1]

Villehardouin enjoyed a remarkable career. As a garrison knight in his twenties and early thirties, he witnessed the evolution of Troyes from a quiescent episcopal town into the capital of the county of Champagne and a center of international commerce. Appointed marshal in his late thirties, he became the senior staff officer responsible for overseeing the defense of the county's thirty walled towns and fortresses. Unlike

---

1. Bull, *Eyewitness and Crusade Narrative*, 260–92, emphasizes the importance of the second half of the memoirs for understanding Villehardouin.

EPILOGUE   183

his contemporary William Marshal in England, who considered tournaments a fine (and profitable) sport and married up to become a great lord, Villehardouin is not known to have participated in tournaments, and he always was aware of his in-between status as a high official of knightly origin: two of his brothers were knights in the count's service and two were canons in the count's chapel; his two wives came from knightly families; his two sons were knights, as were three nephews. He lived within the knightly milieu until his early fifties, when his close personal bond with the young count Thibaut III made him a central figure in the planning of the Fourth Crusade and ultimately in the Latin settlement in the Byzantine Empire.

Villehardouin's memoirs are as remarkable as his life. Recorded in the vernacular for a distant listening audience, they recall what he saw, what he heard, what he said, and what he did over the course of eight years (1200–1207). He describes his acts at critical junctures of the crusade and its aftermath: negotiating transport for the crusaders, choosing Count Thibaut III's successor, serving as chief of staff during the expedition and conquest of Constantinople, becoming leader of the Champenois and garrison commander of Constantinople after the conquest, saving the army from complete destruction at Adrianople, and finally serving as chief military adviser and virtual prime minister to Emperor Henry.

While recalling his own experiences, he provides a precise chronology of events and invaluable observations on the internal dynamics of the crusader army as seen from the command level, especially regarding the leadership, manpower, morale, and cohesion of the main army. He describes the many meetings, speeches, eyewitness reports, and written and oral communications that were critical to military operations. Although he did not divulge the deliberations of the commanders, he was acutely aware of how their decisions and personal conduct affected the army. As a career soldier, he adhered to an ethical code of conduct expected of someone in a position of authority, and he freely comments on infractions of that code by the barons. He thus offers a rare case of someone whom contemporaries would call a *preudomme* who openly critiqued the ethical and professional lapses of his social superiors.

Modern commentators have questioned Villehardouin's "silences" and omissions.[2] Why, for example, does he not mention the machinations of Boniface and Alexios? Why does he obscure his relationship

---

2. The question of Villehardouin's "sincerity" or truthfulness was resolved long ago by Edmond Faral, who found that on close examination, Villehardouin did not deliberately

184   **EPILOGUE**

with Philip II? Why is he reticent about his role in the destruction of Zara and the decision to divert the expedition to Constantinople? Why does he mention the spoils of war in conquered Constantinople but ignore the fate of the conquered residents, which he surely witnessed? Why does he not describe his interactions with the diverse people he encountered, especially the Jews in Estanor and the Italians and the Greek Orthodox Christians in Constantinople? Why does he not mention his role in devising a new constitution under Emperor Henry? And why does he never mention his wife and children, even though he did provide for his sisters and daughters in convents? The short answer is that we do not know; memoirs are, by their very nature, selective, retrospective narratives.

Whatever his intended audience, the memoirs appear not to have reached Champagne, for not a single copy survives in its regional archives or libraries. By the time Peter of Douai returned to Flanders in late 1209 or 1210, presumably with a copy of the memoirs, the events of the crusade had been overtaken in Champagne by the resistance to the succession of Count Thibaut IV. Although Countess Blanche had just obtained the king's promise to receive the boy's homage when he turned twenty-one, the rest of her twenty-one-year regency was dominated by a civil war contesting her lordship and her son's succession.[3] When Villehardouin died overseas, more than a decade after leaving home, he was remembered only by his eldest son Erard, who established memorial services for "my father and my mother" at four religious institutions, but none, not even where his daughters were nuns, entered his name in its obituary, perhaps because he had failed to endow revenues for his own memorial services.

Few veterans of the crusade are known to have returned home to Champagne. The most enduring memory of the crusade resided in relics, notably those sent by Bishop Garnier to his cathedral in Troyes—a piece of the true cross, the head of Saint Philip, and the body of Saint Helen—which helped to finance the reconstruction of the church and a program of windows (ca. 1228–35) that depict Garnier himself in a "procession of relics."[4] Countess Blanche also received relics from Constan-

---

distort or misrepresent; on occasion he might have erred or did not know, but ultimately he was a reliable witness; see Faral, "Geoffroy de Villehardouin."

3. Evergates, "Countess Blanche."

4. Pastan, "Dating the Medieval Work," 249–50; and Pastan and Balcon, *Les vitraux du choeur de la cathédrale de Troyes*, 221, fig. 187; 460, fig. 399. See also Constable, "Troyes,

EPILOGUE 185

tinople, which she gave to Argensolles, the convent she founded and entered in retirement.[5] But there is no record of crusade veterans donating relics to local religious institutions and recording oral histories of their overseas experiences, as Robert of Clari did for Corbie in Picardy.[6]

Geoffroy of Villehardouin's memoirs and the *History* of William Marshal, both written in the early thirteenth century, are unique in depicting the lives of two contemporary marshals who were central participants in the major events of their time. Both are written in Old French, the memoirs in prose addressed to a lay listening audience, the *History* as a biography in verse intended to be sung at memorial services.[7] Both texts are constructed around a firm chronology and are based primarily on oral sources supplemented by written records. Both were copied in the thirteenth century, but the *History* survives as a single copy, unknown until rediscovered in the late nineteenth century, whereas the memoirs survive in multiple copies from the late thirteenth century and in print editions since the sixteenth century. In one other respect the reception of the two lives has diverged. William Marshal's life and deeds are on full display in the *History*, whereas Villehardouin's life and deeds have been overshadowed by the events he described. This book has attempted to recover the marshal of Champagne as one of the central, and most interesting, figures of his time, who still speaks to us of his life and deeds through his memoirs.

Constantinople, and the Relics of St. Helen," and Geary, "Saint Helen of Athyra and the Cathedral of Troyes."

5. Lester, "What Remains," 325. Some of the relics had Greek inscriptions.

6. See Lester, "Translation and Appropriation," and "What Remains."

7. Crouch, *William Marshal*, 1–10.

APPENDIX 1

Geoffroy of Villehardouin's Letters Patent

Catalogued in Longnon, *Recherches* [LR]. Extant letters marked in Bold.

Date	LR#	Recipient	Subject
1189	**21**	Notre-Dame-aux-Nonnains convent	Reception of daughter Alice
1190	24	Foissy priory	Exchange of fields
1197	38	Montiéramey abbey	Pledge for Clarembaud V of Chappes
1197	39	Montiéramey abbey	Pledge for Renaud of Villers's gift
1197	40	Leper house of Troyes	A knight's gift for daughter's reception
1198	**47**	Montiéramey and guild of bakers	Resolution of a dispute over woods
1198	**48**	Montiéramey abbey	Mortgaged lands of Hugh Curebois

APPENDIX 1

Date	LR#	Recipient	Subject
(1198–1201)	50	Cathedral chapter of Troyes	Received safeguard of its village
1199	52	Reclus abbey	Notice of a sale[1]
1200 July	**53**	Templars	Dispute vs. Renaud of Mesnil's widow
1200 October	54	Leper house of Troyes	Girard of Villy's lease of a servant
1200	—	Chapel of Brandonvillers	Gift of tithe at Longeville[2]
1201 December	**64**	Hotel-Dieu of Troyes	Gift of a tithe revenue
1202 February	65	Odo, canon of Troyes	Gift by his nephews
1202 April	**68**	Chapel at Brandonvillers	His brother Jean's gift
1202 April	69	Chapter of Saint-Loup of Troyes	Exchange of a tenant woman
1202	**70**	Larrivour abbey	His brother Guy's gift of a revenue[3]
1202	**71**	Quincy abbey	Gift of land
1202	**71bis**	Quincy abbey	Gift of land, consent of his wife and sons
(1206)	83	Venice	Division of villages with Venetians
120[8] March	**88**	Foissy and Notre-Dame-aux-Nonnains	Gift of tithe of Voué, half to each
120[8] March	89	Foissy and Notre-Dame-aux-Nonnains	Gift of tithe of Brantigny, half to each
1208–9	92	Countess Blanche of Champagne	Fiefholders in Champagne

The twenty-three letters listed here are only the ones that Villehardouin authored or sealed. He appears in sixty-one documents catalogued in Longnon, *Recherches*.

---

1. Joint letter of Geoffroy the marshal and Milo of Saint-Quentin.
2. Buchon, *Recherches et matériaux*, pt. 2:26, no. 2.
3. A green pendant seal reads: "Seal of Geoffroy, marshal of Champagne."

APPENDIX 2

Tables

Table 1. Size of tactical units

KNIGHTS	MOUNTED SERGEANTS	COMMANDER	§
80		Odo of Champlitte	138
80		Villehardouin	343
100		Count Henry	269
100		Boniface	298
100		Macaire of Sainte-Menehould	312, 342, 347
100	100	William of Champlitte	328
100	500	Anselm of Courcelles	382
100	140	Peter of Bracheux	369
120		Count Louis	305
120		Count Henry	310
120		Renier of Trith	311, 345
120		Thierry of Tenremonde	405
140		Peter of Bracheux	319, 453
140		Emperor Baldwin	349
160 (100+60)		Emperor Baldwin and Henry	269, 273
400	plus infantry	Emperor Henry and the marshal	429

Note: Villehardouin does not mention turcopoles and mounted crossbowmen attached to tactical units except for his strike force to rescue Renier of Trith (*La conquête*, §438).

APPENDIX 2

Table 2. Distance of cities from Constantinople

CITY	DAYS TRAVEL	§
Nicomedia	2	312
Selymbria	2	387
Rodosto	3	386
Tchorlu	3	343, 390
Adrianople	5	368
Stenimakos	9	400
Philippopolis	9	345
Thessalonika	12	302

Table 3. Size of garrisons in Greek cities

CITY	KNIGHTS	§
Adrianople	40 (+100 mounted sergeants)	273, 441
Adrianople	20	452
Adrianople	100	273, 496
Bizoë	120 (+ mounted sergeants)	403
Bizoë	120	421
Kibotos	40	464
Nicomedia	100+	342
Philippopolis	120	345
Rhousion	140 (+mounted sergeants)	402
Selymbria	50	411, 421

Table 4. References to Villehardouin as marshal

	BEFORE MAY 1204	AFTER MAY 1204	TOTAL
Geoffroy the marshal	3	20	23
Geoffroy of Villehardouin, the marshal	0	2	2
Geoffroy of Villehardouin, marshal of Champagne	7	2	9
Geoffroy, the marshal of Champagne	7	9	16
Geoffroy of Villehardouin, marshal of Romania and of Champagne	0	9	9
	17 (29%)	42 (71%)	59

Note: Naïs, *Index Complet*, 236–37, lists fifty-nine references to Geoffroy plus one (§392) for another marshal. Table 4 develops a suggestion in Grossel, *Le milieu littéraire en Champagne*, 1:152–53, but with reference here to the scribe's usage rather than to Villehardouin's self-referencing.

APPENDIX 2   191

Table 5. Villehardouin's references to the chancery "Book"

§	SUBJECT
5,6,7,8 (9,10)	Rosters of crusaders at Écry, "in France," at Bruges
54	Names of those at Piacenza who bypassed Venice
99	Names of barons at Zara who swore oaths to aid Alexios
114	Names of the leaders of the depart faction on Corfu
129–31	Record of council's deliberations and doge's speech at Saint Stephen's monastery
141	Notes of Alexios III's letter read to the barons at Scutari
201	Names of the barons who accompanied Alexios IV's expedition, August 1203
231	Fates of those who bypassed Venice at Piacenza (see §54)
236	Account of the second assault on Constantinople
345–46	Report of desertion of Renier of Trith's family and knights at Philippopolis
361	Names of the fallen at Adrianople, April 1205
367	Names of those who left the retreat from Adrianople to ride directly to the capital
376	Names of crusaders who left on Venetian ships for home
409	Survivor report of those who died at Rhousion
464	Survivor report of those who died at Kibotos
*	Vivianus's copy *in libro* of Emperor Henry's pre-coronation oath.
**	Vivianus's two copies *in libro* of the contracts with Venice.

* Tafel and Thomas, *Urkunden*, 2:34–35, no. 174, 12 August 1206.
** Tafel and Thomas, *Urkunden*, 1:362–68, no. 92, and 369–73, no. 3, April 1201.

APPENDIX 3

Manuscripts, Editions, and Translations

The fate of the scribe's fair copy of the memoirs is unknown, but it most likely remained in Constantinople, where it later furnished materials on the Fourth Crusade for the early fourteenth-century *Chronicle of Morea*.[1] The copy brought to Flanders by Peter of Douai in 1209–10, or an early copy of it, may have survived to the sixteenth century, when it was described as "a very old exemplar written on parchment 400 years ago."[2] The earliest known use of the memoirs was by the monks of Corbie in the Ernoul and Bernard *Chronique* (circa 1230).[3] The scribe who embellished Villehardouin's testimony and

---

1. Shawcross, *The Chronicle of Morea*, 70–71, notes that the French version of the *Chronicle of Morea* contains details of the Fourth Crusade known only through Villehardouin. In fact, the Fourth Crusade in *Chronique de Morée*, §§5–75, appears to have been taken directly from the memoirs, enhanced by imagined scenes and speeches.

2. Rouillé, *L'histoire ou chronique du seigneur Geoffroy de Villehardouin*, preface.

3. Natalis de Wailly (Villehardouin, *Geoffroi de Ville-Hardouin*), 430–39, was the first to signal the connection between the memoirs and the Ernoul-Bernard *Chronique*. For a detailed analysis of Ernoul and Bernard, see Edbury, "New Perspectives on the Old French Continuations of William of Tyre," and Gaggero, "Western Eyes in the Latin East." The Anonymous of Béthune may have seen a copy of the memoirs: his *Chronique française des rois de France* (ca. 1220) includes an exact copy of Villehardouin's list of crusaders by region, and in the same order (§§5, 6, 8, 9, 7, 10). Not being interested in the Fourth Crusade, however, which he summarized in one paragraph, he passes to the war in Normandy between the kings of France and England. See Delisle, "Extraits d'une chronique française."

194   **APPENDIX 3**

dramatized the role of Count Louis at the battle of Adrianople as an epic figure inadvertently revealed that he was working directly from the memoirs; realizing that he had skipped over Hugh of Saint-Pol's earlier death, he addressed the reader: "I have forgotten to tell you about the Count of Saint-Pol, who was in Constantinople."[4] The Ernoul-Bernard compilation also borrowed from Clari's oral history.[5]

At about the same time, the Cistercian monk Aubri of Trois-Fontaines apparently consulted both the memoirs and Clari's oral history for his universal chronicle (*Chronica*, 1232–41). He cites many of his sources— chronicles, epics, romances, charters, letters—and he quotes extensively from Baldwin's letter of 1204 and what he heard (*audivimus*), perhaps from old veterans like Clarembaud VI of Chappes (d. 1246).[6] Although he does not cite the memoirs, he appears to have lifted Villehardouin's reference to the fiefs of the *partitio* and the conquest of the Peloponnese by the marshal's eponymous nephew, while he took details of Baldwin's coronation from Clari.[7] However, he ignored the post-conquest years in Constantinople.

A half-century after Ernoul-Bernard and Aubri, the universal *Chronique* attributed to Baldwin of Avesnes (1278–81) was the first to appreciate the memoirs as a structured narrative rather than a source of anecdotes about the crusade.[8] One of the earliest versions of the *Chronique* (BnF, fr. 2633) devotes more than twenty folios to the Fourth Crusade,

---

4. Ernoul and Bernard, *Chronique*, 390. Jacquin, "La mort de deux barons," compares similar accounts of the battle of Adrianople in the memoirs (§§356–57) and the Ernoul-Bernard *Chronique* (382–83).

5. Jacquin, *Le style historique*, 373–74, suggests that similar passages in Clari and Villehardouin appear to have been taken from another source, but in view of what we now know about the Ernoul-Bernard text, it seems more likely that the copyists had direct access to both Clari and Villehardouin, and "enriched" Clari's text with passages from Villehardouin. Bull, *Eyewitness and Crusade Narrative*, 294, agrees that Clari's text is an "artfully crafted and considered piece of writing," that is, not a simple oral history. Dembowski, *La Chronique de Robert de Clari*, 121, regards Clari's narrative not as a spontaneous dictation but "an organized composition," that is, by a scribal rewriter. See Gaggero, "Western Eyes in the Latin East," 93–98, on the similar passages in Clari (*La conquête*, §8) and Ernoul and Bernard (*Chronique*, 374).

6. Chazan, "Aubri de Trois-Fontaines," and "L'usage de la compilation," discuss Aubri's sources and his critical assessment of them.

7. Aubri of Trois-Fontaines, *Chronica*, 885–86, borrows Villehardouin's description of the *partitio* and his nephew's conquest of the Peloponnese (*La conquête*, §§304, 325), and he repeats Clari's statement that Hugh of Saint-Pol carried the imperial sword and Boniface of Montferrat carried the imperial crown at Baldwin's coronation (Clari, *La conquête*, §96).

8. Natalis de Wailly (Villehardouin, *Geoffroi de Ville-Hardouin*), xvii–xviii, was the first to identify the abridged versions of the memoirs and Valenciennes's *Histoire* in the *Chronique dite de Baudouin d'Avesnes* (BnF, fr. 15460), a manuscript that he designated as G and now is dated to the fourteenth century.

APPENDIX 3   195

from the initial cross-taking of Count Thibaut to the death of Boniface of Montferrat.[9] It follows Villehardouin closely, especially for the battle of Adrianople, but omits the speeches in Villehardouin's narrative.[10]

Manuscript Editions

The earliest complete copies of the memoirs (B, C, D, F) were made in the last decades of the thirteenth century, most likely in Douai or Arras.[11] Manuscript B (BnF, fr. 2137), a miscellany of several history-themed vernacular texts, contains perhaps the oldest complete copy.[12] Written in a clear, professional script, it is devoid of title, illustrations, rubrics, and foliation. Jean Dufournet, the modern editor, considers the text to have been "rewritten," in effect translated to make it more accessible to a late thirteenth-century Middle French audience.[13] That practice of translating the memoirs for an audience whose spoken French had evolved from Villehardouin's speech of 1200 continued in print editions, beginning with Blaise de Vigenère's edition and translation of 1585.

Three contemporary manuscripts (C, D, F) copied the memoirs from the same exemplar as B but paired it with Valenciennes's *Histoire*, thus creating a seamless narrative of the brother-counts of Flanders as crusaders and emperors of Constantinople, from their cross-taking in February 1200 to July 1209. That pairing suggests that exemplars of the two texts had been kept together ever since Peter of Douai brought

---

9. BnF, fr. 2633, fols. 180r–206v, begins with an exact copy, in the same order, of Ville-hardouin's rosters of cross-takers at Écry (Villehardouin, *La conquête*, §§5–9) and ends with the death of Boniface at Ipsala. The copyist continues with several folios of Valenciennes's description of the battle of Philippopolis but apparently thought the rest of Valenciennes not sufficiently interesting to include in his chronicle.

10. As noted by Gachet, "Les chroniques de Bauduin d'Avesnes," 308–10.

11. I refer to manuscript "editions" in order to signal the fact that texts collected in bound codex volumes are just as much editions as are printed books. The decision to copy or print a text separately or in conjunction with other selected texts was an editorial decision made by the commissioner or producer of the volume and depended on the availability of exemplars.

12. Manuscript B (BnF, fr. 2137), fols. 47–148, edited and translated by Dufournet. The volume contains in addition: a *Roman des Septs Sages*, a brief *Description des saints lieux*, a *Histoire de Charlemagne* (from the Pseudo-Turpin), and an extract from the Anonymous of Béthune's *Histoire des ducs de Normandie et des rois d'Angleterre* (wrongly attributed to the Anonymous, according to Webster, in the Anonymous's *History of the Dukes of Normandy*, 197). An ex libris names Jean Sala, a Lyonnais bibliophile of ca. 1600. Faral (Villehardouin, *La conquête*), 1:xlix, classifies B, C, and D as belonging to a similar manuscript tradition, as does Dufournet (Ville-hardouin, *La Conquête*), 35.

13. Villehardouin, *La Conquête* (Dufournet), 35.

196   **APPENDIX 3**

them from Constantinople, and that the three copies likely were commissioned for the count of Flanders or someone close to the comital family.[14] In 1748 the three manuscripts entered the French royal library, where they were consulted by the nineteenth-century editor-translators who followed Dom Brial (1822) in pairing the memoirs and the *Histoire* in print editions.[15]

Manuscript D (BnF, fr. 12203) is a well-crafted miscellany of five texts with twelve miniatures.[16] It most likely was commissioned by Guy of Dampierre, count of Flanders (r. 1278–1305), a patron of the arts whose cultural interests included the history of the counts of Flanders.[17] His maternal grandfather Baldwin and granduncle Henry had been emperors of Constantinople, and his grandmother Marie of Champagne would have been empress had she not died in Acre before joining Baldwin in Constantinople. Villehardouin and Valenciennes offered contemporary narratives of his ancestors' exploits overseas. In manuscript D the memoirs are preceded by a framed painting of a crowned Baldwin (identified by his shield's coat of arms) leading several mounted knights to a tower portal, presumably in Constantinople, followed by a rubric: "This begins the history of Emperor Baldwin of Constantinople"

---

14. Longnon, "Sur l'Histoire de l'empereur Henri de Constantinople," 223–27, postulated the existence of an intermediary codex copy but did not consider the possibility that the exemplars were kept unbound in a copy shop and only paired when commissioned by the count of Flanders.

15. Legaré, "Nouveaux documents," 195.

16. Manuscript D (BnF, fr. 12203) contains: Villehardouin's memoirs, fols. 69–112; Valenciennes's *Histoire*, fols. 113–31; *Estoires d'outremer et de la naissance Salehadin*, fols. 1–49; *L'estoire des contes de Flandres*, fols. 50–68 (a translation of a Latin chronicle of the counts of Flanders [792–1164] written in the late twelfth century at Anchin monastery; see Rider, "Vice, Tyranny, Violence," 62–69, and his edition of the *Historia et genealogia comitatum Flandrensium*); and the Anonymous of Béthune's *Li estore des ducs de Normendie et des rois d' Engleterre*, fols. 131–84. Brief analyses of manuscript D are in Faral (Villehardouin, *La conquête*), 1:xxxviii, and Longnon, "Sur l'Histoire de l'empereur Henri de Constantinople," 218–20.

17. Rider, "Vice, Tyranny, Violence," 68–70, concludes that the volume was commissioned by Count Guy of Flanders in 1294. Krause, "Genealogy and Codicology," 334–36, 340n2, argues that the inclusion of the Anonymous of Béthune indicates a workshop in Douai. Caroff, "La narration des croisades," 187, no. 3, and "La quatrième croisade en images," 48, no. 3, suggests a late thirteenth-century copy from Arras. Avril, "Fichier des manuscrits enluminés," 756, agrees in dating the manuscript to the late thirteenth century, probably from Arras. It is also possible that it was produced in Tournai, since its fly leaves are fourteenth-century financial records from Tournai. Manuscript D was first inventoried in 1405 for the estate of Margaret of Flanders (Falmagne, *Corpus Catalogorum Belgii*, 115, no. 41). An identical paper copy of D, designated E (BnF, fr. 24210), was made in 1458 (note by François Avril in his "Fichier des manuscrits enluminés," 173).

APPENDIX 3   197

(Chi commence l'ystore de l'empereur Bauduin de Constantinoble).[18]
Villehardouin's text (fols. 69r–112v) is followed by Valenciennes's *Histoire* (fols. 113r–131r): "This begins the history of Emperor Henry of Constantinople" (Chi commence l'estore de l'empereur Henri de Constantinoble). In effect, Villehardouin's text is appropriated for a "history" of the Flemish count-emperors overseas as if they were proto-Belgians, just as they appear in Pierre Outreman's *Constantinopolis Belgica* (1643) and Charles Verlinden's *Les empereurs belge de Constantinople* (1945).[19]

Manuscript C (BnF, fr. 12204, ca. 1294), a paper copy of only the memoirs and the *Histoire*, is rubricated: "This begins the history of Count Baldwin of Flanders and Hainaut and how by his bravery he conquered the empire of Constantinople and how he was crowned emperor" (Chi commence li histoire dou conte Bauduin de Flandres et de Hainau, comment il conquis par sa proeche l'empire de Constantinoble et comment il en fu couronnes a empereour).[20] Valenciennes's text follows: "This is how Henry, brother of Emperor Baldwin, became emperor after his brother Emperor Baldwin was killed at Adrianople" (C'est de Henri le frere l'empereur Baudin, comment il fu empereour de Constantinoble apre son frere l'empereour Bauduin qui demoura devant Adrenople). Manuscript F (BnF, fr. 15100), a luxury volume most likely a copy of C, also contains only the memoirs and the *Histoire*.[21] Written in a careful gothic hand, it begins with a painting of Fulk preaching the cross to

---

18. Manuscript D (BnF, fr. 12203), fol. 69. See Caroff, "La narration des croisades," 190, fig. 3 (a full-page color photograph of the painting), and "La quatrième croisade en images," 189, plate 7. A painting on folio 78 depicts warriors in ships facing a wall tower; the rubric reads: "How the army arrived at Constantinople." A full-page reproduction is in Baudin, Brunel, and Dohrmann, *The Knights Templar*, 83, illustration no. 58.

19. Verlinden wrote without scholarly apparatus for a general audience in order to correct "une injustice historique" (9) of calling counts Baldwin and Henry (of Flanders and Hainaut) "French" instead of "Belgian" emperors of Constantinople. Pierre d'Outreman's *Constantinopolis Belgica* (1643), a detailed history of the counts written in Latin, was taken directly from Villehardouin's memoirs as edited by Vigenère (1585) or Rouillé (1601); see Zorzi, "Per la storiografia sulla quarta crociata," 724–35. Thirteen years later Du Cange rebranded the brothers as "French" in his *Histoire de l'empire de Constantinople sous le empereurs français* (1656).

20. Manuscript C (BnF, fr. 12204), fols. 1–30 (Villehardouin) and fols. 31–44 (Valenciennes), with endpapers listing fines collected in Tournai. See Faral (Villehardouin, *La conquête*), 1:xxxviii, and Longnon (Valenciennes, *Histoire*), 15. Manuscript C was first inventoried in 1469 for the estate of Philip the Good (Falmagne, *Corpus Catalogorum Belgi*, 227, no. 514).

21. Avril, "Fichier des manuscrits enluminés," 980, dates F to the third quarter of the thirteenth century, while Faral (Villehardouin, *La conquête*), 1:xxxix and Longnon (Valenciennes, *Histoire*, 15) date it to the fourteenth century and regard it as a copy of C. It was first inventoried in 1405 for the estate of Margaret of Flanders (Falmagne, *Corpus Catalogorum Belgii*, 115, no. 52).

198   **APPENDIX 3**

four pilgrims, and by suppressing Valenciennes's prologue, it effectively makes the *Histoire* a continuation of the memoirs.[22]

A second manuscript tradition was produced in Venice from four single copies of the memoirs presumably made in the thirteenth century but now lost. The best known was owned by Marino Sanudo Torsello (ca. 1270–1343), a prominent and well-traveled Venetian who acquired a "book of the conquest of Constantinople" (libro de conquisto Constantinopolitano), most likely in 1321 while visiting Flanders.[23] His testament identifies the *libro de conquisto* by name among the books he bequeathed to the brothers of San Giovanni and San Paolo of Venice but without identifying Villehardouin as its author.[24] If Sanudo did acquire the *libro* in Flanders, it would have derived from the same exemplar copied in manuscripts B, C, D, and F, and it indicates, importantly, that single copies of the memoirs (without Valenciennes) were still available in the early fourteenth century.

Sanudo commissioned two virtually identical copies (A, O) of his *libro* from a Venetian copy shop in the 1320s, most likely after 1328.[25] Manuscript A (BnF, fr. 4972) is a volume consisting of the memoirs and Sanudo's own *Fragmentum*, a brief account of events in the Latin Empire of Constantinople between 1207 and 1262.[26] Manuscript O (Bodleian Library, Laud. misc. 587) contains the memoirs, the *Fragmentum*, and a

---

22. Caroff, "La narration des croisades," 190, fig. 1, is a color photograph; and "La quatrième croisade en images," 185, fig. 1.

23. Vercauteren, "Note sur les rapports de Marino Sanudo." It is also possible that Sanudo acquired his *libro* during his time in Greece, perhaps in 1312 in Glarentsa (modern Killíni) in Achaia, where he wrote book 2 of his *Libro secretorum fidelium crucis*, a detailed proposal for a Venetian naval attack on Egypt that suggests a familiarity with Villehardouin's account of Venice's naval preparations for the Fourth Crusade. For the early fourteenth-century context of Sanudo's proposals for a new crusade, see Laiou, "Marino Sanudo Torsello"; Jacoby, "Catalans, Turcs et Vénitiens"; and Lock, "Sanudo, Turks, Greeks and Latins."

24. Sanudo's will of 9 March 1343 is printed in Magnocavallo, *Marin Sanudo*, 150–54, and translated in Frankfort, "Marino Sanudo Torsello," 274–78. The fate of the *libro* is unknown.

25. The consensus now is that A and O were written in the 1320s, in a copy shop where Marino Sanudo had his books made. See Angold, *The Fourth Crusade*, 123–24, and Devereaux, *Constantinople and the West*, 163–72. Reginato, "Le manuscrit Contarini," 40, dates A and O more precisely to after 1328, during the reign of Philip VI of Valois (1328–50).

26. Natalis de Wailly edited manuscript A (Paris, BnF, fr. 4972, fols. 1–54) in 1874. It was acquired by Cardinal Nicolo Ridolfi in the early sixteenth century and entered the library of Catherine de Medici by 1585; it was loaned to Claude Fauchet, who sold it to the Bibliothèque Royale in 1601, and today it remains in the Bibliothèque nationale de France; see Reginato, "Le manuscrit Contarini," 42–43. Wolff, "Hopf's So-Called 'Fragmentum'" (1953), edited the *Fragmentum*.

APPENDIX 3   199

text related to the history of Venice.[27] In all other respects, manuscripts A and O are identical: in text, in ornamentation, even in their painted scenes, and neither is rubricated. Their first folios begin with a historiated initial "S" of "Sachiez" showing Fulk of Neuilly preaching; across the entire lower borders of folio 1 are nearly identical scenes depicting the first assault on the walls of Constantinople, the Venetians attacking by sea, the mounted French by land.[28] The two "narrative images," beginning with the preaching of crusade and ending with the conquest of Constantinople, frame the first half of Villehardouin's account; they omit the establishment of a Latin regime and the post-conquest pacification of Constantinople's hinterland. Natalis de Wailly, who had access to all the manuscripts except O, regarded A as the best text, while Edmond Faral, who established the filiation of all the extant manuscripts, regarded O (hence also A) as most closely reflecting Villehardouin's Champenois language of a century earlier.[29]

What interested Sanudo in Villehardouin's *libro* was its positive view of the Venetians, with the conquest of Constantinople seen as a precursor of Venetian intervention in the eastern Mediterranean in the early fourteenth century, at the very time he was writing the *Liber secretorum fidelium crucis*, a call for a crusade against the Turks, and the *Istoria del regno di Romania*.[30] Sanudo's copies (A, O) brought the memoirs into the Venetian historiographical tradition, beginning with Andrea Dandolo's *Chronica* (1343–54).[31] With Faral's edition, manuscript O passed beyond

---

27. Villehardouin's memoirs in manuscript O (fols. 1–56r) are followed by Sanudo's *Fragmentum* (fols. 57v–58v) and Bonicontro dei Bovi's account of the Peace of Venice, written in the 1320s (fols. 59r–64r).

28. A photograph of manuscript O, fol. 1r, is in Devereaux, *Constantinople and the West*, 170; a digitized version is available online at Medieval Manuscripts in Oxford Libraries, https://medieval.bodleian.ox.ac.uk/catalog/manuscript_7384. A photograph of manuscript A, fol. 1, is in Caroff, "Le quatrième croisade en images," 186, plate 2.

29. Edmond Faral, who produced the most thorough edition of the memoirs and established the filiation of the earliest manuscripts (Villehardouin, *La conquête*, 1:xliv–xlix), concluded that, despite some Latinisms and Italianisms, manuscript O, with its Champenois usages and discordant case agreements, is the closest to Villehardouin's spoken language, although he conceded that B might be the earliest extant copy (1:l–li). Natalis de Wailly, who edited manuscript A, thought that it was closest to the marshal's language; Poirion, "Les paragraphes et le pré-texte," 53, agrees with him. For the difficulty in detecting Villehardouin's language of 1207 in late thirteenth-century copies, see Rodríguez Somolinos, "Variation et changement," and Naïs, "Reflexions preliminaires."

30. Devereaux, *Constantinople and the West*, 164–67. Reginato, "Marino Sanudo Torsello," shows how Sanudo saw his *Liber secretorum fidelium* as an extension of Villehardouin's *liber* in constituting a dossier for justifying Venetian expansion in the Mediterranean.

31. Madden, "The Venetian Version of the Fourth Crusade," concludes that Martin da Canal was unaware of the memoirs when he wrote *Les estoires de Venise* (1267–76), which simply

200   **APPENDIX 3**

the Venetian context to become the primary scholarly edition of the memoirs in the wider field of crusade studies.

The two sets of codex copies (B, C, D, F and A, O) illustrate what might be called "textual migration," by which the memoirs passed through two distinct political and cultural milieus.[32] For the Flemish, Villehardouin's memoirs and Valenciennes's *Histoire* were recopied in a project celebrating the deeds of counts Baldwin and Henry as emperors of Constantinople, as the rubricators of C and D clearly indicated. For the Venetians, the "book of the conquest of Constantinople" supported a narrative of Venice as the driving force of an expedition in service to then-current political goals of Venetian expansion in the Mediterranean. Those were two separate agendas: the deeds of the Flemish counts overseas versus a joint French-Venetian naval expedition to conquer Constantinople under the pope's direction. Neither was interested in Marshal Geoffroy and his Champenois companions.

Printed Editions

In 1541 Francesco Contarini (1477–1558), Venetian ambassador to the court of Emperor Charles V, returned home with what was described as a very old and barely readable copy of the memoirs that he had acquired from a monastic library in Brussels.[33] His description suggests that it might have been a thirteenth-century copy of the exemplar brought by Peter of Douai from Constantinople. Contarini deposited the manuscript with the Venetian Council of Ten, where it was scrutinized by several humanists working in the council's recently opened archive; they apparently did not know of Sanudo's *libro* or the copies A and

---

repeated a sanitized oral tradition depicting Venetian participation in the crusade (323–38). He argues that the anonymous *Chronicle of Marco* (1292) was the first Venetian work to draw on Villehardouin's details and narrative from an unknown source (335–36), but that Andrea Dandolo was the first to make use of Villehardouin's work in his *Chronica* (336–37). See also Angold, *The Fourth Crusade*, 123–24; Devereaux, *Constantinople and the West*, 158–63; and Saint-Guillain, "Tales of San Marco."

32. Textual migration usually refers to a translated text entering a different linguistic and cultural milieu, but I think the concept is pertinent here, in that Villehardouin's text operated within distinct cultural milieus.

33. For an analysis of Contarini's manuscript, see Reginato, "La manuscrit Contarini." For its importance in framing Venice's history at a time when documents from the Fourth Crusade were being consulted in the archive of the Venetian chancery, see Antonini, "Historical Uses of the Secret Chancery," 159–67. See also Paris (Villehardouin, *De la conquête de Constantinoble*), vii.

APPENDIX 3   201

O made two centuries earlier, which may have already left Venice.[34] In 1556 Giovanni Battista Ramusio, secretary of the Venetian archives, offered to edit Contarini's manuscript and translate it into Italian. He described it as "il libro del signor Geoffredo di Villa Arduin marescalo di Campagna," thus identifying Villehardouin for the first time as its author.[35] Giovanni's son Paolo published the first quire of the manuscript in 1572 but did not complete the project because, he said, he was not always able to transcribe the damaged manuscript accurately, and so he sent printed copies of the first quire to scholars in France who knew medieval French better and who might have access to other copies in better condition.[36]

Paolo Ramusio might have learned that the accomplished translator Blaise de Vigenère was preparing a bilingual edition of the memoirs under the patronage of Louis de Gonzaga, marquis of Montferrat (and descendant of Boniface of Montferrat).[37] Vigenère notes that he saw Ramusio's edition of the first quire but that he relied on the complete Zacco copy (now lost but closely related to A and O) for his bilingual edition, in which he presented Villehardouin's Old French (*vieil langage*) opposite a current (*plus moderne et intelligible*) French translation. The book's title reads: *L'Histoire de Geoffroy de Villehardouyn, mareschal de Champagne et de Romenie* [. . .] *de la Conqueste de Constantinople par les barons françois associez aux Venitiens, l'an 1204* (1585).[38] It is the earliest complete

---

34. Manuscript A was acquired by Claude Fauchet (1530-1602), a Parisian bibliophile and president of the Cour des Monnayes, who sold it to the Royal Library of France on 18 June 1601 (as noted in a blank folio); see Faral (Villehardouin, *La conquête*), 1:xxxviii. Manuscript O, first listed in the Bodleian Laud collection ca. 1790, apparently was acquired after the French Revolution.

35. The Contarini manuscript was subsequently lost, but Reginato's close analysis of Giovanni Battista Ramusio's unpublished Italian translation makes it possible to recover a full and accurate semblance of it; see Reginato, "Le manuscrit Contarini," 49-56, and 47-48n68 for the lost Paradin copy. Reginato concludes (68) that Contarini's copy was related to, but independent of, A and O, which were made from Sanudo's *libro*.

36. Faral, "Pour l'établissement du texte de Villehardouin," 293-94, and Antonini, "Historical Uses of the Secret Chancery," 161-64. The first cahier of Contarini's manuscript was presented to the Council of Ten in 1572; for its fate, see Gazzotti, "Studi cinquecenteschi," and Faral (Villehardouin, *La conquête*), 1:xl.

37. Faral, "Pour l'établissement du texte de Villehardouin," provides a brief history of the early editions of the memoirs. See also Rickard, "Blaise de Vigenère's Translation," 12, and Zorzi, "Per la storiografia sulla quarta crociata," 703-5.

38. Rickard, "Blaise de Vigenère's Translation of Villehardouin," 1-2, 12-15. Rickard notes that the lost Zacco manuscript appears to have been related to manuscripts A and B (13). Buridant, "Blaise de Vigenère," regards Vigenère's vocabulary as "un véritable lexique bilingue" (99). See also Faral (Villehardouin, *La conquête*), 1:xl, and "Pour l'établissement du texte," 292, 303-11.

202   **APPENDIX 3**

print edition of Villehardouin's memoirs with the earliest translation into "modern" French.

Soon thereafter the Lyonnais printer Guillaume Rouillé, who had apprenticed in Venice, acquired Contarini's manuscript, which he described as "a very old exemplar written on parchment 400 years ago in French letters so obsolete and worn that they are scarcely readable."[39] He edited Contarini's manuscript, together with Vigenère's edition and several other now-lost manuscripts, under the title *L'histoire ou Chronique du seigneur Geoffroy de Ville-Hardouin, mareschal de Champaigne et de Romanie. [...] contenant la Conqueste de l'empire de Constantinople faicte par les barons françois, confederez et unis avec les seigneurs Venetiens, l'an 1204* (1601).[40]

Those two editions, Vigenère's in Paris based primarily on the Zacco manuscript (1585), and Rouillé's in Lyon based on the Contarini manuscript (1601), identified Geoffroy of Villehardouin as marshal of Champagne and author of the "history" or "chronicle" of the conquest of Constantinople, thereby placing the memoirs within the French (as opposed to the Flemish or Venetian) experience overseas and ultimately within the French literary tradition as the earliest prose narrative in French.[41] With those two editions, the memoirs underwent their third textual migration, as they moved from late thirteenth-century Flanders (B, C, D, F) to early fourteenth-century Venice (A, O) to late sixteenth-century France (Vigenère, Rouillé), in each case providing material for a cultural appropriation—of Flemish, Venetian, and French identity.

In France, Villehardouin's printed text passed through several iterations. Rouillé's edition of 1601 became the base text of Charles Du Cange's edition (with parallel translation) of 1657, which in its second

---

39. For Rouillé's apprenticeship in Venice, see Davis, "Publisher Guillaume Rouillé," 74–76. Rouillé states in his preface that his edition was based primarily on the copy brought from Belgium by Francesco Contarini in 1541: "Cest exemplaire escrit en parchemin fort vieux, il y a 400 ans, avec characteres françois si caduques et usez qu'à grand peine les peut-on lire." Rouillé also consulted the Paradin manuscript (now lost) and knew of Vigenère's edition-translation of 1585. See also Zorzi, "Per la storiografia sulla quarta crociata," 694–95.

40. Rouillé divided Villehardouin's text into 257 paragraphs, which Du Cange later retained, and included a translation of book 3 of Niketas Choniates's *Annals*. Rouillé's edition was published posthumously by his family.

41. For the provenance of Vigenère's copy, see Rickard, "Blaise de Vigenère's Translation of Villehardouin," 2, 13. The similarity of the two titles raises the suspicion that Contarini and Vigenère knew of each other's impending publication. Vigenère may have seen a copy of the Venice 1572 edition and decided to offer an accessible translation for a general audience in France. Three years after Rouillé's edition (dedicated to Henry IV of Navarre) was published, Paolo Ramusio published an Italian translation as *Della guerra di Costantinopoli* "by the Venetians and French" (1604); see Zorzi, "Per la storiografia sulla quarta crociata," 692–702, and Antonini, "Historical Uses of the Secret Chancery," 94, 161–63.

APPENDIX 3   203

edition of 1729 served as the text of reference for almost two centuries.[42] Dom Brial reprinted Du Cange's text, with variants from manuscripts B and C, in the *Recueil des historiens des Gaules et de la France* (1822), to which he joined Valenciennes's *Histoire* as a continuation of Villehardouin, just as it appears in manuscript C, which he consulted in the royal library.[43] That pairing was followed by the editions of J. A.-C. Buchon (1828) and Paulin Paris (1838), who produced the first critical edition of both texts based on all the extant manuscripts in the Bibliothèque Nationale, with a facing-page translation and extensive notes.[44] Natalis de Wailly (1872) continued the Villehardouin-Valenciennes pairing, provided new translations, and introduced the now-standard classification of the manuscripts by letter (A to F) and the sequential numbering of the paragraphs for Villehardouin (§§1–500) and Valenciennes (§§501–694).[45]

Natalis de Wailly's edition marked the last time that the memoirs and the *Histoire* would be paired as they are in manuscripts C and D. The very next year, 1873, Karl Hopf disrupted that model by publishing an edition of Robert of Clari's *The Conquest of Constantinople* from a hitherto unknown manuscript, thereby introducing a second lay participant's account of the crusade in vernacular prose.[46] Natalis de Wailly, in his second edition of the memoirs (1874), rendered a severe assessment of Clari's text, pointing out the many factual errors that diminished its

---

42. Du Cange states in his preface that he consulted Vigenère's edition of 1585 and Rouillé's superior edition of 1601 with its 257 paragraph divisions. He also consulted other manuscripts in the French royal library, including manuscript A, which Claude Fauchet brought from Venice, and Vigenère's notes made on the printed edition of Contarini's first quire in 1573. See also Faral (Villehardouin, *La conquête*), 1:xl–xli, and "Pour d'établissement du texte de Villehardouin," 311. For Du Cange's more precise translations, see Rickard, "From Villehardouin to Du Cange." Du Cange's edition of 1657 is also notable in offering the first, if brief, biography of Villehardouin (1:235–39, "Eloge de Geoffroy de Villehardouin"), which Buchon expanded in his reedition of Du Cange (1828), i–xiii.

43. For the several editions of Valenciennes, see Longnon, "Sur l'Histoire de l'empereur Henri," 229–37.

44. Buchon republished Du Cange's edition of the memoirs but took Valenciennes's *Histoire* from manuscript C. Paulin Paris (Villehardouin, *De la conquête de Constantinoble*, viii–xxvi), divided the text into 177 paragraphs.

45. Natalis de Wailly (Villehardouin, *Geoffroi de Ville-Hardouin*), xi–xviii, whose edition is based primarily on A, discussed the relationship of all the manuscripts except O, and numbered the paragraphs §§1–500. Poirion, "Les paragraphes et le pré-texte," 51–53, concludes that the divisions did not reflect Villehardouin's spoken testimony but were introduced by later copyists. See also Faral (Villehardouin, *La conquête*), 1:xl–xlii, and Paris (Villehardouin, *De la conquête de Constantinoble*), viii–xxvi.

46. See Edgar Holmes McNeal's introduction to Robert of Clari, *Conquest of Constantinople*, 10–12.

204   **APPENDIX 3**

value in comparison with Villehardouin's account.[47] But the appearance of Clari's oral history broke the link between Villehardouin and Valenciennes, and since then the memoirs and the *Histoire* have been edited separately, most recently in definitive editions of Villehardouin from manuscripts O (Faral, 1939–40) and B (Dufournet, 2004), and of Valenciennes from all known manuscripts (Longnon, 1948).

Translations

Vigenère, who as a professional translator strove to make ancient texts available to a general readership, established the bilingual model for presenting Villehardouin's thirteenth-century text with a facing-page translation in current French for a late sixteenth-century audience (1585). Du Cange followed that model with his side-by-side edition-translation (1657), in which he modified Vigenère's translation to improve its accuracy and to reflect the continuing evolution of French usage during the intervening seven decades.[48] Natalis de Wailly (1872) was the last to offer current translations of both the memoirs and the *Histoire*. In the wake of Hopf's edition of Clari and the severing of the Villehardouin-Valenciennes pairing, Bouchet (1891), Faral (1939), and Dufournet (2004) offered bilingual editions of the memoirs alone. Those "modern" French translations with a facing page in thirteenth-century orthography solidified the marshal's standing as the earliest prose "writer" in French.

Although Philippe Lauer's careful edition of Clari's text (1922) established it as a vernacular account worthy to stand with Villehardouin's, it was Albert Pauphilet who cemented Clari's standing as an early vernacular author of non-fiction prose by placing him in the company of Villehardouin, Jean de Joinville, Jean Froissart, and Philippe de Commynes in his *Historiens et chroniqueurs du moyen âge* (1948).[49] Noël Coulet (1966) and Jean Longnon (1981) followed Pauphilet's example by pairing translations of Villehardouin and Clari as contemporary accounts of the Fourth Crusade.[50] Scholarly studies of the crusade have continued to compare

---

47. Natalis de Wailly (Villehardouin, *Geoffroi de Ville-Hardouin*), 440–48.
48. Rickard, "From Villehardouin to Du Cange," 117–19, notes that Du Cange relied mainly on Vigenère's translation.
49. Pauphilet reproduced Lauer's edition of Clari (1924) and Natalis de Wailly's edition of Villehardouin (1874).
50. Longnon's *Histoire de la conquête de Constantinople*, 43–75, published posthumously, is a modified translation of Natalis de Wailly's translation of 1872.

APPENDIX 3   205

the two texts as foundational accounts of the Fourth Crusade.[51] However, recent questions surrounding the integrity of Clari's text threaten to remove him from the pantheon of earliest "writers" in Old French.[52] A paradigm shift in viewing earlier vernacular texts and translations also promises to relocate both Villehardouin and Clari within a longer tradition of written vernacular.[53] Yet the originality of Villehardouin's memoirs remains: as the earliest war memoirs in medieval Europe, the earliest original Old French prose narrative, and the only contemporary account of the Fourth Crusade and its immediate aftermath.

The earliest English translation of the memoirs, based on Du Cange's 1656 edition, was by Thomas Smith (1829), who noted that Villehardouin's text is far more than an account of a crusade. But the memoirs did not become widely known to Anglophone readers until Frank Marzials published his translation (1908) based on the editions of Natalis de Wailly (1872) and Bouchet (1891). Marzials was the first to pair the memoirs with Joinville's *Life of Saint Louis* in a single volume for general readers because, he explained, Villehardouin and Joinville are "monuments of the French Language, and of French prose at an early stage of development . . . [by] eye-witnesses who had taken an important part, and in the case of Villehardouin a very important part, in what they describe."[54] That Villehardouin-Joinville pairing was followed by M. R. B. Shaw (1963) and Caroline Smith (2008), whose translations of the memoirs and *The Life of Saint Louis* in the Penguin editions consecrated the marshal and seneschal of Champagne as authors of "the earliest full-fledged military memoirs" of the Middle Ages.[55]

Villehardouin could not have imagined the multiple paths that his memoirs would take far beyond Constantinople in the next eight centuries through the hands of scribes, patrons, editors, and translators. It has appeared in both manuscript and print in several formats: as a stand-alone text; in a miscellany of related prose narratives; and paired variously with Valenciennes's *Histoire*, with Clari's oral history, and with

---

51. Notably: Dufournet, *Les écrivains de la IVe croisade* (1973); Jacquin, *Le style historique*, 300–335; Beer, *In Their Own Words*, 38–68; and Bull, *Eyewitness and Crusade Narrative*, 265–336.

52. Gaggero, "Western Eyes in the Latin East," 93–98.

53. Damian-Grint, *The New Historians of the Twelfth-Century Renaissance*, 207.

54. Marzials in Villehardouin and Joinville, *Memoirs of the Crusades*, ix. Marzials goes on to remark that they both deal with "stirring episodes in one of the most stirring chapters in human history." His pairing of Villehardouin and Joinville might have been inspired by Debidour's study, *Les chroniqueurs* (1888), which Marzials cites (xliii).

55. Harari, "Military Memoirs," 291.

APPENDIX 3

Joinville's history of Louis IX. The old marshal would have been satisfied with the high regard his memoirs have earned for providing the only secure narrative of the Fourth Crusade, and for doing so in his spoken vernacular that has entered the canon of early French prose literature.[56]

---

56. In 1959 France honored Villehardouin with a postage stamp in the series "Les grandes personnages," in which his imagined portrait gazes out from a fleet of cross-signed sailing ships.

BIBLIOGRAPHY

Primary Sources

Akropolites, George. *The History*. Translated with an introduction and commentary by Ruth Macrides. Oxford: Oxford University Press, 2007.

Ambroise. *The History of the Holy War: Ambroise's "Estoire de la Guerre Sainte."* Edited by Marianne Ailes and Malcolm Barber. Translated by Marianne Ailes. 2 vols. Woodbridge, UK: Boydell, 2003.

Andrea, Alfred J., ed. and trans. *Contemporary Sources for the Fourth Crusade*. 2nd ed. Leiden: Brill, 2008.

Andrea, Alfred J. "The *Devastatio Constantinopolitana*." Translation in Andrea, *Contemporary Sources*, 205–21.

Andrieu, G., and J. Piolle, eds. *Perceval: Ou le conte du graal de Chrétien de Troyes; Concordancier complet des formes graphiques occurrentes d'après l'édition de M. Félix Lecoy*. Aix-en-Provence: Université de Provence, 1976.

Anonymous of Béthune. *History of the Dukes of Normandy and the Kings of England by the Anonymous of Béthune*. Translated by Janet Shirley. Edited by Paul Webster. London: Routledge, 2021.

Arbois de Jubainville, Henry d'. "Nouvelles recherches sur le chroniquer Geofroi de Villehardouin." *Revue des Sociétés Savantes des départements de l'étranger*, 3e série, 1 (1863): 364–73.

Aubri of Trois-Fontaines. *Chronica*. Edited by Paul Scheffer-Boichorst. *MGH SS*, 23:631–950. Hannover: Hahn, 1874. Partial translation in Andrea, *Contemporary Sources*, 291–309.

Avril, François. "Fichier des manuscrits enluminés du département des manuscrits [de la Bibliothèque Nationale de France]." Nouvelles acquisitions françaises 28935 (40).

Baldwin, John W., et al., eds. *Les registres de Philippe Auguste*. Vol. 1. Paris: Imprimerie nationale, 1992.

Baldwin of Avesnes. "Chronique universelle de Baudoin d'Avesnes." BnF, fr. 2633.

Barthélemy, Anatole de. "Chartes de départ et de retour des comtes de Dampierre-en-Astenois, IVe and Ve croisades." In *Archives de l'Orient latin*, edited by Paul Riant, vol. 2, pt. 2, 184–207. Paris: E. Leroux, 1884.

Beaumanoir, Philippe de. *Coutumes de Beauvaisis*. Edited by Am. Salmon. 3 vols. Paris: A. et J. Picard, 1970–74. Translated by Akehurst as The *"Coutumes de Beauvaisis."*

Beaumanoir, Philippe de. *The "Coutumes de Beauvaisis" of Philippe de Beaumanoir*. Translated by F. R. P. Akehurst. Philadelphia: University of Pennsylvania Press, 1992.

BIBLIOGRAPHY

Benedict of Peterborough. *Gesta Regis Henrici Secundi Benedicti abbatis*. Edited by W. Stubbs. 4 vols. Rolls Series 49. 2 vols. London: Longmans, 1867. Now ascribed to Roger of Howden.

Benton, John F., ed. "Recueil des actes des comtes de Champagne, 1152–1197." Unpublished "pre-edition" of the acts of Count Henry I, Countess Marie, and Count Henry II. Pasadena: California Institute of Technology, 1988.

Benton, John, and Michael Bur et al., eds. *Recueil des actes d'Henri le Libéral, comte de Champagne (1152–1181)*. 2 vols. Paris: De Boccard, 2009–13.

Boutillier du Retail, Armand, and P. Piétresson de Saint-Aubin, eds. *Obituaires de la province de Sens*. Vol. 4, *Diocèses de Meaux et de Troyes*. Paris: Imprimerie nationale, 1923.

Buchon, J. A.-C. *Recherches et matériaux pour servir à une histoire de la domination française au XIIIe, XIVe, and XVe siècles dans les provinces démembrées de l'Empire Grec à la suite de la quatrième croisade*. 2 Vols. Paris: Auguste Desrez, 1840.

Carile, Antonio. "Partitio Terrarum Imperii Romanie." *Studi Veneziani* 7 (1965): 125–305.

Carrière, Victor. *Histoire et cartulaire des Templiers de Provins*. Paris: Honoré Champion, 1919.

Cartulary of Larrivour. AD (Aube), 4 H 1. Thirteenth century.

Cartulary of Vauluisant. BnF, Latin 9901. Thirteenth century.

Choniates, Niketas. *O City of Byzantium: Annals of Niketas Choniates*. Translated by Harry J. Magoulias. Detroit: Wayne State University Press, 1984.

Chrétien de Troyes. *Cligés*. In *Chrétien de Troyes: Romans*, edited and translated by Charles Méla and Olivier Collet, 285–494. La Pochothèque. Paris: Librairie Générale Française, 1994.

Chrétien de Troyes. *Le conte du Graal (Perceval), édités d'après la copie de Guiot (Bib. nat. fr. 794)*. Edited by Félix Lecoy. Les romans de Chrétien de Troyes. 2 vols. Paris: Librairie Honoré Champion, 1984.

Clari, Robert de. *The Conquest of Constantinople*. Translated by Edgar Holmes McNeal. New York: Columbia University Press, 1936.

Clari, Robert de. *La conquête de Constantinople*. Edited and translated by Jean Dufournet. Paris: Honoré Champion, 2004.

Clari, Robert de. *La conquête de Constantinople*. Edited by Philippe Lauer. Paris: Édouard Champion, 1924.

Clari, Robert de. *La conquête de Constantinople*. Edited and translated by Peter Noble. Edinburgh: Société Rencesvals British Branch, 2005.

Conon de Béthune. *Les chansons de Conon de Béthune*. Edited by Alex Wallensköld. Paris: Honoré Champion, 1968.

Delaborde, H.-F., et al., eds. *Recueil des actes de Philippe Auguste*. 4 vols. Paris: Imprimerie nationale, 1916–79.

Delaville Le Roulx, J., ed. *Cartulaire général de l'ordre des Hospitaliers de S. Jean de Jérusalem, 1100–1310*. Vol. 1. Paris: Ernest Leroux, 1894.

Delisle, Léopold. "Extraits d'une chronique française des rois de France, par un Anonyme de Béthune." In *Recueil des historiens des Gaules et de la France*, 24:750–75. Paris: Imprimerie nationale, 1904.

BIBLIOGRAPHY 209

Duba, William O., and Christopher D. Schabel, eds. *Bullarium Hellenicum: Pope Honorius III's Letters to Frankish Greece and Constantinople (1216–1227)*. Turnhout, Belgium: Brepols, 2015.

Ernoul and Bernard. *Chronique d'Ernoul et de Bernard le Trésorier*. Edited by L. de Mas Latrie. Société de l'histoire de France. Paris: Chez Mme Ve Jules Renouard, 1871.

Evergates, Theodore, ed. *The Cartulary of Countess Blanche of Champagne*. Medieval Academy Books 112. Toronto: University of Toronto Press, 2009.

Evergates, Theodore, ed. and trans. *Feudal Society in Medieval France: Documents from the County of Champagne*. Philadelphia: University of Pennsylvania Press, 1993.

Evergates, Theodore, ed. *Littere Baronum: The Earliest Cartulary of the Counts of Champagne*. Medieval Academy Books 107. Toronto: University of Toronto Press, 2003.

Flammarion, Hubert, ed. *Cartulaire du chapitre cathédral de Langres*. Turnhout, Belgium: Brepols, 2004.

Gallia Christiana in provincias ecclesiasticas distributa. 16 vol. Paris, 1715–1865.

Garrigues, Martine, ed. *Le premier cartulaire de l'abbaye cistercienne de Pontigny (XIIe–XIIIe siècles)*. Paris: Bibliothèque Nationale, 1981.

Gautier d'Arras. *Eracle*. Edited and translated by Karen Pratt. London: King's College, 2007.

Gesta Innocentii. In *PL*, 214:17–227. Translated by Powell as *The Deeds of Innocent III*.

Gislebert of Mons. *Chronicle of Hainaut*. Translated by Laura Napran. Woodbridge, UK: Boydell, 2005.

Gislebert of Mons. *La chronique de Gislebert de Mons*. Edited by Léon Vanderkindere. Brussels: Kiessling, 1904.

Guiot de Provins. *Les Oeuvres de Guiot de Provins, poète lyrique et satirique*, edited by John Orr. Manchester: University of Manchester Press, 1915. Reprint, Geneva: Slatkine Reprints, 1974.

Guy of Bazoches. *Ex Guidonis de Bazochiis, Cronosgraphie libro septimo*. Edited by Alexander Cartellieri. Jena: Kämpfe, 1910.

Hageneder, Othmar, et al., comp. *Die Register Innocenz' III*. 15 volumes to date. Graz: Verlag Hermann Böhlaus, 1964–.

Harmand, Auguste. "Notice historique sur la Léproserie de la ville de Troyes." *MSA* 14 (1847–48): 429–669.

Hendrickx, Benjamin. *Regestes des empereurs latins de Constantinople (1204–1261/1272)*. Thessalonika: The Byzantine Research Centre, Aristotelian University of Thessaloniki, 1988.

Holden, A. J., ed. *History of William Marshal*. Translated by S. Gregory. Notes by D. Crouch. 3 vols. London: Anglo-Norman Text Society, Birbeck College, 2002–6.

Ibn Shaddād, Bahā' al-Din. *The Rare and Excellent History of Saladin*. Translated by D. S. Richards. Aldershot, UK: Ashgate, 2001.

John of Salisbury. *The Letters of John of Salisbury*. Edited by W. J. Millor and C. N. L. Brook. Vol. 2. Oxford: Clarendon, 1979.

BIBLIOGRAPHY

Lalore, Charles, ed. *Cartulaire de l'abbaye de Montiéramey*. Paris: Thorin, 1890.

Lalore, Charles, ed. *Cartulaire de l'abbaye de Saint-Loup de Troyes*. Paris: Thorin, 1875.

Lalore, Charles, ed. *Cartulaire de l'abbaye du Paraclet*. Paris: Thorin, 1878.

Lalore, Charles, ed. *Cartulaire de Montier-la-Celle*. Paris: Thorin, 1882.

Lalore, Charles, ed. *Cartulaire de Saint-Pierre de Troyes*. Paris: Thorin, 1870.

Lalore, Charles, ed. *Documents sur l'abbaye de Notre-Dame-au-Nonnains de Troyes*. Paris: Imprimerie de Dufour-Bouquot, 1874.

Lalore, Charles, ed. *Inventaires des pricipales églises de Troyes*. Collection de documents inédits relatifs à la ville de Troyes et à la Champagne méridionale, publié par la Société Académique de Troyes. Vol. 1. Troyes: Imprimerie & lithographie Dufour-Bouquot, 1893.

Lambert of Ardres. *The History of the Counts of Guines and Lords of Ardres*. Translated by Leah Shopkow. Philadelphia: University of Pennsylvania Press, 2001.

Longnon, Auguste, ed. *Documents relatifs au comté de Champagne et de Brie (1172–1361)*. 3 vols. Paris: Imprimerie nationale, 1901–14.

Longnon, Jean, ed. *Le livre de la conqueste de la princée de l'Amorée: Chronique de Morée (1204–1305)*. Paris: Librairie Renouard, 1911. Translated by Van Arsdall and Moody as *The Old French Chronicle of Morea*.

Longnon, Jean. *Recherches sur la vie de Geoffroy de Villehardouin: Suivies du catalogue des actes des Villehardouin*. Paris: Édouard Champion, 1939.

Meinert, Hermann, ed. *Papsturkunden in Frankreich*. Neue Folge. Bd. 1, *Champagne und Lothringen*. Berlin: Wiedermannsche Buchhandlung, 1932.

Meliga, Walter, ed. *L' "Eructavit" antico francese secondo il ms. Paris B.N.Fr. 1747*. Alessandria: Edizione dell'Orso, 1992.

Mesarites, Nicholas. *Nicholas Mesarites: His Life and Works (in Translation)*. Translated with notes and commentary by Michael Angold. Liverpool: Liverpool University Press, 2017.

Migne, J. P., ed. *Patrologiae cursus completus: Series Latina*. 221 vols. Paris, 1844–64.

Newman, William Mendel, ed. *Les seigneurs de Nesle en Picardie (XIIe–XIIIe siècles), leurs chartes et leur histoire: Étude sur la noblesse régionale, ecclésiastique et laïque*. 2 vols. Philadelphia: American Philosophical Society, 1971.

Nicaise, Auguste. *Épernay et l'abbaye Saint-Martin de cette ville*. 2 vols. Châlons-sur-Marne: J.-L. Le Roy, 1869.

Nicholson, Helen J., trans. *Chronicle of the Third Crusade: A Translation of the Itinerarium Peregrinorum et Gesta Regis Ricardi*. Aldershot, UK: Ashgate, 1997.

Nieus, Jean-François, ed. *Les chartes des comtes de Saint-Pol (XIe–XIIIe siècles)*. Turnhout, Belgium: Brepols, 2008.

Pauphilet, Albert, ed. *Historiens et chroniqueurs du moyen age: Robert de Clari, Villehardouin, Joinville, Froissart, Commynes*. Bibliotheque de la Pléiade. Paris: Gallimard, 1952.

Pokorny, Rudolf. "Zwei unedierte Briefe aus der Frühzeit des lateinischen Kaiserreichs von Konstantinopel." *Byzantion* 55, no. 1 (1985): 180–209.

Powell, James M., trans. *The Deeds of Innocent III*. Washington, DC: Catholic University of America Press, 2004.

Prevenier, Walter, ed. *De oorkonden der graven van Vlaanderen (1191–aanvang 1206)*. Vol. 2, *Uitgave*. Brussels: Palais des Académies, 1964.

BIBLIOGRAPHY   211

Raimbaut de Vaqueiras. *The Poems of the Troubadour Raimbaut de Vaqueiras*. Edited and translated by Joseph Linskill. The Hague: Mouton, 1964.

Ralph of Diceto. *Ymagines historiarum*. In *The Historical Works of Master Ralph de Diceto, Dean of London*, edited by William Stubbs, 1:291–440, 2:2–174. London: Longmans, 1876.

Riant, Paul, ed. *Exuviae sacrae Constantinopolitanae*. 2 vols. Geneva, 1877. Reprint, with preface by Jannic Durand. Paris: Éditions du CTHS, 2004.

Rider, Jeff, ed. *Historia et genealogia comitatum Flandrensium*. In *The Earliest Genealogies and Histories of the Counts of Flanders*. Brussels: Académie royale des sciences, des lettres et des beaux-arts de Belgique, forthcoming.

Rigord. *The Deeds of Philip Augustus: An English Translation of Rigord's "Gesta Philippi Augusti."* Translated by Larry F. Field. Edited and annotated by M. Cecilia Gaposchkin and Sean L. Field. Ithaca: Cornell University Press, 2022.

Rigord. *Gesta Philippi Augusti*. In *Histoire de Philippe Auguste*. Edited and translated by Élisabeth Carpentier, Georges Pon, and Yves Chauvin. Sources d'histoire médiévale 33. Paris: CNRS, 2006. Translated by Field as *The Deeds of Philip Augustus*.

Robert, Gaston. "Fondation d'une chapellenie par Jean de Brandonvillers, confirmée par son frère Geoffroy de Villehardouin." *Nouvelle revue de Champagne et de Brie* 10 (1932): 132–33.

Robert of Auxerre. *Chronicon*. Edited by Oswald Holder-Egger. *MGM SS*, 26: 217–76.

Roger of Howden. *Chronica magistri Rogeri de Houedene*. Edited by W. Stubbs. 4 vols. Rerum Britannicarum medii aevi scriptores 51. 4 vols. London: Longmans, 1868–71.

Roserot, Alphonse. "Deux chartes inédites concernant le père et les frères présumés de Geoffroy de Villehardouin." *Bulletin du Comité des Travaux historiques et scientifiques, Section d'histoire et de philologie* (1884): 278–84.

Rzihacek, Andrea, Renate Spreitzer, Brigitte Merta, Christine Ottner-Disenberger, Paul Zinsmaier, and Rainer Maria Herkenrath, eds. *Die Urkunden Philipps von Schwaben*. Vol. 2. Wiesbaden: Harrassowitz Verlag, 2014.

Saint-Étienne of Troyes. "Cartulary of ca. 1271." BnF, Latin 17098.

Shaw, M. R. B., trans. "The Conquest of Constantinople," in Villehardouin and Joinville, *Chronicles of the Crusades*, 29–160.

Smith, Caroline, trans. "The Conquest of Constantinople." In Villehardouin and Joinville, *Chronicles of the Crusades*, 1–135.

Strehlke, Ernst, ed. *Tabulae Ordinis Theutonici*. Berlin: Weidmann, 1869. Reprint, Toronto: University of Toronto Press, 1975.

Stubbs, William, ed. *Itinerarium Peregrinorum et gesta regis Ricardi: Chronicles and Memorials of the Reign of Richard I*. Vol. 1. Rolls Series 38. London: Longman, 1864. Translated by Nicholson as *Chronicle of the Third Crusade*.

Tafel, G. F. L, and G. M. Thomas, eds. *Urkunden zur älteren Handels- und Staatsgeschichte der Republik Venedig: Mit besonderer Beziehung auf Byzanz und die Levante*. 3 vols. Vienna, 1856–57. Reprint, Amsterdam: Verlag Adolf M. Hakkert, 1964.

Teulet, Alexandre, et al., eds. *Layettes du Trésor des Chartes*. 4 vols. Paris: H. Plon, 1863–1909.

212   BIBLIOGRAPHY

Valenciennes, Henri de. *Histoire de l'empereur Henri de Constantinople*. Edited by Jean Longnon. Documents relatifs à l'histoire des Croisades 2. Paris: Librairie Orientaliste Paul Geuthner, 1948.

Van Arsdall, Anne, and Helen Moody, trans. *The Old French Chronicle of Morea: An Account of Frankish Greece after the Fourth Crusade*. Farnham, UK: Ashgate, 2015.

Veyssière, Laurent, Jean Waquet, and Jean-Marc Roger, eds. *Recueil des chartes de l'abbaye de Clairvaux au XIIe siècle*. Paris: Comité des travaux historiques et scientifiques, 2004.

Villehardouin, Geoffroy de. *Ceaux qui conquirent Constantinople: Récits de la quatrième croisade*. Translation by Noël Coulet. Paris: Union général d'éditions, 1966.

Villehardouin, Geoffroy de. *The Chronicle of Geoffry of Villehardouin, Marshal of Champagne and Romania, concerning the Conquest of Constantinople by the French and Venetians, anno MCCIV*. Translated by Thomas Smith. London: William Pickering, 1829.

Villehardouin, Geoffroy de. *Chronique de la prise de Constantinople par les francs, écrite par Geoffroy de Ville-Hardouin, marechal de Champagne et de Romanie*. Edited by J.-A. Buchon. Paris: Verdiêre, 1828.

Villehardouin, Geoffroy de [Josfroi de Vileharduyn]. *La conqueste de Costentinoble, d'après le manuscrit no. 2137 de la B.N.* Edited by O. Derniame, M. Henin, S. Monsonego, H. Naïs, and R. Tomasonne. Nancy: Centre de recherches et d'applications linguistiques, Université de Nancy II, 1978. Based on a digital edition of manuscript B.

Villehardouin, Geoffroy de. *La Conquête de Constantinople*. Edited and translated by Emile Bouchet. 2 vols. Paris: Alphonse Lemerre, 1891. Text based on Natalis de Wailly's edition (Villehardouin, *Geoffroi de Ville-Hardouin*), with a new translation.

Villehardouin, Geoffroy de. *La Conquête de Constantinople*. Edited and translated by Jean Dufournet. Paris: Éditions Flammarion, 2004.

Villehardouin, Geoffroy de. *La conquête de Constantinople*. Edited and translated by Edmond Faral. 2 vols. Paris: Les Belles Lettres, 1938–39. Reprint, 2nd ed., 1961.

Villehardouin, Geoffroy de. *De la conquête de Constantinoble: Édition faite sur les manuscrits nouvellement reconnus [. . .] par Joffroi de Villehardouin et Henri de Valenciennes*. Edited and translated by Paulin Paris. Paris: Jules Renouard, 1838. Based primarily on manuscript D.

Villehardouin, Geoffroy de. *Geoffroi de Ville-Hardouin, Conquête de Constantinople, avec la continuation de Henri de Valenciennes*. Edited and translated by Natalis de Wailly. 2nd ed. Paris: Firmin-Didot Frères, Fils et Cie, 1874; reprinted in 1882. Based on manuscript A.

Villehardouin, Geoffroy de. *L'Histoire de Geoffroy de Villehardouin, mareschal de Champagne et de Romanie, de la Conquest de Constantinople par les barons françois assosiez aux Venitiens, l'an 1204*. Edited and translated by Blaise de Vigenère. Paris: Abel l'Angelier, 1585.

Villehardouin, Geoffroy de. *L'histoire de la conquête de Constantinople*, translation by Jean Longnon. Paris: Tallandier, 1981.

BIBLIOGRAPHY   213

Villehardouin, Geoffroy de. *Histoire de l'empire de Constantinople sous les empereurs François, divisée en deux parties, dont la première contient l'Histoire de la conquête de la ville de Constantinople par les François et les Venitiens, écrite par Geoffroy de Ville-Hardouin, Maréchal de Champagne et de Romanie* [. . .]. 2 vols. Edition and translation by Charles du Fresne Du Change. Paris: Imprimerie Royale, 1657.

Villehardouin, Geoffroy de. *L'histoire ou chronique du seigneur Geoffroy de Ville-Hardouin, mareschal de Champagne et de Romanie* [. . .]. *De nouveau mise en François.* Lyon: Par les heritiers de Guillaume Rouillé, 1601.

Villehardouin, Geoffroy de. *Mémoires de Geoffroy de Ville-Hardouin, maréchal de Champagne et de Romaine, ou Histoire de la conquête de Constaninople par les Français et les Vénetiens.* Edited and translated by Claude-Bernard Petitot. Paris: Foucault, 1819.

Villehardouin, Geoffroy, and Jean de Joinville. *Chronicles of the Crusades.* Translated by Margaret Renée Bryers Shaw. London: Penguin Books, 1963.

Villehardouin, Geoffroy de, and Jean de Joinville. *Chronicles of the Crusades.* Translation and notes by Caroline Smith. London: Penguin Books, 2008.

Villehardouin, Geoffroy de, and Jean de Joinville. *Memoirs of the Crusades.* Translated by Frank Marzials. London: J. M. Dent Sons, 1908.

Secondary Works

Alanièce, Valérie, and François Gilet. "Les fiefs de Geoffroy de Villehardouin en Thrace (Grèce)." *La vie en Champagne* 62 (2010): 2–12.

Allmand, Christopher. *The "De Re Militari" of Vegetius: The Reception, Transmission and Legacy of a Roman Text in the Middle Ages.* Cambridge: Cambridge University Press, 2011.

Andrea, Alfred J. "Adam of Perseigne and the Fourth Crusade." *Cîteaux: Commentarii Cistercienses* 36, no. 1 (1985): 21–37.

Andrea, Alfred J. "Essay on Primary Sources." In Queller and Madden, *The Fourth Crusade,* 299–343.

Angold, Michael. "Byzantine Politics via-à-vis the Fourth Crusade." In Laiou, *Urbs Capta,* 55–68.

Angold, Michael. *The Fourth Crusade: Event and Context.* Harlow: Longman, 2003.

Angold, Michael. "Thomas Morosini, First Latin Patriarch of Constantinople (1205–1211): A Reappraisal." In *Crusading and Trading between West and East: Studies in Honour of David Jacoby,* edited by Sophia Menache, Benjamin Z. Kedar, and Michel Balard, 17–34. London: Routledge, 2019.

Angold, Michael. "Turning Points in History: The Fall of Constantinople." *Byzantinoslavica* 71, no. 1–2 (2003): 11–30.

Antonini, Fabio. "Historical Uses of the Secret Chancery in Early Modern Venice: Archiving, Researching and Representing the Records of State." PhD diss., University of London, 2016.

Arbois de Jubainville, Henry d'. *Histoire des ducs et des comtes de Champagne.* 7 vols. Paris: A. Durand, 1859–69.

BIBLIOGRAPHY

Asdracha, Catherine. *La région des Rhodopes aux XIIIe et XIVe siècles: Étude de géographie historique*. Athens: Verlag der Byzantinisch-Neugriechischen Jahrbücher, 1976.

Barber, Malcolm. "The Impact of the Fourth Crusade in the West: The Distribution of Relics after 1204." In Laiou, *Urbs Capta*, 325–34.

Barker, John W. "Late Byzantine Thessalonike: A Second City's Challenges and Responses." *Dumbarton Oaks Papers* 57 (2003): 5–33.

Barthélemy, Édouard de. "Les seigneurs et la seigneurie d'Arzillières." *Revue de Champagne et de Brie* 23 (1887): 161–78.

Baudin, Arnaud. "De la Champagne à la Morée: L'héraldique de la maison de Villehardouin." In Villela-Petit, *1204*, 97–112.

Baudin, Arnaud. *Emblématique et pouvoir en Champagne: Les sceaux des comtes de Champagne et de leur entourage (fin XIe–début XIV siècle)*, including a CD-ROM, Corpus des Sceaux. Langres: Éditions Dominique Guéniot, 2012.

Baudin, Arnaud. "Larrivour, trentième fille de Clairvaux: Origines et constitution du temporel (v. 1137/1140–v. 1235)." *Société académique de l'Aube* 139 (2015): 441–66.

Baudin, Arnaud, Ghislain Brunel, and Nicolas Dohrmann, eds. *The Knights Templar: From the Days of Jerusalem to the Commanderies of Champagne*. Paris: Somogy Éditions d'Art, 2012.

Beer, Jeanette M. A. *In Their Own Words: Practices of Quotation in Early Medieval History-Writing*. Toronto: University of Toronto Press, 2014.

Beer, Jeanette M. A. *Narrative Conventions of Truth in the Middle Ages*. Geneva: Droz, 1981.

Beer, Jeanette M. A. *Villehardouin: Epic Historian*. Geneva: Droz, 1968.

Bell, Gregory D. "Unintended Consumption: The Interruption of the Fourth Crusade at Venice and Its Consequences." *Journal of Medieval Military History* 6 (2008): 79–94.

Brader, David. *Bonifaz von Montferrat bis zum Antritt der Kreuzfahrt (1202)*. Historische Studien 55. Lübeck: Matthiesen Verlag, 1907.

Brand, Charles M. *Byzantium Confronts the West, 1180–1204*. Cambridge, MA: Harvard University Press, 1968.

Brown, Elizabeth A. R. "The Cistercians in the Latin Empire of Constantinople and Greece." *Traditio* 14 (1958): 63–120.

Bull, Marcus. *Eyewitness and Crusade Narrative: Perception and Narration in Accounts of the Second, Third and Fourth Crusades*. Woodbridge, UK: Boydell and Brewer, 2018.

Bur, Michel, et al. *Vestiges d'habitat seigneurial fortifié en Champagne méridionale*. Inventaire des sites archéologiques non monumentaux de Champagne 4. Reims: Cahiers des lettres et sciences humaines de l'Université de Reims, 1997.

Burgtorf, Jochen. *The Central Convent of Hospitallers and Templars: History, Organization, and Personnel (1099/1120–1310)*. Leiden: Brill, 2008.

Buridant, Claude. "Blaise de Vigenère, traducteur de *La Conquête de Constantinople* de Geoffroy de Villehardouin." *Revue des sciences humaine* 52, no. 180 (1980): 95–118.

Caroff, Fanny. "La narration des croisades dans l'iconographie française et flamarde." In Laiou, *Urbs Capta*, 175–92.

Caroff, Fanny. "La quatrième croisade en images." In Villela-Petit, *1204*, 39–53.

Chapin, Elizabeth. *Les villes de foires de Champagne, des origines au début du XVIe siècle*. Paris: Honoré Champion, 1937.

Chassel, Jean-Luc. *Sceaux et usage de sceaux: Images de la Champagne médiévale*. Paris: Somogy Éditions d'Art, 2003.

Chazan, Mireille. "Aubri de Trois-Fontaines, un historien entre la France et l'Empire." *Annales de l'Est* 36 (1984): 163–92.

Chazan, Mireille. "L'usage de la compilation dans les chroniques de Robert d'Auxerre, Aubri de Trois-Fontaines et Jean de Saint-Victor." *Journal des savants* (1999): 261–94.

Chrissis, Nikolaos G. *Crusading in Frankish Greece: A Study of Byzantine-Western Relations and Attitudes, 1204–1282*. Turnhout, Belgium: Brepols, 2012.

Ciggaar, Krijnie. *Western Travellers to Constantinople: The West and Byzantium, 962–1204*. Leiden: Brill, 1996.

Civel, Nicolas. *La fleur de France: Les seigneurs d'Ile-de-France au XIIe siècle*. Turnhout, Belgium: Brepols, 2006.

Claverie, Pierre-Vincent. "Un *Illustris amicus Venetorum* du début du XIIIe siècle: L'évêque Nivelon de Quierzy et son temps." In Ortalli, Ravegni, and Schreiner, *Quarta Crociata*, 485–523.

Constable, Giles. "Troyes, Constantinople, and the Relics of St. Helen in the Thirteenth Century." In *Mélanges offerts à René Crozet*, edited by Pierre Gallais and Yves-Jean Rion, 2:1035–42. Poitiers: Société d'études médiévales, 1966.

Courroux, Pierre. *L'Écriture de l'histoire dans les chroniques françaises (XIIe–XVe siècle)*. Paris: Classiques Garnier, 2016.

Crépin-Leblond, Thierry. "Louis, comte de Blois et de Chartres: De Blois à Adrianople." In Villela-Petit, *1204*, 17–20.

Crouch, David. *The Chivalric Turn: Conduct and Hegemony in Europe before 1300*. Oxford: Oxford University Press, 2019.

Crouch, David. *Tournament*. London: Hambledon Continuum, 2005.

Crouch, David. "When Was Chivalry? Evolution of a Code." In *Knighthood and Society in the High Middle Ages*, edited by David Crouch and Jeroen Deploige, 277–95. Leuven: Leuven University Press, 2020.

Crouch, David. *William Marshal*. 3rd ed. London: Routledge, 2016.

Damian-Grint, Peter. *The New Historians of the Twelfth-Century Renaissance: Inventing Vernacular Authority*. Woodbridge, UK: Boydell, 1999.

Davis, Natalie Zemon. "Publisher Guillaume Rouillé, Businessman and Humanist." In *Editing Sixteenth-Century Texts*, edited by R. J. Schoeck, 62–112. Toronto: University of Toronto Press, 1966.

Debidour, Antonin. *Les chroniqueurs: Première série; Villehardouin-Joinville*. Paris: Lecène et Oudin, 1892.

Dectot, Xavier. "Les tombeaux des comtes de Champagne (1151–1284): Un manifeste politique." *Bulletin Monumental* 162, no. 1 (2004): 3–62.

Delisle, Léopold. "Chroniques et annales diverses." *Histoire littéraire de la France* 32 (1898): 182–264.

216 **BIBLIOGRAPHY**

Delisle, Léopold. *Mémoire sur les opérations financières des Templiers*. Paris: Imprimerie nationale, 1889. Reprint, Geneva: Slatkine Reprints, 1975.

Dembowski, P. F. *La Chronique de Robert de Clari: Étude de la langue et du style*. Toronto: University of Toronto Press, 1963.

Devereaux, Rima. *Constantinople and the West in Medieval French Literature: Renewal and Utopia*. Cambridge: D. S. Brewer, 2012.

Donnachie, Stephen. "Crown and Baronage in the Latin Kingdom of Jerusalem after the Battle of Hattin, 1187–1228." *Medieval Prosopography* 32 (2017): 87–124.

Du Cange, Charles du Fresne, ed. *Glossarium mediae et infimae Latinitatis*. 10 vols. Niort: L. Favre, 1883–87.

Dufournet, Jean. "La bataille d'Adrianople." In *Les écrivains de la IVe croisade*, 2:245–81.

Dufournet, Jean. *Les écrivains de la IVe croisade: Villehardouin et Clari*. 2 vols. Paris: Société d'édition d'enseignement supérieur, 1973.

Dufournet, Jean. "Villehardouin et les Champenois dans la quatrième croisade." In *Les Champenois et la croisade: Actes des quatrièmes journées rémoises 27–28 novembre 1987*, edited by Yvonne Bellenger and Danielle Quéruel, 55–69. Paris: Aux amateurs de livres, 1989.

Edbury, Peter W. "Ernoul, Eracles, and the Collapse of the Kingdom of Jerusalem." In Morreale and Paul, *The French of Outremer*, 44–67.

Edbury, Peter W. "New Perspectives on the Old French Continuation of William of Tyre." *Crusades* 9 (2010): 107–36.

Evergates, Theodore. *The Aristocracy in the County of Champagne, 1100–1300*. Philadelphia: University of Pennsylvania Press, 2007.

Evergates, Theodore. "Countess Blanche, Philip Augustus, and the War of Succession in Champagne, 1201–1222." In *Political Ritual and Practice in Capetian France: Studies in Honour of Elizabeth A. R. Brown*, edited by Jay Rubenstein and M. Cecilia Gaposchkin, 77–104. Turnhout, Belgium: Brepols, 2021.

Evergates, Theodore. *Henry the Liberal: Count of Champagne, 1127–1181*. Philadelphia: University of Pennsylvania Press, 2016.

Evergates, Theodore. *Marie of France: Countess of Champagne, 1145–1198*. Philadelphia: University of Pennsylvania Press, 2019.

Falkenstein, Ludwig. "Wilhelm von Champagne, Elekt von Chartres (1164–1168), Erzbischof von Sens (1168/69–1176), Erzbischof von Reims (1176–1202), Legat des apostolischen Stuhles, im Spiegel päpstlischer Schreiben Privilegien." *Zeitschrift der Savigny-Stiftung für Rechtsgeschichte* 120. *Kanonistische Abteilung* 89 (2003): 107–284.

Falmagne, Thomas, and Baudouin van den Abeele, eds. *Corpus Catalogorum Belgii: The Medieval Booklists of the Southern Low Countries*. Vol. 5, *Dukes of Burgundy*. Leuven: Peeters, 2016.

Faral, Edmond. "Geoffroy de Villehardouin: La question de sa sincérité." *Revue historique* 177, no. 3 (1936): 530–82.

Faral, Edmond. "Pour l'établissement du texte de Villehardouin: Manuscrits conservés et manuscrits perdus." *Romania* 64, no. 255 (1938): 289–312.

BIBLIOGRAPHY 217

Frankfort, Frank. "Marino Sanudo Torsello: A Social Biography." PhD diss., University of Cincinnati, 1974.

Frappier, Jean. "Les discours dans la chronique de Villehardouin." In *Histoire, Mythes et Symboles: Études de littérature française*, 55–83. Geneva: Droz, 1976.

Gachet, Émile. "Les chroniques de Bauduin d'Avesnes." *Compte-rendu des séances de la commission royale d'histoire*, 2e série, no. 9 (1857): 265–319.

Gaggero, Massimiliano. "Western Eyes in the Latin East: The *Chronique d'Ernoul et de Bernard le Trésorier* and Robert of Clari's *Conquête de Constantinople*." In Morreale and Paul, *The French of Outremer*, 86–109.

Gaposchkin, M. Cecilia. "Nivelon of Quierzy, the Cathedral of Soissons, and the Relics of 1205: Liturgy and Devotion in the Aftermath of the Fourth Crusade." *Speculum* 95, no. 4 (2020): 1087–1129.

Gaunt, Simon. *Marco Polo's "Le Devisement du Monde": Narrative Voice, Language and Diversity*. Cambridge: D. S. Brewer, 2013.

Gazzotti, M. "Studi cinquecenteschi su 'La conquête de Constantinople' di Geoffroy de Villehardouin." *Aevum* 63, no. 2 (1989): 284–335.

Geary, Patrick. "Saint Helen of Athyra and the Cathedral of Troyes in the Thirteenth Century." *The Journal of Medieval and Renaissance Studies* 7, no. 1 (1977): 149–76.

Gillingham, John. *Richard I*. New Haven: Yale University Press, 1999.

Gillingham, John. "Richard I and the Science of War in the Middle Ages." In his *Richard Coeur de Lion*, 111–26.

Gillingham, John. *Richard Coeur de Lion: Kingship, Chivalry and War in the Twelfth Century*. London: Hambledon, 1994.

Gillingham, John. "Roger of Howden on Crusade." In his *Richard Coeur de Lion*, 141–53.

Gjuzelev, Vassil. "La quatrième croisade et ses conséquences pour la Bulgarie médiévale: Le Tzar Kaloyan, les Latins, et les Grecs (1204–1207)." *Studia Ceranea* 3 (2013): 29–37.

Grasso, Christian. "Folco di Neuilly: *Sacerdos et Predicator Crucis*." *Nuova Rivista Storica* 94, no. 3 (2010): 741–64.

Grossel, Marie-Geneviève. *Le milieu littéraire en Champagne sous les Thibaudiens: 1200–1270*. 2 vols. Orléans: Paradigme, 1994.

Haberstumpf, Walter. "Bonifacio di Montferrato e il mondo greco." In *Atti del Convegno internazionale Bonifacio, marchese di Montferrato, re di Tessalonica*, edited by Roberto Maestri, 23–55. Genoa: San Giorgio, 2009.

Haberstumpf, Walter. *Dinastie Europee nel Mediterraneo Orientale: I Monferrato e i Savoia nei secoli XII–XV*. Turin: Scriptorium, 1995.

Harari, Yuval Noah. "The Assassination of King Conrad: Tyre, 1192." In *Special Operations in the Age of Chivalry, 1100–1550*, 91–108. Woodbridge, UK: Boydell and Brewer, 2007.

Harari, Yuval Noah. "Knowledge, Power and the Medieval Soldier, 1096–550." In Shagrir, *In Laudem Hierosolymitani*, 345–55.

Harari, Yuval Noah. "Military Memoirs: A Historical Overview of the Genre from the Middle Ages to the Late Modern Era." *War in History* 14, no. 3 (2007): 289–309.

218   **BIBLIOGRAPHY**

Hendrickx, Benjamin. "À propos du nombre des troupes de la quatrième croisade et de l'empereur Baudouin I." *Byzantina* 3 (1971): 29–41.

Hendrickx, Benjamin. "Les chartes de Baudouin de Flandre comme source pour l'histoire de Byzance." *Byzantina* 1 (1969): 61–80.

Hendrickx, Benjamin. "Le contrat féodal et le fief dans l'Empire latin de Constantinople." *Byzantiaka* 20 (2000): 223–42.

Hendrickx, Benjamin. "Les *parlements* dans l'Empire latin de Constantinople, le Royaume des Montferrat à Thessalonique et le Principauté d'Achaïe." *Byzantiaka* 30 (2012–13): 211–28.

Hendrickx, Benjamin. "Recherches sur les documents diplomatiques non conservés, concernant le quatrième croisade et l'empire latin de Constantinople pendant les premières années de son existence (1200–1206)." *Byzantina* 2 (1970): 107–84.

Hodgson, Natasha. "Honour, Shame and the Fourth Crusade." *Journal of Medieval History* 39, no. 2 (2013): 220–39.

Hosler, John D. *The Siege of Acre, 1189–1191: Saladin, Richard the Lionheart, and the Battle That Decided the Third Crusade*. New Haven: Yale University Press, 2018.

Humphreys, R. Stephen. *From Saladin to the Mongols: The Ayyubids of Damascus, 1193–1260*. Albany: State University of New York Press, 1977.

Jacoby, David. "Catalans, Turcs et Vénitiens en Romanie (1305–1332): Un nouveau témoignage de Marino Sanudo Torsello." *Studi medievali* 15, no. 1 (1974): 217–61. Reprinted in his *Recherches sur la Méditerranée orientale*.

Jacoby, David. "Conrad, Marquis of Montferrat, and the Kingdom of Jerusalem." In *Atti del congress internazionale "Dai feudi Monferrini e dal Piemonte ai nuovi mondi oltre gli oceani": Alessandria, 2–6 aprile 1990*, edited by Laura Balletto, 187–237. Alessandria: Società di storia, arte e archeologia, 1993. Reprinted with the same pagination in his *Trade, Commodities and Shipping*.

Jacoby, David. "The Greeks of Constantinople under Latin Rule, 1204–1261." In Madden, *The Fourth Crusade*, 53–73.

Jacoby, David. "Les quartiers juifs de Constantinople à l'époque byzantine." *Byzantion* 37 (1967): 167–227. Reprinted in his *Société et démographie*.

Jacoby, David. *Recherches sur la Méditerranée orientale du XIIe au XVe siècle: Peuples, sociétés, économies*. London: Variorum Reprints, 1979.

Jacoby, David. *Société et démographie à Byzance et en Romanie latine*. London: Variorum Reprints, 1975.

Jacoby, David. *Trade, Commodities and Shipping in the Medieval Mediterranean*. Aldershot, UK: Variorum, 1997.

Jacoby, David. "The Venetian Government and Administration in Latin Constantinople, 1204–1261: A State within a State." In Ortalli, Ravegnani, and Schreiner, *Quarta Crociata*, 1:19–79.

Jacquin, Gérard. "Geoffroy de Villehardouin, le récit de l'ambassade à Venise: Informer et convaincre." In *Récits d'ambassades et figures du messager*, edited by Gérard Jacquin, 119–35. Rennes: Presses universitaires de Rennes, 2007.

Jacquin, Gérard. "La mort de deux barons dans les chroniques françaises du la IVe crosiade." In *Le récit de la mort: Écriture et histoire*, edited by Gérard Jacquin, 93–108. Rennes: Presses universitaires de Rennes, 2004.

Jacquin, Gérard. *Le style historique dans les recits français et latins de la quatrième croisade.* Geneva: Champion-Slatkine, 1986.

John, Simon. "Historical Truth and the Miraculous Past: The Use of Oral Evidence in Twelfth-Century Latin Historical Writing on the First Crusade." *English Historical Review* 130 (2015): 263–301.

Jones, Andrew W. "Fulk of Neuilly, Innocent III, and the Preaching of the Fourth Crusade." *Comitatus: A Journal of Medieval and Renaissance Studies* 41, no. 1 (2010): 119–48.

Joris, André. "Un seul amour . . . ou plusiers femmes?" In *Femmes: Mariages-lignages, XIIe–XIVe siècles; Mélanges offerts à Georges Duby*, edited by Jean Dufournet, André Joris, and Pierre Toubert, 197–214. Brussels: De Boeck Université, 1992.

Kazhdan, Alexander P., et al., eds. *The Oxford Dictionary of Byzantium.* 3 vols. New York: Oxford University Press, 1991.

Kedar, Benjamin Z. *Crusaders and Franks: Studies in the History of the Crusades and the Frankish Levant.* London: Routledge, 2016.

Kedar, Benjamin Z. "The Fourth Crusade's Second Front." In Laiou, *Urbs Capta*, 89–110. Reprinted with the same pagination in his *Crusaders and Franks*.

Kittell, Ellen E. "Was Thibaut of Champagne the Leader of the Fourth Crusade?" *Byzantion* 51, no. 2 (1981): 557–65.

Köhler, Erich. *L'aventure chevaleresque: Idéal et réalité dans le roman courtois.* Translated from the German by Éliane Kaufholz. Paris: Gallimard, 1974.

Kolias, Taxiarchis. "Military Aspects of the Conquest of Constantinople by the Crusaders." In Laiou, *Urbs Capta*, 123–38.

Krause, Kathy M. "Genealogy and Codicology: The Manuscript Contents of the 'Fille de Comte de Pontieu.'" *Romance Philology* 59, no. 2 (2006): 323–42.

Laiou, Angeliki. "Marino Sanudo Torsello, Byzantium and the Turks: The Background to the Anti-Turkish League of 1332–1334." *Speculum* 45, no. 3 (1970): 374–92.

Laiou, Angeliki, ed. *Urbs Capta: The Fourth Crusade and Its Consequences.* Paris: Lethielleux, 2005.

Legaré, Anne-Marie. "Nouveaux documents concernant l'histoire de la bibliothèque des ducs de Bourgogne." *Scriptorium* 54, no. 1 (2000): 193–96.

Lerond, Alain, ed. *Chansons attribuées au chastelain de Couci, fin du XIIe–début du XIIIe siècle.* Paris: Presses universitaires de France, 1964.

Lester, Anne E. "Translation and Appropriation: Greek Relics in the Latin West in the Aftermath of the Fourth Crusade." *Studies in Church History* 53 (2017): 88–117.

Lester, Anne E. "What Remains: Women, Relics and Remembrance in the Aftermath of the Fourth Crusade." *Journal of Medieval History* 40, no. 3 (2014): 311–28.

Lippiatt, G. E. M. "Duty and Desertion: Simon de Montfort and the Fourth Crusade." *Leidschrift: Historische Tijdschrift* 27, no. 3 (December 2012): 75–88.

Lock, Peter. *The Franks in the Aegean, 1204–1500.* London: Longman, 1995.

Lock, Peter. "Sanudo, Turks, Greeks and Latins in the Early Fourteenth Century." In *Contact and Conflict in Frankish Greece and the Aegean, 1204–1453:*

BIBLIOGRAPHY

Crusade, Religion and Trade between Latins, Greeks and Turks, edited by Nikolaos G. Chrissis and Mike Carr, 135–49. Farnham, UK: Ashgate, 2014.

Longnon, Jean. "Le chroniqueur Henri de Valenciennes." *Journal des Savants* 3, no. 1 (1945): 134–50.

Longnon, Jean. *Les compagnons de Villehardouin: Recherches sur les croisés de la quatrième croisade.* Geneva: Droz, 1978.

Longnon, Jean. *Recherches sur la vie de Geoffroy de Villehardouin, suivies du catalogue des actes des Villehardouin.* Paris: Honoré Champion, 1939.

Longnon, Jean. "Sur l'histoire de l'empereur Henri de Constantinople par Henri de Valenciennes." *Romania* 69 (1946–47): 198–41.

Mack, Merav. "A Genoese Perspective of the Third Crusade." *Crusades* 10 (2011): 45–62.

Madden, Thomas F. *Enrico Dandolo and the Rise of Venice.* Baltimore: Johns Hopkins University Press, 2003.

Madden, Thomas F. "The Fires of the Fourth Crusade in Constantinople, 1203–1204: A Damage Assessment." *Byzantinische Zeitschrift* 84, no. 1 (1991): 72–93.

Madden, Thomas F. "Food and the Fourth Crusade: A New Approach to the 'Diversion Question.'" In *Logistics of Warfare in the Age of the Crusades,* edited by John H. Pryor, 209–28. Farnham, UK: Ashgate, 2006.

Madden, Thomas F., ed. *The Fourth Crusade: Event, Aftermath, and Perceptions.* Crusades–Subsidia 2. Ashgate, UK: Aldershot, 2008.

Madden, Thomas F. "The Latin Empire of Constantinople's Fractured Foundation: The Rift between Boniface of Montferrat and Baldwin of Flanders." In Madden, *The Fourth Crusade,* 45–52.

Madden, Thomas F. "The Venetian Version of the Fourth Crusade: Memory and the Conquest of Constantinople in Medieval Venice." *Speculum* 87, no. 2 (2012): 311–44.

Madden, Thomas F. "Vows and Contracts in the Fourth Crusade: The Treaty of Zara and the Attack on Constantinople in 1204." *The International History Review* 15, no. 3 (1993): 441–68.

Madgearu, Alexandru. *The Asanids: The Political and Military History of the Second Bulgarian Empire (1185–1280).* Leiden: Brill, 2017.

Magdalino, Paul. "Prophecies on the Fall of Constantinople." In Laiou, *Urbs Capta,* 41–53.

Magnocavallo, Arturo. *Marin Sanudo, il Vecchio, e il suo progetto di crociata.* Bergamo: Istituto italiano d'arti grafiche, 1901.

Maleczek, Werner. *Petrus Capuanus: Kardinal, Legat am Vierten Kreuzzug, Theologie (†1214).* Vienna: Österreichischen Akademie der Wissenschaften, 1988.

Marnette, Sophie. "Narrateur et point de vue dans les chroniques médiévales: Une approache linguistique." In *The Medieval Chronicle: Proceedings of the First International Conference on the Medieval Chronicle,* edited by Erik Kooper, 174–90. Amsterdam: Rodopi, 1999.

Mayer, Hans Eberhard. *Die Kanzlei der lateinischen Könige von Jerusalem.* 2 vols. Monumenta Germaniae Historica Schriften 40. Hannover: Hahn, 1996.

Milland-Bove, Bénédicte. "Miracles et interventions divines dans la 'Conquête de Constaninople' de Geoffroy de Villehardouin et Robert de Clari." In

BIBLIOGRAPHY 221

Miracles d'un autre genre: Récritures médiévales en dehors de l'hagiographie, edited by Olivier Biaggini and Bénédicte Milland-Bove, 85–103. Madrid: Casa de Velázquez, 2012.

Mitchell, Russell. "Light Cavalry, Heavy Cavalry, Horse Archers, Oh My! What Abstract Definitions Don't Tell Us about 1205 Adrianople." *Journal of Medieval Military History* 6 (2008): 95–118.

Moore, John C. "Count Baldwin IX of Flanders, Philip Augustus, and the Papal Power." *Speculum* 37, no. 1 (1962): 79–89.

Moore, John C. "Peter of Lucedio (Cistercian Patriarch of Antioch) and Pope Innocent III." *Römische historische Mitteilungen* 29 (1987): 221–49.

Morganstern, Ann McGee. *Gothic Tombs of Kinship in France, the Low Countries, and England.* University Park: Pennsylvania State University Press, 2000.

Morreale, Laura K., and Nicholas L. Paul. *The French of Outremer: Communities and Communications in the Crusading Mediterranean.* New York: Fordham University Press, 2018.

Murray, Alan V. "The Place of Egypt in the Military Strategy of the Crusades, 1099–1221." In *The Fifth Crusade in Context: The Crusading Movement in the Early Thirteenth Century*, edited E. J. Mylod, Guy Perry, Thomas W. Smith, and Jan Vandeburie, 117–34. London: Routledge, 2017.

Naïs, Hélène. "Reflexion preliminaires à un traitment automatique des textes médiévaux sur ordinateur à propos de 'La Conqueste de Constantinople' par G. de Villehardouin." In *Mélanges de langue et de la littérature du moyen âge et de la renaissance offerts à Jean Frappier*, 2:867–75. Geneva: Droz, 1970.

Naïs, Hélène, et al., eds. *Index complet du manuscrit O de la Conquête de Constantinople.* Nancy: Université de Nancy II, 1972.

Naïs, Hélène, et al., eds. *Index général des lemmes des manuscrits B et D de Villehardouin et des "Sept Sages de Rome."* Nancy: Université de Nancy II, 1984.

Neocleous, Savvas. "Financial, Chivalric or Religious? The Motives of the Fourth Crusaders Reconsidered." *Journal of Medieval History* 38, no. 2 (2012): 183–206.

Nicholas, Karen S. "Countesses as Rulers in Flanders." In *Aristocratic Women in Medieval France*, edited by Theodore Evergates, 111–37. Philadelphia: University of Pennsylvania Press, 1999.

Nieus, Jean-François. "Pairie et 'estage' dans le comté de Saint-Pol aux XIIIe siècle: Autour d'une texte publié par Charles du Cange." *Revue du Nord* 81 (1999): 21–42.

Nieus, Jean-François. *Un pouvoir comtal entre Flandre et France: Saint-Pol, 1000–1300.* Brussels: De Boeck, 2005.

Noble, Peter. "1204: The Crusade without Epic Heroes." In *Epic and Crusade: Proceedings of the Colloquium of the Société Rencesvals British Branch Held at Lucy Cavendish College, Cambridge, 27–28 March 2004*, edited by Philip E. Bennett, Anne Elizabeth Cobby, and Jane E. Everson, 89–104. Edinburgh: Société Rencesvals British Branch, 2006.

Noble, Peter. "Epic Heroes in Thirteenth-Century Chronicles." In *The Medieval Chronicle III: Proceedings of the 3rd International Conference on the Medieval Chronicle, Doorn/Utrecht, 12–17 July 2002*, edited by Erik Kooper, 135–48. Amsterdam: Rodopi, 2004.

BIBLIOGRAPHY

Noble, Peter. "Eyewitnesses of the Fourth Crusade: The War against Alexius III." *Reading Medieval Studies* 25 (1999): 75–89.

O'Brien, John. "Fulk of Neuilly." *Proceedings of the Leeds Philosophical and Literary Society* 13, no. 4 (1969): 105–48.

Oikonomides, Nicolas. "La décomposition de l'Empire Byzantin à la veille de 1204 et les origines de l'empire de Nicée: À propos de la "Partitio Romaniae." In *XVe Congrès international d'études byzantines: Rapports et co-rapports, histoire*, 3–28. Athens: XVe Congrès international d'études byzantines, 1976.

Ortalli, Gherardo, Giorgio Ravegnani, and Peter Schreiner, eds. *Quarta Crociata: Venezia, Bisanzio, Imperio Latino*. 2 vols. Venice: Istituto Veneto de scienze, lettere ed arti, 2006.

Outreman, Pierre d'. *Constantinopolis Belgica, sive de rebus gestis a Balduino et Henrico impp. Constantinopolitanis ortu Valentianensibus Belgis*. Tournai: Adriani Quinqué, 1643.

Page, Gill. *Being Byzantine: Greek Identity before the Ottomans*. Cambridge: Cambridge University Press, 2008.

Painter, Sidney. *William Marshal: Knight-Errant, Baron, and Regent of England*. Baltimore: Johns Hopkins University Press, 1933.

Park, Danielle E. A. *Papal Protection and the Crusader: Flanders, Champagne and the Kingdom of France, 1095–1222*. Woodbridge, UK: Boydell, 2018.

Parkes, M. B. *Scribes, Scripts, and Readers: Studies in the Communication, Presentation, and Dissemination of Medieval Texts*. London: Hambledon, 1991.

Parkes, M. B. "Tachygraphy in the Middle Ages: Writing Techniques Employed for 'Reportationes' of Lectures and Sermons." *Medioevo a rinascimento* 3 (1989): 159–69. Reprinted in his *Scribes, Scripts and Readers*, 19–33.

Pastan, Elizabeth C. "Dating the Medieval Work: The Case of the Miracles of Saint Andrew Window from Troyes Cathedral." In *Feud, Violence and Practice: Essays in Medieval Studies in Honor of Stephen D. White*, edited by Belle S. Tuten and Tracey L. Billado, 239–57. Farnham, UK: Ashgate, 2010.

Pastan, Elizabeth C., and Sylvie Balcon. *Les vitraux du choeur de la cathédral de Troyes (XIIIe siècle)*. Corpus Vitrearum Medii Aevii France 2. Paris: Comité des travaux historiques et scientifiques, 2006.

Perry, David M. *Sacred Plunder: Venice and the Aftermath of the Fourth Crusade*. University Park: Pennsylvania State University, 2015.

Perry, Guy. *The Briennes: The Rise and Fall of a Champenois Dynasty in the Age of the Crusades, c. 950–1356*. Cambridge: Cambridge University Press, 2018.

Perry, Guy. *John of Brienne: King of Jerusalem, Emperor of Constantinople, c. 1175–1237*. Cambridge: Cambridge University Press, 2013.

Petit, Ernest. *Histoire des ducs de Bourgogne de la race Capétienne*. 9 vols. Paris: Picard, 1885–1909.

Petit, Ernest. *Les sires de Villehardouin*. Troyes: Imprimerie J.-L. Paton, 1913.

Phillips, Jonathan. *Defenders of the Holy Land: Relations between the Latin East and the West, 1119–1187*. Oxford: Oxford University Press, 1996.

Phillips, Jonathan. *The Fourth Crusade and the Sack of Constantinople*. Rev. ed. New York: Penguin, 2005.

BIBLIOGRAPHY   223

Piatti, Pierantonio, ed. *The Fourth Crusade Revisited: Atti della Conferenza internazionale nell'ottavo centenario della IV crociata, 1204–2004, Andros, Grecia, 27–30 maggio 2004*. Vatican City: Libreria Editrice Vaticana, 2008.

Pippenger, Randall Todd. "Lives on Hold: The Dampierre Family, Captivity, and the Crusades in Thirteenth-Century Champagne." *Journal of Medieval History* 44, no. 5 (2018): 507–28.

Poirion, Daniel. "Les paragraphes et le pré-texte de Villehardouin." *Langue française* 40, no. 1 (1978): 45–59.

Polemis, Dimitrios. "Andros on the Eve of the Fourth Crusade." In Piatti, *The Fourth Crusade Revisted*, 11–17.

Poull, Georges. *La maison souveraine et ducale de Bar*. Nancy: Presses universitaires de Nancy, 1994.

Prevenier, W. "La chancellerie de l'empire latin de Constantinople (1204–1261)." In *The Latin Empire: Some Contributions*, edited by V. D. van Aalst and K. N. Ciggaar, 63–81. Hernen, The Netherlands: A. A. Bredius, 1990.

Pryor, John H. "The Chain of the Golden Horn, 5–7 July 1203." In Shagrir, *In Laudem Hierosolymitami*, 369–84.

Pryor, John H. "The Venetian Fleet for the Fourth Crusade and the Diversion of the Crusade to Constantinople." In *The Experience of Crusading*. Vol. 1, *Western Approaches*, edited by Marcus Bull and Norman Housely, P. W. Edbury, and Jonathan Phillips, 1:103–22. Cambridge: Cambridge University Press, 2003.

Putter, Ad. "Knights and Clerics at the Court of Champagne: Chrétien de Troyes's Romances in Context." *Medieval Knighthood V: Papers from the Sixth Strawberry Hill Conference, 1994*, edited by S. D. Church and Ruth Harvey, 243–66. Woodbridge, UK: Boydell, 1995.

Queller, Donald E. "Diplomatic 'Blanks' in the Thirteenth Century." *English Historical Review* 80 (1965): 476–91. Reprinted with same pagination in his *Medieval Diplomacy and the Fourth Crusade*.

Queller, Donald E. *Medieval Diplomacy and the Fourth Crusade*. London: Variorum Reprints, 1980.

Queller, Donald E., Thomas K. Compton, and Donald A. Campbell. "The Fourth Crusade: The Neglected Majority." *Speculum* 49 (1974): 441–65.

Queller, Donald E., and Thomas F. Madden. *The Fourth Crusade: The Conquest of Constantinople, 1201–1204*. 2nd ed. Philadelphia: University of Pennsylvania Press, 1997.

Reginato, Irene. " 'Le manuscrit Contarini' de *La Conquête de Constantinople* dans un témoin indirect: Ramusio traducteur de Villehardouin." *Romania* 134 (2016): 31–76.

Reginato, Irene. "Marino Sanudo Torsello e la Conqueste de Constantininople di Geoffroy de Villehardouin." In *La prosa medievale: Produzione e circolazione, atti del convegno Università degli Studi di Milano, 9–10 aprile 2018*, edited by Massimiliano Gaggero, 59–74. Filologia classica e medievale 4. Rome: L'Erma di Bretschneider, 2020.

Rhodes, Hilary. *The Crown and the Cross: Burgundy, France, and the Crusades, 1095–1223*. Turnhout, Belgium: Brepols, 2020.

224   **BIBLIOGRAPHY**

Rickard, Peter. "Blaise de Vigenère's Translation of Villehardouin." *Zeitschrift für französische Sprache und Literatur* 91, no. 1 (1981): 1–40.

Rickard, Peter. "From Villehardouin to Du Cange via Vigenère." *Zeitschrift für französische Sprache und Literatur* 103, no. 2 (1993): 113–43.

Rider, Jeff. "Vice, Tyranny, Violence, and the Usurpation of Flanders (1071) in Flemish Historiography from 1093 to 1294." In *Violence and the Writing of History in the Medieval Francophone World*, edited by Noah D. Guynn and Zrinka Stahuljak, 55–70. Cambridge: D. S. Brewer, 2013.

Riley-Smith, Jonathan. "The Hospitaller Commandery of Éterpigny and a Postscript to the Fourth Crusade in Syria." In Shagrir, *In Laudem Hierosolymitani*, 385–93.

Riley-Smith, Jonathan. "Toward an Understanding of the Fourth Crusade as an Institution." In Laiou, *Urbs Capta*, 71–87.

Robert, Gaston. "La maison d'Aulnay." *Nouvelle Revue de Champagne et de Brie* 11 (1933): 168–93.

Rodríguez Somolinos, Amelia. "Variation et changment de l'ancien au moyen français: L'ordre des mots et de l'emploi du sujet." In *The Dawn of the Written Vernacular in Western Europe*, edited by Michèle Goyens and Werner Verbeke, 273–88. Leuven: Leuven University Press, 2003.

Roserot, Alphonse. *Dictionnaire historique de la Champagne méridionale (Aube) des origines à 1790*. 3 vols. Langres: Imprimerie Champenoise, 1942–48. Reprint, Marseilles: Laffitte Reprints, 1983.

Ryan, Vincent. "Richard I and the Early Evolution of the Fourth Crusade." In Madden, *The Fourth Crusade*, 3–13.

Saenger, Paul. "Books of Hours and the Reading Habits of the Later Middle Ages." In *The Culture of Print: Power and the Uses of Print in Early Modern Europe*, edited by Roger Chartier, 141–73. Princeton: Princeton University Press, 1989.

Saint-Guillain, Guillaume. "Comment les Vénitiens n'ont pas acquis la Crête: Note à propos de l'élection impériale de 1204 et du partage projeté de l'empire byzantin." In *Mélanges Cécile Morrisson*, edited by Denis Feissel, Vincent Deroche, and Jean-Claude Cheynet, 713–58. Travaux et Mémoires 16. Paris: College de France, 2010.

Saint-Guillain, Guillaume. "Tales of San Marco: Venetian Historiography and Thirteenth-Century Byzantine Historiography." In *Identities and Allegiances in the Eastern Mediterranean after 1204*, edited by Judith Herrin and Guillaume Saint-Guillain, 265–90. Farnham, UK: Ashgate, 2011.

Saint-Phalle, Edouard de. "Les seigneurs de Chappes aux XIe et XIIe siècles." *Mémoires de la Société académique du département de l'Aube* 131 (2007): 31–65.

Savetiez, Charles. "Maison de Dampierre-Saint-Dizier." *Revue de Champagne et de Brie* 17 (1884): 113–25.

Schmandt, Raymond. "The Fourth Crusade and the Just-War Theory." *Catholic Historical Review* 61, no. 2 (1975): 191–221.

Schon, Peter M. *Studien zum Stil der frühen französischen Prosa (Robert de Clari, Geoffroy de Villehardouin, Henri de Valenciennes)*. Analecta Romanica: Beihefte zu den Romanischen Forschungen, Heft 8. Frankfurt am Main: Klosermann, 1960.

BIBLIOGRAPHY   225

Shagrir, Iris, Ronie Ellenblum, and Jonathan Riley-Smith, eds. *In Laudem Hierosolymitani: Studies in Crusades and Medieval Culture in Honour of Benjamin Z. Kedar*. Aldershot, UK: Ashgate, 2007.

Shawcross, Teresa. *The Chronicle of Morea: Historiography in Crusader Greece*. Oxford: Oxford University Press, 2009.

Short, Ewan. "The Agency and Authority of Agnes of France and Margaret of Hungary in the Aftermath of the Fall of Constantinople (1204–1206)." *Question: Essays & Art from the Humanities* 3 (2019): 28–37, 96–103.

Sivéry, Gérard. *L'économie du royaume de France au siècle de Saint Louis*. Lille: Presses universitaires de Lille, 1984.

Smalley, Beryl. *Historians in the Middle Ages*. New York: Scribner, 1974.

Stephenson, Paul. *Byzantium's Balkan Frontier: A Political Study of the Northern Balkans, 900–1204*. Cambridge: Cambridge University Press, 2000.

Stoyanov, Aleksandar. "The Size of Bulgaria's Medieval Field Armies: A Case Study of Military Mobilization Capacity in the Middle Ages." *Journal of Military History* 83 (2019): 719–46.

Thompson, Kathleen. *Power and Border Lordship in Medieval France: The County of the Perche, 1000–1226*. Woodbridge, UK: Boydell, 2002.

Van Tricht, Filip. "The Byzantino-Latin Principality of Adrianople and the Challenge of Feudalism (1204/6–ca. 1227/8): Empire, Venice, and Local Autonomy." *Dumbarton Oaks Papers* 68 (2014): 325–42.

Van Tricht, Filip. "The Duchy of Philippopolis (1204–ca. 1236/37): A Latin Border Principality in a Byzantine (Greek/Bulgarian) Milieu." *Crusades* 21 (2022): 91–120.

Van Tricht, Filip. "La gloire de l'empire: L'idée impériale de Henri de Flandre-Hainaut, deuxième empereur Latin de Constantinople (1206–1216)." *Byzantion* 70 (2000): 211–41.

Van Tricht, Filip. "De jongelingenjaren van een keizer van Konstantinopel: Hendrik van Vlaanderen en Henegouwen (1177–1202)." *Tijdschrift voor geschiedenis* 111 (1998): 187–217.

Van Tricht, Filip. *The Latin Renovatio of Byzantium: The Empire of Constantinople (1204–1228)*. Leiden: Brill, 2011.

Vásáry, István. *Cumans and Tatars: Oriental Military in the Pre-Ottoman Balkans, 1185–1365*. Cambridge: Cambridge University Press, 2005.

Verbruggen, J. F. *The Art of Warfare in Western Europe during the Middle Ages, from the Eighth Century to 1340*. 2nd ed. Translated by Sumner Willard and R. W. Southern. Woodbridge, UK: Boydell, 1997.

Vercauteren, Fernand. "Note sur les rapports de Marino Sanudo avec le Hainaut, le Brabant et la Flandre (1321–1337)." *Bulletin de l'Institut historique Belge de Rome* 28–29 (1953–55): 5–20.

Verdier, François. *L'aristocratie de Provins à la fin du XIIe siècle: L'exemple de Milon le Bréban, chambrier des comtes de Champagne, bouteiller de l'empereur de Constantinople*. Provins: Société d'histoire et d'archéologie de l'arrondissement de Provins, 2016.

Verlinden, Charles. *Les empereurs belges de Constantinople*. Brussels: Charles Dessart, 1945.

BIBLIOGRAPHY

Villela-Petit, Inés, ed. *1204: La quatrième croisade; De Blois à Constantinople & éclats d'empires*. With an exhibition catalogue. Revue française d'héraldique et de sigillographie 73–75. Paris: Le Léopard d'Or, 2005.

Weijers, Olga. "Note sur une expérience de *reportatio*." In *Du copiste au collectioneur: Mélanges d'histoire des textes et des bibliothèques en l'honneur d'André Vernet*, edited by Donatella Nebbiai-Dalla Guarda and Jean-François Genest, 85–90. Bibliologia 18. Turnhout, Belgium: Brepols, 1998.

Williams, John R. "William of the White Hands and Men of Letters." In *Anniversary Essays in Medieval History by the Students of C. H. Haskins*, edited by John L. LaMonte and Charles H. Taylor, 365–87. Boston: Houghton Mifflin, 1929.

Wolff, Robert Lee. "Baldwin of Flanders and Hainaut, First Latin Emperor of Constantinople: His Life, Death, and Resurrection, 1177–1225." *Speculum* 27 (1952): 281–322. Reprinted in his *Studies in the Latin Empire*.

Wolff, Robert Lee. "Hopf's So-Called 'Fragmentum' of Marino Sanudo Torsello." In *The Joshua Starr Memorial Volume: Studies in History and Philology*, 149–59. New York: Conference on Jewish Relations, 1953. Reprinted in his *Studies in the Latin Empire*.

Wolff, Robert Lee. *Studies in the Latin Empire of Constantinople*. London: Variorum Reprints, 1976.

Zorzi, Niccolò. "Per la storiografia sulla quarta crociata: Il *De Bello Constantinopolitano* de Paolo Ramusio et la *Constantinopolis Belgica* de Pierre d'Outreman." In Ortalli, Ravegni, and Schreiner, *Quarta Crociata*, 2:683–746.

INDEX

Placenames are in France or Greece unless otherwise identified.

Abydos (modern Çanakkale, Turkey), 81–82, 114

Acre, 39, 56, 67; siege of, 29

Adam, abbot (Cistercian) of Perseigne, 59, 67

Adele (of Champagne), queen of France, 9, 38, 54, 170

Adeline of Villehardouin, 12, 13n43

Adramyttion (near modern Edremit, Turkey), 114, 118

Adrianople (modern Edirne, Turkey), 108, 131, 136–38, 140; battle of, 119–27, 161; principality of, 134, 136

Agnes (of France), Byzantine empress, wife of Theodore Branas, 11, 99, 132, 134

Ainos (Enos, modern Enez, Turkey), port, 128

Alexander III, pope, 10

Alexios III Angelos Komnenos, emperor (1195–1203), 83, 89, 109

Alexios IV Angelos, emperor (August 1203–January 1204), 70–71, 75, 78, 83, 89–95

Alice of Villehardouin, nun, 25–27, 60, 144, 150

Andreas Capellanus, author of *De amore*, 21, 152

Andros, 81

Anonymous of Béthune, 193n3

Anseaux of Cayeux, commander, 76, 134

Anselm of Courcelles, knight, 3, 114, 121, 128

Apros (also Naples, modern Kermeyan, Turkey), 131–32, 134

Arcadiopolis (modern Lüleburgaz, Turkey), 120, 131

army: amphibious landing, 86; *battailes* (battalions) and companies, 84n10, 85; desertions, 76–78, 92, 120, 136;

dispersal, 52, 65, 67–68, 113–14, 116, 139; diversions, 69–72, 76, 81; garrisons, size of, 190 (table 3); leadership of, 51–52, 56–60; manpower, 44, 50–51, 91–92, 116, 130, 138–39; morale, 68–69, 74–77, 79–80, 120; recruitment of, 36, 117, 130, 138; return home, 121, 125–26; supreme commander of, 57–58, 70, 77; tactical units, 52, 78, 116, 189 (table 1); Turcopoles, 116–17, 123, 136–37. *See also* "second front" of the Fourth Crusade

Athyra (modern Büyükçekmeçe, Turkey), destroyed, 133–34

Aubri of Trois-Fontaine, Cistercian chronicler, 59, 194

Aulnay. *See* Erard of Aulnay; Helvide of Aulnay; Oudard of Aulnay; Vilain of Aulnay; William of Aulnay

Baldwin of Avesnes, author (attributed) of the *Chronique*, 194–95

Baldwin V, count of Hainaut, 9–10, 76

Baldwin VI, count of Hainaut, IX of Flanders, 35, 43–44, 65, 76, 85, 175–76; at Adrianople, 120–24, 137; chancery of, 163; council of, 107, 109, 111; death, 137, 175; emperor of Constantinople, 102–27; letters of, 105–6, 112, 119, 194; seal of, 105; war versus Boniface, 108–13

Béla III, king of Hungary (1173–96), 33, 69

Bera (modern Pherrai/Ferres), monastery with church of Kosmosoteira, 114

Berengar of Villemaur, knight, 3

Berengaria of Navarre, 38

Bertrand of Vitry, knight, 12, 14

Bizoë (modern Vize, Turkey), 131, 134, 136

227

228　　**INDEX**

Blanche (of Navarre), countess of
　Champagne, 38–39, 53–57, 145
Boniface, marquis of Montferrat, 51–52;
　king of Thessalonika and lord of
　Crete, 104–5, 118, 172; death, 141–42;
　supreme commander, 57–58, 85,
　99–100, 70–74, 78, 85, 172; war versus
　Baldwin, 108–13
Boril, king of Bulgaria (1207–18), 146
"the Book" (*li livres*), 76, 79, 120, 164–67,
　191 (table 5). *See also* Vivianus
Boulgarophygon (modern Babaeski,
　Turkey), 121
Brandonvillers, 60
Buchet, Émile, xi

castleguard, 3, 7, 14, 50, 61 (table 3)
Chalcedon, 83
Châlons (-en-Champagne): bishops,
　12–13, 38; canons, 12–13
Champagne, county of, 1–5, 14, 17–18,
　19 (map 1); trade fairs, 1, 4–5, 22
chancery, 105, 107, 163–38
Chane of Lézinnes, wife of the marshal,
　16, 26, 61–62; *marescalisse*, 145
Chariopolis (modern Hayrabolu,
　Turkey), 127
Choniates, Niketas, author of the *History*,
　89, 91–92, 100, 112–13
Chrétien de Troyes, 180; *Cligés*, 20;
　Perceval, 170–71
Chronique de Morée, 169, 193
Cistercian crusade abbots, 59, 75–76
Cîteaux (Cistercian monastery), 65, 106;
　chapter general meetings, 36, 59–60
Clairvaux (Cistercian monastery), 65, 150
Clarembaud of Broyes, canon of Troyes,
　archbishop of Tyre, 68
Clarembaud V of Chappes, 32, 54
Clarembaud VI of Chappes, 79, 85,
　126–27, 178, 194
Clari, Robert of, 70, 72, 101–2, 126, 194,
　203–5
Compiègne, council of, 45
concordia (March 1204), 97–98
Conon of Béthune, 44, 65, 76;
　commander, 136–41; councilor, 107,
　121, 129, 132, 150; envoy, 45, 47, 94,
　149; returns home, 126; seal of, 149;
　speeches, 84, 94
Conrad of Montferrat, 29–30, 51, 57
Constantinople (modern Istanbul,
　Turkey), 61(fig. 3); Blachernai, 87, 89,

94, 97, 110, 119, 132; Boukoleon, 97,
　99, 119, 139; Column of Theodosius,
　116–17; fires in, 93–94, 99; first assault
　on, 86–90; Hagia Sophia, 91, 97, 102,
　138; harbor chain, 86–87; Saint George
　of Mananga, 119; sack of, 100; second
　assault on, 95–100. *See also* relics
constitution: *concordia*, 97–98; *pactum
　scriptum*, 132, 137; *partitio terrarum*,
　113–14
Contarini, Francesco, 200, 202
Corbie, monastery, 193
Corfu, 78–80, 177–78
Cortacopolis, 128
councils: advisory, 107, 121, 129–30, 132,
　134, 139, 140; collegial, 44–45, 58, 75,
　97–98, 101, 104, 157. *See also parlement*
couriers, 110–12, 125, 134, 136, 139,
　141, 162
Cumans, 123–24, 128, 133–34, 140
Cyzicus (near modern Erdek, Turkey),
　138, 140

Dameron of Villehardouin, nun, 26,
　144, 150
Didymoteichon, 109, 113, 120, 136, 138
Dreux of Etroeungt, 174
Du Cange, Charles, editor and translator,
　202–3
Dyrrachion (Durazzo, modern Durrës,
　Albania), 78

Écry-sur-Aisne (modern Asfeld), 41; lords
　of, 41
Emeline of Villehardouin, nun, 8, 26,
　144, 150
Emeric, king of Hungary (1196–1204),
　69, 103
Engeurrand of Boves, 78, 92
Enrico Dandolo, doge of Venice, 47–49,
　74, 83, 88, 124, 128–29, 175
Erard of Aulnay, marshal, 12–15
Erard of Villehardouin, marshal, 62, 145,
　149–50
Ernoul-Bernard *Chronique*, 193–94
Eructavit, 170
Espigal (modern Spiga, Turkey), 121,
　129, 138
Estanor, Jewish suburb of
　Constantinople, 86, 90
Eustace of Conflans, 52, 53
Eustace of Salperwick, commander,
　109–10, 174

INDEX 229

Evrat, translator of Genesis, 153
eyewitness reports, 161–62. *See also* "news"

Faral, Edmond, editor and translator, ix, 199
fiefs, 13, 35, 45, 98, 113–14; distribution of (*partitio*), 113–16, 115 (map 5); *Feoda Campanie*, 3, 23–24, 50, 145
Foissy (Notre-Dame), priory of Fontevraud, 8, 26, 144, 150
Fontaine-les-Nonnains, priory of Fontevraud in Meaux, 33
French Road, in Italy, 56, 65, 68
Fulk of Neuilly, preacher, 36–37, 58–59, 153, 172

Galata, tower of, 86
Gardiki, bishop versus Hospitallers, 149
Garnier, bishop of Troyes, 33, 39, 41, 98, 102, 107–8, 176
Gautier d'Arras, *Eracle*, 20
Geoffroy V of Joinville, seneschal, 32, 39, 54–56
Geoffroy of Villehardouin: acts of, 25–27, 32, 46, 187–88 (app. 1); captivity on Third Crusade, 29–31; chief of staff, 44; councilor, 34, 38, 43; at court, 13–14, 20–21, 32–33; culture of, 19–21, 160–61; envoy, 45–51, 89, 94, 148–49; fiefs in Champagne, 3, 23–24, 114; fiefs in Thrace, 114; field commander, 121–26 (at Adrianople), 137, 146–47; garrison commander of Constantinople, 106–8, 158; garrison knight in Troyes, 3–8; knightly milieu, 1, 7–8, 14–16, 129, 182–83; leader of the Champenois, 93; letters patent, 1, 26–27, 37, 46, 60–62, 187–88 (app. 1); marshal of Champagne, 13, 18–19, 43; marshal of Romania, 132, 144; Masses for, 150; mediator, 37, 46, 110–13; oaths of, 13, 35, 49, 55, 76, 80, 177; as a *prodom*, 169–70, 176–81; properties in Champagne, 16, 60, 61 (map 3); religious sensibilities of, 141–42, 181; seals of, 26, 144, 149; speeches, 159–61; as a Templar, 3. on the Third Crusade, 23, 25–26, 28–29
Geoffroy of Villehardouin, memoirs of, ix, 142–44, 147, 183–85; assessment of colleagues, 170–81; author, 153–55, 201; composition, 152–58; 167–68; date, 142–44; dictation of, 152–55; eyewitness reports, 161–62; manuscripts, 184–85, 193–200; modern translations, 204–6; print editions, 200–204; scribe of, 152–55, 167–68; speeches, 159–61 (*see also* Geoffrey of Villehardouin, speeches of); third-person narrator, 131, 154–55, 190 (table 4); written records, 162–67 (*see also* "the Book")
Geoffroy of Villehardouin, speeches of, 159–61; at Adrianople, 124–25; at Constantinople, 89–90, 94–95; at Nicomedia, 140; at Pamphilon, 125; at Philippopolis, 146; at Sens, 55; at Soissons, 57; at Venice, 48. *See also* speeches
Geoffroy of Villehardouin, son of the marshal, 62, 145, 150
Geoffroy of Villehardouin, son of Jean, 41, 67, 118–19; prince of Achaia, 148–50, 174
Gislebert of Mons, chancellor of Hainaut, 9, 11
Greek cities, revolt of, 120
Guiot of Provins, author of *La Bible*, 29–30, 173, 180
Guy (of Joinville), bishop of Châlons, 12–13
Guy, castelan of Coucy, 42, 81, 160
Guy, (Cistercian) abbot of Vaux-de-Cernay, 59, 74–75, 78, 92
Guy II of Dampierre (le-Château), 13–14, 21–23, 25–26, 35, 54
Guy le Grive of Villehardouin, knight, 61
Guy of Chappes, 24–25, 35, 67, 79, 85, 126–27, 178
Guy of Dampierre, count of Flanders, 196–97

Haice (of Plancy), count's chancellor, bishop of Troyes (1190-93), 3, 7, 27, 30
Haye of Villehardouin, nun, 8, 26, 144, 150
Helvide of Aulnay, 12, 15
Henry of Arzillières, 41, 67
Henry I the Liberal, count of Champagne, 2, 5, 7–9, 10, 17; crusade of 1179, 11–12
Henry II, count of Champagne, 8, 13, 18, 21; on the Third Crusade, 22–33, 34–35, 51

230 INDEX

Henry of Hainaut, count of Flanders, 85, 88, 121, 128; emperor of Constantinople, 137–47; fief of Adramyttion, 114; leadership team of, 129–30, 132–33; letters of, 130, 133, 138; marriage, 138; raid at Philia, 96; regent emperor, 129–37. *See also* Vivianus

Henry of Valenciennes, author of the *History*, 108, 142–43, 145–48, 195

homage, 15, 34–35, 54–55, 105, 110, 112, 141

honor, 1, 6, 74, 76, 79, 92, 179–80

Hospitallers, 28, 42, 44, 96, 149

Hugh IV, count of Saint-Pol, 43, 65–66, 76, 85–86, 88, 91–92, 113, 119–20

Hugh of Berzé and son Hugh (the poet), 60, 160

Hugh of Boves, 92

Hungary, kings of. *See* Bélla III; Emeric

indulgences, 36–37

Innocent III, pope, 49, 59, 77, 91; letters of, 36, 42, 44, 70, 82, 96, 117

Ipsala (Turkey), 141

Isaac II Angelos, emperor (1185–95, 1203–04), 89, 103

Itinerarium Peregrinorum, 29

Jean of Noyon, chancellor of Count Baldwin, 77, 102, 111

Jean of Villehardouin, knight, 2, 4, 14, 26, 149

Jean of Villers, 96

Kalojan, king of Bulgaria, 93; at Adrianople, 123; campaign of 1205–6, 120, 130–34, 141

Kibotos (modern Dinar, Turkey), 139

knightly society, 3, 7, 13–16, 129–30, 182–83

Larrivour, Cistercian monastery, 127, 150

letters: of credence, 45, 47, 83; correspondence, 58, 75, 77, 91–92, 105–6, 112, 117, 130, 133, 138, 146, 163–64. *See also* Innocent III; speeches

Libro de conquisto Constantinopolino, 198

Longnon, Jean, x–xi, 169

Louis, count of Blois, 35–36, 39, 43, 54, 85, 88, 108, 175–76, 178; at Adrianople, 123–24; fief of Nicaea, 113; illness, 93, 99, 107, 113, 119; at Pavia, 66

Louis VII, king of France (1137–80), 9–10

loyal/disloyal, 178–79

Lucas of Ervy, garrison knight, marshal, 12

Macaire of Sainte-Menehould, 41, 76, 85, 107, 127; butler of Romania, 132; commander, 121, 129, 133–34, 136–38, 140; fief of Nicomedia, 114

Makri, Aegean port, 114, 121, 128, 133–34, 148

Manasses (of Pougy), bishop of Troyes, 7, 25, 30

Manessier of L'Isle-Adam, 41, 76, 85, 107, 111; commander, 83, 110, 121, 124, 127, 129, 132

Manuel Komnenos, Byzantine emperor, 10–11

Marie of Champagne, countess of Flanders, 8, 10–11, 42–43, 65, 117–18

Marie of France, countess of Champagne, 8, 12–16, 18–21, 32–33

Marino Sanudo Torsello, 198–99

Marino Zeno, podesta in Romania, 132, 137

Margaret of France, wife of Henry the Young King, then of Bela III of Hungary, 33, 170

Margaret of Hungary, wife of Isaac III, then of Boniface of Montferrat, 89, 99, 103–4, 109, 112

marshals of Champagne. *See* Erard of Aulnay; Erard of Villehardouin; Lucas of Ervy; Oudard of Aulnay; William *Rex* of Provins; William of Villy

Mathieu (of Provins), bishop of Troyes, 8

Mathieu of Montmorency, lord of Marly(-le-Roi), 42, 44, 55; leader of the Champanois, 64, 67, 72, 74, 76, 85, 89, 93

Mesarites, Nicholas, author of the *History*, 99–100, 119–20

Milo Breban (of Provins), knight and treasurer of Champagne, 11, 15–16, 20–21, 24, 35, 41, 44, 76, 85; butler of Romania, 132, 145, 150; in Constantinople, 107, 112, 121, 129, 138–39; commander, 136–37, 140, 147, 150; at court, 32–33, 152; envoy, 45, 49, 94, 149; on Third Crusade, 24, 27, 39, 62, 67–68, 145

misfortune (*mesaventure*), 68, 93, 125, 141

Modon (modern Methone), 118

INDEX 231

Moniac (modern Kardjali, Bulgaria), 137
Morosini, Thomas, Venetian patriarch of Constantinople, 137
Mosynopolis, 109, 141
Mourtzouphlos, Alexios V Doukas, emperor (January–April 1204): coup of, 95; execution, 116–17; flight, 96, 99, 107, 109

Natalis de Wailly, editor and translator, 199, 203–4
"news," 107–10, 120, 125, 133, 137, 147–49, 154, 156, 162
Nicaea (modern Iznik Turkey), 113
Nicomedia (modern Izmit, Turkey), 114, 138, 140
Nikitza, 121, 167
Nivelon, bishop of Soissons, 42, 56–59, 77, 98, 102, 108, 130, 176
Notre-Dame-aux-Nonnains of Troyes, Benedictine convent, 8, 26, 144, 150

oaths, 49n55, 76: not observed, 53, 76, 177; at Sézanne, 24–25; sworn on relics, 13, 177; sworn on Scripture, 35, 49, 53, 55, 76–77, 80, 177–78
Odo of Arzillières, 1
Odo (the Champenois) of Champlitte, 60, 64, 77, 83, 85, 102–3
Odo III, duke of Burgundy, 28, 35, 54–55
Oger of Saint-Chéron, 12–14, 41, 79, 83, 85, 126, 178
Oudard of Aulnay, marshal, 13, 25, 63, 150

Pamphilon (modern Uzunköprü, Turkey), 125, 131, 147
Paris, Paulin, 203
parlement, 44, 80, 82, 92–93, 95–98, 101–2, 112, 148; on horseback, 84–85
partitio terrarum imperii Romanie, 113
Peloponnese, conquest of, 118–19
Peter, (Cistercian) abbot of Lucedio, 58, 70–71, 102
Peter of Bracheux, commander,113, 121, 125, 138, 396
Peter Capuano, papal legate, 36, 59, 69, 77, 121, 126
Peter of Douai, bailiff of Flanders, 143, 147, 193; at battle of Philippopolis, 145–46
Philadelphia, duchy, 114
Philia (near modern Karaburun, Turkey), raid at, 96

Philip (of Dreux), bishop of Beauvais, 22, 25
Philip of Beaumanoir, bailiff of Beauvais, 161
Philip I, count of Flanders, 22, 24–25, 65, 171
Philip II, king of France, 9, 18, 21–23, 35, 38; and Fourth Crusade, 49, 54–55, 58–59, 64, 119, 138; on Third Crusade, 28, 50
Philip of Swabia, 71, 75
Philippopolis (modern Plovdiv, Bulgaria), 113, 120, 128, 131–32; battle of, 145–46
Pontigny, Cistercian monastery, 28
preud'homme, prodom, 57, 169–71, 174–75, 176–81; collective (= barons), 56, 101, 173

Raimbaut of Vaqueiras, Provençal poet, 52, 109, 111–12, 173
Ramusio, Paolo, editor, 201
Ravennika (near modern Lamia), Resignation of, 148
relics, 91, 119
Renaud (of Bar-le-Duc), bishop of Chartres, 22, 38–39
Renaud II of Dampierre (-le-Château), 41, 67, 96
Renaud of Montmirail, 76, 92, 124, 177
Renier of Mons, 111, 172–73
Renier of Trith, 65, 76; commander, 111, 113, 120, 128, 131, 138, 178
Rhousion (modern Rusköy, near Kesan, Turkey), 132–33
Robert of Auxerre, author of the Chronicon, 27, 106n8
Robert of Boves, 77, 177
Rodosto (Rheidestos, modern Tekur-Dagh, Turkey), 125, 128, 133; destroyed, 134
Roger of Howden, author of Gesta Henrici and Chronica, 29
Roscelin of Villehardouin, cathedral canon of Troyes, 2, 7, 30
rosters of crusaders, 41, 165
Rouillé, Guillaume, Lyonnais printer, 202

Saint-Étienne of Troyes, comital chapel, 5, 145
Saint-Loup of Troyes (Augustian chapter), 4
Saladin, 22, 29, 31, 51
Sanudo, Marino Torsello, 198–99

INDEX

Scutari, 83
"second front" of the Fourth Crusade, 52, 66–68, 96, 117–18
Selymbria (modern Silivi, Turkey), 129, 133–34
Sens, 55
Serres, 109, 131, 138
shame (*honte*), 74, 76, 79–80, 120, 136, 179–80
Simon, abbot (Cistercian) of Loos, 59, 75, 94, 172
Simon V of Montfort, 55, 78, 92
Soissons, councils at, 44, 56
speeches, 48, 70–71, 74, 83, 89–90, 94, 109, 125; collective, 79–80, 92–94, 101, 136, 140, 159–60; letters read as, 71, 75, 83–84. *See also* Geoffroy of Villehardouin, speeches of
Stenimachos (modern Asenovgrad, Bulgaria), 131, 137
Stephen, count of Perche, 92, 114, 124
Syria, 67–68, 78, 92–93

Templars, 42, 44; in Acre, 31, 67, 127; in Champagne, 21, 46, 53, 127; in Provins, 31; in Troyes, 5. *See also* William (Templar)
Tchorlu (modern Çorlu, Turkey), 107, 120–21, 131, 134
Theodore Branas, lord of Adrianople, 132, 134–37
Theodore Lascaris, 118, 139
Thessalonika, kingdom of, 104–5
Thibaut I, count of Bar-le-Duc, 55–56
Thibaut V, count of Blois, royal seneschal, 9, 18, 22, 28, 145
Thibaut III, count of Champagne, 8, 11, 24, 34–35, 38–39, 155; at Écry, 41; death, 53
Thierry of Tenremonde, 133
Third Crusade, 27–30, 39, 41
tournaments, 9–10; tournament rolls, 9–10, 165
Trajanopolis, 114, 128
Troyes, capital of Champagne, 4–8, 6 (fig. 1)

Vegetius, author of *De re militari*, 19–20, 180
Venice, 36; fleet, 68, 72, 95; fleet negotiations, 47–51; muster, 66–72
Via Egnatia, 78, 109, 113–14, 128, 133–34, 141

Via Militaris, 108, 110, 121, 131
Vigenère, Blaise de, editor and translator, 201–2, 204
Vilain of Aulnay, 13, 67, 127
Vilain of Nully, 41, 96
Vilain I of Villehardouin, knight, 1, 26; fief of, 3, 30
Vilain II of Villehardouin, canon of Troyes, 2–3, 30
Villehardouin, genealogy 1. *See* Alice of Villehardouin; Dameron of Villehardouin; Emeline of Villehardouin; Erard of Villehardouin; Geoffroy of Villehardouin (son of Jean); Geoffroy of Villehardouin (son of the marshal); Guy la Grive of Villehardouin; Haye of Villehardouin; Jean of Villehardouin; Roscelin of Villehardouin; Vilain I of Villehardouin; Vilain II of Villehardouin; Walter of Villehardouin; William of Villy
Villy, later Villy-le-Maréchal, 3, 26, 150
Vivianus, chief scribe of Emperor Henry, 166–67

Walter III, count of Brienne, 31–32, 39, 52, 68, 79, 154, 178
Walter of Chappes, chancellor of Champagne, 35, 54
Walter of Châtillon, 35, 39, 54
Walter of Villehardouin, knight, 26
war memoirs, xi
William (Templar), almoner of the count, 11, 31
William of Arzillières, marshal of the Temple of Acre, 67, 127
William of Aulnay, 79
William (of Champagne), archbishop of Sens, Reims, 7, 9, 13, 18, 35, 38, 54
William (the Champenois) of Champlitte, 60, 64, 77, 83, 88, 110–11, 118; prince of Achaia, 119, 174
William of Lézinnes, knight, 16
William Marshal, ix–x, 9, 185
William of Nully, 41, 96
William Rex of Provins, marshal of Champagne, 3, 7, 11–12, 23, 28
William of Villy, marshal, 151

Zara (mordern Zadar, Croatia), 69–78

Printed in the USA
CPSIA information can be obtained
at www.ICGtesting.com
LVHW092105271223
767549LV00023B/412/J